SUPERVENIENCE

Supervenience

New Essays

Edited by

ELIAS E. SAVELLOS

ÜMIT D. YALÇIN

CAMBRIDGE
UNIVERSITY PRESS

Published by the Press Syndicate of the University of Cambridge
The Pitt Building, Trumpington Street, Cambridge CB2 1RP
40 West 20th Street, New York, NY 10011-4211, USA
10 Stamford Road, Oakleigh, Melbourne 3166, Australia

© Cambridge University Press 1995

First published 1995

Printed in the United States of America

Library of Congress Cataloging-in-Publication Data
Supervenience: new essays / Elias E. Savellos, Ümit D. Yalçın.
p.   cm.
ISBN 0-521-45002-0
1. Metaphysics.   I. Savellos, Elias E.   II. Yalçın, Ümit D.
BD111.S86   1995
110 – dc20   94-38590
                                                CIP

A catalog record for this book is available from the British Library.

ISBN 0-521-45002-0 Hardback

For Vivian Ackerson, Miranda Yalçın, and Ayten İmer

Contents

Contributors

Felicia Ackerman is Professor of Philosophy at Brown University. She has published papers on a wide range of philosophical subjects, including methodology of philosophy, philosophy of language, and related issues in epistemology and metaphysics.

John Bacon is Reader in Philosophy at the University of Sydney. He has written in metaphysics, philosophical logic, and modal and predicate-functor logic. A book on tropes, *Relations Particularized: The Alphabet of Being,* is in press (Blackwell).

Daniel Bonevac is Professor and Chair of the Department of Philosophy at the University of Texas at Austin. He is the author of *Reduction in the Abstract Sciences* (Hackett, 1982), *Deduction* (Mayfield, 1987), *The Art and Science of Logic* (Mayfield, 1990); editor of *Today's Moral Issues* (Mayfield, 1991); and coeditor of *Beyond the Western Tradition* (Mayfield, 1992) and *Understanding Non-Western Philosophy* (Mayfield, 1993). He has published articles on Kant, metaphysics, semantics, and philosophical logic.

Earl Conee is Associate Professor of Philosophy at the University of Rochester and Book Review Editor of *Noûs.* He is the author of various papers, largely of a critical nature, on topics in epistemology, ethics, metaphysics, and philosophy of mind. Currently his philosophical opposition is directed primarily toward naturalism in epistemology and imputations of begging the question.

Berent Enç, Professor of Philosophy at the University of Wisconsin-Madison, has published papers on scientific reduction, metaphysics, and the philosophy of mind. His current interests range from studies in animal behavior, action theory, and functional explanation to the philosophy of Hume.

Thomas R. Grimes is Professor of Philosophy at Arkansas State University. He received his Ph.D. from the University of Arizona. He has published articles on ontology, confirmation, and explanation and is currently working on a project on scientific realism.

John Heil is Professor of Philosophy at Davidson College and the author of *The Nature of True Minds* (Cambridge University Press, 1990).

James C. Klagge is Associate Professor of Philosophy at Virginia Polytechnic Institute and State University. He is the author of several articles on supervenience published over the past dozen years. He has coedited a collection of essays, *Methods of Interpreting Plato and His Dialogues*, published as the 1992 supplementary volume to Oxford Studies in Ancient Philosophy, and also a collection of Wittgenstein's shorter writings, *Philosophical Occasions: 1912–1951* (Hackett, 1993).

Keith Lehrer is Regents Professor of Philosophy at the University of Arizona, Honorary Professor at the University of Graz, Austria, and Chair of the Board of Officers of the American Philosophical Association. He is the author and editor of many books and articles on freedom, knowledge, and consensus, including, most recently, *Metamind* (Oxford University Press, 1990), *Thomas Reid* (Routledge, 1991), and *Theory of Knowledge* (Westview Press and Routledge, 1991).

Barry Loewer is Professor of Philosophy at Rutgers University. He works on issues in philosophy of physics, philosophy of mind, and philosophical logic and has published widely in these areas.

Cynthia Macdonald is Senior Lecturer in Philosophy at the University of Manchester. She is the author of *Mind–Body Identity Theories* (Routledge, 1989), coeditor of *Philosophy of Psychology: Debates on Psychological Explanation* (Blackwell, 1994) and of *Connectionism: Debates on Psychological Explanation*, Vol. 2 (Basil Blackwell, forthcoming), and author of articles on the philosophy of mind, metaphysics, and the philosophy of psychology.

Brian P. McLaughlin is Associate Professor of Philosophy at Rutgers University. He has published numerous articles on the philosophy of mind, philosophy of psychology, and metaphysics.

Paul K. Moser is Professor of Philosophy at Loyola University of Chicago. He has authored three books, *Epistemic Justification* (Reidel, 1985), *Knowledge and Evidence* (Cambridge University Press, 1989), and *Philosophy after Objectivity* (Oxford University Press, 1993), and edited a variety of anthologies, among them *A Priori Knowledge* (Oxford University Press, 1986) and *Rationality in Action* (Cambridge University Press, 1990). He has published numerous papers in the areas of epistemology, philosophy of mind, and rationality.

David Papineau is Professor of Philosophy of Science at King's College, London. He is the author of *Philosophical Naturalism* (Basil Blackwell, 1993), *Reality and Representation* (Basil Blackwell, 1987), *Theory and Meaning* (Clarendon Press, 1979), and *For Science in the Social Sciences*

(Macmillan, 1978). He has written articles on a wide range of philosophical topics and is currently editor of the *British Journal for the Philosophy of Science*.

John F. Post is Professor of Philosophy at Vanderbilt University. He is the author of *The Faces of Existence: An Essay in Nonreductive Metaphysics* (Cornell 1987), *Metaphysics: A Contemporary Introduction* (Paragon, 1991), and numerous articles in metaphysics, epistemology, philosophy of religion, and philosophical logic.

Elias E. Savellos is Associate Professor of Philosophy at the State University of New York at Geneseo. His research interests lie in contemporary analytical philosophy, and he has published several papers on topics of current interest in philosophical logic, metaphysics, and the philosophy of language.

J. D. Trout is Associate Professor of Philosophy at Loyola University of Chicago and Adjunct Assistant Professor at the Parmly Hearing Institute. He has also taught at Bryn Mawr College and Virginia Tech. Professor Trout is coeditor (with Richard Boyd and Philip Gasper) of *The Philosophy of Science* (MIT Press, 1991), has recently completed a book, *Measuring the Intentional World*, on quantitative methods in the social and behavioral sciences, and has published various papers on the philosophy of science, philosophy of mind, and speech perception.

James Van Cleve teaches philosophy at Brown University. His principal interests are epistemology, metaphysics, and the history of philosophy from Descartes to Kant. He has published several papers on supervenience, including "Semantic Supervenience and Referential Indeterminacy" (*Journal of Philosophy* 89, 1992).

Ümit D. Yalçın teaches at East Carolina University. His research interests lie in epistemology, metaphysics, the philosophy of science, and the philosophy of mind.

Introduction

ELIAS E. SAVELLOS AND ÜMIT D. YALÇIN

1. The Basic Concept

For most people who are not familiar with its many manifestations, analytical philosophy is the philosophy of reductionism par excellence. And the title is well earned when one recalls the string of reductionist programs that have left their mark on the first part of this century, ranging from the purported *analytical* reductions proposed by phenomenalism and behaviorism, to the weaker *theoretical* reductions of the later generations. Yet, starting with sporadic suggestions in the 1960s and 1970s, the philosophical literature is now rife with pronouncements of the wrongheadedness of all reductive programs. Perhaps surprisingly, the current literature associated with analytical philosophy is being swept by a wave of antireductionism.

Reductionism might be dead or dying, but the idea that certain entities we seem to talk and think about depend on others for their existence (and that they are somehow less real?) is still alive and kicking. This had led philosophers to search for a topic-neutral *nonreductive* dependence relationship that can be easily incorporated into the analytical toolbox of a variety of philosophical endeavors, performing at least part of the function reductive relationships were supposed to fulfill. Hence the recent philosophical interest in *supervenience*, which purports to be precisely this sort of relationship. Although the concept that the modern use of 'supervenience' aims to express has been around for some time, widespread interest in it is a relatively recent phenomenon.[1]

The basic idea behind the philosophical concept of supervenience is perhaps best introduced by an example. Take the property of being a beautiful piece of music.[2] When we consider the various musical works that instantiate this property, it is highly dubious that we can come up with any one sequence of musical notes or sounds[3] that is common to all and only the pieces that instantiate it. With the terminology that is quite commonly utilized in such circumstances, one could express this point by saying that the beauty of a musical piece seems to be *multiply realizable*. Hence, it is highly improbable that the

1

property in question can be correlated with any such sequence of notes or sounds. This is enough to convince most of us that being a beautiful piece of music cannot be *identified with* or be *reduced to* having any given sequence of sounds as a part.[4] But at the same time, we are still convinced that the beauty of any musical piece has to do with the sequence of sounds that constitutes it. If a musical piece is beautiful and some other piece is not, they cannot be constituted of exactly the same sequence of sounds; their aesthetic difference has to be somehow due to some difference in the sequence of sounds that constitutes each piece. The beauty of a musical piece seems to be *grounded in* the sequence of sounds that constitutes a musical work without being *identifiable* with any unique property of such sequences of sounds. The concept of supervenience is supposed to denote this dependence relationship that appears to be weaker than reducibility.

Hence, whether one talks about the supervenience of concepts, properties, phenomena, entities, or what have you, the basic notion of *A*s supervening on *B*s appears to subsume (a) *covariance,* where variations in *A*s are correlated with variations in *B*s, (b) *dependence* of *A*s on *B*s (or, if these are different,[5] the *determination* of *A*s by *B*s), and (c) the *nonreducibility* of *A*s to *B*s.

Given the character of the example we used, it might sound odd at this point to characterize supervenience as incorporating nonreducibility but not *irreducibility.* For it was the apparent irreducibility of the beauty of a musical piece that led us to look for a weaker dependence relationship. As we shall see later, the same goes for other fields in philosophy: it was the apparent irreducibility of mental properties to physical properties in the philosophy of mind, and of moral properties to natural properties in ethics, that opened the door to supervenience. Nevertheless, it has become common practice these days to explicate the notion of supervenience only in terms of nonreducibility,[6] and we shall stay with this perhaps controversial practice. This is undoubtedly an important issue that needs more attention, since the stand one takes will have a bearing on how one attempts to provide a more detailed explication of supervenience and the philosophical work one expects from this notion. Beyond this point, the issues become even more controversial.

2. The Logic of Supervenience

Mainly due to Jaegwon Kim's pioneering work on the topic, the prevalent understanding of supervenience is that of a relation between families of properties closed under a set of property-forming operations. That is, a set of properties, *A*, supervenes on another set of properties, *B*, if and only if there is a certain kind of relationship between each

A-property and a property that can be constructed from the *B*-properties by means of a set of specified property-forming operations. Yet, even if this is the intuitive understanding of supervenience, there still remains the task of clearly formulating specific theses that capture it. By the time the supervenience literature had ripened, there were at least five supervenience theses (more accurately, schemata) that purportedly expressed a relationship that could ground the ontic priority claims supervenience was supposed to support.[7] We give these theses below together with their symbolic representations, following Kim (1990a) in calling them "covariance" theses for reasons that will become clear in the further course of our discussion. Where *A* ranges over the properties in the supervenient set of properties, and *B* over the subvenient or base set of properties, and $=_x$ is used to indicate indiscernibility with respect to *X*-ness, we have the following:

(WC₁) Weak Covariance 1   For any possible world w and objects x and y in w, if x and y are indiscernible with respect to properties in B, they are indiscernible in respect of properties in A.

$\forall w \ \forall x \ \forall y \ ((x \text{ is in } w \text{ and } y \text{ is in } w) \rightarrow (\forall B \ (Bx \leftrightarrow By) \rightarrow \forall A \ (Ax \leftrightarrow Ay)))$

(WC₂) Weak Covariance 2   Necessarily, if anything has some property A_i in A, there exists a property B_j in B such that the thing has B_j, and everything that has B_j has A_i.

$\Box \ \forall x \ \forall A \ (Ax \rightarrow \exists B \ (Bx \ \& \ \forall y \ (By \rightarrow Ay)))$

(SC₁) Strong Covariance 1   For any objects x and y and worlds w_1 and w_2, if x in w_1 is *B*-indiscernible from y in w_2 (i.e., x has in w_1 precisely those *B*-properties that y has in w_2), then x in w_1 is *A*-indiscernible from y in w_2.

$\forall w_1 \ \forall w_2 \ \forall x \ \forall y \ ((x \text{ is in } w_1 \text{ and } y \text{ is in } w_2) \rightarrow (\forall B(Bx \leftrightarrow By) \rightarrow \forall A \ (Ax \leftrightarrow Ay)))$

(SC₂) Strong Covariance 2   Necessarily, if anything has some property A_i in A, there exists a property B_j in B such that the thing has B_j, and *necessarily*, everything that has B_j has A_i.

$\Box \ \forall x \ \forall A \ (Ax \rightarrow \exists B \ (Bx \ \& \ \Box \ \forall y \ (By \rightarrow Ay)))$

(GC) Global Covariance   For any worlds w_1 and w_2, if w_1 and w_2 are *B*-indiscernible, then they are *A*-indiscernible.[8]

$\forall w_1 \ \forall w_2 \ (w_1 =_B w_2 \rightarrow w_1 =_A w_2)$

These should be understood as schemata that can be particularized in various ways so as to be a component of this or that supervenience thesis. A particularization will consist of a specific choice for the supervenient and subvenient properties, and a specific construal of the necessity operators (or alternatively, the range of the world-binding quantifiers). Whether any interesting thesis can be formulated by assigning different interpretations to different modal operators occurring in the same schema (or by using different ranges for different world-binding quantifiers in the same schema) is an intriguing, yet not much discussed question.

Weak supervenience is so called because, roughly, it only requires B-indiscernibles in the *same* world to be A-indiscernible. Strong supervenience is stronger in that it also requires B-indiscernibles *across* possible worlds to be A-indiscernible. To put it in terms of a concrete example, if entities in a given world that had indiscernible brain states had to be in indiscernible mental states, weak supervenience would obtain. Further questions such as If there were other entities with brain states indiscernible from the entities in that world, what would their mental states be like? or Could there have been other entities with brain states indiscernible from the entities in that world, but with different mental states? are irrelevant to a weak supervenience claim, but not to a strong supervenience claim.[9] Finally, unlike both strong and weak supervenience, global supervenience characteristically takes whole worlds as the relata of the supervenience relation.

Given this proliferation of theses, one is naturally led to wonder which (if any) of these formulations is the most suitable. This, in turn, raises questions about the relationship of these various theses to each other. A significant portion of the supervenience literature, including some of the essays in this volume, is devoted to settling such questions.

With the foregoing characterizations, it is fairly certain that particularizations of (SC$_1$) entail comparable particularizations of (WC$_1$) and that the same goes for (SC$_2$) and WC$_2$.[10] But what about other relationships between these theses?

Initially, Kim (1984) and (1987) suggested that the alternative formulations of weak and strong covariance were equivalent and that so were (SC$_2$) and (GC). Both of these claims have come under attack in subsequent years. Van Cleve (1990) disputes the putative equivalence of (WC$_1$) and (WC$_2$), as well as Kim's argument to that effect, by objecting to Kim's use of complementation as a property-forming operation.[11] Perhaps the easiest way to motivate this objection is as follows: (WC$_1$), as applied to mental on physical covariance, would be trivially true if in any given possible world no two entities had the same physical properties. But intuitively, (WC$_2$) could still be false if in one of these possible worlds there were an entity e with some mental property but no physical properties (e.g., a Cartesian ego). This seems to suggest that (WC$_1$) does not entail (WC$_2$). It is easy to appreciate that, with minor complications, a similar thought experiment would militate against the purported equivalence of (SC$_1$) and (SC$_2$).

But if we take the base set to be closed under negation (as well as conjunction), e ends up having a physical property after all, and the conclusion that (WC$_1$) does not entail (WC$_2$) is blocked. For there is a property in the base set that is the conjunction of the complements of all the basic physical properties, namely, $\neg B_1$ & $\neg B_2$ & ... & $\neg B_n$, and e instantiates this "physical" property. McLaughlin's essay in this volume incorporates a comprehensive discussion of this controversy.

The purported equivalence of (SC_2) and (GC) has also come under attack, the most well-known dissent appearing in Petrie (1987).[12] Kim (1987) seemed to accept Petrie's criticisms, but this was not enough to lay the dispute to rest.[13] The discussion is continued in this volume in the essays of Klagge and McLaughlin.

Let us return to the question, Which formulation of supervenience should be preferred? pretending that it can be answered without settling questions regarding the entailment relationships between various purported formulations. In our volume, we get different answers from Bacon and Post. The former observes that weak supervenience entails strong supervenience under an understanding of properties as functions from possible worlds to individuals, but not when properties are construed as tropes. Favoring the trope account, Bacon prefers weak supervenience as the only formulation that does not entail some sort of necessary coextension. Post first defends global supervenience against charges of excessive permissiveness. Then, he contrasts it with other supervenience claims he characterizes as "individualistic" and, citing Milikan,[14] suggests that there is empirical evidence at least for some restricted global supervenience claims.

3. Supervenience and Reduction

At the same time, there is a further consideration that plays a major role in guiding various choices. As already indicated, supervenience is minimally supposed to be a nonreductive relationship, yet there is the danger that certain strong formulations of supervenience might imply reduction, which will render such formulations unsuitable for the proponents of nonreductive positions in various areas of philosophy. But first, some more background.[15]

It has now become the established lore of the supervenience literature to pinpoint Putnam (1967) and Davidson (1970) as the two main sources of the final critique of reductionism in the philosophy of mind, a critique that has had wide-ranging consequences for reductionist positions in all areas of philosophy. Both Putnam's and Davidson's arguments can be seen as undermining a necessary condition of the most popular model of reduction in the 1960s: the bridge laws of Nagel-type theoretical reductions.[16] According to the Nagel model, T_1 reduces T_2 if and only if, roughly, all the laws of T_2 (or close approximations thereof) can be derived from the laws of T_1 in conjunction with bridge laws that connect the terms of the two theories.[17] Now Putnam's arguments can be taken to imply that such bridge laws will not be forthcoming because of the multiple realizability of the mental,[18] whereas Davidson's arguments seem to once again undermine the possibility of bridge laws by establishing the "anomaly of the mental," that is, the lack of strict lawlike relationships between the mental and the physical. On the one hand, if mental properties are multiply realizable, then no mental property will be correlated with a unique physical property;[19] on the other hand, if the mental domain is anomalous, then there will be no room for strict psychophysical correlations between mental and physical properties.[20]

Just when supervenience was becoming entrenched as the favored nonreductive notion of dependence in analytical philosophy, Kim (1983, 1984) argued that (SC_2)-type covariance between As and Bs entails the reducibility of As to Bs. The reducibility is supposed to be entailed by the fact that such a strong covariance relation entails what amounts to bridge laws or, as Kim (1990a) puts it, "strong connectibility" between theories about As and Bs, defined as follows:[21]

T_1 is strongly connectible with respect to T_2. $=_{\text{def}}$ Each n-place predicate of T_2 has a nomological coextension in the vocabulary of T_1; that is, for each n-place predicate P of T_2, there is an n-place open sentence, P^*, of T_1 such that the following is a bridge law:

$$\forall x_1 \ldots \forall x_n [P(x_1 \ldots x_n) \leftrightarrow P^*(x_1 \ldots x_n)]$$

The suggestion that (SC_2) implies reducibility was disputed by Teller and Post as early as 1983.[22] The key objection is that Kim's argument uses disjunction, specifically, infinitary disjunction, as a property-forming operation, whereas disjunctive properties have been held suspect for some time.[23]

In this volume, Bonevac argues that even if infinitary disjunctions are allowed, what results from strong covariance is something weaker than what is commonly understood by reduction. Strong covariance implies reduction in an infinitary language, and with such languages being incomprehensible to humans, we only get "reduction in the mind of God." Nevertheless, Bonevac suggests, this is only an *epistemological* difference: the *ontological* point, that strong covariance implies reducibility in an important sense, remains. Grimes defends the claim that similar reductive consequences also follow from global supervenience. Also arguing that neither thesis captures the intuitive idea of determination, he suggests that there are no general grounds on which to choose between (SC_2) and (GC). Macdonald attempts to give an account of psychophysical supervenience that is captured by (SC_2) without being reductive. Drawing from the example of biological properties, she argues that the existence of necessary coextensivity between two kinds of properties is not sufficient for reducibility insofar as the types of relations the supervenient properties bear to each other do not just replicate the pattern of causal relations between the physical properties that realize them.

It is worth noting here a point that is not emphasized in the supervenience literature: we have seen that if we do not assume that complementation is a property-forming operation under which all families of properties are closed, there is reason to believe that (SC_1) is not equivalent to (SC_2). If so, does (SC_1)-covariance between *A*s and *B*s entail the reducibility of *A*s to *B*s?

The answer appears to be in the negative, unless we assume the base family to be closed both under infinitary disjunction *and* complementation. To take up the second of these, for there to be a necessary coextension between *A*s and *B*s, there need to be one-way conditionals connecting *A*s to *B*s. As Kim puts it, for each property A_i in *A*, we need to have in each world conditionals of the form $\forall y\ (A_i y \rightarrow B^* y)$, where B^* designates the infinite disjunction of the *B*-maximal properties (i.e., the strongest consistent properties constructible in *B* relative to the property-constructing operations allowed) that ground A_i in various possible worlds. But (SC_1) can be true in models incorporating a world containing an entity with no physical properties, such as the Cartesian ego mentioned in Section 2 (again assuming that the conjunction of the complements of physical properties need not be a physical property), insofar as any two entities from the worlds in such a model are physically distinct.[24] But then, trivially, in such a world, $\forall y(A_i y \rightarrow B^* y)$ will not hold for some value of A_i, and this will be sufficient to block necessary coextensiveness of the two families of properties.

Of course, such a conclusion can be resisted by restricting the quantifiers in (SC_1) to worlds where everything has some physical properties. But as noted earlier, this opens another can of worms about the strength of the various covariance theses, specifically about the strength of the various modalities they purport to express.

4. Arguments for and against Supervenience

That a supervenience relation holds between this or that family of properties (or what have you) is a substantial thesis that goes beyond formulating various covariance principles and determining their logical properties. How does one establish such a substantive thesis? Bonevac (1988) argues that supervenience claims do not go far in supporting the ontic priority claims they are supposed to support unless backed by actual reductions. Some of the contributors in this volume appear to disagree. Loewer argues for a thoroughgoing physicalism by defending the supervenience of any physically detectable property on basic physical properties. A crucial premise of his argument is that physics is closed and complete. This, roughly, amounts to the claim that all physical events are determined by prior physical events according to physical laws. Papineau considers an argument for a similarly strong supervenience of mental properties on the physical, which, he suggests, can be extended to show the supervenience of all real properties on the physical. Both the closed and complete character of physics, and the "manifestability of the mental" (i.e., that difference in mentally different systems will display differing physical consequences at least in some physical contexts) are key suppositions of this argument. Papineau tries to argue for the manifestability of the mental by showing that mental facts have to be realized by physical facts. Heil's contribution is a sustained effort to answer the triviality and symmetricity charges raised against physicalism in Miller (1990), where the "symmetricity charge" amounts to the claim that, given certain assumptions, physical properties also supervene on other kinds of properties.

Moser and Trout focus on global supervenience and raise problems both against the epistemic support for it and against various attempts to furnish an account of the nonreductive dependency relation it tries to capture. They conclude that such an account in terms of global supervenience that also upholds the primacy of the physical has bleak prospects. Lehrer takes issue against claims that epistemic properties supervene on nonepistemic properties and extols the virtues of the coherence theory of justification as entailing the rejection of such supervenience. The entailment follows from the fact that the notion of coherence cannot be used except in terms of epistemic concepts such as *trustworthiness* and *comparative reasonableness*. Van Cleve formulates antirealism as a thesis that claims that truth supervenes on evidence. He argues that once we focus on such a clear formulation, antirealism is faced with a number of insurmountable objections.

Ackerman and Savellos are concerned with the application of supervenience to ontological matters. Ackerman proposes a technique for transforming questions that prima facie imply the existence of certain kinds of entities (e.g., numbers, events, objects) to questions that are ontologically noncommittal and argues that the answers to the former questions supervene on the answers to the latter. Savellos examines whether events could supervene on a subvenient base consisting of objects, properties, and times, and concludes that given certain assumptions about the individual essences of events, there is no place for a nonreductive account of event supervenience.

5. Supervenience and Causation

Focusing our discussion on the philosophy of mind for the moment, if we assume that mental properties supervene on physical properties, can we also maintain our usual talk about mental causes? As we saw earlier (Loewer, Papineau), such supervenience claims are usually based on the assumption that basic physical conditions and laws are sufficient to account for any physical change that can be explained. But now, think about some mental effect that is putatively caused by a mental cause. Since the mental effect supervenes on some physical condition, and the occurrence of this physical condition can be fully explained in terms of the operation of physical laws on antecedent physical conditions, there is no work left for the original mental cause to do unless we assume large-scale causal overdetermination. Mental to physical supervenience seems to lead to epiphenomenalism about the mental.

An argument along these lines is suggested by Kim (1989a) as raising the problem of "explanatory exclusion" and is further investigated in Kim (1989b, 1990b).[25] The problem has been a source of headache for nonreductive materialists but can be appreciated by any philosopher who wishes to maintain a supervenience thesis about anything, while preserving the causal efficacy of the supervenient domain. Enç meets the challenge head-on and argues for the existence of what he calls "nonreducible supervenient causal properties." According to Enç, these properties, which include representational properties, have causal efficacy "that does not get fully accounted for by the causal role played by [their] micro base properties." Conee addresses the problem in the context of theories of meaning and retreats from supervenience to type-identity between mental and physical properties. He argues that the standard multiple-realizability arguments, contrary to common belief, do not present type materialism with insurmountable problems.

6. Is Supervenience Enough?

On a final note, we would like to consider two ways in which supervenience has been criticized for not delivering what it promises. To begin with, it has been suggested that without the specification of the particular determination or dependence relationship that underlies it, the claim of supervenience is "simply an empty sound expressing a faith that two levels of properties are somehow related."[26] As Schiffer puts it, "Invoking a primitive metaphysical relation of supervenience to explain how non-natural moral properties were related to physical properties was just to add mystery to mystery, to cover one obscurantist move with another."[27]

Let us, for the sake of simplicity, focus on global covariance between the mental and the physical. The problem that the preceding complaints raise seems to be the following: establishing that worlds alike in physical respects have to be alike in mental respects does not seem, by itself, to explain either why this relationship obtains between the mental and the physical or why the physical is in some sense prior to the mental. The proponent of the covariance just presents such a relationship as a brute metaphysical fact and often accompanies his claim with the somewhat dogmatic pronouncement that the physical is, somehow, ontologically the more basic of the two. But a materialist who wants to make assertions about the ontic priority of the physical has to say more than this to explain *how* and *why* the covariance relation between the mental and the physical amounts to dependency. Perhaps he can appeal to microdetermination, conceptual dependence or part–whole relationships to make his point, but one must appeal to something more than mere covariance.[28] The point can be generalized, mutatis mutandis, to covariance between other domains.

One might attempt to minimize the force of this objection by granting that it would be desirable to explain why and how supervenience obtains by appealing to more familiar dependence or determination relationships *when this is possible*. At the same time one can insist that sometimes supervenience can be a brute fact as little in need of explanation as the basic laws of physics or logic.[29] That is, if we cannot discover some familiar dependence or determination relationship between As and Bs, but we are still confronted with the fact that As covary with Bs (and not vice versa?), we might after all be forced and entitled to postulate an unexplained, perhaps primitive dependence relationship between them. Needless to say, the final word on whether this is a fully satisfactory maneuver is not in.

At this point, we can turn to an alternative criticism of supervenience. It has been frequently observed that satisfaction of even the strongest covariance thesis considered in Section 2 is by no means sufficient to establish dependence or determination between the properties that covary in this manner.[30] For example, (SC_2)-type mental to physical covariation can be satisfied in a single world model in which psychophysical parallelism is true. Is this not, then, a serious shortcoming of the theses under consideration? And more importantly, if all supervenience claims are based on the existence of such covariations that need not be explained by appeal to a dependency, does this not undermine the recently made suggestion that such covariation entitles us to postulate an unexplained, perhaps primitive dependence relationship between the covarying domains?

The answer has to be a qualified yes. Among other things, if supervenience purports to capture dependence or determination relations, and if the latter are asymmetric relations, then none of the covariance theses we have been considering can be adequate to the task since they do not formulate asymmetric relations. On the other hand, the same can be said about various popular formulations of reduction: although reducibility is often taken to imply ontological priority, and the latter is taken to be an asymmetric relation, formulations of reduction are not asymmetric. Take, for example, Nagel-type reductions. First, the intertheoretic *identity* claims based on such reductions cannot be just a function of the Nagel-reducibility of one theory to another, which is a purely syntactic relation between the two theories. We must, at least, make additional assumptions about the best explanation of the bridge laws that connect the two theories.[31] Second, even if, say, the identity of the mental and the physical is established, there remains the fact that identity is a symmetric relation. To claim the ontic priority of the physical, it is not sufficient to show that mental properties are identical to physical properties. More needs to be proved, or assumed.

Ultimately, ontic priority claims have to establish more than just showing that two domains of properties are related in a manner that satisfies covariance concerns. And if the vast literature on reduction is any indication, we still have a lot to say about what else needs to be added to covariance to get the mileage we wish to get out of it.

NOTES

1. Moore (1922) formulates a concept of supervenience without calling it by that name. Hare (1952), perhaps erroneously, is often cited as the modern source for the philosophical usage of the term.
2. Treating 'beautiful' in 'beautiful piece of music' as an attributive adjective, defined as follows in Geach (1956):

    In a phrase 'an *A B*' . . . '*A*' is a predicative adjective if the predication 'is an *A B*' splits up logically into a pair of predications 'is a *B*' and 'is an *A*'; otherwise I shall say that '*A*' is a (logically) attributive adjective. (p. 33)

3. Obviously, these have to be sound *types* rather than *tokens*. Also, we are ignoring a whole set of complicated considerations about scoring, tempo, etc.
4. And similar considerations (e.g., the existence of radically different musical traditions) go against identifying the beauty of a musical piece with less obvious structural properties of the sequence of sounds that constitutes it.
5. See Grimes (1991) for the claim that dependency and determination are different concepts.
6. See, e.g., Kim (1990a), esp. note 20.
7. But see also Bacon (1986), among others, for additional alternatives.
8. Perhaps first formulated in Hellman and Thompson (1975) as a *determina*

tion relation between facts. See Post (1987) for an in-depth treatment of physicalism in terms of global supervenience.

9. We try to formulate these questions in a manner that avoids explicit commitment to possible worlds.

10. Restricting the discussion, for the sake of simplicity, to (SC_2) and (WC_2), we can understand comparable particularization in the following sense: if the first modal operator in (SC_2) is interpreted as physical necessity and the one in (WC_2) is interpreted as logical necessity, the particularizations are not comparable. Obviously, the former of these particularizations does not entail the latter.

11. Objections against the claim that families of properties are closed under complementation date back, at least, to Post (1983). See Klagge in this volume for an attempt to answer Post's objection.

12. See Kim (1987), p. 318, note 6, for a more complete list of dissenters.

13. Paull and Sider (1992) reconsider Petrie's criticism, find it wanting, and try to improve it.

14. Specifically, Milikan (1984, 1986, 1989, 1990, 1993).

15. The causes of the shift from reductionism to antireductionism are many, and a full accounting lies beyond the scope of this introduction. Nevertheless, one cannot help but speculate that the shift has been partially due to the winds of fashion that seem to play some role in changing philosophical currents and partially due to simple failure. We can start with the failure of purported analytical reductions in epistemology and the philosophy of mind to respond to the crisp and penetrating criticisms of Chisholm and Sellars, among others (see, e.g., Chisholm 1948, 1952). At the same time, the Moorean idea that identifying moral concepts with any nonmoral concepts would commit the "naturalistic" fallacy had been presenting a formidable challenge to many a reductionist in ethics (for a discussion of Moore's argument, see Ball 1988). Nevertheless, for a while, it appeared as if reductionists could give up analytical reduction claims and take refuge in theoretical reductions. The idea was that even if one could not maintain that the properties designated by certain predicates were identical because of the analytical equivalence of the predicates, one could still hold on to the idea that these predicates designated the same property as a matter of contingent fact. Moreover, one could establish such contingent property identities by producing "theoretical" reductions, where the predicates of one theory were reduced to those of the other as specified by one or the other of the currently popular models of reduction. Thus arose, for example, the once-popular contingent type-identity theories in the philosophy of mind.

16. See Nagel (1961, chap. 11).

17. It is also a matter of dispute whether these bridge laws have to be biconditional or whether one-way conditionals connecting the two theories would be sufficient.

18. But Kim (1992) suggests the interesting point that multiple *realization* is not needed to jeopardize Nagel-type reductions; all one needs is that for some key predicates in the to-be-reduced theory, there is no unique predicate in the reducing theory that can be correlated with it.

19. See Bickle (1992) for an attempt to develop a notion of reduction that is compatible with multiple realizability.
20. As a matter of fact, Davidson argues that there are no strict psychophysical laws. However, in a not altogether uncontroversial move, this has been taken to amount to there being no strict psychophysical correlations.
21. The following formulation was presented by Kim in 1990 in his NEH seminar entitled "Supervenience and Its Philosophical Applications." See also Kim (1990a) for an alternative formulation.
22. See Post (1983) and Teller (1983).
23. For example, in Armstrong (1978).
24. And, of course, there would have to be a *unique* Cartesian entity; if there were more than one, assuming that their distinctness requires their having different mental properties, there would be a mental difference without a physical difference.
25. Kim (1993), appealing to similar considerations with a new twist, confronts the nonreductive materialist with the further problem of "downward causation."
26. Georgalis (forthcoming).
27. Schiffer (1987, pp. 153–4).
28. Horgan (1993) uses 'superdupervenience' to designate ontological supervenience that can be further explained by materialistically respectable explanations.
29. This seems to be the general drift of Kim (1990a).
30. See, e.g., Grimes (1988).
31. See, e.g., Sklar (1967).

REFERENCES

Armstrong, D. M. (1978). *A Theory of Universals*, Vol. 2 of *Universals and Scientific Realism*. Cambridge University Press.

Bacon, J. (1986). "Supervenience, Necessary Coextension and Reducibility," *Philosophical Studies* 49: 163–76.

Bickle, J. (1992). "Multiple Realizability and Psychophysical Reduction," *Behavior and Philosophy* 20: 47–58.

Bonevac, D. (1988). "Supervenience and Ontology," *American Philosophical Quarterly* 25: 37–47.

Chisholm, R. M. (1948). "The Problem of Empiricism," *Journal of Philosophy* 45. Reprinted in *Perceiving, Sensing and Knowing*, R. J. Swartz (ed.). Los Angeles: University of California Press, pp. 347–54.

(1952). "Intentionality and the Theory of Signs," *Philosophical Studies* 3: 81–92.

Davidson, D. (1970). "Mental Events," in *Experience and Theory*, L. Foster and J. W. Swanson (eds.). Amherst: University of Massachusetts Press, pp. 79–101.

Geach, P. (1956). "Good and Evil," *Analysis* 17, no. 2: 33–42.

Georgalis, N. (forthcoming). "Review of John Heil's *The Nature of True Minds*," *Philosophical Psychology*.

Grimes, T. R. (1988). "The Myth of Supervenience," *Pacific Philosophical Quarterly* 69: 152–60.

(1991). "Supervenience, Determination and Dependency," *Philosophical Studies* 62: 81–92.

Hare, R. M. (1952). *The Language of Morals.* New York: Harcourt, Brace and World.

Hellman, G., and Thompson, F. (1975). "Physicalism: Ontology, Determination and Reduction," *Journal of Philosophy* 72: 551–64.

Horgan, T. (1993). "From Supervenience to Superdupervenience: Meeting the Demands of a Material World," *Mind* 102: 555–86.

Kim, J. (1983). "Supervenience and Supervenient Causation," *Southern Journal of Philosophy* 22, Supplement: 45–56.

(1984). "Concepts of Supervenience," *Philosophy and Phenomenological Research* 45: 153–76.

(1987). "'Strong' and 'Global' Supervenience Revisited," *Philosphy and Phenomenological Research* 48: 315–26.

(1989a). "The Myth of Non-Reductive Materialism," *Proceedings of the American Philosophical Association* 63: 31–47.

(1989b). "Mechanism, Purpose and Explanatory Exclusion," in *Philosophical Perspectives*, Vol. 3, J. Tomberlin (ed.). Atascadero, Calif.: Ridgeview, pp. 77–108.

(1990a). "Supervenience as a Philosophical Concept," *Metaphilosophy* 21: 1–27.

(1990b). "Explanatory Exclusion and the Problem of Mental Causation," in *Information, Semantics and Epistemology,* E. Villanueva (ed.). Oxford: Basil Blackwell, pp. 36–56.

(1992). "Multiple Realization and the Metaphysics of Reduction," *Philosophy and Phenomenological Research* 52: 1–26.

(1993). "The Non-Reductivist's Troubles with Mental Causation," in *Mental Causation,* J. Heil and A. Mele (eds.). Oxford: Clarendon Press, pp. 189–210.

Miller, R. (1990). "Supervenience is a Two-Way Street," *Journal of Philosophy* 87: 695–701.

Millikan, R. (1984). *Language, Thought and Other Biological Categories.* Cambridge, Mass.: MIT Press.

(1986). "Thoughts without Laws: Cognitive Science without Contents," *Philosophical Review* 95: 47–80.

(1989). "Biosemantics," *Journal of Philosophy* 86: 281–97.

(1990). "Truth-Values, Hoverflies and the Kripke–Wittgenstein Paradox," *Philosophical Review* 99: 323–53.

(1993). "Explanation in Biopsychology," in *Mental Causation,* J. Heil and A. Mele (eds.). Oxford University Press, pp. 211–32.

Moore, G. E. (1922). "The Conception of Intrinsic Value," in *Philosophical Studies.* London: Routledge and Kegan Paul, pp. 253–75.

Nagel, T. (1961). *The Structure of Science.* New York: Harper, Brace and World.

Paull, C. P., and Sider, T. R. (1992). "In Defense of Global Supervenience," *Philosophy and Phenomenological Research* 52: 833–54.

Petrie, B. (1987). "Global Supervenience and Reduction," *Philosophy and Phenomenological Research* 48: 119–30.

Post, J. (1983). "Comments on Teller," *Southern Journal of Philosophy* 22, Supplement: 163–7.

——— (1987). *The Faces of Existence.* Ithaca, N.Y.: Cornell University Press.

Putnam, H. (1967). "Psychological Predicates," in *Art, Mind and Religion,* W. H. Capitan and D. D. Merrill (eds.). Pittsburgh: University of Pittsburgh Press, pp. 37–48.

Schiffer, S. (1987). "The Fido-Fido Theory of Belief," in *Philosophical Perspectives,* Vol. 1, J. Tomberlin (ed.). Atascadero, Calif.: Ridgeview, pp. 455–80.

Sklar, L. (1967). "Types of Inter-theoretic Reduction," *British Journal for the Philosophy of Science* 18: 109–24.

Teller, P. (1983). "Comments on Kim's Paper," *Southern Journal of Philosophy* 22: Supplement: 57–62.

Van Cleve, J. (1990). "Supervenience and Closure," *Philosophical Studies* 58: 225–38.

Varieties of Supervenience

BRIAN P. McLAUGHLIN

In recent years, supervenience has been the subject of extensive philosophical analysis.[1] Varieties of supervenience have been distinguished, their pairwise logical relationships examined, and their usefulness for various purposes scrutinized. However, despite extensive analysis, some details are askew, some controversies unresolved. I will by no means attempt to straighten out all the details or to settle all the controversies. But I will take a detailed look at what others have said and add a couple of wrinkles.

In Section 1, I present and explore the core intuitive idea of supervenience. In Section 2, I argue that the possible-world versions of weak and strong supervenience do not imply, respectively, the modal-operator versions of weak and strong. In Section 3, I discuss an aspect of global supervenience, in particular what it is for two worlds to have the same total pattern of distribution of properties of a certain sort. In Section 4, I examine the logical relationships between weak and global supervenience, and between strong and global. In Section 5, I make some observations about multiple-domain weak and strong supervenience. In Section 6, I consider whether any variety of supervenience implies reduction. Finally, in Section 7, I briefly note two theoretical uses of supervenience.

1. The Core Idea

There is a vernacular use of 'supervene'. Dr. Samuel Johnson's *A Dictionary of the English Language* (1775), Vol. 2, informs us that 'supervene' derives from the Latin *super*, meaning "on," "above," or "additional," and from the Latin verb *venire* meaning "to come." And Dr. Johnson's dictionary defines 'supervene' as "to come as an extraneous addition," and 'supervenient' as "added, additional."[2] More recently, *Webster's New International Dictionary*, 3d edition (1986), defines 'supervene' as "coming or occurring as something additional, extraneous, or unexpected" and cites the following use by George Santayana: "An event supervened that brought disaster to my uncle's family."

I mention the vernacular use of 'supervene' only to set it aside as irrelevant to understanding its current philosophical use. 'Supervene' is today used in philosophy as a term of art. The current philosophical use of 'supervene' is different from the vernacular use in ways that will be apparent shortly, and it is not intended to be *in any way* beholden to the vernacular use. (In this way, the use of 'supervene' in current philosophical discourse differs from, say, the use of 'cause' in such discourse, which is to some extent constrained by vernacular usage.) The literature on supervenience contains various nonequivalent definitions that purport to be definitions of types of supervenience, types with labels such as "strong supervenience," "weak supervenience," and "global supervenience." The point to note for now is that the definitions are in no sense intended to capture ways in which, or senses in which, something can "come or occur as something additional, extraneous, or unexpected."[3]

What, then, is supervenience in the (current) philosophical sense? We noted that there are various definitions of types of supervenience. Before looking at them, let us ask, What is supervenience *itself*? Of supervenience, David Lewis says: "The idea is simple and easy: we have supervenience when [and only when] there could be no difference of one sort without differences of another sort" (1986, p. 14).[4] Suppose that there could be no difference of sort A without some difference of sort B. Then, and only then, A-respects supervene on B-respects. Thus, for example, mental respects supervene on physical respects if and only if there could be no difference of a mental sort without some difference of a physical sort; moral respects supervene on "natural" respects if and only if there could be no difference of a moral sort without some difference of a natural sort; and so on.[5]

We see, then, that supervenience has to do with sameness and difference, topics of philosophical discussion since the pre-Socratics. More specifically, it has to do with the fact that sameness in certain respects can exclude the possibility of difference in certain other respects. Suppose that there could be no difference of sort A without some difference of sort B. Then, difference in any A-respect requires difference in some B-respect. Thus, if there is no difference in any B-respect, then there can be no difference in any A-respect. Exact similarity in B-respects excludes the possibility of difference in A-respects. Moreover, if exact similarity in B-respects excludes the possibility of difference in A-respects, then there could be no difference in A-respects without some difference in B-respects. Thus, A-respects supervene on B-respects if and only if exact similarity in B-respects excludes the possibility of difference in A-respects. So, for example, mental respects supervene on physical respects if and only if exact similarity in every physical respect excludes the possibility of difference in any mental respect.[6]

This simple and easy idea of supervenience – hereafter, to be called "the *core idea* of supervenience" – is the idea of *dependent-variation*, where the dependency is of a *purely modal* sort. Variation in *A*-respects depends on variation in *B*-respects in that *A*-respects *cannot* vary without variation in *B*-respects. Variation in the *supervenient A*-respects *requires* variation in the *subvenient B*-respects. *A*-respects *fail* to supervene on *B*-respects when and only when *A*-respects can vary *independently* of variations in *B*-respects. I will thus sometimes refer to the relation of supervenience as the relation of dependent-variation.[7] Supervenience, so understood, is a purely modal dependent-variation relation that is reflexive, transitive, and neither symmetrical nor asymmetrical (cf. Kim 1984).

We could, of course, modify the core idea in various ways. We could weaken it by eliminating the modal aspect of the dependency. We could say that *A*-respects supervene on *B*-respects when and only when there is no difference of sort *A* without a difference of sort *B*. We might call this "de facto supervenience." However, as far as I can see, this weaker idea is without theoretical interest. We could also, of course, strengthen the core idea by modifying it so as to ensure irreflexivity. We could say that we have supervenience of *A*-respects on *B*-respects when and only when there could be no difference of sort *A* without some *further* difference of sort *B*. While I have no objection to this modification, there seems little point in making it. As a final example, we could, of course, strengthen the core idea as follows. We could stipulate that we have supervenience of *A*-respects on *B*-respects when and only when there could be no difference of sort *A* without some further difference of sort *B* that *makes it the case* that there is the difference of sort *A* in question.[8] The strengthened idea is that for *A*-respects to supervene on *B*-respects, *A*-differences must hold *in virtue* of *B*-differences. 'In virtue of' implies 'because of'. Thus, supervenience, so understood, would require an explanatory relationship: for *A*-differences to supervene on *B*-differences, *A*-differences must be explainable by *B*-differences. Supervenience would, then, fail to be a purely modal dependent-variation relation. For the explanatory relationship in question cannot be defined solely in modal terms.[9]

The core idea of supervenience is, however, much simpler and easier than the stronger idea under consideration; the core is far better understood. The core idea gives us a firm intuitive grip on supervenience; the stronger idea cries out for explication. And while the in-virtue-of relation cannot be explicated *solely* in modal terms, it has been hoped that some type of purely modal dependent-variation relation will at least figure significantly in an explication of it (see Kim 1984). Moreover, the types of supervenience one finds characterized in the current literature are almost all purely modal dependent-variation relations, rather than explanatory relations.[10] For these reasons, let us continue to take supervenience itself to be a purely modal dependent-variation relation. On our conception of supervenience, A-respects can supervene on B-respects even if B-differences fail to explain A-differences. In what remains of this section, let us explore the core idea further and comment on how it relates to the various technical definitions of types of supervenience one finds in the literature.

To begin, suppose that some x and some y differ in some A-respect. According to the core idea, then, if A-respects supervene on B-respects, must x and y differ in some B-respect, or is it enough that there is some appropriate v distinct from x and some appropriate w distinct from y such that v and w differ in some B-respect? One could allow for either possibility and remain faithful to the core idea of supervenience – the idea that there could be no difference of sort A without a difference of sort B. One could say that (1) no x and no y can differ in some A-respect without differing in some B-respect. Or one could say that (2) no x and y can differ in some A-respect without some v that bears a certain relation R to x and some w that bears R to y differing in some B-respect. While nonequivalent, (1) and (2) are both faithful to the core idea. Kim (1988) counts supervenience theses of sort (1) as "single-domain" and those of sort (2) as "multiple-domain." Multiple-domain supervenience may well serve theoretical purposes not served by single-domain supervenience. For example, there may be dependent-variation relationships between certain properties of certain objects and certain properties of distinct objects that wholly constitute them. Suppose, for instance, that clay statues are not lumps of clay, that they are, instead, constituted at any time by some lump of clay.[11] Then, the following would be a plausible instance of multiple-domain supervenience: no two clay statues can differ in shape at a certain time without some difference in the shapes of the lumps of clay that constitute them at that time. But of multiple-domain supervenience, more in Section 5.[12]

In the clay statue example, we spoke of A-differences and B-differences holding at the same time. However, supervenience need not be a synchronic relation. We can allow for diachronic supervenience while remaining faithful to the core idea. A supervenience thesis might imply that there could be no A-difference at a certain time t without a B-difference at some appropriate time t^*, distinct from t. For example, according to some historical-externalist theories of intentional content, there could be no difference in the intentional contents of the thoughts of two individuals at a time without some difference in their causal interactions with the environment at some earlier time or else some intrinsic difference. Or a supervenience thesis might imply that there could be no A-difference from a time t to a time t^* without

some B-difference from t to t^*. For example, it may be that there could
be no mental difference in an object from a time t to a time t^* without
some physical difference in the object from time t to time t^*.[13] Moreover, there are *atemporal* supervenience relations. Here is one: two
numbers could not differ with respect to the property of being a prime
without their differing with respect to the property of being divisible
only by themselves and by 1. The differences between sychronic, diachronic, and atemporal supervenience will not, however, be explored
in what follows.

Consider the claim that there could be no *big* A-difference with a *big*
B-difference, the claim that *extensive* similarity in B-respects excludes
the possibility of extensive differences in A-respects. This is a purely
modal dependent-variation relation. Indeed, it, arguably, does not
even involve a modification of the core idea that there could be no
difference of one sort without a difference of another sort; for perhaps
we could take big A-differences, for instances, to be one sort of A-
difference. In any case, this idea is not widely discussed. However, Kim
calls this "similarity-based supervenience" and contrasts it with "indiscernibility-based supervenience," the sort we have been considering
thus far (see Kim 1987, 1988). And he has suggested that it may serve
theoretical purposes not served by indiscernibility-based supervenience. Similarity-based supervenience will be discussed in Section 3.

There are, of course, as many sorts of differences as there are ways
of sorting anything that can be sorted. And anything that is a subject
of predication can be sorted: for example, events, states, processes,
objects, stuff, persons, social institutions, waves (of the ocean sort and
of the electromagnetic sort), space-time regions, strings (in the physicist's sense), sets, numbers, universals, tropes, possible worlds, facts,
conditions, propositions, and properties can differ in respects, if each
of these is among what there is. Moreover, by differences of sort A may
be meant, for example, differences with respect to what A-type objects
there are, to what A-type events occur, to what A-conditions obtain,
to what A-properties are exemplified, to what A-states of affairs obtain, to what A-facts hold, to what A-sentences are true, to what
A-propositions are true, to what A-laws there are, to what A-events
something undergoes, to what A-conditions something is in, to what
A-properties something has, to what the A-facts about something are,
and/or to what A-predicates are true of something. The relata of supervenience relations, it appears, are many and varied indeed.

The question naturally arises as to whether there are *primary* relata
of the supervenience relation. Consider the causal relation. Events are
often claimed to be the primary relata of the causal relation; objects,
it is claimed, are only causes in a derivative way, by virtue of their
participation in events which are causes. (The rock broke the window,

but it did so only in virtue of, say, the impact of the rock breaking the window.) Is there some uniform ontological category whose members are the primary relata of the supervenience relation?

Kim (1984) suggests that properties (more accurately, nonempty sets of properties) may be such relata.[14] Differences in A-respects may invariably hold, ultimately, in virtue of differences with respect to what A-properties some x and some y have, that is, in virtue of some x having some A-property some y lacks. However, Kim appears to use 'property' in its most liberal philosophical sense: he appears to take every meaningful predicate to express a property and two predicates to express different properties if they are nonsynonymous. (He speaks even of impossible properties, properties expressed by predicates of the form 'is F and is not F'.) I take such a use of 'property' to be *pleonastic*, rather than to designate an ontological category, a mode of being.[15] I have used 'respect' rather than 'property' to try to avoid the impression that I was speaking of a mode of being. My use of 'respect' is pleonastic. Taking properties in Kim's sense to be the primary relata of the supervenience relation would, I believe, be no different from taking respects in my sense to be such. If 'property' is used pleonastically, then it does not answer our question of whether there is any uniform ontological category whose members are the primary relata of supervenience relations to say that properties are. If, however, 'property' is intended to designate an ontological category, then it is very much an open question whether properties are the primary relata of supervenience relations. For it may not be the case that A-differences invariably hold, ultimately, in virtue of some x having some A-property some y lacks.

Instead of employing a pleonastic use of 'property', one might, of course, appeal directly to predicates, taking them to be the primary relata of supervenience relations (see Davidson 1985, 1993). It may be that A-differences invariably hold, ultimately, in virtue of some A-predicate being true of some x and failing to be true of some y. Unlike the case of properties, one finds little dispute over whether predicates are among the things that there are; that is an attraction of this proposal. However, it may well not be the case that A-differences invariably hold, ultimately, in virtue of some A-predicate being true of some x and failing to be true of some y. It may be that when some A-predicate is true of some x and fails to be true of some y, that is so in virtue of some A-difference between x and y. If so, A-predicate differences would be secondary to those A-differences.

Whether there is some uniform ontological category whose members are the primary relata of supervenience relations will be left open here. As should be apparent, this issue turns, in part, on difficult questions about the relationship between certain ontological categories. Some of the would-be relata of the supervenience relation mentioned four paragraphs back may be analyzable in terms of others: facts may just be obtaining states of affairs; events may just be exemplifications of certain sorts of properties; possible worlds may just be maximally consistent states of affairs or, instead, just be "maximal" universals or, instead, just be complete space-times; laws may just be certain kinds of true sentences or just be certain kinds of singular relations between certain universals. Also, some of the would-be relata may be relevantly dependent on others: for example, predicates may be true of things in virtue of the things' having properties expressed by the predicates; sentences may be true in virtue of expressing true propositions. Moreover, as should also be apparent, the issue of the primary relata of supervenience relations turns on the issue of what there is. Some of these would-be relata may not be among what there is. (My use of 'some' in the previous sentence is, of course, substitutional.) For example, perhaps there are no facts. If so, then facts are not among the relata of supervenience relations since there are none. I will leave all such ontological issues open and continue to use 'respect' in a pleonastic sense. Like most philosophers who do metaphysics, I have opinions about these issues. But this is not the place to air them. The issues turn on broad theoretical considerations that have nothing especially to do with supervenience. An investigation of supervenience can proceed quite a long way without settling any of them. Suffice it to note that should the relata of supervenience relations prove to be a heterogeneous lot with no uniform ontological category serving as primary, nothing disturbing would follow about supervenience itself. Perhaps there is a uniform ontological category whose members are the primary relata of supervenience relations; then, again, perhaps there is not. Either way, the core idea of supervenience remains simple and easy enough: we have supervenience when and only when there could be no difference of one sort without a difference of another sort.

A final preliminary point: Lewis complains that one finds an "unlovely proliferation of nonequivalent definitions of supervenience" in the current literature and warns that "a useful notion threatens to fade into confusion" (1986, p. 14). There are, however, many ways in which there could be no difference of one sort without a difference of another sort. It is important to sort out at least the basic ways; some are stronger than others; some are entirely logically independent of others; and some may serve theoretical purposes others won't. We have already noted at least two ways – single-domain and multiple-domain supervenience – and there are many more specific ways of each of these sorts. Moreover, it should be noted that virtually all of the relevant definitions one finds in the literature are billed as definitions of *types* of supervenience, rather than as definitions of supervenience itself. Most of these specify relations that are *determinates* of the *determinable* relation expressed by the core idea, the relation of (purely modal) dependent-variation. Distinguishing determinates of this determinable relation is useful and important for the reasons just mentioned and is not something to be discouraged. (It should be noted that from the fact that there are different determinates of the supervenience relation, it does not follow that 'supervenience' is ambiguous. There are different determinates of color; that is to say, there are many ways in which something can be colored: it can be red, or blue, etc. That does not make 'color' ambiguous.)

Embracing the core idea of supervenience gives us a test for whether a would-be definition of a type of supervenience succeeds in characterizing a type. To do so, it must succeed in characterizing a determinate of the determinable relation of dependent-variation. One question to ask of a would-be definition of a type of supervenience, then, is whether any supervenience relation – that is, any dependent-variation relation – answers to it. If no relation answers to such a definition, or if the relation that answers to it is not a dependent-variation relation, then the definition fails to specify a type of supervenience in our intended sense.

Purported definitions of supervenience are sometimes presented as entirely stipulative, to be judged solely in terms of their theoretical fruits. If such a definition is *entirely stipulative*, then, of course, it need not meet our test; it is to be judged solely in terms of its theoretical fruits. However, if what answers to such a definition is not a dependent-variation relation, then the stipulated sense of 'supervenience' is different from ours. When that happens, there would be little point in fighting over who gets to keep the word 'supervenience'. Nevertheless, the difference should be pointed out. If there are different senses of 'supervenience' in the philosophical literature, they should be flagged as such. Otherwise, there is indeed a danger that a useful notion will "fade into confusion."

Of course, what we really want to know about a would-be definition of a type of supervenience is whether anything of theoretical interest answers to it. Some dependent-variation relations may be interesting for certain theoretical purposes and others not. But it should go without saying that there is no theoretical interest that a dependent-variation relation must serve to be a supervenience relation. Philosophers have hoped to characterize how mental properties depend on physical properties and how moral properties depend on natural properties by appealing to supervenience. But a relation need not be one that mental properties bear to physical properties or one that moral properties bear to natural properties in order to be a supervenience relation. We have supervenience when and only when there could be no difference of one sort without a difference of another sort.

It is a separate matter whether a supervenience relation will serve a certain theoretical purpose. Given that we have fixed on the core idea of supervenience, if (a purely modal) dependent-variation relation answers to a would-be definition of a type of supervenience, then the definition succeeds in characterizing a type of supervenience, theoretically interesting or not. There are a variety of supervenience relations we will examine in what follows. However, the issue of the theoretical interest of supervenience will not be addressed until Section 7.

2. Strong and Weak Supervenience

Suppose that there could be no difference of sort A between any x and any y without some difference of sort B between them.[16] That will be so if and only if any x and any y that are exactly alike in every B-respect must be exactly alike in every A-respect. Let us stipulate that any x and any y are A[or B]-*twins* if and only if x and y are exactly alike in every A[or B]-respect. ('Twins' is used here such that everything is, trivially, an A[or B]-twin of itself. That may seem odd, but it should lead to no misunderstanding.) Given this use of 'twins', there could be no difference of sort A between any x and any y without some difference of sort B between them if and only if any x and any y that are B-twins must be A-twins. (The 'must' must, of course, be coordinate with the 'could'.) We have supervenience of A-respects on B-respects when and only when being B-twins excludes the possibility of failing to be A-twins.

As is well known, one way Kim (1987, 1988, 1990) has distinguished weak and strong supervenience is by using quantification over possible worlds, rather than using modal locutions such as 'could' and 'must'. Let us present weak and strong supervenience using our notion of twins and joining Kim in quantifying over possible worlds:[17]

Weak Supervenience A-respects weakly supervene on B-respects $=_{df}$ for any possible world w, B-twins in w are A-twins in w.

Strong Supervenience A-respects strongly supervene on B-respects $=_{df}$ for any possible worlds w and w^* and any individuals x and y, if x in w is a B-twin of y in w^*, then x in w is an A-twin of y in w^*.

Strong supervenience and weak supervenience are so called, respectively, because strong implies weak and weak does not imply strong. Of course, subvariants of both weak and strong supervenience are possible by restricting the universe of discourse of the quantifiers. The worlds in the range of the quantifiers may include all logically possible worlds, only the causally possible worlds, only the nomologically possible worlds, or something else.[18] Thus, for example, it is a weak supervenience thesis that for any causally possible world w, B-twins in w are

A-twins in *w;* it is also a weak supervenience thesis that for any logically possible world *w, B*-twins in *w* are *A*-twins in *w;* and the second thesis entails the first, but not conversely. Weak and strong supervenience, so defined, are determinates of the determinable relation of (purely modal) dependent-variation. Each is a way that there could be no *A*-difference without a *B*-difference; each is a way that exact sameness in *B*-respects can exclude the possibility of difference in *A*-respects. In the case of weak supervenience, exact sameness in *B*-respects within a world is always accompanied by sameness in *A*-respects within that world; in the case of strong, exact sameness in *B*-respects across any two worlds is always accompanied by sameness in *A*-respects across them.

As is also well known, Kim (1984, 1987, 1990; see also Sosa 1984) has offered would-be definitions of weak and strong supervenience using 'necessity', rather than quantification over possible worlds. But Kim holds (1987, 1990) that the "modal operator" definitions of weak and strong are equivalent to the possible-worlds definitions of weak and strong, respectively. I think that he is mistaken. But let us first turn to the modal operator definitions and then to the question of equivalence.

Following Kim, we will focus on property-supervenience, taking the relata of property-supervenience relations to be nonempty sets of properties. Kim's modal-operator definitions can be fomulated as follows, where *A* and *B* are nonempty sets of properties:

> **Modal-Operator Weak Supervenience** *A* weakly supervenes on *B* $=_{df}$ necessarily, if anything has some property *F* in *A*, then there is at least one property *G* in *B* such that that thing has *G*, and everything that has *G* has *F.*

> **Modal-Operator Strong Supervenience** *A* strongly supervenes on *B* $=_{df}$ necessarily, if anything has some property *F* in *A*, then there is at least one property *G* in *B* such that that thing has *G*, and necessarily everything that has *G* has *F.*

There is, you will notice, a one-word difference between the definitions of modal-operator strong and weak supervenience: the definition of strong supervenience contains one more occurrence of 'necessarily' than does the definition of weak. Thus, strong implies weak, but not conversely. Of course, subvariants of these modal-operator notions are possible that employ different notions of necessity (e.g., causal necessity as opposed to logical necessity).

Let us use 'WS$_p$' and 'WS$_m$' to abbreviate 'possible-world weak supervenience' and 'modal-operator weak supervenience', respectively; and let us use 'SS$_p$' and 'SS$_m$' to abbreviate 'possible-world strong supervenience' and 'modal-operator strong supervenience', respectively.[19] Kim (1984) argues that WS_p and WS_m characterize equivalent relations. Kim (1987) argues that "the relation $[SS_p]$ characterizes is equivalent to strong supervenience as given by $[SS_m]$" (p. 317). Kim (1990) explicitly qualifies these claims of equivalence, saying that the relations in question are equivalent given certain assumptions about property composition; but this qualification is implicitly understood in Kim (1984, 1987). Of the assumptions about property composition, more shortly.

Another assumption that Kim makes in arguing for these equivalences is that talk of necessity can be replaced by universal quantification over possible worlds. Two observations are worth reporting. The first is that SS_m uses 'necessarily' twice, and it need not be used with the same modal force in each occurrence. The two occurrences need not express the same kind of necessity; one might express (say) metaphysical necessity, and the other nomological necessity. But SS_p uses two quantifications over worlds of the same sort (e.g., metaphysically possible worlds). Having noted this difference, however, I will pass it by since the two modalities in an SS_m thesis can be captured by an SS_p thesis using the notion of *accessibility* relations between worlds.[20]

It should also be observed, however, that 'necessary' is sometimes used in ways that cannot be captured by quantification over possible worlds (even assuming that there are possible worlds). For example, by 'logically necessary', philosophers often mean 'logically true'; and by 'analytically necessary', they often mean 'analytically true'. W. V. O. Quine (1953, pp. 22–3) noted that on (one of) the logical positivist conception(s) of analyticity, there are two types of analytical truths: logical truths, and truths that can be turned into logical truths by substitution of synonyms.[21] On this conception, logical truths are analytical truths. But there are analytical truths that are not logical truths; for instance, it is arguable that it is an analytical truth that brothers are males, but this truth is not a logical truth. Nevertheless, the logically possible worlds = the analytically possible worlds. It is true in every logically possible world that brothers are males. Of course, if by 'logically necessary' one means true in every logically possible world, then it is logically necessary that brothers are males. But, as we noted, it is not a logical truth that brothers are males. And all and only the logical truths are logically true. The point is that quantification over possible worlds will not capture the difference between 'logically necessary' and 'analytically necessary', when 'logically necessary' is used as a synonym of 'logically true' and 'analytically necessary' is used as a synonym of 'analytically true'. Moreover, it is arguable that there are metaphysically necessary truths that are neither logical truths nor analytical truths; for example, the truth that water is H_2O is arguably such (cf.

Kripke 1971). If it is indeed metaphysically necessary that water is H_2O, then it is true that water is H_2O in every metaphysically possible world. But the metaphysically possible worlds = the logically possible worlds = the analytically possible worlds. Logical truths, analytical truths, and "metaphysical truths" are all true in literally every possible world. The differences between them are not captured by quantification over worlds.[22]

Of course, Kim intends his uses of 'necessary' in WS_m and SS_m to be replaceable by universal quantification over possible worlds. But they are not always so used in would-be supervenience theses. Consider the following thesis suggested by Dreier (1992), in which C is the set of moral properties and D is the set of natural properties:

> It is analytically necessary that for any object x and any property F in C, if x has F, then there exists a property G in D such that x has G, and it is metaphysically necessary that if any y has G, it has F.

Dreier intends a contrast between 'analytically necessary' and 'metaphysically necessary'. But, as we just noted, there is none when talk of necessity is to be replaceable by quantification over possible worlds. Thus, Dreier's supervenience thesis is not an instance of SS_m, as intended by Kim. Dreier might reformulate his proposal as follows:

> It is analytically true that it is metaphysically necessary that for any object x and any property F in C, if x has F, then there exists a property G in D such that x has G, and it is metaphysically necessary that if any y has G, it has F.

But this too fails to be an instance of an SS_m thesis. It is, rather, a claim that a certain SS_m thesis is analytically true. (The claim is awkward, for the first occurrence of 'metaphysically necessary' is redundant.)

Given that occurrences of 'necessarily' in a WS_m and in an SS_m thesis are to be replaced by universal quantification over worlds, WS_m implies WS_p, and SS_m implies SS_p.[23] However, in what remains of this section, I will argue that, in each case, the implication fails in the other direction: WS_p fails to imply WS_m, and SS_p fails to imply SS_m. Thus, the relation characterized by WS_p is not equivalent to the relation characterized by WS_m, and the one characterized by SS_p is not equivalent to the one characterized by SS_m. Indeed, as we will see, SS_p fails to imply even WS_m. The relations of SS_p and WS_m are thus entirely logically independent: neither implies the other.

Here is one reason why the implications in question fail. Both the WS_m and SS_m of a nonempty set, A, of properties on a nonempty set, B, of properties imply that it is necessarily the case that if something has an A-property (i.e., a member of set A), then it has some B-property. But neither the WS_p nor the SS_p of A-properties on B-

properties implies that. Indeed, neither implies that it is even as a matter of fact the case that if something has an A-property, then it has some B-property. For one way in which two things can be twins (i.e., exactly alike) with respect to B-properties is for both of them to lack any B-property whatsoever.[24] Thus, WS_p fails to imply WS_m, and SS_p fails to imply SS_m. Indeed, SS_p fails to imply even WS_m.

Kim's assumptions about property composition would block this line of argument for nonequivalence *if* by a B-property one were to mean a property of some type B, rather than a property that is a member of some nonempty set B of properties. For one of Kim's assumptions is this:

(N) For any B-property P, not having P is itself a B-property.

Given (N), for any type of property B, everything must have B-properties.[25] There are, however, at least two reasons one might reject (N). First, one might deny (N) because one denies

(N*) If P is a property, then not having P is too.

One might deny that complementation is a property-forming operation. One might thus deny that there are any "negative" properties. If one takes (empirical) properties to be ways things might be that endow them with causal powers, then one might deny (N). For one might hold that not being a certain way is not a way of being that endows anything with causal powers.[26] If (N*) is false, so is (N). Of course, if one uses 'property' in a pleonastic sense, then trivially (N*) is true. But one can still be neutral on (N). In fact, one can even consistently countenance negative properties in a "robust sense" while denying (N). For one might deny that properties that are complements of B-properties are ipso facto B-properties. For example, one might concede that there is such a property as lacking mass but deny that the property is a physical property. Numbers lack mass but, one might claim, they do not thereby have physical properties (cf. Post 1983; 1987, pp. 178–80). (And was Descartes committed to the view that lacking extension is a physical property?) (N) might be false even if (N*) is true.

Moreover, Kim makes further assumptions about property composition. He assumes that both infinitary conjunction of and infinitary disjunction of B-properties are B-property-forming operations, and thus that for any type of property B, there are infinitary conjunctive and infinitary disjunctive B-properties. He speaks of "families" of properties closed under complementation, infinitary conjunction, and infinitary disjunction (1984, 1987). But if 'property' is understood in a nonpleonastic sense, then it is controversial whether there are such property-forming operations.[27]

Suppose, for the sake of argument, that for any type of property B, complementation, infinitary conjunction, and infinitary disjunction are B-property-forming operations. Even if this is so, it is still not the case that the relation characterized by WS_p is equivalent to the relation characterized by WS_m or that the relation characterized by SS_p is equivalent to the relation characterized by SS_m. Let us use 'closed under Boolean operations' as shorthand for 'closed under the operations of property complementation, and infinitary conjunction or infinitary disjunction'. Then, granting that there are the property-forming operations in question, and following Kim in taking the relata of property-supervenience relations to be nonempty sets of properties, Kim has at best shown:

(I) A set of A-properties WS_p on a set of B-properties iff the set of A-properties closed under Boolean operations WS_m on the set of B-properties closed under Boolean operations.

(II) A set of A-properties SS_p on a set of B-properties iff the set of A-properties closed under Boolean operations SS_m on the set of B-properties closed under Boolean operations.

However, it does not follow from (I) that if the members of a set of A-properties WS_p on a set of B-properties, then that set of A-properties WS_m on that set of B-properties; and from (II) it does not follow that if a set of A-properties SS_p on a set of B-properties, then that set of A-properties SS_m on that set of B-properties. Even if the set of all B-properties must include all properties formed by the Boolean operations in question on B-properties, there are proper subsets of this set that include no negative properties, ones that include no conjunctive properties, ones that include no disjunctive properties, and ones that include no negative, conjunctive, or disjunctive properties. A set of A-properties can bear the WS_p relation to a proper subset of the set of all B-properties, even when it fails to bear the WS_m relation to that proper subset. Thus, a set of A-properties can bear the WS_p relation to a set of B-properties, even when the set fails to bear the WS_m relation to that set of B-properties. Indeed, a set of A-properties can bear the SS_p relation to a set of B-properties, even when the set of A-properties fails to bear the WS_m relation to that set of B-properties. However, two relations, R and R^*, are equivalent relations only if it is impossible for some x to bear R to some y and it not be the case that x bears R^* to y. Thus, the weak and strong relations characterized by the modal-operator definitions are not equivalent, respectively, to the weak and strong relations characterized by the possible-world definitions. They are nonequivalent, even if the controversial assumptions about property-forming operations are accepted. From those assumptions,

(I) and (II) may follow. But even given the assumptions, it does *not* follow that "the relation [SS_p] characterizes is equivalent to strong supervenience as given by [SS_m]" (Kim 1987, p. 317), and likewise for WS_p and WS_m. Indeed, as I indicated, the relation characterized by SS_p does not even require the relation characterized by WS_m.

As we noted earlier, WS_p and SS_p are determinates of the determinable relation of (purely modal) dependent variation. In contrast, if we take the relata of property-supervenience relations to be nonempty sets of properties, then WS_m and SS_m property-supervenience go beyond the core idea of supervenience: they are not determinates of the relation of dependent-variation. WS_m and SS_m appear to characterize what we might call "dependence–determination" relations. If a nonempty set, *A*, of properties WS_m or SS_m on a nonempty set, *B*, of properties, then (i) having any property *F* in *A requires* having at least one property *G* in *B* such that (ii) having *G suffices* (materially or modally) for having *F*. Condition (i) is the dependency component; (ii) is the determination component (cf. Van Cleve 1990). WS_m and SS_m do not characterize supervenience relations in our intended sense. If it is insisted that the definitions are, by stipulation, characterizations of supervenience relations, then 'supervenience' is being used differently from our intended sense. WS_m and SS_m do not characterize supervenience relations in the same sense of 'supervenience' as do WS_p and SS_p. The latter characterize determinates of the determinable relation of dependent-variation, while the former do not. As we noted earlier, there is no point in fighting over the word 'supervenience'. But it is important to flag such differences when we find them; otherwise "a useful notion threatens to fade into confusion."

It should go without saying that nothing I have argued in this section gives us any reason to eschew the notions of WS_m and SS_m. These notions may well serve theoretical purposes not served by WS_p and SS_p, or indeed by any supervenience relation. Dependence-determination relations are interesting in their own right.

3. Global Supervenience

We have thus far considered two determinates, WS_p and SS_p, of the determinable relation of dependent-variation. Let us turn to a third determinate, global supervenience, a type of supervenience that is being appealed to with increasing frequency in philosophical literature.[28] We might initially formulate global supervenience using our notion of twins:

Global Supervenience   *A*-respects globally supervene on *B*-respects $=_{df}$ all worlds that are *B*-twins are *A*-twins.

Things begin to get complicated, however, when we ask what it is for two worlds to be A-twins (i.e., exactly alike in A-respects). The notion of twin worlds admits of no simple characterization.

What is it, for instance, for two worlds to be twins with respect to, say, A-*properties*?[29] A natural suggestion is that two worlds are twins with respect to A-properties if and only if they have all and only the same A-properties. However, if the notion of A-property twin worlds is understood in that way, then, as Paull and Sider (1992) correctly note in an important paper,

> global supervenience would be trivial in typical cases. For example, if [the set of properties] A contains only intentional properties like *believing that snow is white*, then any two worlds will have the same A-properties because possible worlds do not have beliefs. (p. 834)

Indeed, intentional properties would globally supervene on any set or kind of property whatsoever since two worlds will always be twins with respect to intentional properties: for any such property, two worlds will both lack it.

When theorists talk of worlds that are indiscernible with respect to A-properties, they typically mean not that the worlds have all and only the same A-properties, but rather that the worlds have exactly the same total pattern of distribution of A-properties. One might, of course, claim that having a certain total pattern of distribution of A-properties is an A-property, one possessed by the world itself. I take that claim to be controversial, if 'property' is used in a nonpleonastic sense. But in any case, whether or not one countenances such a "constructed" A-property, it is important to see that by worlds that are indiscernible (i.e., twins) with respect to A-properties is typically meant worlds that have the same total pattern of distribution of A-properties. The intuitive idea of global property-supervenience is that there could be no difference in the worldwide pattern of distribution of A-properties without a difference in the worldwide pattern of distribution of B-properties.

But what does it mean, exactly, for two worlds to have the same total pattern of distribution of B[or A]-properties? Kim (1984, p. 168) has made the following proposal: two worlds w and w^* are indiscernible with respect to B-properties just in case for any B-property F and any individual x, x has F in w if and only if x has F in w^*. Kim has provided a *sufficient* condition for two worlds to be B[or A]-property twins; that is, he has specified a way in which two worlds *can be* B[or A]-property twins. But one may well want to deny that he has stated a *necessary* condition for two worlds to be such. Let us see why.

To begin, one might want a notion of the same total pattern of distribution of B-properties which requires that if worlds w and w^* are

B-property twin worlds, then if something in w lacks a B-property, then it must lack that property in w^*. For in the total pattern of distribution of B-properties, one might want to include absences of exemplifications of B-properties in parts of the world. Kim's proposal does not yield the requirement in question. For there are two ways in which it can fail to be the case that some x has F in a world. One way is for x to exist in the world but to lack F. Another way is for x to fail to exist (or to fail to have a counterpart in Lewis's [1986] sense) in the world. On Kim's proposal, two worlds, w and w^*, can be B-property twins when some x exists in w but not in w^*, as long as x in w lacks every B-property.[30] By 'x lacks F in w' let us mean that x exists in w, but it is not the case that x has F in w. Then, to accommodate the concern in question, one could recast Kim's proposal as follows: for any B-property F and any individual x, x has F in w if and only if x has F in w^* and x lacks F in w if and only if x lacks F in w^*.

However, on this proposal two worlds can be B[or A]-property twins only if they contain exactly the same individuals. But one might be interested in the total pattern of distribution of B-properties irrespective of whether they are distributed over numerically the same individuals. Further, if two worlds must contain exactly the same individuals to be B-property twins, then the set of essential properties of individuals in a world will globally supervene on any set of properties whatsoever. For two worlds can be property twins of any sort only if they contain the same total pattern of distribution of the essential properties in question. Finally, both Kim's proposal and the modification of it we have considered face the following concern. On some accounts of possible worlds, individuals are world-bound (Lewis 1986). If individuals are indeed world-bound, then, on Kim's proposal and on the modification of it, no two worlds will be B[or A]-property twins. Both Kim's proposal and the modification of it arguably provide sufficient conditions for two worlds to be property twins. But, as we have seen, there are reasons for denying that either provides a necessary condition for two worlds to be property twins.

Paull and Sider (1986, p. 834) claim that worlds are indiscernible with respect to B-properties if and only if there is the same total pattern of distribution of B-properties in each. And they say that

> sameness of distribution of properties means roughly 'sameness of distribution throughout time and space among the objects of that world'. When two worlds have the same distribution of [B]-properties for a set of properties [B], we will call them '[B]-indiscernible'. (1992, p. 835)

Paull and Sider tell us that the intuitive idea of B-indiscernible worlds is "that worlds are B-indiscernible iff their objects exist at the same places and times, and corresponding objects have the same B-properties" (p. 848). They sharpen the notion of B-indiscernible worlds as follows:

Let w and z be possible worlds, $D(w)$ and $D(z)$ be the set of objects existing at w and z, respectively, and B be a nonempty set of properties . . .

(D1) w and z are B-indiscernible $=_{df}$ there is a bijection Γ from $D(w)$ onto $D(z)$ such that for any x that is a member of $D(w)$ and time t, $L(x)$ has the same position and the same B-properties at t as does x (at t). (1992, p. 852)[31]

Γ is a one-to-one function that maps objects in $D(w)$ onto their "counterparts," so to speak, in $D(z)$.[32] Paull and Sider, however, do not use the term 'counterpart'. They are not committed to Lewis's (1986) theory of counterparts and world-bound individuals. If I understand them, $\Gamma(x)$ may be x, even when w is not z, though $\Gamma(x)$ may fail to be x when w is not z. The issue is left open. I will use 'counterpart' in a "loose intuitive" sense, not in Lewis's technical sense. It will be left open whether an object x in a world w can be a counterpart of itself in a distinct world w^*.

Paull and Sider have provided a sufficient condition, distinct from Kim's and the modification of Kim's, for two worlds to be property twins. Unlike those proposals, Paull and Sider's proposal allows that two worlds can be B-property twins even though B-properties are distributed over numerically different individuals. Moreover, on their proposal, two distinct worlds can be B-property twins even if individuals are world-bound. There is, however, a reason why one might not want to appeal to their bijection in formulating a global supervenience thesis. Recall that they tell us that "worlds are B-indiscernible iff their objects exist at the same places and times, and corresponding objects have the same B-properties" (1993, p. 848). Let us call, by stipulation, the property of having a certain spatial position at a certain time "a spatiotemporal property." Paull and Sider's bijection Γ is such that $\Gamma(x)$ will always have the same position as x at a time, and thus, the same spatiotemporal properties. Hence, given Γ, if two worlds are B-indiscernible, then they will be indiscernible with respect to their spatiotemporal properties. The set of spatiotemporal properties will globally supervene on the set whose sole member is the property *believing that snow is white*. Indeed, for any set B of properties, spatiotemporal properties will globally supervene on B. One may well want to avoid this result. However, as should be apparent, *whatever* bijection one chooses to map the individuals of a world onto the individuals of another, the property *being in a world with such and such cardinality* will globally supervene on any property whatsoever. Moreover, whatever property is used to identify the counterparts in one world of the individuals in another world will ipso facto globally supervene on any set of properties whatsoever. To elaborate, suppose that "counterpart-identifying properties" are used in specifying a function from the set of individuals in one world onto the set of individuals in another. Then, for any set B of properties, the counterpart-identifying properties will globally supervene on B-properties; for to be B-property twins, two worlds must be counterpart-identifying-property twins. The automatic global supervenience of the counterpart-identifying properties on every set of properties may or may not be intolerable. Whether it is intolerable will depend, I suppose, both on what the counterpart-identifying properties are and on the purposes to which one intends to put global supervenience.

Kim (1988) considered some of the problems indicated earlier for using *identity* as the bijection from individuals in one world to individuals in another in characterizing property twin worlds. He pointed out that requiring that two worlds contain exactly the same individuals to be property twins seems unacceptably strong, because it requires both that property twin worlds have the same cardinality and, for two worlds to be property twins, that the relevant properties be distributed over numerically the same individuals in each. In response to these problems, Kim made a strikingly different proposal. He suggested that in the face of issues raised by a requirement of property-indiscernibility, theorists might do best to appeal to "similarity in A (or B) respects" rather than appealing to "indiscernibility" (1988, p. 139). He says that "by replacing [indiscernibility] with [similarity] we can keep the theory [of global supervenience] itself simple and elegant, relegating the complications (the "dirty work") to its applications" (1988, p. 139; cf. 1987, p. 325). "Similarity," he correctly notes, "has enough intuitive content to keep us going at least some distance" (1988, p. 139). In short, Kim suggested that metaphysicians focus on "similarity-based" supervenience, rather than "indiscernibility-based" supervenience, and made the following proposal (1988, p. 139):

> **Similarity-based GS** A globally supervenes on B iff any two worlds that are pretty much similar in respect of B are pretty much similar in respect of A.

Of course, weak and strong similarity-based supervenience can also be defined. As we noted earlier, similarity-based supervenience is a determinate of the determinable relation of purely modal dependent-variation. I have no objection to the notion of similarity-based supervenience. Let a thousand varieties of supervenience bloom.

Similarity-based global supervenience can hold when indiscernibility-based global supervenience fails to hold. However, it is likewise the case that indiscernibility-based global supervenience can hold when similarity-based global supervenience fails to hold. These varieties of supervenience are logically independent. Of the similarity-based variety, suffice it for me to note that the relation characterized by Kim's definition of similarity-based global supervenience will fail to hold if there are any "critical points of *B*-difference" for *A*-differences. That is to say, it will fail to hold if there are any small *B*-differences that are enough for huge *A*-differences. It is worthwhile noting that this seems to be what we find in the psychophysical case, in the moral-natural case, and in the aesthetic-natural case. A few small neural changes in the central nervous systems of creatures in our world may well be enough to "pull the mental plug" in our world. A world physically just like ours except for the small neural differences in question will be pretty much like our world in physical respects. But it will be devoid of mentality. Likewise, in the moral-natural property case, a few small changes in natural properties may well be enough for vast moral differences. A few small neural changes in the central nervous systems of organisms capable of self-reflection might "pull the plug on self-reflection." A world naturalistically just like our world except for those small changes and the resulting absence of self-reflection would be devoid of moral properties. Still, such a world would be pretty much like our world in natural respects. Turn to the case of aesthetic and natural properties. Small differences in natural properties can be enough for vast differences in aesthetic properties. A world pretty much like ours in its naturalistic properties may be quite different from ours in its aesthetic properties. Indeed, I venture to say that in most cases of philosophical interest, there are critical points of *B*-difference for *A*-differences; certain small *B*-differences will be enough for vast *A*-differences. In such cases, Kim's similarity-based global supervenience will fail to hold. Various varieties of indiscernibility-based global supervenience, however, may well hold. (Analogous points can be made, of course, for similarity-based weak and similarity-based strong supervenience.) Similarity-based supervenience deserves our attention. But I see no reason whatsoever for ceasing work on indiscernibility-based supervenience.

John Haugeland (1982, p. 96) has characterized a supervenience relation that takes *truths* as relata, "without regard to how (or even whether) those truths are decomposed into properties of individuals." More specifically, Haugeland takes the relata to be true sentences within a language. *A*-truths would be true sentences with an *A*-language. For example, physical truths would be true sentences within a physical language (a language in which the physics true of our world can be expressed). Where W is a set of worlds (say, the logically possible ones, the causally possible ones, etc.), Haugeland tells us, "Two worlds in W are discernible with language L just in case there is a sentence of L which is true at one, and not true at the other" (1982, p. 96). Haugeland's brand of supervenience falls under our general notion of global supervenience.[33] Here the notion of twin worlds is easy, at least at first blush. Two worlds, w and w^*, are twins with respect to sentences in language B if and only if exactly the same sentences of B are true at each. We have global supervenience of sentences in language A on sentences in language B if and only if worlds that are twins with respect to what sentences in language B are true at them are twins with respect to what sentences in language A are true at them. Here we have necessary and sufficient conditions for twin worlds in the respects in question.

It is not the shift to language that makes the issues concerning cardinality, essential properties, and counterpart-identifying properties disappear, or at least appear to disappear. Global state of affairs supervenience and global fact supervenience can appear to avoid the issues. Two worlds are twins with respect to what B-states of affairs (e.g., physical states of affairs) obtain in them if and only if all and only the same B-states of affairs obtain in each. Two worlds are twins with respect to B-facts if and only if all and only the same B-facts are in each. (Of course, if facts just are obtaining states of affairs, then two worlds are twins with respect to B-facts if and only if they are twins with respect to what B states of affairs obtain in them.)

Haugeland speaks generally of sentences. It should be noted that his proposal will avoid the issues concerning cardinality, essential properties, and counterpart-identifying properties only if the thesis is restricted to sentences that are universally or existentially quantified and contain no singular terms. For if any of the sentences contain singular terms, terms that purport to refer to individuals, then we must be told what it is for such sentences to be true at two worlds, w and w^*. Issues about cardinality, essential properties, and counterpart-identifying properties will arise and need to be addressed. (Must exactly the same individuals be present in two worlds for the same such sentences to be true, or will counterparts do? And if counterparts will do, what properties pick out the counterparts? Will the relations that pair entities in one world with their counterparts in another require that the worlds have the same cardinality?) Similarly, global *singular* fact supervenience and *singular* state of affairs supervenience will also raise the same issues. For singular facts and singular states of affairs contain individuals (or else special functions from worlds to individuals) as constituents (cf. Kim 1988, p. 137).

I have no bright idea about what way that two worlds can have exactly the same total pattern of distribution of B[or A]-properties is the optimal way to appeal to in formulating global property-supervenience (or singular fact supervenience, etc.). Perhaps there is no way that is optimal for all the purposes global supervenience has been hoped to serve. When philosophers talk of B-property twin worlds as having exactly the same total pattern of distribution of B-properties, they need to tell us what this means.

4. Pairwise Logical Relationships

Global supervenience implies neither SS_m nor even WS_m. From the fact that A-properties globally supervene on B-properties, it does not follow that if something has an A-property, then it has some B-property.[34] Both WS_m and SS_m imply that, in every world, if something has an A-property, then it has some B-property. Thus, global supervenience implies neither SS_m nor WS_m. Do the implications go in the other direction? Does either SS_m or WS_m imply global supervenience? I will address this question in the context of examining the logical relationship between WS_p and global supervenience, and between SS_p and global. For ease on the eye, let us simply use 'weak supervenience' and 'strong supervenience' instead of 'WS_p' and 'SS_p'. And, to avoid prolixity, let us focus exclusively on indiscernibility-based property-supervenience.

To begin, then, weak supervenience does not imply global. The weak supervenience of some set A of properties on some set B of properties is consistent with there being two worlds that are twins with respect to B-properties (in any of the ways we have discussed), but in one of them nothing has any A-property, while in the other A-properties are liberally distributed throughout the world. Global supervenience is inconsistent with that; thus, weak supervenience does not imply global. (For the same reason, WS_m does not imply global.) This is quite straightforward. Other cases are complicated.

Consider an elegant proof by Kim that strong property-supervenience implies global property-supervenience:

> To show that strong supervenience entails global supervenience: assume w_1 and w_2 are B-indiscernible but A-discernible. Then for some F in A and some x, $F(x)$ in w_1 but $-F(x)$ in w_2. Let B^* be the B-maximal property of x in w_1; then by strong supervenience of A on B, necessarily $(y) [B^*(y) \rightarrow F(y)]$. Since w_2 is B-indiscernible from w_1, $B^*(x)$ in w_2. Hence, $F(x)$ in w_2, yielding a contradiction. (1984, p. 168)

This proof employs Kim's notion of a B-maximal property, which I take to be a controversial notion; for a B-maximal property is a consistent infinitary conjunction of positive and negative B-properties (see Kim 1984). Moreover, given that the relata of property-supervenience relations are nonempty sets of properties, the set B may well fail to contain any "maximal" properties (see note 29). Kim's proof won't work for sets of properties that are not closed under Boolean operations (as we understood that notion in Section 2). Furthermore, the proof presupposes Kim's definition of what it is for worlds to be indiscernible with respect to A-properties. Suppose that in some global property-supervenience thesis, the notion of A-property indiscernible worlds is not understood in Kim's way. Then, it may not follow from the fact that w_1 and w_2 are A-discernible that there is some F in A and some x, such that x has F in w_1 and x has $-F$ in w_2. There may be no such x.

However, suppose that 'the same total pattern of distribution of A[or B]-properties' is so understood that two worlds, w_1 and w_2, have the same total pattern of distribution of A[or B]-properties only if there is a bijection, J, from individuals in w_1 onto individuals in w_2 such that for any B[or A]-property, F, and for any x in w_1, x has F in w_1 if and only if $J(x)$ has F in w_2. The bijection J may be identity, or it may be, say, Paull and Sider's bijection, or some other bijection. In any case, given J, Kim's proof can be easily recast as follows (without using the notion of a B-maximal property). Assume w_1 and w_2 are B-indiscernible but A-discernible. Then, given B-indiscernibility, for every property G in B and for every x, x has G in w_1 if and only if $J(x)$ has G in w_2; but, given A-discernibility, for some F in A and some x, either x has F in w_1 and $L(x)$ lacks F in w_2 or x lacks F in w_1 and $L(x)$ has F in w_2. However, given B-indiscernibility and given strong supervenience of A on B, for any A-property F, and for any x, either x has F in w_1 and $L(x)$ has F in w_2 or x lacks F in w_1 and $L(x)$ lacks x in w_2. From that and the assumption that, for some x in w_1, either x has F in w_1 and $L(x)$ lacks F in w_2 or x lacks F in w_1 and $L(x)$ has F in w_2, we can derive a contradiction. (Of course, since SS_m implies SS_p, SS_m also implies global supervenience in any case in which a bijection of type J is employed.)

There is controversy concerning whether global supervenience implies strong, and even whether it implies weak. Kim (1984) argues that strong and global supervenience are equivalent, that "global supervenience is nothing but strong supervenience" (p. 168). In response, Petrie (1987) argues that global supervenience does not imply strong. He employs the following strategy: he attempts to show how there could be a counterexample to a strong supervenience thesis that is not a counterexample to the corresponding global supervenience thesis. He asks us to consider two worlds, w and w^*. World w contains exactly two objects, x and y. World w^* contains exactly two objects, x^* and y^*. And in w and w^* only the following hold, respectively:

World w	World w^*
x has P	x^* has P
x has S	x^* lacks S
y has P	y^* lacks P
y lacks S	y lacks S

Suppose that set A contains just one property, S, and that set B contains just one property, P. Then, the fact that there are worlds w and w^* is a counterexample to the claim that A strongly supervenes on B. For x in w is a B-twin of x^* in w^*, but x in w is not an A-twin of x^* in w^*. That there are worlds w and w^*, however, is not a counterexample to the thesis that A globally supervenes on B. Since w and w^* do not have the same total pattern of distribution of B-properties (in any relevant sense), and thus are not B-property twins, it does not matter to the truth of the global supervenience thesis in question that the worlds are not A-property twins. Petrie (1987) tells us that "since global super-venience is, and strong supervenience is not, consistent with this ex-ample, the two concepts of supervenience are not equivalent" (p. 121).

Kim (1987, p. 318) concedes to Petrie that global supervenience in-deed fails to imply strong for the reason Petrie claims it so fails. More-over, Kim claims that Petrie's example serves to show something else too, namely, that global supervenience does not imply weak. For, he points out, the existence of w is a counterexample to weak super-venience: w contains B-twins that are not A-twins, namely, x and y. But the existence of w is not, of course, a counterexample to global super-venience. From this, Kim concludes that global supervenience does not imply weak.

For reasons I will give shortly, I think that global supervenience indeed fails to imply either strong or weak supervenience. I do not, however, think that Petrie (1987) succeeds in showing that global fails to imply strong or that Kim (1987) succeeds in showing that global fails to imply weak. For from the fact that there are counterexamples to a strong or weak supervenience thesis that are not themselves coun-terexamples to a global supervenience thesis, it does not follow that the global supervenience thesis does not imply the strong or weak su-pervenience thesis. We knew prior to Petrie's discussion that there are such counterexamples: the existence of a single world of a certain sort can be a counterexample to strong and weak supervenience theses, but it takes two worlds to have a counterexample to a global supervenience thesis. Global supervenience theses do not imply strong or weak supervenience theses in virtue of logical form. But it is another matter whether global supervenience theses *metaphysically necessitate* corresponding weak and strong supervenience theses. What matters is whether it is metaphysically necessary that (true in every possible world that) *if* there is a counterexample to a strong or weak supervenience thesis, then there is a counterexample to the corresponding global supervenience thesis.

Paull and Sider (1992, p. 838) have stated a plausible metaphysical principle that yields this result for Petrie's type of counterexample to a strong or weak supervenience thesis. One can appeal to the principle to show that if there is a pair of worlds such as Petrie describes, then there would have to be a pair of worlds that is a counterexample to the global supervenience of A on B. The principle is what Lewis (1986) calls a "recombination" principle. Paull and Sider (1992) tell us, "Recombination principles share a common form: *if* certain possibilities exist, *then* certain other possibilities must exist" (p. 838). Their specific recombination principle comes into play in this way. They appeal to it to show that if there are worlds such as w and w^*, then there is a pair of worlds that is a counterexample to the global supervenience of A on B:

> We will need the undefined notion of *duplicate*. The idea is that duplicates are exactly qualitatively similar considered "as they are in themselves" and not in relation to other things. Imagine indistinguishable marbles, or identical twins exactly similar down to the last detail. Following Lewis [1986, pp. 59–63], *intrinsic properties* are those that can never differ between duplicates. We believe these notions are very intuitive. Likewise for the following rather weak recombination thesis based on them:
>
> (I) For any object x in any world w, there is a world w_1 containing a duplicate of x in isolation
>
> (where an object y exists *in isolation* in a world iff that world contains only (i) y, (ii) y's parts, and (iii) objects whose existence is entailed by the existence of any of the objects mentioned in (i) and (ii)). We call this the principle of *isolation*. The idea is that if it is possible for an object to exist as part of a larger system of objects and relations, then it is (metaphysically) possible for a duplicate of that object to exist all alone in some possible world. (pp. 838–9)

This recombination principle does the job.[35] Suppose that there is a pair of worlds such as w and w^*, described by Petrie. Petrie purports to characterize the worlds in question in full. Thus, S and P are, presumably, supposed to be intrinsic properties, and x, y, x^*, and y^* are, presumably, supposed to be "atomic," and thus to lack proper parts.

Then, according to (I), there is a world z that contains an isolated duplicate of x, call it "v," and a world z^* that contains an isolated duplicate of x^*, call it "v^*." As Paull and Sider note (1992, p. 839), the worlds would be as follows:

World z	**World z^***
v has P	v^* has P
v has S	v^* lacks S

World z and world z^* are B-twins. But they are not A-twins. Thus, A does not globally supervene on B. Given the principle of isolation, if there were a pair of worlds such as Petrie describes, then there would be a pair of worlds that is a counterexample to the relevant global supervenience thesis. Thus, Petrie fails to establish that global supervenience fails to imply strong supervenience.

However, Paull and Sider (1992, p. 840) deny that global supervenience implies strong supervenience. They describe a pair of worlds that is a counterexample to a certain strong supervenience thesis, but *not* to the corresponding global supervenience thesis; and the pair of worlds is not such that, if it exists, then, by the isolation principle, there is a pair of worlds the existence of which is a counterexample to the global supervenience thesis. They ask us to consider a set B containing just two properties, P and Q. And they ask us to consider a set A that contains only one property, M, a property that they define as follows: $Mx =_{df} Px$ & (Ey) Qy. They elaborate: "In English: an object has M just in case it has P, and some object or other in the universe has Q" (1992, p. 840). They point out that "since 'M' is *defined* solely in terms of properties in B, if two worlds have the same distribution of B-properties then the definition of 'M' will apply in the same way within each world. Consequently, they will have the same distribution of A-properties as well" (p. 840).[36] Thus, A globally supervenes on B. They then go on to characterize two worlds, w and w^*, that are counterexamples to the claim that A strongly supervenes on B. World w contains two individuals, a and b; world w^* contains one individual, c. And the worlds are as follows:

World w	**World w^***
a has M	c lacks M
a has P	c has P
b lacks M	
b has Q	

If there are worlds such as w and w^*, then A does not strongly supervene on B. However, as we noted, A globally supervenes on B. Paull and Sider conclude, "Hence global and strong supervenience are not equivalent" (1992, p. 841).[37]

Paull and Sider do not say whether they think global supervenience implies weak. As we noted, Kim (1987) claimed that Petrie's example shows that global does not imply weak, since Petrie's world w is a counterexample to weak, but not to global. But we have already noted what is wrong with that line of argument. We already knew that there are counterexamples to weak supervenience that are not counterexamples to global; for a single world can be a counterexample to a weak supervenience thesis, but it takes two worlds to have a counterexample to a global supervenience thesis. Global supervenience theses do not imply weak supervenience theses in virtue of logical form. What matters, however, is whether it is necessary that *if* there is a counterexample to a weak supervenience thesis, then there is a counterexample to the corresponding global thesis. By employing Paull and Sider's principle of isolation, we can see that if there is a world such as Petrie's world w, then there is a pair of worlds that is a counterexample to global supervenience.[38]

But global supervenience indeed fails to imply weak. Suppose that one employed Paull and Sider's counterpart-identifying properties in a bijection from individuals in one world onto those in another. Then, spatiotemporal properties (in the sense stipulated earlier) will globally supervene on any set of properties whatsoever – for instance, on the set of properties whose sole member is the property *believing that snow is white*. But spatiotemporal properties will not weakly supervene on the set of properties whose sole member is that property. Two individuals might both have that property yet have different spatiotemporal properties. Recall that whatever counterpart-identifying property one picks will trivially globally supervene on any set of properties whatsoever. But surely, virtually any counterpart-identifying property will be such that there is some set of properties on which it fails to supervene weakly. Thus, global supervenience does not imply weak supervenience (and so does not imply strong either).

Suppose a global supervenience thesis employs the identity bijection function; then, no counterpart-identifying properties need be appealed to. The global supervenience thesis would still fail to imply weak supervenience. As Haugeland (1982) has emphasized, the definitions of strong and weak supervenience imply that the bearers of subvenient properties are the bearers of supervenient properties. However, the definition of global supervenience has no such implication. Let me provide a "real philosophical life" example that exploits this fact to illustrate how a global supervenience thesis could fail to imply the corresponding weak supervenience thesis. The example will use Kim's well-known theory of events (see, e.g., Kim 1973). I will proceed in three stages. First, according to Kim's theory, a (monadic) event is an object's having a(n) (appropriate) property at a time (or throughout an interval of time).[39] An event has a constitutive object, a constitutive property, and a constitutive time. Events are individuated in accordance with the following nonduplication principle: no two events can have exactly the same constitutive object, constitutive property, and constitutive time. Suppose that Kim's theory of events is correct.[40] Suppose further that certain empirical mental and physical properties can be constitutive properties of events, that the constitutive properties of mental events are mental properties, and that the constitutive properties of physical events are physical properties. Furthermore, suppose that no mental property is a physical property. Then, it follows that no mental event is a physical event; for no mental and physical events will have the same constitutive property. On these assumptions, token–event dualism is true. This completes stage one.

Second, notice that the constitutive object of an event will have the constitutive property of the event, but the event itself will also have the constitutive property. The object and event will have the property, however, in different ways. The constitutive object will exemplify the constitutive property (at the time in question); but the event itself will have the constitutive property as a constituent, that is, as a constitutive property. The object will exemplify the property, but the event will be an exemplification of the property. Let's call a property of having such and such a mental property as a constitutive property a "second-order mental event-constituting property," and let's call a property of having such and such a physical property as a constitutive property a "second-order physical event-constituting property." Given our suppositions, the bearers of second-order mental event-constituting properties are not the bearers of second-order physical event-constituting properties. For the former are mental events, while the latter are physical events, and by assumption, no mental event is a physical event. Notice, then, that any two mental events will be exactly alike with respect to second-order physical event-constituting properties, and thus will be twins (i.e., indiscernible) with respect to those properties. The reason is simply that, for any such property P and for any mental event m, m will lack P. However, not all mental events will be twins with respect to second-order mental event-constituting properties. Two mental events can differ with respect to what second-order mental event-constituting properties they have, since the events can have different mental properties as constitutive properties. One event may have, say, *believing that many are called but few are chosen* as a constitutive property, and the other *desiring that one not be called*. This completes stage two.

Finally, we are in a position to see that second-order mental event-constituting properties do not weakly supervene on second-order physical event-constituting properties. For even two events within the same world that are twins with respect to second-order physical event-constituting properties may fail to be twins with respect to second-order mental event-constituting properties. One may have a second-order mental event-constituting property that the other lacks. If the events have the same constitutive object and the same constitutive time but are distinct mental events, then they will have distinct second-order mental event-constituting properties. The reason is simply that they will have distinct mental properties as constitutive properties. But mental events will be twins with respect to physical event-constituting properties: for any such property P, they will lack P. Thus, second-order mental event-constituting properties fail to weakly supervene on second-order physical event-constituting properties. However, it may well be that second-order mental event-constituting properties *globally* supervene on second-order physical event-constituting properties. Take the identity function as the bijection function mapping the individuals in one world onto the individuals in the other. It may be that two worlds with exactly the same total pattern of distribution of second-order physical event-constituting properties will have exactly the same pattern of distribution of second-order mental event-constituting properties. Or take Paull and Sider's bijection function and let it map events in one world onto events in the other world that occur at the same place and time. Then, again, it may be that two worlds with exactly the same total pattern of distribution of second-order physical event-constituting properties will have exactly the same total pattern of distribution of second-order mental event-constituting properties. But weak supervenience will fail.

5. Multiple-Domain Supervenience

Thus far we have discussed only single-domain weak and strong supervenience. Kim (1988) has formulated multiple-domain versions of weak and strong supervenience. He says:

> Let D_1 and D_2 be two nonempty domains . . . and let R be a relation whose domain is D_1 and whose range is a subset of D_2. For any member x of D_1 R/x is the "image" of x under R (that is, the set of all objects in D_2 to which x is related by R). We can then define the following analogues of weak and strong supervenience:
>
> **(MWS)** $\{A, D_1\}$ weakly supervenes on $\{B, D_2\}$ relative to relation R just in case necessarily [or for any world w] for any x and any y in D_1 [in w] if

R/x and R/y are B-indiscernible [in w], then x and y are A-indiscernible [in w].

(MSS) $\{A, D_1\}$ strongly supervenes on $\{B, D_2\}$ relative to relation R just in case for any x and y in D_1 and worlds w_1 and w_2, if R/x in w_1 is B-indiscernible from R/y in w_2, x in w_1 is A-indiscernible from y in w_2.

The expression "R/z in w" designates the image R picks out in w of z; to say "u in w_i is A-indiscernible from v in w_j" where A is a set of properties, means that u has in w_i exactly those A-properties that v has in w_j. (p. 143)

Kim calls R "the coordinating relation." If the coordinating relation is identity, we have single-domain supervenience; but, of course, R need not be identity. Thus, single-domain supervenience is a special case of multiple-domain supervenience. My example of second-order event-constituting properties does not show that global supervenience will not imply weak and strong supervenience across different domains. If there is a suitable coordinating relation between mental and physical events, then the global supervenience of second-order mental event-constituting properties on second-order physical event-constituting properties implies some strong supervenience thesis (and thus some weak supervenience thesis), albeit (if token physicalism is false) one concerning supervenience across different domains. Indeed, as Kim suggests (1988, p. 137), it seems that for any global supervenience thesis, there should be *some* coordinating relation relative to which both a weak multiple-domain supervenience thesis and a strong multiple-domain supervenience thesis will be implied by it.[41]

As we indicated earlier, multiple-domain supervenience is a determinate of the determinable relation of *purely modal* dependent-variation. Without going into detail that would us take over territory we covered in our discussion of global supervenience, it is worthwhile simply mentioning here that given that multiple-domain supervenience is a purely modal notion, whatever coordinating relation one chooses, the resulting multiple-domain supervenience thesis will have some awkward and perhaps unwanted consequences. Let the theorist decide which awkward consequences are to be avoided and which can be tolerated. Of course, there is always the option of similarity-based supervenience, as well. But, as I noted, I doubt that notion has wide applicability. It is particularly relevant to mereological supervenience, an interesting variety of multiple-domain supervenience, that often small micro differences are enough for vast macro differences.

6. Supervenience and Reduction

There has been some discussion in the literature on supervenience of whether any variety of supervenience implies reducibility (see Kim

1984, 1990). One difficulty in addressing this issue is that there is no received view of reduction. Indeed, it is fair to say that there is not even a leading contender for general acceptance; there are some discernible trends, but none is dominant. There are ideas that are somewhat helpful in seeing what philosophers have in mind by reduction. There is, for instance, the idea that sometimes possessing certain properties is *nothing but* possessing certain other properties; there is the idea that two distinct concepts may apply in virtue of the same property or kind; and there is the idea that sometimes scientific laws can be derived from others with only the help of analytical truths. But the philosophical idea of reduction seems fixed, to the extent that it is fixed, mostly by various paradigm cases of scientific successes (e.g., the explanation of chemistry by quantum mechanics). Philosophical theories of reduction attempt to characterize these and like successes. The issue of whether any variety of supervenience implies reducibility can, however, be pursued for quite some distance without taking a stand on controversial issues in the theory of reduction. We will focus on property-supervenience and property-reduction.

Discussions of whether supervenience ever suffices for reduction have focused on modal-operator strong supervenience, SS_m. We earlier called into question whether SS_m is a kind of supervenience in our sense. However, whether it is or not, it is useful to focus on SS_m. For SS_m implies every variety of supervenience we have considered.[42] If it does not imply reducibility, no variety of supervenience does. Let us, then, address the issue of whether the SS_m of A-properties on B-properties implies the reducibility of A-properties to B-properties.

Kim (1988) says:

> In "Concepts of Supervenience" I argued that, on certain assumptions . . . each strongly supervening [SS_m] property has a necessary coextension in the [supervenience] base properties, that is, a coextensive base property invariant from world to world. Similar results should hold for the special case of coordinated multiple-domain . . . strong supervenience in which the coordinating relation is one–one. The notion of coextensive properties must of course be reconstrued in obvious ways so that it may be applied across two domains relative to a one–one coordinating relation. (pp. 145–6)

The assumptions needed are that complementation of, and either infinitary conjunction of or infinitary disjunction of, B-properties are B-property-forming operations. Let us concede these controversial assumptions, for the sake of argument. Given those assumptions, it is indeed the case that the SS_m of A-properties on B-properties implies that every A-property is necessarily coextensive with some B-property (perhaps an infinitary disjunctive B-property).[43] Does that imply that A-properties reduce to B-properties?

Kim (1984, 1990) has speculated that the answer may be yes. However, I think the answer is no, at least where the relevant modality is only nomological necessity. I say this even though there is no received view of reduction, nor even a leading contender for general acceptance. For, despite controversies over the nature of reduction, there are cases involving nomologically coextensive properties that no one would count as cases of reduction. I will start with an example I owe to Kim. Consider the Wiedemann–Franz law, which links thermal and electrical conductivity in metals under normal conditions. Since the same free electrons carry charge and heat, under normal conditions, the thermal conductivity properties of metals are nomological necessary and sufficient for their thermal conductivity properties. But the thermal conductivity properties of metals do not reduce to the electrical conductivity properties of metals, even together with conditions that make up normal conditions, nor conversely. Contra Ernest Nagel's (1961) model of reduction, nomological equivalence does not suffice for reduction.[44]

Two other related examples can be found in Grimes (1988):

> Consider the way in which the family of properties describing the lengths of pendulums uniquely determines the family of properties describing the periods of pendulums. Given this relation it is necessarily the case (in a nomic sense) that for each pendulum of a certain length it will have a particular period and that necessarily for any pendulum with that period it will also have just that length, but surely the family of properties describing the periods of pendulums does not determine, not even in a supervenient way, the family of properties describing the lengths of the pendulums. (p. 160)

I do not understand why Grimes says "surely the family of properties [characterizing] the periods of pendulums does not determine, *not even in a supervenient way*, the family of properties describing the lengths of the pendulums" (emphasis mine). Given appropriate boundary conditions, there is SS_m (with nomological necessity) here. But this is not a case of reduction. Consider a second case described by Grimes (but attributed to Richard Grandy): "The viscosity and flammability of fluids seem to be independently determined by the microphysical structure of fluids in such a way that the family of viscosity properties satisfies the requirements for strongly supervening on the family of flammability properties, and vice versa" (1988, p. 160). Here again, we have SS_m (with nomological necessity), but not reducibility. These cases show that SS_m with only nomological necessity fails to imply reducibility.

It is, however, a more controversial issue whether, if A-properties SS_m on B-properties with *metaphysical necessity*, A-properties reduce to B-properties. For it is more controversial whether metaphysically necessary and sufficient conditions suffice for reduction. However, as we indicated earlier, even SS_m does not imply *explanatory* connections between supervenient and subvenient properties. As also noted earlier, the in-virtue-of relation cannot be captured solely in modal terms. *If* reduction is an explanatory relation, then the SS_m of A-properties on B-properties with metaphysical necessity fails to suffice for reduction.

However, whether reduction is an explanatory relation is controversial. Perhaps we should draw a distinction between ontological reduction and epistemic reduction, requiring explanation for the latter, but not for the former. Then, neither any supervenience relation nor SS_m will suffice for epistemic reduction. But whether SS_m with metaphysical necessity suffices for ontological reduction is an issue that calls for further investigation. I must leave such matters for another occasion.

7. Two Uses of Supervenience

To begin, note that nonreductive materialists will take it as all to the good that not even SS_m with nomological necessity implies *reduction*. For they want to appeal to supervenience without being committed to the reducibility of supervenient properties to subvenient properties (e.g., Davidson 1970). The nonreductive materialist can concede various varieties of psychophysical supervenience to the reductionist but deny reducibility. Here, then, we see one use for supervenience.

Of course, one might well find nonreductive materialism unacceptable. One might regard SS_p across only nomologically possible worlds as kind of "ontological emergence."[45] And one might regard *unexplainable* psychophysical SS_p across metaphysically possible worlds as a kind of "epistemic emergence."[46] One might regard one or both sorts of emergence as unacceptable for various reasons. If mental properties are ontologically emergent, then it is hard to see how they could fail to be either such that they endow things with fundamental causal powers or such that they are epiphenomenal.[47] Neither alternative seems the least bit plausible. If mental properties are epistemically emergent, then their intimate connection with physical properties would be an utter mystery. That may well seem unacceptable. But, in any case, these are among the issues that arise in the debate between reductive and nonreductive materialists. The point remains, however, that nonreductive materialists and reductive materialists can agree that there is psychophysical supervenience of various varieties.

Let's turn to a second use of supervenience. Whether any variety of supervenience entails reducibility, it is generally acknowledged that reduction at least requires SS_p with nomological necessity. That makes SS_p theses useful in evaluating reductive programs. Suppose, for example, there were a research program that was attempting to reduce intentional properties to neurophysiological properties. One could await each proposed reduction of intentional properties to neurophysiological properties and attempt to refute it. That strategy, however, is unsatisfying; for it leaves open whether some other such would-be reductive proposal could succeed. However, intentional properties are reducible to neurophysiological properties only if a certain supervenience thesis is true: the thesis that intentional properties SS_p across nomologically possible worlds on neurophysiological properties. A single example could show that this supervenience thesis is false. And if it is false, then no research program for reducing intentional properties to neurophysiological properties can succeed. Refuting a reductive research program by giving a counterexample to a supervenience thesis required for it to succeed is a strategy I have elsewhere called "refutation by appeal to a false implied supervenience thesis," or for short, refutation by appeal to a FIST (see McLaughlin 1984).

Refutations by appeal to FISTs are common both in science and in philosophy. Any philosophical program for analyzing some A in terms of some B (e.g., empirical knowledge in terms of causal connections between beliefs and facts) will presuppose the truth of a certain SS_p thesis, where the relevant worlds are the metaphysically possible worlds. Rather than addressing each would-be analysis as it is proposed, one can, instead, find an SS_p thesis that would be implied by any such would-be analysis and attempt to show it is false by appeal to a counterexample. If a counterexample can be found, then the program of analysis will have been shown to be untenable. It will have been shown that no such analysis can succeed (e.g., that empirical knowledge cannot be analyzed in terms of causal connections between beliefs and facts). To provide such a counterexample would be to provide a refutation by appeal to a FIST.[48]

Here, then, are two uses for supervenience. First, nonreductionists can concede various varieties of supervenience to reductionists but deny reducibility. Second, reductive programs and programs of philosophical analysis can be shown to be untenable by appeals to FISTs.

NOTES

I owe a deep debt to Jaegwon Kim. In addition to acknowledging the great influence that his work on supervenience has had on my thinking (I have studied all of his papers), I wish to acknowledge my debt to him for many illuminating discussions of supervenience over the past ten years. I wish also to thank my colleague Van McGee for many hours of helpful discussion of this essay; his influence is present in every section. Finally, in addition to the acknowledgments in subsequent notes, I wish to thank David Chalmers, Barry Loewer, Elias Savellos, and the participants in Kim's 1988 NEH Sum-

mer Institute on Supervenience, where, as an invited speaker, I read a very
early version of this essay.

1. See, especially, Hellman and Thomson (1975, 1977), Kim (1978, 1984,
   1987, 1988, 1990), Armstrong (1982), Horgan (1982, 1983, 1987, 1993),
   Haugeland (1982), Teller (1983), Lewis (1983; 1986, pp. 14–17), Hare
   (1984), Lewis (1985), Blackburn (1985), Lycan (1986), Petrie (1987), Post
   (1987), Grimes (1988), Heil (1992), and Paull and Sider (1992). I shall be
   concerned here only with what Klagge (1988) calls "ontological supervenience," and not at all with what he calls "ascriptive supervenience."

2. Kim (1990, pp. 2–3) instructively notes:

   > The O.E.D. lists 1594 for the first documented occurrence of the adjective
   > "supervenient" [citing "By reason of the cold supervenient winter, I was tied
   > to the bed" Alex Hume] and 1647–48 for the verb "supervene"; the noun
   > "supervenience" occurred as early as 1664, according to the O.E.D. In these
   > uses, however, "supervene" and its cognates were almost without exception
   > applied to concrete events and occurrences in the sense of "coming upon" a
   > given event as something additional and extraneous (perhaps as something
   > unexpected), or coming shortly after an occurrence, as in "Upon a sudden
   > supervened the death of the king" (1647–48) and "The king was bruised by
   > the pommel of his saddle; fever supervened, and the injury proved fatal"
   > (1867). There is also this entry from Charlotte Bronte's *Shirley* (1849): "A
   > bad harvest supervened. Distress reached its climax."

3. It is not for nothing that I speak in this paragraph of the *current* philosophical use of 'supervene'. Beginning at least with Lloyd Morgan (1923) and
   lasting until the early 1960s, there was a philosophical use of 'supervene'
   connected with the notion of emergence; but that use is different from the
   current philosophical use of 'supervene'; it is much more closely related to
   the vernacular use of 'supervene' than is the current philosophical use. (For
   some references, see Kim 1990, Van Cleve 1990, and Beckerman 1992. For
   a discussion of the relevant emergentist tradition, see McLaughlin 1992.) I
   simply lack the space here to discuss the differences between the philosophical use of 'supervene' in the emergentist tradition and the current philosophical use. Let me simply warn the reader that there is a great deal of
   misinformation in the literature on this topic. Suffice it for me to note here
   that the current philosophical use of 'supervene' traces back to Davidson
   (1970) (see note 5). Davidson apparently encountered the term in Hare
   (1952) (see Davidson 1992, p. 4). (Hare's version of supervenience is discussed in note 8.) Kim has informed me that he first encountered 'supervene' in Davidson (1970). Hare (1984) claims that he was certain he was
   not the first to use 'supervene' and its cognates in philosophical discourse.
   He claimed that its use at Oxford University preceded his own but that he
   did not recall who so used it. Harry Lewis (1985, p. 159n) reports that
   Peter Geach suggested to him "that the term 'supervenient' entered our
   philosophical vocabulary by way of Latin translations of Aristotle's *Nicomachean Ethics* 1174B31–3." The Greek at 1174B31–3 reads: "hos epiginomenon ti telos, hoion toise akmaiois he hora." Robert Grosseteste's Latin
   translation of this passage translated 'epiginomenon' as 'supervenire' (Gau-

thier 1973). Sir David Ross used 'supervenient' to translate 'epiginomenon'. In Ross's English, 1184B31–3 becomes "as an end which supervenes as the bloom of youth does on those in the flower of their age." Ross's translation of 1174B31–3 appears to have been completed by at least 1923. I say this because Ross (1923, p. 229) contains the sentence "It is like the bloom of youth, something that supervenes on the activity produced under these conditions" in explicating 1174B31–3 and surrounding text. No doubt Hare encountered 'supervene' in the *Nicomachean Ethics* (a work frequently cited in Hare 1952). I am uncertain, however, whether Geach is right that 'supervenient' entered our philosophical vocabulary by way of Latin translations of Aristotle. For 'supervenient' was, as I said, used by Lloyd Morgan (1923) at least as early as it was used by Ross, perhaps even earlier. However, while Morgan's use may be as early as Ross's, Ross's is historically related to the current philosophical use of 'supervene', and as I said, I do not believe that Morgan's is. The use of 'supervene' in Ross's translation of 1174B31–3 is fairly close to Hare's (1952) use, and that use is historically connected to current philosophical use.

4. While I have added "and only when," it is clear from the context that Lewis intends this.

5. Lewis's characterization of supervenience is faithful to Davidson's use of 'supervene' in contemporary philosophy of mind. After claiming that the mental characteristics of events are dependent on the physical characteristics of events in that the former supervene on the latter, Davidson remarked, in an often quoted passage, "Such supervenience might be taken to mean that there cannot be two events exactly alike in all physical respects but differing in some mental respect" (1970, p. 214). Thus, such supervenience might be taken to mean that there could be no mental difference between two events without some physical difference between them. What about R. M. Hare's earlier use of 'supervenience'? See note 8.

6. See, however, the upcoming discussion of so-called similarity-based supervenience.

7. A strictly terminological point: I speak of dependent-variation, rather than following Kim (1990) in speaking of "co-variation." The reason is that, to my ear at least, 'co-variation' *suggests* both that A-respects cannot vary without variation in B-respects and that B-respects cannot vary without variation in A-respects. But the claim that A-respects supervene on B-respects does not, of course, imply that there can be no difference in B-respects without a difference in A-respects. For example, even if there can be no difference in mental respects without a difference in physical respects, it may nevertheless be that physical respects can vary without variation in mental respects. We could distinguish one-way covariation from two-way covariation, and claim that supervenience entails only one-way covariation. But I think it is preferable to speak instead of 'dependent-variation'. My differences with Kim here are, of course, merely verbal.

8. This appears to be how Hare (1952, p. 81) initially characterized supervenience. Hare claimed that value terms such as 'good' are "names of 'supervenient' . . . properties" (1952, p. 80). To explicate the notion of a supervenient property, he remarked that if two pictures differ in that one

is a good picture and the other is not, then "there must be some *further* difference between them to *make* one good and the other not" (p. 81; emphases mine). (Davidson 1970 intended nothing so strong by 'supervenience'.) It should be noted, however, that Hare (1984) claims that he had in mind weak supervenience in 1952. But the idea expressed in the quoted passage is stronger than the idea of weak supervenience, which, as we will discuss in detail in Section 2, is a purely modal dependent-variation relation that does not imply that differences in subvenient respects *make for* differences in supervenient respects. It may well be that if two pictures differ in that one is a good picture and the other is not, then "there must be some further difference between them to *make* one good and the other not" (Hare 1952, p. 81). But that the property of goodness (for pictures) weakly supervenes on some distinct type of property *B* would *not* imply that if two pictures differ in that one is a good picture and the other is not, then there is some *B*-difference between them to *make* one good and the other not. Finally, it should be noted that Hare (1952) seems to use 'consequential property' as a synonym for 'supervenient property'. His talk of consequential properties is reminiscent of Aristotle's talk of certain properties "naturally following" from other properties, in the text surrounding 1174B31–33, *Nicomachean Ethics*.

9. After proposing definitions of two types of supervenience, weak and strong, equivalent to two types defined by Kim (1984), Sosa (1984, p. 280), speaking of himself and Kim, remarked, "We agree . . . (in conversation) in recognizing stronger forms of supervenience that invoke a kind of formal causation (a by-virtue-of relation) apparently not definable by the modal notions." I do not know what Sosa and Kim, in their conversations, took supervenience itself to be such that the by-virtue-of relation is a form or type of supervenience. However, their stipulative definitions of types of supervenience indeed fail to imply by-virtue-of relations, for their definitions characterize types of purely modal relations. (Of the definitions in question, more in Section 2.) And the by-virtue-of relation is indeed not definable in purely modal terms. The basic reason is a familiar one: sufficiency, even minimal sufficiency, does not suffice for explanation.

10. See note 9. Moreover, Grimes (1988) correctly points out that neither weak, strong, nor global supervenience implies that differences in subvenient respects explain differences in supervenient respects.

11. Here is an argument that clay statues are not lumps of clay. A clay statue is essentially a statue. A lump of clay is not essentially a statue. Therefore, a clay statue is not a lump of clay. It makes no difference for present purposes whether this is a sound argument.

12. Multiple-domain supervene is put to work in Van Cleve (1990); see McLaughlin (1992) for a discussion of Van Cleve (1990).

13. It appears that Davidson had this kind of diachronic supervenience in mind when he said, "An object cannot alter in some mental respect without altering in some physical respect" (1970, p. 214). See Davidson (1992, pp. 7–8).

14. Kim (1984, p. 169) suggests how singular fact supervenience may be derivative upon property supervenience, as may event supervenience also, at least if events are certain kinds of property exemplifications.

15. See Schiffer (1987) for a discussion of the pleonastic sense of 'property'.

16. In this section, we will focus exclusively on single-domain, indiscernibility-based supervenience and will suppress references to times.

17. I mean to remain neutral concerning what possible worlds are. I will rely, for present purposes, on the intuitive idea that they are ways the world might be and on the idea that possible worlds must be such that (a) every possible world w is such that something can be true at it; (b) if something is true at a possible world w, then it is necessarily true at w if and only if it is true at all possible worlds (or at all possible worlds "accessible" from w); (c) if something is false at a world w, then it is necessarily false at w if and only if it is false at all possible worlds (accessible from w); (d) if something is contingently true at a world w, then it is false at some possible world; and (e) if something is contingently false at a world w, then it is true at some possible world. Whether possible worlds are *possibilia* that, with the exception of the actual world, exist yet do not actually exist or whether they are instead abstract entities that, with the exception of the actual world, do not obtain (or are not exemplified, or not instantiated, or not semantically satisfied) will be left open.

18. Nothing would bar us from formulating weak or strong supervenience theses that quantify over only technologically possible worlds.

19. My formulations of WS_p, WS_m, SS_p, SS_m differ only verbally from the formulations in Kim (1984, 1987, 1990).

20. For a detailed discussion of how, see Meskin (forthcoming). I wish to thank Aaron Meskin both for calling my attention to this issue and for showing how it can be resolved.

21. There is no received view of logical truth. Moreover, since there is no received view of meaning there is no received view of what, exactly, synonymy (sameness of meaning) consists in. On the Tarskian conception of logical truth, a truth is a logical truth if and only if it is true however its nonlogical terms are interpreted. However, this won't do if interpretation must be interpretation in some model, given the standard conception of a model; for, as Etchemendy (1990) argues, on this conception of logical truth, it would be a matter of contingent fact what truths are logical truths. And that seems unacceptable, for logical truths should be necessarily true. Moreover, as McGee (1992) has argued, being true in every model may be no guarantee that a sentence is even true; he proposes a candidate for a false sentence that is true in every model. Controversies over the nature of logical truth and the nature of meaning must, however, be set aside here.

22. The explanation of why logical truths are true in every world will be different from the explanation of why nonlogical analytical truths are; and the explanation of why metaphysical truths are true in every world will be different from the explanation of why logical truths are and of why analytical truths are. But I cannot discuss these matters further. (I have benefited here from correspondence with David Chalmers.)

23. Keep in mind, however, the first observation that an SS_p thesis will have to appeal to accessibility relations between worlds if it is equivalent to an SS_m, which involves two kinds of necessity (see Meskin, forthcoming).

24. This point is often missed. Speaking of his psychophysical event super-

venience thesis (quoted in note 5), Davidson says: "To hold that there cannot be two events alike in all physical respects is to hold that there is a physical predicate uniquely true of every event (assuming there is a predicate for each 'respect'). Such an event is, however, what I would call a physical event (since it is *the* event that has such and such physical characteristics)" (1985, p. 244). Two points are in order to avert misunderstanding. First, that there cannot be two events alike in all physical respects does not imply that there is a physical predicate uniquely true of every event (even assuming there is a predicate for each "respect"). Second, even if there is a physical predicate uniquely true of an event, it does not follow that the event is a physical event. I will elaborate on these claims, taking them in reverse order. The physical predicate uniquely true of an event might be a negative predicate, of the form 'is an event such that it is not . . .', where what fills in the dots is a (perhaps infinite) disjunction of physical predicates. From the fact that there is such a physical predicate uniquely true of an event, it would not follow that event is a physical event. Davidson's psychophysical event supervenience thesis is consistent with the existence of a single nonphysical event, say a spiritual event, which is unchanging in any physical or mental respects. Second, if there are respects that are neither physical respects nor mental respects, then Davidson's supervenience thesis is consistent with there being infinitely many nonphysical events, albeit ones that are exactly alike physically and mentally. Davidson's event supervenience thesis does not imply token-physicalism for events.

25. I am, of course, assuming classical logic.

26. Armstrong (1978) offers this and other reasons for denying that there are negative properties. Whether not being a certain way could endow something with causal powers is, however, a controversial issue we can leave open here.

27. Armstrong (1978) has argued that there are no disjunctive properties.

28. Global supervenience is discussed in Horgan (1982, 1983, 1987, forthcoming), Haugeland (1982), Lewis (1983, pp. 61–4; 1986, pp. 14–17), Kim (1984, 1987, 1988, 1989), Petrie (1987), Post (1987), Grimes (1988), Paull and Sider (1992), Chalmers (1993), and Byrne (1993). Hellman and Thomson (1975, 1977) are widely viewed as having formulated global supervenience theses. There are two points, one important, one not: Hellman and Thomson speak of emergence, rather than of supervenience; but that is neither here nor there. However, it is also the case that Hellman and Thomson (1975, 1977) quantify over models, while the other discussions cited quantify over possible worlds. And this is a difference that makes a difference. Models cannot do all the theoretical work of possible worlds (at least if models do not include sets of possibilia or are not used in conjunction with modal operators). (Here I am indebted to Vann McGee.) But I must leave this for another occasion.

29. Here and in what remains, when I speak of A-properties, I mean simply a nonempty set, A, of properties. I will follow Kim in taking property-supervenience to be a relation between nonempty sets of properties. To say that some x and y differ with respect to an A-property is just to say that

there is some member of the set A of properties such that x has it and y does not, or conversely. If there are the sorts of "families" of properties Kim describes, then supervenience between them is just a special case of property-supervenience.

30. Of course, that is impossible if complements of B-properties are themselves B-properties. For, then, an object must have some B-property in any world in which it exists. If complements of B-properties are ipso facto B-properties, then, given Kim's proposal concerning what it is for two worlds to be B-property twins, B-property twin worlds must contain exactly the same individuals. However, as we noted, property-supervenience is a relationship between nonempty sets of properties. It is thus possible for there to be an individual in a world that lacks any B-properties (i.e., any member of the nonempty set of properties B) whatsoever.

31. I have corrected one typographical error on page 852.

32. Paull and Sider should have used a broader ontological category than the category of objects, perhaps that of individuals. Concrete events are individuals, but not objects. I will pass by this issue. I will also ignore the issue of whether places and times are world-bound; but on Lewis's (1986) view, they would be.

33. Haugeland (1982) uses "weak supervenience" to refer to essentially what Kim calls "global supervenience." Kim's use of "weak supervenience" has wider currency, however; so I have followed it.

34. Recall that, by A-properties, we mean simply properties that are members of a nonempty set, A, of properties; likewise for B-properties.

35. In his NEH seminar on supervenience in the summer of 1990, Kim proposed an equivalent metaphysical principle, the one that Klagge (this volume) calls the "restriction principle."

36. Paull and Sider offer a rigorous proof of this claim in an appendix (1992, pp. 852–3).

37. Klagge (this volume) has objected that Paull and Sider have not shown that global supervenience fails to imply strong. His objection fails, however, even though he makes an interesting point – first the interesting point, then why his objection fails. Paull and Sider include an *extrinsic* property, M, in the supervenient set, but include only *intrinsic* properties, P and Q, in the subvenient set. But if we allow that there are the sorts of property-forming operators needed to generate an *extrinsic* property such as M, then it is implausible that Paull and Sider have exhaustively described worlds w and w^*. For, then, it is plausible that there will be, for instance, a property, $P\#$, that can be defined as follows: $P\#x =_{df} Px \ \& \ (Ey)$ $(y \neq x)$. And in world w, a will have $P\#$, while in world w^*, c will lack $P\#$. Klagge may well be right about this; perhaps Paull and Sider have not exhaustively characterized w and w^*. Perhaps w and w^* are as he says they are. However, Klagge goes on to claim that if w and w^* are as he says they are, then the existence of w and w^* does not show that A fails to supervene strongly on B. If Klagge were right about that, then Paull and Sider would have failed to describe a case in which strong supervenience fails even though global supervenience holds. However, Klagge is not right about that. Paull and Sider get to say which sets of properties they wish to speak

about. By *stipulation*, set B contains only the properties P and Q, and set A contains only M. (Property-supervenience, you will recall, is a relationship between nonempty sets of properties.) Thus, the existence of w and w^* would indeed falsify the thesis that A strongly supervenes on B, just as Paull and Sider claim. Klagge's claim that a has $P\#$ in w and that c lacks $P\#$ in w^* simply does not affect their point.

38. To see how, recall that Petrie takes set A to include only one property, S, and set B to include only one property, P; and recall that w contains only two individuals, x and y, and that the following is an exhaustive characterization of world w: x has P, x has S, y has P, y lacks S. The existence of world w is a counterexample to the weak supervenience of A on B. But, by the principle of isolation, if there is a world such as w, then there are two worlds that are counterexamples to the global supervenience of A on B. Each of the two worlds will contain only one individual. In one of the worlds, $w\#$, its sole inhabitant, an isolated duplicate of x, call it "d," will have P and have S. In the other world, $w@$, its sole inhabitant, an isolated duplicate of y, call it "e," will have P but lack S. Worlds $w\#$ and $w@$ will be B-twins, but they will not be A-twins. Hence, the existence of worlds $w\#$ and $w@$ is a counterexample to the global supervenience of A on B.

39. Two points: first, I say "appropriate" property, since Kim thinks that only the members of a certain proper subset of the set of properties can be constitutive properties of events. Second, a polyadic event is an n-tuple of objects having an n-adic property at a time (or throughout an interval of time). We will, however, stick with the simpler case of a monadic event.

40. Actually, it does not matter for present purposes whether the theory is a correct theory of *events*. It is enough that there are entities of the sorts in question, even if they proved to be, say, states, or singular facts, or situations, or something else, rather than events properly so-called.

41. It should be noted, however, that this is not so where multiple-domain WS_m and multiple-domain SS_m are concerned. For a global property-supervenience thesis will not imply that if something has an A-property, then it or an appropriately related object has some B-property.

42. I focus here on indiscernibility-based supervenience; for, plainly, similarity-based supervenience does not imply reduction. Moreover, I won't pause here to distinguish single- from multiple-domain supervenience.

43. Kim (1984) offers a rigorous proof of this, which I will not repeat here. If you have not seen the proof, it is well worth looking at, for it is quite ingenious.

44. See, e.g., Causey (1977), McLaughlin (1992), and Beckermann (1992) for further reasons for denying that Nagelian reduction suffices for genuine reduction. For the record, contingent bridge laws are, I believe, insufficient for reduction.

45. See Van Cleve (1990) and McLaughlin (1992). Chalmers (1993) plausibly takes global supervenience, where the worlds are only the nomologically possible ones, as a kind of emergence.

46. Byrne (1993) plausibly regards unexplainable global supervenience, even where the relevant worlds are all the metaphysically possible worlds, as a

kind of emergence. It should be noted that even if psychophysical global supervenience is *unexplainable,* a psychophysical global supervenience thesis may, nevertheless, be *justifiable.*

47. The possibility of emergent fundamental powers is discussed in McLaughlin (1992). Chalmers (1993) argues that conscious properties globally supervene on physical properties, where the relevant worlds are only the nomologically possible worlds, and opts for epiphenomenalism for conscious properties.

48. For a wide variety of examples of refutations of programs of philosophical analysis by appeal to FISTs, see McLaughlin (1984).

REFERENCES

Armstrong, D. M. (1978). *Universals and Scientific Realism.* 2 vols. Cambridge University Press.

(1982). "Metaphysics and Supervenience," *Critica* 14, 3–17.

Beckermann, A. (1992). "Supervenience, Emergence, and Reduction," in A. Beckermann, H. Flohr, and J. Kim (eds.), *Emergence or Reduction?* Berlin: de Gruyter, pp. 94–118.

Blackburn, S. (1985). "Supervenience Revisited," in I. Hacking (ed.), *Exercises in Analysis.* Cambridge University Press.

Byrne, A. (1993). *The Emergent Mind.* Ph.D. dissertation, Princeton University.

Causey, R. L. (1977). *Unity of Science.* Dordrecht: Reidel.

Chalmers, D. (1993). *A Theory of Consciousness.* Ph.D. dissertation, Indiana University.

Davidson, D. (1970). "Mental Events," in L. Foster and J. W. Swanson (eds.), *Experience and Theory.* Amherst: University of Massachusetts Press, pp. 79–101.

(1985). "Reply to Lewis," in B. Vermazen and M. Hintikka (eds.), *Essays on Davidson: Actions and Events.* Oxford: Clarendon Press, pp. 159–72.

(1993). "Thinking Causes," in A. Mele and J. Heil (eds.), *Mental Causation.* Oxford University Press, pp. 1–10.

Dreier, J. (1992). "The Supervenience Argument against Moral Realism," *Southern Journal of Philosophy* 30, 13–38.

Etchemendy, J. (1990). *The Concept of Logical Consequence.* Cambridge, Mass: Harvard University Press.

Gauthier, R. A. (1973). *Aristotleles Latinus* XXVI. Leiden.

Grimes, T. R. (1988). "The Myth of Supervenience," *Pacific Philosophical Quarterly* 69, 152–60.

Hare, R. M. (1952). *The Language of Morals.* Oxford University Press.

(1984). "Supervenience," *Aristotelian Society Supplementary Volume.*

Haugeland, J. (1982). "Weak Supervenience," *American Philosophical Quarterly* 19, 93–103.

Heil, J. (1992). *The Nature of True Minds.* Cambridge University Press.

Hellman, G. P., and Thomson, F. W. (1975). "Physicalism: Ontology, Determination, and Reduction," *Journal of Philosophy* 72, 551–64.

(1977). "Physicalist Materialism," *Nous* 11, 309–45.

Horgan, T. (1982). "Supervenience and Microphysics," *Pacific Philosophical Quarterly* 63, 29–43.

(1983). "Supervenience and Cosmic Hermenuetics," *Southern Journal of Philosophy* 22, Supplement, 19–38.

(1987). "Supervenient Qualia," *Philosophical Review* 96, 491–520.

(forthcoming). "From Supervenience to Superdupervenience: Meeting the Demands of a Material World," *Mind*.

Johnson, S. (1775). *A Dictionary of the English Language*. Vol. 2. Rpt. New York: AMS Press, 1967.

Kim, J. (1973). "Causation, Nomic Subsumption, and the Concept of Event," *Journal of Philosophy* 70, 217–36.

(1978). "Supervenience and Nomological Incommensurables," *American Philosophical Quarterly* 15, 149–56.

(1984). "Concepts of Supervenience," *Philosophy and Phenomenological Research* 45, 153–76.

(1987). "'Strong' and 'Global' Supervenience Revisited," *Philosophy and Phenomenological Research* 48, 315–26.

(1988). "Supervenience for Multiple Domains," *Philosophical Topics* 16, 129–50.

(1990). "Supervenience as a Philosophical Concept," *Metaphilosophy* 21, 1–27.

Klagge, J. (1988). "Supervenience: Ontological and Ascriptive," *Australasian Journal of Philosophy* 66, 461–70.

Kripke, S. (1971). "Identity and Necessity," in M. K. Munitz (ed.), *Identity and Individuation*. New York University Press, pp. 135–64.

Lewis, D. K. (1983). "New Work for a Theory of Universals," *Australasian Journal of Philosophy* 61, 343–77.

(1986). *On the Plurality of Worlds*. Oxford: Basil Blackwell.

Lewis, H. A. (1985). "Is the Mental Supervenient on the Physical?" in B. Vermazen and M. Hintikka (eds.), *Essays on Davidson: Actions and Events*. Oxford: Clarendon Press, pp. 159–72.

Lycan, W. (1986). "Moral Facts and Moral Knowledge," *Southern Journal of Philosophy* (Spindel Supplement), 79–94.

McGee, V. (1992). "The Problem with Tarski's Theory of Consequence," *Proceedings of the Aristotelian Society*, 273–92.

McLaughlin, B. P. (1984). "Perception, Causation, and Supervenience," *Midwest Studies in Philosophy* 9, 569–92.

(1992). "The Rise and Fall of British Emergentism," in A. Beckermann, H. Flohr, and J. Kim (eds.), *Emergence or Reduction?* Berlin: de Gruyter, pp. 49–93.

Meskin, A. (unpublished manuscript), "Woops Didn't Visit Everywhere He Had To."

Morgan, L. (1923). *Emergent Evolution*. London: Williams and Norgate.

Nagel, E. (1961). *The Structure of Science*. New York: Harcourt, Brace and World.

Paull, C. P., and Sider, T. R. (1992). "In Defense of Global Supervenience," *Philosophy and Phenomenological Research*, 32, 830–45.

Petrie, B. (1987). "Global Supervenience and Reduction," *Philosophy and Phenomenological Research* 48, 119–30.

Post, J. F. (1983). "Comments on Teller," *Southern Journal of Philosophy,* 22, Supplement, 165–6.

——— (1987). *The Faces of Existence.* Ithaca, N.Y.: Cornell University Press.

Quine, W. V. O. (1953). "Two Dogmas of Empiricism," in *From a Logical Point of View.* Cambridge, Mass.: Harvard University Press, pp. 20–47.

Ross, W. D. (1923). *Aristotle.* London: Methuen.

Schiffer, S. (1987). *Remnants of Meaning.* Cambridge, Mass: MIT Press.

Sosa, E. (1984). "Mind–Body Interaction and Supervenient Causation," *Midwest Studies in Philosophy* 9, 276–81.

Teller, P. (1983). "A Poor Man's Guide to Supervenience and Determination," *Southern Journal of Philosophy* 22, Supplement, 137–62.

Van Cleve, J. (1990). "Emergence vs. Panpsychism: Magic or Mind Dust?" in J. E. Tomberlin (ed.), *Philosophical Perspectives.* Vol. 4. Atascadero, Calif.: Ridgeview, pp. 215–26.

Supervenience: Model Theory or Metaphysics?

JAMES C. KLAGGE

There are two problems concerning the implications of certain forms of supervenience that I wish to discuss. The problems are connected in that their resolution depends on deciding what sort of enterprise we are engaged in when we approach the problems. Supervenience can be formulated and discussed as a purely logical set of formulas, which are indeed quite engaging in their own right. On the other hand, much of the interest in supervenience has been generated by its apparent usefulness in understanding certain philosophically perplexing realms of life, for example, mentality and morality. These two conceptions of supervenience can come into conflict with one another, as we will see. The conflicts provide the opportunity to assess our motivations.

1. The First Problem

Suppose we accept supervenience in the form of the Quinean slogan "No difference without a physical difference," or, as Davidson puts it for one particular case, "There cannot be two events alike in all physical respects but differing in some mental respects."[1] Does it follow from this that there are principles, that is, universal generalizations, in which sufficient conditions are given in physical (or subvening) terms for the presence of certain supervening qualities?[2]

It might seem as though there obviously are such principles. Consider some mental state that I am now in, say one of anxiety. By our assumption, no one can be nonanxious without also differing from me in some physical way. In other words, if someone were exactly like me physically, that person would have to be anxious, too. Now, one may despair of ever giving a complete physical description of me, but nevertheless our assumption commits us to the principle that if someone has my physical description completely and exactly, that person is anxious. So, whatever my physical state is, call it P, it follows that

$(\forall x)(Px \rightarrow x$ is anxious$)$.

Thus, the assumption of supervenience entails the existence of principles that are one-directional and in which the antecedent states only physical conditions and the consequent attributes some supervening condition. As Richard Hare put it, "Supervenience brings with it the claim that there is some law [by which he seems to mean simply a universal generalization] which binds what supervenes to what it supervenes upon."[3]

Let us formalize the original assumption as

(1) $\sim \Diamond (\exists x)(\exists y)[(\exists M)(Mx \,\&\, \sim My) \,\&\, (\forall P)(Px \equiv Py)]$

(where M ranges over the supervening properties – e.g., mental properties – and P ranges over the subvening properties – e.g., physical properties). Or, more smoothly,

(2) $\Box (\forall x)(\forall y)[(\forall P)(Px \equiv Py) \rightarrow (\forall M)(Mx \rightarrow My)]$.

And let us formalize the assertion of the existence of principles as

(3) $\Box (\forall x)(\forall M)\{Mx \rightarrow (\exists P)[Px \,\&\, (\forall y)(Py \rightarrow My)]\}$.

In other words, for any supervening condition, there is a sufficient condition that can be articulated in subvening terms. The subvening characterization may have to be an exhaustive, or maximal, characterization, as we supposed it was in giving the sufficient condition for my anxiety, but it may not be. Intuitively we can think of P in formula (3) as ranging over conjunctions of "mentally relevant" properties. But since we cannot generally delimit the set of mentally relevant properties in advance, we allow P to range over all (conjunctions of) physical properties.

Now we can formally state the first problem as whether (2) implies (3). (In the technical terminology of the literature, this is the problem of whether possible-worlds supervenience implies modal-operator supervenience.) I have already given an intuitive argument that it does, in which I was simply repeating a more formal proof offered by Jaegwon Kim.[4]

Kim's proof is impeccable from a model-theoretic point of view. However, the assumptions that lie behind this proof have been questioned by John Post.[5] Post objects as follows: the proof employs the notion of an exhaustive (or maximal) physical characterization of something. Presumably this characterization will indicate for each physical property whether or not the thing has the property.[6] Thus, the exhaustive characterization will be a conjunction of some physical properties and negations of the other physical properties. Post claims,[7] quite plausibly, that the negation of a physical property is not in general itself a physical property. For example, the property *not being an electron* is not a physical property, since it is had by the number 5, but the number 5 has no physical properties. Thus, a conjunction of physical properties and negations of physical properties is not in general a physical property. The assumption that the class of physical properties is closed under negation and conjunction, while admissible from a purely model-theoretic point of view, seems questionable after a metaphysical examination of the nature of physical properties. So the principle whose existence is asserted by formula (3) does not necessarily offer a sufficient condition *in physical terms* for the supervening property after all, and we cannot infer the existence of physicopsychical principles from the assumption of physicopsychical supervenience. It seems that metaphysics has to take precedence over model theory in our understanding of supervenience.

As a point about the metaphysical nature of the physical in general, I think Post's argument has to be accepted. The interest of the original proof is not mainly logical, but metaphysical – it purports to tell us something about the nature of the relationship between certain realms, such as the physical and the mental, or the natural and the moral. I agree that it is from a metaphysical perspective that we have to assess the assumptions that lie behind the proof. But Post's handling of the assumptions is still too abstract for the issue at hand.

Let us call the negations (or complements) of physical properties "quysical" properties. (That is short for "*qu*asi-phy*sical*" properties.) Post's point is that the set of physical properties is not closed under complementation. Let us call a set of properties a "physical *description*" of an object if the set of properties

(a) holds of the object in question,
(b) includes only physical and quysical properties, and
(c) includes at least one physical property.

Then it is intuitively true that, if supervenience is assumed, and an object with a set of *physical* properties has a supervening property, then there is a physical description (in my defined sense) such that any object that has that physical description will also have the supervening property in question.[8] So the physicopsychical principles are back in business.

Is this an ad hoc trick? From the point of view of Post's metaphysical reflections on the nature of the physical, it may seem to be. But from the point of view of the metaphysics of mind and morality, I think it is not. What, then, are its motivations?

In morality it is not generally sufficient, when justifying a moral judgment (i.e., an all-things-considered judgment, not a prima facie judgment), to list some of a person's or an action's natural qualities – for a list of qualities may be "defeated" by the presence of some additional quality. For example, it may not be enough to explain Socrates' goodness to say he is honest, courageous, and wise if being bad-tempered would cause us to rescind the judgment. So our moral principles may need to exclude some qualities as well as assert others. Until we have accounted for all the (potentially) morally relevant properties, our judgment must remain tentative (or prima facie). Thus, a principle can achieve some kind of closure only by asserting either the negation of every other morally relevant property or a negative existential to the effect that there are no other morally relevant properties.[9]

Perhaps, however, the search for closure (which is what led to the need for negations of physical properties) has more of a psychological than logical motivation. (If so, then we could ignore Post's metaphysical qualms about negations.) By calling a principle (or the resulting judgment) "prima facie," we mean that it holds so far as *these* considerations (covered in the antecedent of the principle) are concerned but may not hold once a wider range of considerations are brought to bear. By contrast, a principle (or resulting judgment) holds all things considered just insofar as all (relevant) considerations have been brought to bear. We cannot tell, just by examining a principle, whether it is (to be treated as) prima facie or not. Explicit indication of closure is a psychologically useful way to let us know that the principle (or the resulting judgment) is (meant as) all things considered. But it is not logically necessary. If being bad tempered would preclude Socrates from being good, then we should not assert:

$$(\forall y)[(y \text{ is honest } \& y \text{ is courageous } \& y \text{ is wise}) \rightarrow y \text{ is good}].$$

On the other hand, if we do assert this, then we would be logically committed to the irrelevance of Socrates' temper.

But this is too simplistic. Indication of closure – that a principle is meant as all things considered – is *not* just a psychological aid. In many contexts we could indicate closure by prefixing Frege's assertion sign ("⊢") to the principle. But what of other contexts in which contemplation or discussion of the principle is of interest or in which the principle is being assumed in the course of a derivation? In these contexts, since they are explicitly nonassertoric, we cannot rely on the assertion sign. If we want to draw out the implications of a principle without asserting it, we need to know and indicate whether the principle is prima facie or all things considered. So in nonassertoric contexts we will need an intrinsic indication of the status of the principle. Thus, indicators of closure seem to remain important logically, not just psychologically. And so we need to be willing to countenance negations of physical properties in our principles.

But by doing this, by introducing some elements that are not physical properties (namely, negations of physical properties), we are not introducing anything problematic. It is not as though we are introducing divine commands or queer metaphysical qualities into our description. The conditions are still limited to the physical and (occasionally) its absence.

By this provision, numbers will still not have physical descriptions because they do not have *any* physical properties (though they have a bunch of quysical properties). But maximal descriptions of people or actions with respect to their physical properties *will* be physical descriptions. The principles that result from supervenience will not introduce transphysical or only quysical properties. Post's metaphysical point would certainly protect us from this, too, but in far too sweeping a manner.

If we are interested in doing metaphysics, it is relevant and important to consider *what* we are talking about and why we are talking about it. To call "not being an electron" a physical description has much different implications when discussing numbers, which, after all, have no physical properties, from the implications of calling "not being bad tempered" a part of a physical (or, in this case, naturalistic) description when discussing Socrates, who, after all, has lots of physical (or natural) properties. It is condition (c) that ensures we are talking about something that already has physical properties.

It is a little-noticed fact about the supervenience condition we have assumed that it is consistent with the possibility of a wholly nonphysical entity having mental states, or moral qualities.[10] The supervenience condition simply assures that all nonphysical entities will have the same mental or moral characterization. (Since two nonphysical things have no physical differences between them, they can have no mental or moral differences between them.) And further, their mental or moral state is eternally unchanging.

As a matter of model theory (where we assume closure of the physical under complementation), this possibility will not block the entailment from supervenience to principles, because the condition of having no physical properties will count as a physical property, and thus be fit to serve in the antecedent of the conditional. But from Post's point of view, it will block the implication, since nonphysical things are, after all, nonphysical, and so can have no physical properties that will serve in an antecedent.

Again, however, in doing metaphysics, we need to attend to why we are doing it. Anyone who accepts the supervenience condition as it is stated believes that mental or moral qualities must be physically or naturalistically realized. Not only do the mental and the moral not vary independently of the physical, they cannot be instantiated in the absence of the physical. (I am not asserting that all philosophers of mind are physicalists. I am simply claiming that all philosophers of mind who accept the supervenience of the mental on the physical are physicalists. Cartesians would have no reason to accept such supervenience in the first place.) So anyone who asserts the supervenience of the mental on the physical, for example, is also committed to the physical realization of the mental, and from these conditions follows the existence of physicopsychical principles.

So when we ask ourselves the question that is at issue in my first problem, we have to decide whether we are asking it as model theorists or as metaphysicians. It is to Post's credit that he saw the need to ask the question as a metaphysician. But Post's metaphysical approach remains too abstract. For metaphysicians of mind or morality, certain presuppositions might be natural that could not be justified in a generalized metaphysical setting. Whether the set of physical properties is closed under complementation is a metaphysical question that depends on our intuitions and decisions about the nature of the physical (or the natural), as well as the context in which the question is being asked. Whether mental or moral qualities can be instantiated by entities that are nonphysical is also a metaphysical question. A requirement of physical (or naturalistic) realization would seem to be a presupposition of anyone who was willing to assert supervenience.

Since the idea of supervenience is most naturally used in the realm of ethics and philosophy of mind, it is reasonable to consult our thoughts about what function the notion of the physical is playing in those realms. And if we do so, I think it is natural to see the existence of principles as following from the assertion of supervenience. While metaphysical considerations seem to overturn conclusions reached from a model-theoretic point of view, deeper reflection on those metaphysical considerations takes us back to the original conclusions, but for much better reasons.[11]

2. The Second Problem

Some philosophers have been attracted by a form of supervenience known as global supervenience that seems to be weaker (in the sense of being less ambitious) than other forms of supervenience commonly considered. Global supervenience makes supervening properties depend not on the subvening properties of particular individuals, but on the distribution of subvening properties over the entire possible world. Thus, it is formulated as follows:

(4) Possible worlds that coincide in respect of truths involving subvenient properties coincide in respect of truths involving supervenient properties.

And this is thought to be weaker than strong supervenience, which seems to localize the supervenience relation to the properties of particular individuals, as follows:

(5) For any objects x and y and any possible worlds w and v, if x in w coincides in respect of truths involving subvenient properties with y in v, then x in w coincides in respect of truths involving supervening properties with y in v.

It is agreed all around that (5) implies (4). Kim originally claimed that (4) also implies (5) but more recently has conceded that it does not.[12] The following situation illustrates the failure of the latter implication.[13]

World w: There are exactly two objects x and y such that Px, Mx, Py, $\sim My$ (where P is a subvening property, and M is a supervening one).

World v: There are exactly two objects x and y such that Px, $\sim Mx$, $\sim Py$, $\sim My$.

Possible worlds w and v, so described, constitute a model in which (4) holds but (5) fails. Thus (4) does not imply (5).

It is worth pondering what we mean by a "model." In particular, are there any constraints on the stipulation of models? After all, the situation described in w and v is rather odd. For if w and v are indeed possible worlds, it would seem that the following must also be possible worlds:

World w^*: There is exactly one object x such that Px, Mx.

World v^*: There is exactly one object x such that Px, $\sim Mx$.

So can we consider w and v to be a model in isolation from w^* and v^*? If we insist that any model involving w and v must also include w^* and v^*, then the resulting more robust model fails to satisfy global supervenience after all.[14]

If we are only doing model theory here, then we can dismiss this proposed solution immediately: one needn't rule out the worlds w^* and v^*; one simply doesn't include them in the stipulation. But perhaps there can be metaphysical constraints on the stipulation of models.[15] The problem with w and v seems to be that they try to paste inconsistent things together. The inconsistency is hidden by placing it in a larger context, but we can draw it out by a method of isolation. For example, consider the following restriction principle: any restriction of a possible world is itself a possible world.[16] One question would be, Under what conditions does it hold? A further question would be, Even if it is true, should it constrain the stipulation of models? If we allow this principle to constrain stipulation, then we force global supervenience to be "fine-grained" in just the sense that its advocates wished to avoid.

Paull and Sider have proposed a way of reestablishing the independence of global supervenience as follows:[17] we simply need to construct a supervening property that cannot be subjected to the restriction principle for generating further possible worlds. They suggest the property *M*, which they define as holding of an object just in case it has *P and* some object has *Q*. (Intuitively, *M* is a nonintrinsic property.) Then *M* will supervene globally, but it will not supervene intrinsically on its possessor. The following situation is now supposed to illustrate the failure of (4) to imply (5):

World *s*: There are exactly two objects *a* and *b* such that *Pa*, *Qb*, *Ma*, ~*Mb*.

World *t*: There is exactly one object *c* such that *Pc* and ~*Mc*.

And now there is no further possible world:

World *s**: There is exactly one object *a* such that *Pa* and *Ma*,

because we know from the definition of *M* that (given only *Pa*) ~*Ma*.

But it seems that if Petrie was guilty of ignoring further possible worlds that were entailed by his stipulated worlds, Paull and Sider are guilty of ignoring further subvening properties that are entailed by their stipulated properties. In particular, it seems that if *P* is a property, then there is also a property *P*# that holds of an object just in case *P* holds of the object *and* there is another object in the world (formally: $P\#x \equiv [Px \,\&\, (\exists y)y \neq x]$). (Intuitively, *P*# is a nonintrinsic subvening property – i.e., it is a relational property.) So the correct description of the worlds would be:

World *s*: There are exactly two objects *a* and *b* such that *Pa*, *P*#*a*, *Qb*, *Ma*, ~*Mb*.

World *t*: There is exactly one object *c* such that *Pc*, ~*P*#*c*, ~*Mc*.

So now, while this model does not violate (4), it does not violate (5) either, and so does not establish their independence.

Just as Paull and Sider urge us to transcend the purely formal approach to independence that Petrie takes and to consider the metaphysical question of which possible worlds there really are, we must also transcend their stipulative approach to the description of a possible world and consider the metaphysical question of which properties there really are (in the world). In doing so, we are brought back to the original model-theoretic conclusion, but for good metaphysical reasons.

A more radical challenge to the equivalence of (4) and (5) can be gleaned from an article by John Haugeland.[18] He points out that what he calls "weak supervenience," essentially equivalent to (4), is consistent with the possibility that the truths in the supervening realm are about individuals that, as a set, are disjoint from the set of individuals that the subvening truths are about. Yet (5) requires that the supervening truths be about the same (domain of) individuals as the subvening truths. As long as the supervening domain is not constructible from the subvening domain, (4) can be true while (5) is not.

As a point about model theory, Haugeland is right. And he goes on to illustrate his point with examples drawn from plane geometry and wave physics. But a further question is what this means for the realms of mentality and morality.

Haugeland, in fact, argues that his point holds for mentality as well.[19] He uses, as a model, a chess-playing computer to which we ascribe intentional states. Haugeland claims that since the intentional states are a function of a large number of internal data structures, it is impossible to specify any particular data structures as *the* ones on which a certain intentional state (token) supervenes (or, with which it is token-identical).[20]

A response to this, however, can be constructed from the progress made on the first problem in this essay. An advocate of (5) can forsake the sort of specificity that Haugeland seems to require in a subvening characterization, and instead fall back on the idea of a possibly exhaustive characterization at the subvening level.[21] The key issue then turns out to be whether the individuals (or entities) to which mental or moral properties are ascribed can also be the subject of whatever properties are in question at the subvening level. It seems that they can, since the subvening level can just be treated as a different level of description *of that individual.* If that were *not* ultimately possible, then there would be a fundamental lacuna in our mental or moral practices.[22] The connection asserted between the levels by supervenience would seem to be nonlocalized and hence ungrounded. The possibility of a common domain assures this localizable grounding for the determination of one level by another.[23] We at least must be able to say that there is something (subvening and possibly relational) about these individuals that makes them whatever (supervening) they are.

In assessing Haugeland's attempt to separate (4) and (5), we have had to focus on the nature of token-identity and on the notion of domains of individuals. Here our motivations have been mixed: I have objected to his narrow construal of token-identity, one that I think is too motivated by epistemological considerations, and replaced it with a wider construal. I am not sure if this takes us to metaphysics, or all the way back to model theory. But I have objected to his model-theoretic separation of domains on metaphysical grounds.

Research on supervenience over the past fifteen years has flourished both because of its theoretical elegance and because of its apparent metaphysical importance. It is time to articulate our motivations and recognize that they do not always point us in the same direction. Only then can we hope for progress.

NOTES

In writing this essay I benefited from the stimulating ideas of Jaegwon Kim and the support of the NEH during Kim's NEH summer seminar entitled "Supervenience and Its Philosophical Applications" at Brown University, 1990. In revising the essay, I was helped by comments from Tom Grimes, John Heil, Bradford Petrie, Tadeusz Szubka, and Nick Zangwill. An unrevised version of part of the essay was presented to the 1992 meeting of the Southern Society for Philosophy and Psychology, Memphis, Tennessee, and was on that occasion subjected to helpful commentary by John Post.

1. What I am calling the "Quinean slogan" is approximated by Quine himself at several points in his essay "Facts of the Matter," *Essays on the Philosophy of W. V. Quine*, ed. R. Shahan and C. Swoyer (Norman: University of Oklahoma Press, 1978), pp. 162–6. The quotation from Donald Davidson appears in "Mental Events," *Essays on Actions and Events* (Oxford University Press, 1980), p. 214.

2. An assertion of *reducibility* entails that such conditions exist *and* are *necessary* as well as sufficient. I am not concerned with that more ambitious assertion. Of course, if there are not even sufficient conditions, reducibility will fail a fortiori.

3. R. M. Hare, "Supervenience," *Aristotelian Society Supplementary Volume*, 58 (1984): 1–16, at 3. See also p. 16.

4. Jaegwon Kim, "Concepts of Supervenience," *Philosophy and Phenomenological Research*, 45 (1984): 153–76, at 163–4. Following Kim, I have presented the issue in the particular case of whether weak supervenience implies principles. In fact, however, all the same considerations apply to strong supervenience as well. John Post has objected to formula (3), and by implication anything that (allegedly) implies it, as being excessively individualistic. Instead, he argues, we should endorse only global supervenience rather than (1) and (2). One might be able to surmount the apparent individualism of (1), (2), and (3) by allowing P to range over relational properties as well (see, e.g., Section 2). But whether that succeeds or not, the issue of interest to me – whether supervenience implies principles – arises for global supervenience too: from the assumption of global supervenience (no difference between two possible worlds without a physical difference between those worlds), does it follow that there is a physical description of (part of) a world that is a sufficient condition for (part of) the world to possess a supervening property? Again, the same considerations apply. So, as I see it, the issue of individualistic versus global construals of supervenience (or, narrow

versus wide construals of mental states) is not relevant to the issue of whether supervenience implies principles.

5. John Post, *The Faces of Existence: An Essay in Nonreductive Metaphysics* (Ithaca, N.Y.: Cornell University Press, 1987), pp. 178–80.

6. Though one might have qualms about whether we can make sense of such an exhaustive characterization, which would involve considering a totality of physical properties, Post expresses no qualms about that. Insofar as not all subvening properties are "relevant" to the possession of certain supervening properties, it should be possible to get by with something less than an exhaustive characterization. Whether such a limitation could quell the qualms is a further question.

7. Post, *Faces*, p. 178. Post first made this point in his "Comments on Teller," *Southern Journal of Philosophy*, 22, Supplement: *Spindel Conference on Supervenience* (1983): 163–7, at 165–6.

8. If, in the relevant contexts, the absence of a physical (or, natural) property could always be "represented" by the presence of some (other) physical property, then we wouldn't have to involve ourselves with the metaphysical status of negations of physical properties at all. (In such contexts, negation would amount to choice-negation rather than exclusion-negation, since we would be dealing with objects that already had some physical properties.) But if, as seems more likely, precluding some physical properties cannot always be represented as (or, replaced by) including others, then we do need to consider the strategy proposed in the text.

9. While my essay supposes that closure will be achieved in the first way, Bradford Petrie has informed me that he prefers the second method, which he finds less ad hoc. Given a principle of the form $(\forall x)(Px \to Mx)$, where P is the conjunction of the subvening properties true of x, we would conjoin with it the following closure condition:

$$\forall y \{[(\forall Q) [(Q \in P) \to Qy] \& \sim(\exists R) [(R \in N) \& (R \notin P) \& Ry]] \to My\}$$

(where Q and R range over subvening properties, M is the supervening property attributed by the principle, N is the *set* of all subvening properties, and P is the sub*set* of N containing all subvening properties true of x – i.e., the set [not conjunction] of subvening properties attributed by the principle). I have pursued the first way because it seems to me that quysical properties do not deserve to be dismissed out of hand, but I do not reject the second. The second method seems purely model-theoretic.

10. But see, e.g., T. Grimes, "Supervenience, Determination, and Dependency," *Philosophical Studies*, 62 (1991): 31–92, at 82.

11. The argument of this section is my attempt to substantiate a claim I made in note 4 of "Rationalism, Supervenience, and Moral Epistemology," *Southern Journal of Philosophy*, 29, Supplement: *Spindel Conference on Moral Epistemology* (1990): 25–8, at 28. This section also corrects a mistake in the last paragraph of note 4 of my paper "Davidson's Troubles with Supervenience," *Synthese*, 85 (1990): 339–52, at 349.

12. Kim argued for the equivalence in "Concepts of Supervenience," p. 168, and then conceded the inequivalence in "'Strong' and 'Global' Supervenience Revisited," *Philosophy and Phenomenological Research*, 48 (1987): 315–26, at 318.

13. The example is taken from Bradford Petrie, "Global Supervenience and Reduction," *Philosophy and Phenomenological Research*, 48 (1987): 119–30, at 121. Its use in this context is endorsed by Post.

14. This way of reestablishing that (4) implies (5) was described by Jaegwon Kim in the seminar mentioned in the acknowledgment note above, though he does not necessarily endorse it. A similar strategy is employed by R. Cranston Paull and Theodore R. Sider in "In Defense of Global Supervenience," *Philosophy and Phenomenological Research*, 52 (1992): 833–54, at 836.

15. Kim writes, "David Lewis and Joseph Mendola have raised the possibility of using metaphysical considerations to disarm Petrie-type examples" ("'Strong' and 'Global,'" p. 319n). Perhaps it was this sort of strategy they had in mind.

16. See principle (1) in Paull and Sider, "In Defense," p. 838. This principle strikes me as being analogous to insisting that S5 is the proper interpretation of modal logic. If one were to opt for a weaker relation of accessibility between worlds, then one could resist this principle by appealing to the limits of accessibility. An advocate of this principle seems to be committed to holding that the proper interpretation of modal logic is a metaphysical issue. If we follow this line of thought, we would probably wish to hold that the proper interpretation is relative to the domain about which modal assertions are being made. Then our metaphysical understanding of mentality, or morality, would be brought to bear in reflecting on the notions of mental, or moral, possibility.

17. Paull and Sider, "In Defense," p. 840.

18. John Haugeland, "Weak Supervenience," *American Philosophical Quarterly* 19 (1982): 93–103.

19. Haugeland, "Weak Supervenience," section 6. His point is specifically about token-identity, but the common-domain issue for supervenience is parallel.

20. Haugeland writes, ". . . there is less reason to suppose that the metabolic constituents of mental events can be identified in the midst of all the irrelevant physiological housekeeping; and there is more reason to suppose that distinct mental events will each 'supervene on' (the activity in) extended brain regions, which may largely, or even entirely coincide" ("Weak Supervenience," p. 101).

21. The principles asserted to exist in Section 1 can be used to generate token-identities as follows: the instantiation of subvening properties in the antecedent of a principle are (token-)identified with the instantiation of a supervening property in the consequent. Haugeland's notion of token-identity assumes a high degree of specificity at the subvening level, which, he is probably correct in assuming, could not be achieved. But the kind of token-identity that (5) commits us to turns out to be quite unspecific. Thus, I believe, Haugeland's argument ultimately equivocates on the notion of token-identity: we should not accept a form of supervenience that commits us to token-identity (in the specific sense), but (5) commits us to token-identity (in the unspecific sense); therefore, we should reject (5).

Once we understand the notion of unspecific principles and token-identities, we realize how little epistemological work they can do. (See my essay "Rationalism, Supervenience, and Moral Epistemology.") Then the question beyond that becomes, How specific can they be made, and will they then be able to do any epistemological work? That is, I believe, an open question that cannot be answered by any model theoretic or metaphysical considerations. (Perhaps what I have shown in this essay is how far we can go if we are willing to lower our expectations enough.)

22. The scope of this argument is actually limited to supervenience claims involving those levels of subvening descriptions that are actually used in our moral or mental practices. A similar argument, but without this limitation, is given by Jaegwon Kim in "Supervenience for Multiple Domains," *Philosophical Topics*, 16 (1988): 129–50, sections 3 and 4. Roughly, Kim argues that, for a variety of reasons, we are committed to there being some kind of coordinating relation between the domains such that (4) implies (5).

23. Of course, the possibility of common (or coordinated) domains does not yet explain supervenience in a comprehensive fashion. Some would hold that where a supervenience claim does not reach as far as proper reduction, it is itself no more than a lacuna in our understanding. Still, some lacunae may be more tolerable than others. For more on these questions, see my essay "Wittgenstein and Neuroscience," *Synthese*, 78 (1989): 319–43, sections 6–10.

"Global" Supervenient Determination: Too Permissive?

JOHN F. POST

1. Introduction

Everything whatever is determined by the physical. So goes the sweeping physicalist slogan. The thesis is "global" in the sense, among others, of being about all things and their properties everywhere everywhen. For each thing in the world and for any nonphysical property it may have – mental, semantic, valuational, whatever – physical conditions determine whether it has that property. An equivalent formulation of the thesis, current in the literature, is this: given the physical conditions that obtain in our world, and given any other world in which the same physical conditions obtain, the two worlds are the same as regards what things have what nonphysical properties. Worlds that are physical duplicates are duplicates in nonphysical conditions as well.

Which worlds? Probably the physically possible worlds (the ppws) – those in which the laws of physics hold. The sweeping thesis is not meant as a logically or conceptually necessary truth, and as we will see in Section 5, the empirical evidence for it warrants generalization only over the ppws. In any case, the thesis is "global" in a further sense: it generalizes over *all* the relevant worlds and over *whole* worlds to boot. This is especially clear in the following formulation, also current: in ppws, the physical conditions ϕ determine the nonphysical conditions ψ iff

> **(D)** Given any two ppws, if the same ϕ-conditions obtain in both, the same ψ-conditions obtain in both,

where the same physical (or other) conditions obtain in both of two worlds just in case, for each such condition χ, χ obtains in one iff χ obtains in the other. (D) has the same form as explications presented by Hellman and Thompson, Horgan, Lewis, Post, Currie, Petrie, and others, which differ mainly in what kind of possible world to quantify over in (D).[1] Instead of *conditions* or *properties* as the relata in the determination relation, these and other explications sometimes speak of phenomena, states of affairs, facts, truths, or predicates. Mostly these

73

differences will make no difference for what follows, which speaks of one or another as needed.

Another name for the thesis expressed by (D) is 'global supervenience'.[2] Thus, (D) expresses a sweeping thesis of supervenient determination. No matter what the details of how the disparate specific nonphysical conditions are determined by specific physical conditions peculiar to them, physicalists need a way of generalizing over them all and summing them up. This is one of (D)'s jobs. So too is (D) meant to be neutral on whether all these specific determinations should entail (or even hold only in virtue of), say, connective laws, type–type identities, or (nomic) equivalences of physical and nonphysical properties. (D) is meant to be neutral also on the truth or falsity of causal-role functionalism, internalism, individualism, eliminativism, and so on. Hence, (D) is supposed to be nonreductive in the sense of entailing no universalized biconditionals (hence, no identities) and no connective laws from the physical properties of an individual to its nonphysical properties. At the same time, (D) is compatible with their existence, as it should be, since many higher-level properties do seem (nomologically) equivalent if not identical to physical properties. Thus, (D) is neutral on whether reductivism is true of our world, allowing that further research may be needed to settle the issue.

It follows from this that (D) "is silent about the relations between micro-physical and higher-level . . . properties," and "entails nothing about the ways . . . properties are distributed over individuals within possible worlds"[3] (beyond there being no difference in the distribution without a difference in physical conditions). But it does not follow – indeed, in Sections 2–5 it will begin to seem a surprisingly flagrant non sequitur – that (D) "does not entail that the microphysical determines the mental" or that (D) "is compatible with the falsity of 'all truth is determined by physical truth'."[4]

Some such sweeping thesis of physical determination is essential to physicalism, from Democritus on. It is not sufficient. Any adequate characterization of physicalism requires further theses, not all of them metaphysical.[5] Among the metaphysical, for instance, physicalists often need to affirm specific cases of determination that are among those the sweeping thesis is meant to sum up. That is, they often need to affirm, of some specific nonphysical property N and some given individual x, that whether x has N is determined by certain specific physical condition(s); for some cases of x and N, they need to deny this. For example, they may need to affirm (or deny) that whether Jones has the property of dreaming is determined by the (micro)physical conditions in Jones's reticular activating system (RAS) – that given the physical conditions in Jones's RAS and given any other (experimental) situation in which the same physical conditions obtain in Jones's RAS, the two situations are the same as regards whether Jones is dreaming.

Presumably the situations relevant here are those in which certain background conditions obtain, such as Jones's being a live, functioning human being whose RAS enjoys the normal connections to the rest of the central nervous system. (Section 6 considers how one might define the needed notion of relevance.) It is against this background of normal conditions that the determination claim is made. The idea is that the physical conditions in Jones's RAS, conjoined with the relevant background conditions, determine whether Jones is dreaming. Since these conditions and situations are physically possible, and since counterfactual situations are or can be construed as possible worlds, it looks as though this specific supervenient determination claim about Jones amounts to:

(1) Given any two ppws, if the relevant background conditions obtain in both, and also the physical conditions in Jones's RAS, so does whether Jones is dreaming.

The specific (1) is a kind of restriction or "case" of the sweeping (D): In place of ϕ-conditions generally, (1) talks about a subset of them composed of the relevant background conditions conjoined with the physical conditions in Jones's RAS; in place of ψ-conditions, it talks specifically about whether Jones is dreaming.[6] Pile up enough empirically warranted such cases of (D), across a wide variety of sciences at various levels, and you have substantial inductive evidence for (D).[7] Like indefinitely many other specific supervenient determination claims, (1) has the form

(DS) Given any two ppws, if the relevant background conditions as well as specific physical conditions ϕ' obtain in both, so does nonphysical condition ψ'.

Like (1), (DS) is a restriction or "case" of (D). And like (D), (DS) is meant to be nonreductive, in the sense of entailing no universalized biconditionals (hence, no identities) between an individual's nonphysical properties and its physical (though, like (D), (DS) is compatible with their existence).

This raises one of a nest of questions about (D) and (DS), many of them current in the literature: Are (D) and (DS) nonreductive, or can they be shown to entail appropriate biconditionals or connective laws? Do they at least entail one-way conditionals or laws, say from the physical properties of a thing to its nonphysical (i.e., do they entail sufficient conditions in the thing's own physical properties)? Should they? What is the *evidence* for (D) and (DS)? What would counterexample them?

Does the evidence warrant their quantifying over whole worlds? Over *physically* possible worlds? Over all of them? Does asserting a case of (D) and (DS) ever explain anything? Is it meant to? Or does what the sciences antecedently provide by way of explanations and explanatory theories count as our best evidence for cases of (DS) and thereby for (D)? What would explain why a particular case of (DS) holds? Why (D) holds? Does (D) capture what physicalists see as the *dependence* of the nonphysical on the physical? Is it meant to? In this connection, is the relation of supervenient determination asymmetric? Should it be? What must be added to (D) to give a complete characterization of physicalism, in addition, say, to a token-identity thesis or other inventory of the physicalist ontology?

This list is incomplete, but it outlines a substantial research program to which much of the literature is in effect a contribution. Even if the program is not still in its infancy, much remains to be explored. Here we can explore only the following problem about (D) (though along the way we'll learn a bit about some other questions in the nest).

Some philosophers object that (D), being "global," is too permissive, indeed permissive to the point of licentiousness. For (D) allows "there to be a world which differs physically from this world in some most trifling respect . . . but which is entirely devoid of consciousness, or has a radically different . . . distribution of mental characteristics over its inhabitants."[8] To see why (D) allows this, suppose worlds W_1 and W_2 are the same as regards the physical conditions that obtain in them except that W_2 contains a hydrogen atom at some point in deep space where W_1 does not. This makes the antecedent of the conditional in (D) false, so that (D) remains satisfied no matter how wildly W_1 and W_2 differ as regards mental conditions. "As long as this world differs from that one in some physical respect, however minuscule or seemingly irrelevant, it could be as different as you please in any psychological respect you choose."[9]

How is this licentiousness supposed to undermine (D)? We are told that (D) is meant to capture or express the dependence of the ψ-phenomena on the ϕ-phenomena – say the dependence of the mental on the physical. But this dependence of the mental on the physical is said to be incompatible with the failure of (D) to exclude wild mental difference given only some unrelated physical difference. "How is it possible," goes the rhetorical question, "to advance a claim of physical dependency of the mental if, as permitted by the global supervenience of the mental on the physical, there should exist a human being physically indiscernible from you in every respect who has . . . the mentality of a fruit fly?"[10]

Call this line of thought "the argument from licentiousness" (ARFL) against "global" supervenient determination. Is ARFL sound? Elsewhere I argue that (D) is not meant to capture or express, by itself, the dependence of the nonphysical on the physical, but only in conjunction with other, if closely related, matters, and that the dependence derives largely from those other matters.[11] (D)'s permissiveness spells no failure of (D) to express the dependence, since (D) was not meant to do so in the first place; travelers bound for Nashville can hardly be charged with failure to reach Providence.

However, let's assume for the sake of argument that (D) is meant, by itself, to express some sort of dependence of the nonphysical on the physical. The question then is whether ARFL shows that (D) cannot express this dependence. Sections 2 and 3 argue that whether or not (D) is too permissive, there are would-be principles of supervenient determination in the neighborhood that are too restrictive – principles accepted, as it happens, by those who advance ARFL. These principles require that individualism be true not only of our world, but of *every* physically possible world, where individualism is the view that the nonphysical properties of an individual are always determined by its own physical properties (relational properties included). If it comes to replacing (D), then, we should not do so with any of these too-restrictive principles.

Sections 4 and 5 untangle a number of charges lurking in ARFL. They are of uneven force and include the charge that determination ought not be "global" but local. Neither this charge of nonlocality nor any of the other charges proves effective against (D). Still, ARFL does contain an important truth: the sweeping thesis (D) of "global" supervenient determination does not itself express or entail any restriction of the determining conditions to the relevant ones, namely, to those specific physical conditions that determine given nonphysical properties.

The significance of this truth is another matter, as we see in Section 6. Indeed, were it to count against the intended nonreductive determination expressed by (D), it would count equally against the reductive thesis that any nonphysical property must be identical or at least equivalent to some physical property and against the "strong supervenience" thesis SS that for any instantiated nonphysical property N, there is an instantiated physical property P such that, necessarily, whatever has P has N.[12] But it proves to count against none of these, and there is a better way to accommodate the truth contained in ARFL than to reject "global" supervenient determination. Better to invoke a relation developed elsewhere for this purpose some time ago, that of *relevant* or *focused* determination. Focused determination is defined with the help of (D), making use mainly of a simple case of (D) that is essentially (DS) with relevance defined.

2. Individualism and Supervenient Determination

How can we tell whether a principle of supervenient determination is too permissive, too restrictive, or perhaps just right? This is largely an empirical matter of what in the world physically determines what. If the empirical evidence implies that some given nonphysical phenomenon ψ' is determined by certain specific physical conditions ϕ', yet one's principle of supervenient determination entails that ψ' could not be determined by ϕ', the principle is too restrictive. To persist in formulating physicalism in such terms would be to legislate a priori what can possibly determine what. What can determine what in our world is often a matter of considerable empirical complexity, not to be settled by appeals to intuition from the comfortable depths of the philosopher's armchair. For example, rather than adopt (D), some physicalist philosophers adopt

> **(D₁)** Given any two ppws W_1 and W_2, and any two individuals x and y, if x has the same physical properties in W_1 as y has in W_2, then x has the same nonphysical properties in W_1 as y has in W_2.

(In symbols, (D₁) is $\forall W_1, W_2, x, y[\forall P(W_1 Px \leftrightarrow W_2 Py) \rightarrow \forall N(W_1 Nx \leftrightarrow W_2 Ny)]$.) (D₁) entails that interworld indiscernibility as regards a thing's own physical properties implies interworld indiscernibility as regards its nonphysical properties. Suppose the properties restricted for the moment to the nonrelational or intrinsic properties. Then (D₁) expresses a form of individualism: what determines an individual's nonphysical properties can only be its own intrinsic physical properties.[13]

This nonrelational individualism does hold in many cases but apparently not all. Much of the evidence to this effect is empirical, from the sciences, often in the form of interlevel theories that connect higher-level with lower-level properties (such as a kinetic theory of temperature, a quantum theory of the chemical bond (quantum chemistry), molecular theories of water, molecular cell biology, and the neurological activation-synthesis model of dreaming). Typically it is by means of such explanatory theories that we see what determines what.[14] We see that the temperature of a volume of gas is determined by the mean kinetic energy of its constituent molecules, that the freezing point of water is determined by physical properties of its molecules, *and* that whether a given sequence of amino acid molecules serves as a biological signal sequence is *not* determined by the molecules' intrinsic properties alone but by these in relation to what else is going on in the cell.[15]

Empirically, then, ours is a world in which nonrelational individualism is false. Physicalists would be ill advised to formulate their characteristic determination thesis as (D₁) (restricted to intrinsic properties) or as anything that entails (D_1). For even if you and I are unconvinced that ours is a nonindividualist world, formulations of physicalism should remain officially uncommitted, letting further empirical research in the relevant sciences settle the matter.[16] Why define physicalism in such a way as to prejudge one of its fundamental questions? And even if *our* world is a nonrelational individualist world, it does not follow that *every* ppw is such a world, which is entailed by (D_1) (via universal instantiaton: 'W_1' for 'W_2').

A number of physicalists conclude that (D_1) should be revised or replaced, in the direction of greater permissiveness. One possibility is

(D_{1r}) Given any two ppws W_1 and W_2 and any two individuals x and y, if x has the same physical properties *and relations* in W_1 as y has in W_2, then x has the same nonphysical properties (and relations) in W_1 as y has in W_2.[17]

According to (D_{1r}), interworld indiscernibility as regards x's own physical properties and relations implies interworld indiscernibility as regards x's nonphysical properties (via universal instantiation, 'x' for 'y'). Via further instaniation ('W_1' for 'W_2'), (D_{1r}) entails "weak supervenience": indiscernibility in W_1 as regards x's own physical properties and relations implies indiscernibility in W_1 as regards x's nonphysical properties.[18]

Is (D_{1r}) itself too permissive or perhaps just right? According to nonrelational individualists, (D_{1r}) is too permissive, indeed licentious. They think it allows there to be a human being indiscernible from you in every relevant physical respect – that is, in every intrinsic physical property – who yet has the mentality of a fruit fly. And of course, if the intrinsic physical properties were the *only* relevant ones, (D_{1r}) would indeed allow mental difference where there is indiscernibility not just in every intrinsic physical respect, but in every relevant physical respect. Yet physical relations can also be relevant, in the sense that they are often required for the physical determination of nonphysical properties. So the fault lies not with (D_{1r}) for being too permissive but with (D_1) for being too restrictive.

However, (D_{1r}) could be too permissive in another way. For if x in W_1 is only minutely physically different from y in W_2 as regards physical properties *or relations* – say person x is a millimeter closer to the sun than person y is – then the antecedent of the operative conditional in (D_{1r}) is false, and the conditional remains satisfied no matter how radically x and y differ in nonphysical properties. This is the licentiousness problem all over again. If ARFL works against (D), it works equally against (D_{1r}) (and against (D_1)).

Champions of (D_{1r}) might therefore replace it with a thesis that focuses on just those specific physical properties and relations that are not "minuscule" but relevant to – in the sense of doing real work in – the determination of given nonphysical conditions ψ'. (The needed notion of relevance will be explored in Section 6.) Dub these specific physical properties and relations "determinationally relevant" relative to given x, y, and ψ'. Then we have

> **(DS$_{1r}$)** Given any two ppws W_1 and W_2, and any two individuals x and y, if x has the same determinationally relevant physical properties and relations in W_1 as y has in W_2, then x has the same nonphysical properties (and relations) in W_1 as y has in W_2.

(DS$_{1r}$) stands to (D$_{1r}$) as (DS) stands to (D). Is (DS$_{1r}$) too permissive or perhaps just right?

Note that (DS$_{1r}$), like (D$_1$), implies a form of individualism. By (DS$_{1r}$), what determines an individual x's nonphysical properties are x's own physical properties and relations. This *relational* individualism is what some call "nonindividualism" or "holism."[19] By whatever name, what matters is that an individual's nonphysical properties are determined by its own physical properties and relations. Like (D$_1$), therefore, (DS$_{1r}$) risks not being permissive enough. For the empirical evidence might conflict even with this more permissive form of individualism. Ours might be a nonindividualist world, as indeed many think it is. While one or the other form of individualism does hold in many if not most cases, there might also be cases in which one of x's nonphysical properties N is determined not by x's own physical properties and relations alone, but only together with the physical properties of items that bear no determinationally relevant physical relation to x – no physical relation that does any real work in the determination of whether x has N. (The objection that there must always be some physical relation between x and the items that complete the determination is considered in Section 3.) A physicalism open to this possibility is immune to the antiindividualist arguments in the literature.[20]

Are there such cases? If not, are they at least physically possible? Either way, (D$_{1r}$) would be false. Of course, it may seem completely contrary to one's intuitions that there could ever be an x whose nonphysical properties depend (even in part) on the physical properties of something that bears no determinationally relevant physical relation to x. Perhaps the intuition that this cannot happen "is a manifestation of our micro-reductive proclivities."[21] Nevertheless, there are empirically plausible accounts according to which this does happen, as we see next.

3. Individualism and Propertyhood

Consider Millikan's or a like account of teleofunction (biological proper function). Hearts have the teleofunction of pumping blood; to be a heart is to have that function, to be supposed to pump blood. A token heart, like any token, has a given teleofunction only in virtue of being a descendant in a reproductively established family of items in which a critical mass or proportion of ancestors – it can sometimes be a tiny proportion – performed that function and performed it, I have argued elsewhere, in virtue of having certain physical properties and relations to their physical environments.[22] It follows that it is not the present token heart's intrinsic physical properties that determine it is a member of the biological kind "heart" (its physical structure and causal or other dispositions included), but rather a history in which it is a late arrival. This means that the token heart, though it is supposed to pump blood, may be so defective as to be totally unable to do so (through trauma, disease, deformity, etc.). It follows further that a thing's having "a teleo-function is a causally impotent fact about it. Especially, it is never directly *because* a thing *has* a certain function that it performs that function or any other," or that it has this or that partic-ular causal or other disposition.[23]

On such an account, as on some others, it is just false that "kinds in science are individuated on the basis of causal powers; that is, objects and events fall under a kind, or share in a property, insofar as they have similar causal powers."[24] Kim relies on this "principle of causal individuation of kinds," as if on a bit of settled wisdom, in his discus-sion of mental and other downward causation and in his argument that nonreductive physicalism is committed to a mysterious sort of downward causation "that no underlying physical-biological proper-ties can deliver."[25] Settled wisdom it may be, but the principle suffers numerous empirical counterexamples if Millikan and others are right. Any teleofunction kind – hearts, eyes, signal sequences, honeybee dances, beliefs, whatever – is not so individuated that its tokens fall under the kind, or share the property, "insofar as they have similar causal powers." For in each case, a token of the kind may be so defective as totally to lack the relevant powers. Furthermore, there can be and often are items that have the powers (e.g., artificial hearts) but are not members of the kind (not members of the biolog-ical kind "heart").

Among the teleofunctions a device or behavior may have is that of being supposed to map onto some affair in the world. For example, a certain honeybee dance is supposed to map onto nectar that lies in a specific direction and distance. The dance does so map if and only if nectar exists just there. So too, roughly, for what makes a belief true.[26] Millikan's teleosemantics entails that beliefs can map onto affairs in the world, via rules based on the belief's derived proper function, even when affair and belief are not only not causally related to each other, but not related by a physical relation that does any work in determin-ing whether the belief does map onto the affair. Nevertheless, the truth of such beliefs is determined by – they are made true by – physical conditions, in accord with (D) (and (DS)), just not physical conditions that are a matter only of the belief's physical properties and relations.[27] Since they are not a matter only of its physical properties and relations, there is no connective law from them to the belief's truth. Since the truth of the belief is physically determined in the absence of such a law, it does not follow in the least that (D) "is compatible with the falsity of 'all truth is determined by physical truth'."[28]

Someone might object that "physical relations can be arbitrarily complex, diachronic, context encompassing, etc.," so that "if y's physical properties, in conjunction with x's, determine x's nonphysical properties, that is just a relevant physical relation."[29] Perhaps so, but this is another of those issues about which physicalism should be uncommitted, remaining open to further exploration. Indeed, the issue is far more complex than most realize. Does the predicate 'y's physical properties, in conjunction with x's, determine x's nonphysical properties' express a *physical* relation (given among other things the predicate's talk of the *non*physical)? Is it even a physical *predicate* (meaning a [first-order] compound of basic physical predicates – of those atomic predicates that do the real explanatory work in the papers, treatises, and textbooks of today's best physics)?[30] Even if we assume it is, not every physical predicate expresses a physical property, relational properties included; physical relations can be complex, diachronic, context-encompassing, but not arbitrarily so.

For example, 'is an electron of' is a basic physical relational predicate, and 'is not an electron of' would therefore be a compound physical predicate. But not being an electron of something appears not always to be a physical relational property. Were it so, completely nonphysical spooks would have a physical property after all, that of not being an electron of something, and so too for Cartesian mental substance, numbers, and more. Nor would there be any reason not to allow the same for the complement of any other kind of relational property. The complement of a moral relational property would itself be a moral property, and we would have to say that electrons have moral traits simply because they are not morally good for someone (and not morally bad). Worse, we would have to say that everything whatsoever has properties of every kind, since each thing would have the complement of many a relational property of each kind.[31]

Armstrong goes so far as to deny that negations of physical universals are universals at all, let alone physical; so too for disjunctions of them. His idea is that for something to count as a physical property, it must be among those that would actually be used by physicists, entering smoothly and informatively into their laws, counterfactual generalizations, and explanations. Such a property should do the kind of focused explanatory work performed by the straightforward physical universals or kinds involved in connective theories, like a kinetic theory of temperature, quantum chemistry, and various physical theories of sound and color. From this point of view, a physical property is hardly just whatever is projected by the recursive predicate- or sentence-forming operations of logic and set theory. We should not mindlessly chase propertyhood up the tree of syntax.

Now let's consider, as promised, whether (D_{1r}) is "simply the conjunction of (D) . . . and the token identity thesis," so that under token identity, (D) entails (D_{1r}). Were it so, any problems for (D_{1r}) would be problems for (D) as well. However, talk of *the* token-identity thesis is misleading. There are several, and only one requires type–type identity of the constitutive properties of identical tokens.[32] This requirement is deeply problematic, enough so at any rate that it cannot be assumed without substantially more argument than it has received.[33] Failing the requirement, the situation is as follows.

Suppose (D) is true and every individual is token-identical with some physical individual; this will guarantee that the individuals x and y mentioned in (D_{1r}) have physical properties – x and y are not completely nonphysical spooks (to which (D_{1r}) may not be meant to apply). Suppose further that among the ppws there are W_1 and W_2 such that W_1 contains only two individuals x and $z;$ W_2 contains only y and $z;$ in W_1, x has only the physical property P (there is no other physical property it has in W_1, relational physical properties included), z has the physical property Q, and x has the nonphysical property $N;$ in W_2, y has only P (again there is no other), z does not have Q, and y does not have N. In this example, x has in W_1 the same physical properties and relations – namely, P – that y has in W_2 (which satisfies the antecedent of the conditional in (D_{1r})), yet they differ in the nonphysical property N (which falsifies the consequent; they differ according to whether z has Q). Yet (D) remains true, and true in particular of W_1 and W_2: because z has Q in W_1, but not in W_2, W_1 and W_2 differ in the physical conditions that obtain in them, which falsifies the antecedent of the conditional in (D), making (D) true of W_1 and W_2. Since a physical relational property is not just whatever is projected by the predicate-forming operations of logic and set theory, one cannot object in this way that there *must* be a physical relational property of x involving z in virtue of which x has N while y does not. Thus, the example looks to be a counterexample to the alleged entailment of (D_{1r}) by (D) under token-identity.[34]

Why then is it allegedly impossible for a belief to map onto an affair, via rules based on the belief's derived proper function, when affair and belief are not related by a physical relation that does any work in determining whether the belief does so map? Consider this further objection to the claim that, so far from being impossible, this mapping is actual: suppose you have the true belief that a certain ammonia molecule – call it Ammon – exists in the rings of a distant planet, even one outside your backward light cone. Abbreviate this as the belief that Fa (where F is the physical property of being in the planet's rings). That Fa is true entails that a exists, which in ppws entails that a is in space-time, hence that a bears a physical relation to you (the space-time interval), in particular the physical relation of being at this interval from you and having F. But in ppws, that Fa is true entails and is entailed by a's bearing the physical relation to you of being at that interval and having F. So the truth of your belief is relevantly determined by physical conditions that include this physical relation.[35]

To begin with, the objection overlooks ppws in which a is not in space-time, but on a boundary or edge of space-time (hence, occupies a space of less than four dimensions). And it overlooks ppws that satisfy a many-universe inflationary cosmology, in which a could occupy a universe disjoint from the one occupied by you, so that a and you do not occur in the same space-time and cannot be related by a space-time interval. Much more importantly, however, the objection presupposes that in ppws, at least, anything entailed by what relevantly determines a condition χ (what makes it the case that χ) is part of what relevantly determines χ (part of what makes it the case that χ). That is, it presupposes that the set of conditions doing the real work in determining χ is closed under entailment (in ppws). It is not. The temperature of a cup of coffee is determined (let us suppose) by the mean kinetic energy of its molecules. In ppws, the molecules, assuming they are in space-time, bear some space-time interval to your left little finger, whence it follows that, in ppws, the molecules' having a certain mean kinetic energy entails that they bear a certain space-time interval to your left pinky. But what makes the coffee hot – what relevantly determines this – is the molecules' mean kinetic energy, not their mean kinetic energy in conjunction with their distance from your pinky. Or suppose you have the true belief that Jones is bald. Jones's being bald entails that Jones exists, and in ppws like ours it entails that Jones is in space-time, hence that Jones is at some space-time interval from you the believer. But what makes your belief that Jones is bald true is that Jones is bald, not that he's bald and on the other side of the room. Jones's distance is not part of what relevantly determines the truth of your belief (though it could be relevant to whether you have adequate *evidence* for your belief).

Teleosemantics provides but one of a number of empirical considerations that should make us wonder: is it "highly plausible to regard weak supervenience as minimally necessary for any claim of determination or dependency between sets of properties"?[36] For according to weak supervenience, indiscernibility as regards x's own physical properties and relations implies indiscernibility as regards its nonphysical properties, which is just a form of individualism.[37] Even if Millikan's or a like teleosemantics eventually proves wrong, naturalists in general and physicalists in particular risk a kind of a priorism, if, instead of being officially uncommitted, they build the falsity of teleosemantics into the very statement of their position. Moreover, there would remain nonsemantic phenomena that resist an individualist account. Various social-scientific properties of institutions and roles appear not to be determined by or supervenient on the physical properties or relations of the individuals who occupy them.[38] And recent work in the philosophy of quantum physics suggests that some of what might be called the "higher-level" quantal properties of particles – certain of their entangled-statistical relations – are not determined by or supervenient on the particles' own "lower-level" state-function properties, whether intrinsic or extrinsic (and in that sense relational).[39]

In light of all this, how can we be so sure, in advance of further research, that in every case whatsoever, an individual's higher-level properties must be relevantly determined only by the individual's own lower-level properties and relations, or in particular "that the psychological nature of each such unit is wholly determined by its physical nature"?[40] And even if ours happens ever so conveniently to be a world in which individualism does obtain in every case, what guarantees that *every* ppw is a completely individualist world, as entailed by (D_{1r}) (via instantiation: 'W_1' for 'W_2')? Why define physicalism in such a way as to prejudge some of its fundamental questions?

Better to try formulating the physicalist's characteristic sweeping determination thesis so as to leave open the possibility (some would say the certainty) not only that (i) our world is not completely individualist, but (ii) even if ours is a completely individualist world, not every ppw is. Then (D) looks very attractive. For (D) is neutral on the individualism issue, being compatible with individualist and with nonindividualist physical determination of a thing's nonphysical properties. On the other hand, despite this initial attractiveness, (D) might prove too permissive, indeed licentious. Can (D) be defended against ARFL?

4. The Minuteness Charge

ARFL contains not just one charge against (D) but several. Consider the charge that, according to (D), there could be a world that differs physically from this one in some minuscule or trifling respect, yet differs radically in the distribution of mental properties over its inhabitants. Here it is the *minuteness* of the physical difference that matters. This minuteness charge against (D) is that (D) allows wild mental or other nonphysical difference given only a minute physical difference.[41] (D) is "global" in the sense that it lumps the minute together with the rest of the physical differences.

Suppose we were to revise or replace (D) so as to exclude the possibility of radical nonphysical difference given only minute physical difference. This would exclude too much; from the frying pan of (allegedly) too great a permissiveness into the fire of too little. Consider a world physically just like ours, except that at or just after the Big Bang, certain fundamental physical quantities have minutely different values – for example, baryon-number charge, the quark masses, or specific entropy. These are among the physical quantities that must lie within an extremely narrow range if the universe is to be as it is. Outside this range, stars, galaxies and life would not exist – nor would consciousness. A world minutely different from ours in one of these fundamental physical-cosmological respects could indeed be entirely devoid of consciousness or have a radically different distribution of psychological characteristics over its inhabitants. It seems doubtful, therefore, that "any two worlds that are *physically pretty much the same*" – provided of course this is to include the worlds' distant past – "must be *pretty much the same psychologically* as well" or that "the degree to which any two worlds are similar in respect of [physical] properties is matched by the degree to which they are similar in respect of [nonphysical] properties."[42]

Perhaps, though, any two worlds physically pretty much the same *today* must be nonphysically pretty much the same today. Furthermore, whole worlds or universes are one thing, individuals within them another. As long as we are talking about individuals today rather than whole worlds and their distant past, surely, radical difference in an individual's nonphysical properties should never be possible given only a minute difference in the individual's physical properties and relations; even (D_1) and (D_{1r}) must go.

This too would exclude too much. Chaos theory, among other things, tells us that minute differences, at the level of physics, in the initial conditions of individual processes or systems can make radical differences in their outcomes. Since the outcomes are often expressed in higher-level nonphysical terms – as in weather forecasting, say, or in neurology if recent applications of chaos theory to the brain are sound – an individual system's nonphysical properties can indeed be radically different given only a minute difference in its physical properties.[43] Then there is Schrödinger's cat, to whom it is a matter of life or death whether by chance a single exosomatic atom emits a barely detectable quantum of radiation in the next few seconds.

So the minuteness charge against (D) (and (D_1) and (D_{1r})) is unpersuasive. To revise or replace (D) (or (D_1) or (D_{1r})) in order to exclude the possibility of radical nonphysical difference given only minute physical difference would conflict with our empirical knowledge of the world and of the individuals within it. If ARFL is to have force, it must contain some other charge.

5. Varieties of Globality/Locality

Consider what might be called the charge of "nonlocality": (D) is too permissive because it allows nonphysical properties of an individual to be determined by conditions that obtain not at the local level but only at the "global"; contrary to (D), "determination must hold at the local as well as the global level."[44]

The trouble is, 'local' can mean more than one thing here. So too, correspondingly, for 'global', which often is equally ambiguous in the literature – hence its quarantine in scare quotes whenever used in this essay. Suppose 'local' means that conditions are local only if they are properties or relations of the individual. This seems to be the sense of 'local' in the following: "If psychophysical determination . . . means anything, it ought to mean that the psychological nature of each . . . unit is wholly determined by its physical nature. That is, . . . determination must hold at the local as well as the global level."[45] To require locality in this sense, however, is just to require individualism; the psychological nature of each individual is to be determined by its own physical nature, meaning its own physical properties (relational properties included). So the nonlocality charge, construed this way, is just that (D) is "global" in the sense that it allows nonindividualism and, therefore, is too permissive.

Of course, nonindividualism could someday prove mistaken. But to repeat, this is an empirical question, not to be settled by our philosophical intuitions and not to be built into the very formulations of our naturalism, physicalist or otherwise. And even if our world someday proves to be an individualist world, we have no guarantee that *every* ppw is, as locality in the present sense would require (since this locality is expressed by (D_{1r}), which, as seen, entails individualism for every such world). Rejecting (D) in order to exclude this sort of nonlocality would be too restrictive.

Perhaps, then, 'local' should not be construed to mean "individual." Suppose it means that the physical conditions that determine x's nonphysical properties must be spatially and temporally close to x, or at least not too distant; (D) is "global" in the sense of allowing distant determining conditions. The trouble is, in our world the physical determining conditions can include affairs at enormous distance from x. Whether an astronomer sees a galactic image on a monitor (and not only in the achievement sense of 'sees') may be determined in part by processes billions of light-years away. So too for temporal distance; think again of how baryon-number charge and quark masses at the Big Bang enter the determination of whether there is life or consciousness today. This also reminds us that the determining conditions often are not synchronous with what they determine, so 'local' had better not mean "synchronous."

Suppose 'local' means instead that *whole worlds* are not to be compared, contrary to what happens in the "global" determination expressed by (D). The nonlocality charge would be that (D) "only refers to indiscernibility holding for worlds." (D) is "global," not local, "in that worlds rather than individuals within worlds are compared for discernibility or indiscernibility in regard to sets of properties."[46] But requiring that only individuals be compared for such in-/discernibility amounts to individualism; we've been here before.

Maybe the charge is simply that whole worlds are not to be compared for in-/discernibility in regard to sets of properties (leaving it open whether it is the individuals within them that should alone be thus compared). In line with this, suppose we required locality in the sense that whole worlds are not to be compared for in-/discernibility in regard to sets of properties or conditions.

On one interpretation, this requirement would be too restrictive. For it seems unwise to exclude the possibility that only the totality of the physical conditions, or the whole physical world, however distant and scattered, is what determines certain nonphysical matters – say, the truth (or falsity) of the physicalist's own sweeping generalizations about all of being *qua* being. But even aside from this possibility, there are specific workaday cases in which we must compare whole worlds in regard to sets of conditions.

Consider a uniform steel rod suspended in a vacuum isolated from perturbing forces. Imagine one end of the rod is made to vibrate longitudinally; call it the north end. A moment later the south end will vibrate, and the amplitude of the vibrations at the north end determines the amplitude of those at the south. Strictly speaking, of course, the north-end amplitude does not by itself determine the south-end amplitude, but only given the imagined conditions. It is against the background of those conditions that we make the determination claim. What we have in mind is that the north-end amplitude and the relevant background conditions together determine the south-end's. That is, given any experimental or other situation identical to this one in respect of the relevant background conditions, which include the laws of physics, if the north-end amplitude is the same in both situations, so is the south-end's.

Counterfactual situations are or can be construed as possible worlds, and those in which the laws of physics obtain can be construed as physically possible worlds. Thus, a natural way to express this specific determination claim is by

(2) Given any two ppws, if the relevant background conditions are the same in both, and also the rod's north-end amplitude, so is the south-end amplitude.

In (2), whole worlds are being compared for in-/discernibility in regard to sets of properties or conditions: on the one hand, the set consisting of the relevant background conditions plus the north-end amplitude; on the other, the set consisting of the south-end amplitude. By (2), any two ppws indiscernible in regard to the first set are indiscernible in regard to the second. If requiring locality means we ought not compare whole worlds in this way, we will be deprived of innocent expressions like (2) of quite specific workaday determinations. Once again, the charge of nonlocality or "globality," if pressed, would move us from the (allegedly) too permissive to the too restrictive.

Note that the empirical evidence for the determination of the south-end amplitude by the north-end's warrants the generalization over all the ppws.[47] The most basic reason is that in and across the experimental and other situations in which evidence for the determination is gathered, certain background conditions are held constant, as required by standard inductive method. The evidence is to the effect that given a pair of experimental or other situations in which the relevant background conditions are the same – suspension in a vacuum, isolation from perturbing forces, the laws of physics – then if the north-end amplitude is the same in both so is the south-end's. If the laws of physics are not the same, not constant, all bets in this steel rod case are off. Were we instead testing hypotheses about a law of physics – say, Newton's gravitation law – that law would not be in the presupposed background. The evidence, being empirical and about contingent experimental and other situations in which at least some of the laws of physics obtain, does not warrant generalizations over all the logical or conceptual possibilities, but only those pws in which these physical laws obtain.

All this applies as well to the indefinitely many cases of (DS). Suppose molecular biologists repeatedly find that in "standard conditions," if certain amino-acid molecules occur in the same order in a couple of sequences, and if what else is going on in relevant parts of the cell is the same, then whether the sequences behave as signal sequences (of a certain sort) is also the same. Even though molecular biologists do not normally think about the laws of physics, or list them among the "standard conditions," still those laws are part of the presupposed background. Were the laws to change, all bets would be off about the sequences' behavior. Since counterfactual situations can be construed as possible worlds, and those in which the laws of physics obtain can be construed as ppws, the empirical evidence warrants the following generalization:

(3) Given any two ppws, if the relevant background conditions are the same in both (including the "standard conditions"), and also the amino-acid sequences plus the relevant parts of the cell, so is whether the sequences behave as signal sequences (of a certain sort).

Pile up enough evidence for enough such cases of (DS), and you have strong evidence that the biomolecular conditions determine the cell-biological conditions, as molecular biology implies.[48] So too for those cases of (DS) that connect biology with psychology and, in general, any cases that connect lower-level sciences with the higher. Thus, empirical evidence can quickly accumulate that the physical determines the chemical, the chemical the biochemical, the biochemical the cell-biological, and so on, and that certain of these and other lower-level families in turn determine the psychological, certain others the social, the semantic, whatever (the series of determinations of the higher by the lower forming not a linear chain but a complex trellis). Since determination is transitive, it follows that the evidence supports the claim that the physical determines all the higher levels, in the sense that, given any two ppws, if the physical conditions are the same in both, so are the higher-level conditions, which is just what (D) says.

Like (1) in Section 1, (2) and (3) are restrictions or "cases" of (D). So they are "local" in that they are specific cases of the "global" (D) (formed by replacing talk of ϕ-conditions with talk specifically of those subsets of them comprising the relevant background and other physical conditions, and correspondingly for the ψ-conditions). But they are "local" in another, more significant sense as well. Consider (2). The sets of conditions or properties mentioned in (2) are expressly those *relevant* to the determination of the south-end amplitude. The north-end amplitude is relevant, clearly, and the relevant background conditions are just those required in the imagined experimental situations – suspension in a vacuum, uniformity of the rod, isolation from perturbing forces (which could be listed), and the like. The relevant background conditions, in this specific case of amplitude determination, do not include, say, an extra hydrogen atom somewhere in deep space; so too for (3).

On this interpretation, then, the nonlocality charge is that the "global" determination thesis (D) does not express or entail any restriction of the ϕ-conditions to those that are *relevant* to the determination of some given ψ-condition or conditions. For example, if we applied (D), unrestricted, to the signal-sequence case, we would have to say something like

(4) Given any two ppws, if the physical conditions are the same in both, so is whether the sequences behave as signal sequences.

In (4), the physical conditions mentioned are all physical conditions whatsoever. By (4), then, as long as one world differs from the other in some physical condition, "however . . . irrelevant, it could be as different as you please in any . . . respect you choose,"[49] as regards whether the sequences behave as signal sequences.

6. Focused Determination

This does tell us an important truth about the "global" determination thesis (D): (D) does not specify any restriction of the φ-conditions to those that are *relevant* to the determination of given ψ-conditions. But what exactly is the significance of this truth? Is it that because (D) "only refers to indiscernibility holding for worlds," it *follows* that (D) "does not give us a way of speaking of supervenience of specific . . . properties on specific physical properties"?[50] It would seem this does not follow. For as seen, the innocent (2) also refers to indiscernibility holding for whole worlds, yet speaks of the determination of specific properties by specific physical properties.

Nor is it quite correct to say that (D) does not give us a way of speaking of the determination of specific properties by specific physical properties. All we need do is what we already do, in effect, namely, form various specific cases of (D), such as (1)–(3), in order to speak of the determination of a specific property (dreaming, say) by specific physical properties (the conditions in Jones's RAS conjoined with the relevant background conditions). These cases all have the form of (DS), itself a case of (D), and express "local" property-to-property determinations, meaning the determinations are of and by specific relevant properties.

It follows that those physicalists who formulate their sweeping determination thesis by the "global" (D) are not at all committed to the slogan "Global determination without local determinations!"[51] Local determinations are expressed by specific cases of (D), via restriction of the φ-conditions to those that are relevant in a given case. Nor are such physicalists committed to (D) in the absence of adequate empirical evidence, as seen, including evidence in the form of the many specific cases of (D). In this sense much of the evidence for (D) is entirely local, not "global."

However, the charge that (D) gives us no way of speaking of determination by specific φ-conditions may mean something else. Perhaps the idea is that (D) fails to tell us what *kind* of φ-condition is or can be relevant to the determination. And it is true that (D) tells us no such thing (nor does (DS)). Thus, ARFL contains the truth that not only does (D) not itself restrict the determining φ-conditions to the relevant ones, but (D) tells us nothing about what kind of φ-condition is or can be relevant (nor does (DS)).

Before considering whether this is a reason to reject (D) or ((DS)), let's consider some ways we might be tempted to define relevance. One is to require that the physical conditions relevant to determining whether x has a given nonphysical property N all be physical properties or relations of x. But this is just to require individualism; not a good move. Another is to require the relevant physical conditions to include none that is minuscule or minute; also not a good move. So too if we required the conditions all to be synchronous with x, or in spatiotemporal proximity to x, or if we required that whole worlds never be compared for in-/discernibility in regard to sets of properties. However relevance is defined, the definition should not presuppose any of these too restrictive principles.

How else might relevance be defined? Let's try defining irrelevance first. What we want to exclude as irrelevant to the physical determination of whether x has N are those physical conditions that do no work in determining whether x has N. Intuitively, φ does no work in a given set Γ of conditions that determines whether x has N if φ may be excluded from Γ without disrupting the determination – that is, if there is a subset Δ of Γ that does not contain φ but nevertheless determines whether Nx. For example, consider the set Γ that both determines whether I have the mentality of a fruit fly and contains the condition of there being an extra hydrogen atom somewhere in deep space. Presumably there is a subset A of Γ that does not contain this condition yet determines whether I have fruit fly mentality.

In this kind of case, which is representative of many others, it seems safe to assume that Γ satisfies "determinational uniqueness": either (a) there are not two subsets A and B of Γ, neither one a subset of the other, such that A determines whether Nx and so does B; or at least (b) if there are two such subsets, there is a third subset C of Γ that both determines whether Nx and contains the conditions in virtue of which both A and B determine this. Roughly, C is the "common case" or at least the common factor we would appeal to in explaining what it is A and B share in virtue of which, though otherwise different, they both determine whether Nx (whether what they share are conditions that are members of both, or some relation their members bear to conditions in neither one). When there is such a subset of C, it is the conditions in C that do the real work in determining whether Nx and in this sense are relevant.

Provided Γ satisfies determinational uniqueness, we may say that for any condition φ in Γ, if there is a subset Δ of Γ such that Δ both determines whether Nx and does not include ϕ, then ϕ is irrelevant to the determination of whether Nx. In other words, and putting the matter positively:

> (5) Let Γ be a set of physical conditions ϕ that satisfies determinational uniqueness. Then $\phi \in \Gamma$ is relevant to – does work in – the determination of whether Nx iff ϕ is a member of the least set $\Delta \subseteq \Gamma$ that suffices to determine whether Nx,

where (i) Δ is a least or smallest such set iff Δ is nonempty, and Δ but no proper subset of Δ determines whether Nx; and (ii) Δ but no proper subset of Δ determines whether Nx iff, given any two ppws, if the conditions in Δ obtain in both, so does x's having N (or x's not having N), but for no proper subset of Δ does this hold.[52] Note that the key clause in (ii) – 'given any two ppws, if the conditions in Δ obtain in both, so does x's having N' – is just a case of (D) in the same sense that (1)–(3) are, but with 'Δ' in place of 'ϕ' and 'Nx' in place of 'ψ'. It follows that (5), like (1)–(3) and (DS), makes use of the same core notion of determination as does the "global" (D).

What if Γ fails to satisfy determinational uniqueness? That is, what if there are two subsets A and B of Γ, neither a subset of the other, such that A determines whether Nx, and so does B, and there is no C that both determines this and contains the conditions in virtue of which both A and B do? In this kind of case, there is no one least set $\Delta \subseteq \Gamma$ that suffices to determine whether Nx. We might try arguing that in our world this can never happen – there is always some further such set C. Perhaps some such argument can be given, but until then it seems wise for the physicalist to remain officially uncommitted; let the empirical evidence about what can determine what settle the issue.

Thus, we need a characterization of determinational relevance that is neutral on whether determinational uniqueness always holds:

> (R) Condition $\phi \in \Gamma$ is relevant to – does real work in – the determination of whether Nx iff ϕ is a member of *a* least set $\Delta \subseteq \Gamma$ that suffices to determine whether Nx.

(R) works because if there are two subsets A and B of Γ, neither one a subset of the other, and both determine whether Nx, still either (a) A and B are both least sets in the sense of clause (i), or (b) if one is not a least, then it has a subset that is (which is to assume that successive partitions of it into nonempty sets of conditions via the subset relation does not go on forever, if only because it must stop with the singletons).

Thus, a physical condition ϕ is relevant to the determination of whether Nx, in the sense of (R), iff ϕ is a member of a least set of physical conditions that determines whether Nx. Provided there being an extra hydrogen atom somewhere in deep space is not a member of the least set to determine whether I have fruit fly mentality, it is irrelevant to the determination. And, of course, ϕ can be a member of such a least set, hence relevant, whether or not ϕ is a property or relation of the individual x, and whether or not ϕ is minute, synchronous with x, in spatiotemporal proximity to x, or we require that whole worlds never be compared for in-/discernibility in regard to sets of properties. According to (R), there need be no one kind of physical condition that can be relevant to the determination of whether Nx. Nor should there be. Our empirical knowledge, of what in the world determines what, informs us that no one kind of physical condition is relevant, but many, some on one occasion, others on another. So (D) should not be faulted for failing to tell us what one kind of physical condition can be relevant.

Still, (D) might be faulty in another way. After all, (D) as stated does not restrict the kind of determining physical condition to the kind that is relevant in a given case N, nor, kinds aside, does it restrict the determining conditions to those that are relevant to a given N. It just says, in effect, that *somewhere or other* in the world there are physical conditions, of whatever kind, possibly quite distant and scattered, that determine N. This is a further sense in which (D) compares whole worlds: (D) compares whole worlds rather than the relevant subregions of them. Surely this is too unfocused and disqualifies (D) from expressing the wanted relation of dependence of the nonphysical on the physical. But . . .

Does this lack of restriction or focus count against the "global" supervenient determination expressed by (D)? It would only if (D) were meant, by itself, to express the dependence of the nonphysical on the physical, which, as I have said, it is not meant to do. But even if (D) had been meant by itself to express such dependence, ARFL would not show that (D) cannot do so. To see why, begin by considering the dependence that *reductive* physicalists believe the nonphysical bears to the physical. Their characteristic thesis is that the nonphysical conditions depend on the physical in the sense that the former are identical or at least equivalent (nomologically) to the latter. Like (D), this is a sweeping thesis, and like (D) it does not itself express a restriction of the physical conditions of which it speaks to those that are relevant in a given case N. It just says in effect that *something or other* in the world is the (compound) physical condition or property to which N is identical or equivalent. The reductivist's characteristic thesis therefore suffers the same lack of restriction or focus as (D). So does the strong supervenience thesis (SS) that, for any instantiated N, there is some or another instantiated physical property P such that, necessarily, whatever has P has N. It follows that if ARFL works against the nonreductive supervenient determination thesis (D), it works equally against re-

ductivism and SS. Since those who have so far advanced ARFL against
(D) tend to be reductivists or SS theorists, they would be hoist by their
own petard.

Of course, this does not show that ARFL fails against the claim, were
one to make it, that (D) expresses dependence of the nonphysical on
the physical. It only shows that reductivists and SS theorists are in the
same boat. All three might fail as expressions of dependence, for reasons given by ARFL. We need, therefore, to test ARFL directly.

Consider the dependence, in an axiom system, of the theorems on
the axioms. Each theorem ψ depends on the set Γ of the axioms in the
sense that ψ is entailed by Γ. Some theorems, however, may be entailed
by proper subsets of Γ. Suppose ψ' is such a theorem. Now think of
the "global" assertion that ψ' is dependent on the axioms in the sense
that ψ' is entailed by the whole set Γ of the axioms. This assertion is
"global" in that it does not specify which axioms are relevant (in the
sense of being in a proper subset of Γ that entails ψ') and does not
restrict the entailing axioms to the relevant ones (specified or not),
since it generalizes over them all. Thus, the "global" assertion of the
entailment of ψ' by the axioms is unfocused.

Do we conclude from this lack of focus, as on the present interpretation ARFL would require of us, that this "global" assertion of entailment fails to express dependence of ψ' on the axioms? Hardly. Such
focus is not its job, which among other things is to give us a quite
general or sweeping way of speaking not only of the dependence of the
theorems on the axioms, but of the dependence of a *given* theorem ψ'
on them, *whatever* the details about how ψ' is entailed by specific subsets Δ of the axioms. For this purpose, and in this sense, we want the
assertion of entailment to be quite permissive.

If for some reason we do need a notion of focused entailment, one
is ready to hand: ψ' is focus-entailed by (a set of) $\Delta_i \subseteq \Gamma$ iff, for each
Δ_i, Δ_i but no proper subset of Δ_i entails ψ'. That is, focused entailment
is just entailment by (the set of) these least sets Δ_i. Any axiom outside
the Δ_i does no work in entailing ψ and, in that sense, is irrelevant.
Rather than reject "global" entailment – which is just plain entailment – as a relation of dependence, we do better to adopt this notion of focused entailment on those occasions when we need the focus.

As with entailment, so too with determination. As seen, one of the
jobs of the "global" assertion (D) of physical determination, whether
the determination is of all the nonphysical conditions or of a *given* such
condition, is to give us a quite *general* way of speaking of this determination *whatever* the details about how a given nonphysical condition is
determined by some specific subset(s) Δ of the physical conditions. For
this purpose, and in this sense, naturalists in general and physicalists
in particular need the assertion (D) of determination to be quite per-

missive. To complain that this "global" assertion (D) is unfocused, because it does not restrict the physical conditions to those that are relevant in a given case, would be to miss the point of (D). The complaint would no more show that (D) cannot express a relation of dependence, even had that been its unaided job, than would the parallel complaint about entailment by axioms. All this applies equally to the reductivist's unfocused general thesis that the nonphysical conditions are identical, or at least equivalent to physical conditions, and to the SS thesis that, for any instantiated N, there is some instantiated P such that, necessarily, whatever has P has N.

When we do need a notion of focused determination, or determination by the relevant conditions, one is ready to hand. According to (R), the conditions that are relevant to the determination of ψ' are those that form the least sets that suffice to determine ψ'. Now define:

(FD) ψ' is focus-determined by (a set of) subsets Δ_i of ϕ-conditions iff Δ_i are the least sets to determine ψ'.

Focused determination of ψ' is just determination by sets of conditions relevant to ψ' in the sense of (R) and is essentially (DS) with relevance defined by (R). Like (1)–(3) and (DS), (FD) can be obtained from the more general (D) by replacing unrestricted talk of ϕ-conditions with talk of those ϕ-conditions that are relevant to ψ' in the sense of (R). Adopting this notion of focused determination on those occasions when we need the focus is a more sensible way to accommodate the truth contained in ARFL than is rejecting "global" determination, just as adopting focused entailment, when we need it, makes more sense than rejecting entailment by axioms as a relation of dependence.

NOTES

For comments on earlier drafts of this essay, I am indebted to George Bailey, John Bickle, John Heil, Terry Horgan, David Lewis, Bill Lycan, Paul Moser, Stefan Sençerz, Ümit Yalçın, and an anonymous referee for another occasion.

1. (D) is a possible-worlds rendition (in terms of conditions rather than sentences) of the model-theoretic explication of determination first offered by Hellman and Thompson (1975, p. 558, number (4)), appearing as (TT*) (near enough) in Post (1987, 185) and (D2) in Post (1991, p. 118). Cf. Horgan (1982; 1984, n3), Lewis (1983, p. 364), Currie (1984, p. 350, number (2)); Petrie (1987).
2. Kim (1984, p. 168). See also Kim (1987, p. 318; 1989, p. 41; 1990, p. 22).
3. Baker (1993, p. 80), where (GS) is equivalent, near enough, to (D).
4. Contrary to Baker (1993, pp. 79–80), who follows Kim (1989).

5. See Poland (1994) and Post (1987); personal communication with Poland.
6. Cf. Petrie (1987, p. 129). (1) is not a specialization or "case" of (D) in any sense in which (1) is entailed by (D). Cf. Teller (1984, pp. 145–6).
7. Not that this is the only kind of evidence for (D), or always the most significant; see Post (1987, chap. 5; forthcoming a, b).
8. Kim (1987, pp. 321). See also Kim (1989, p. 41; 1990, p. 23).
9. Kim (1987, p. 321).
10. Ibid., p. 320. See also Kim (1990, p. 23). Baker (1993, p. 80) follows Kim here.
11. Post (forthcoming a).
12. Kim (1984, pp. 163–5). Baker (1993) also accepts SS.
13. This seems equivalent to the supervenience form of individualism rejected by Burge (1986, p. 4), and endorsed by Owens (1993).
14. And typically they provide much of our best evidence for supervenient determination of one level by another. Post (1987, chap. 5; 1991, chap. 6; forthcoming a).
15. On this case of context sensitivity, see Kincaid (1990, pp. 578–83).
16. As Burge (1986, p. 18) says, questions of what supervenes on what "are epistemically posterior to questions about the success of explanatory and descriptive practices in and out of the sciences."
17. Kim (1987, pp. 323–4) endorses what amounts to (D$_{1r}$), which he attributes to Brian McLaughlin. Baker (1993, pp. 79–83) is committed to (D$_{1r}$), if only because it is entailed by SS. Post (1991, pp. 117–29) discusses (D$_{1r}$) and its problems.
18. So-called by Kim (1987, p. 315). Section 3 this chapter explains why (D$_{1r}$) is not "simply the conjunction of D . . . and the token identity thesis," contrary to the same anonymous referee.
19. What Baker (1987) calls individualism amounts to what I am calling nonrelational individualism; what she calls physicalist nonindividualism amounts to (a kind of) relational individualism.
20. For example, the arguments in Baker (1987) and Macdonald (1992) have no effect on a minimal physicalism, which is committed only to (D) in the way of a sweeping determination thesis and is, therefore, nonindividualist and (hence) nonreductive (as is (DS)). See Post (1991, pp. 103–29, 129n12).
21. Kim (1987, p. 322).
22. Millikan (1984, chaps. 1–2) and Post (1991, pp. 49–59, 121–30).
23. Millikan (1993, p. 226).
24. Kim (1992a, p. 17), following Fodor among others. Kim (1992b, p. 135) also accepts the closely related "Alexander's Dictum": "*To be real is to have causal powers.*" Macdonald (1992, p. 140–1) argues against both.
25. Kim (1993, sec. 5).
26. Millikan (1984, 1986, 1989, 1990).
27. Post (1991, pp. 49–58, 113–29). The account of belief in Burge (1979) may have the same consequence; so too for Macdonald (1992). All this causes trouble as well for Kim's "Structure-Restricted Correlation Thesis," Kim (1992a, p. 5).

28. Contrary to Baker (1993, pp. 79–80) and Kim (1989).
29. Same anonymous referee.
30. Post (1987, sec. 3.1.1).
31. Post (1987, p. 178).
32. Rowlands (forthcoming) contains what amounts to a survey with references. See also Macdonald (1989, chap. 4).
33. See Macdonald (1989, chap. 4; 1990; 1992) and Rowlands (1989, forthcoming).
34. The upcoming true-belief case, which is at least physically possible, reinforces the idea that the present example represents a genuine physical possibility. Examples like this also cause trouble for the Identity of Physical Indiscernibles (x and y are identical if they share all their physical properties, relational properties included). IPI cannot be used, unargued, to show that (D) entails (D$_{1r}$) (as (D) does under IPI).
35. Objection due to John Heil, in correspondence.
36. Kim (1987, p. 320).
37. Currie (1984, pp. 348–9), makes a closely related objection to Kim. I too accepted a version of (D$_{1r}$), namely, MND in Post (1987, p. 176) and only later concluded it would not do as one of physicalism's minimal theses. Cf. Post (1991, p. 120n20).
38. Currie (1984).
39. French (1989, p. 16).
40. Kim (1989, p. 42).
41. Kim (1987, p. 321). See also Kim (1989, p. 41; 1990, p. 23). As noted in Section 2, if this minuteness charge works against (D), it works equally against (D$_1$) and (D$_{1r}$), one or the other of which is accepted by physicalists who reject (D).
42. Kim (1987, pp. 324–5).
43. Heil (1992, chap. 3) makes a similar point.
44. Kim (1989, p. 42). See also Kim (1987, pp. 320–3).
45. Kim (1989, p. 42). See also Kim (1987, pp. 321–2).
46. Kim (1989, pp. 46, 41).
47. This and the next paragraph outline a reply to Moser (1992). Some of the necessary further details occur in Post (forthcoming a, b).
48. Again, not that this is the only kind of evidence or always the best; see Post (1987, chap. 5; forthcoming a, b).
49. Kim (1987, p. 321). Cf. Kim (1990, p. 16) on the *relevant* base property.
50. Kim (1989, p. 46).
51. Kim (1987, p. 320) who may have another sense in mind as well, in which 'local' means reductive property-to-property connections, a sense considered in Post (1991, pp. 105–29).
52. This notion of relevance appears in Post (1984, pp. 124–5; 1987, pp. 36, 188), though not by that name. An anonymous referee (same one again) has objected that clause (ii) presupposes transworld identity of x whereas (D$_1$) and (D$_{1r}$) do not. But (D$_1$) and (D$_{1r}$) *are* committed to this transworld identity, via universal instantiation: 'x' for 'y'. In any case, all these principles can easily be reformulated in terms of counterparts.

REFERENCES

Baker, Lynne Rudder. (1987). *Saving Belief: A Critique of Physicalism* (Princeton, N.J.: Princeton University Press).

(1993). "Metaphysics and Mental Causation," in *Mental Causation,* ed. John Heil and Alfred Mele (Oxford University Press), pp. 75–95.

Burge, Tyler. (1979). "Individualism and the Mental," in P. French et al., eds., *Midwest Studies in Philosophy 4:* 73–121.

(1986). "Individualism and Psychology," *Philosophical Review, 95:* 3–45.

Currie, Gregory. (1984). "Individualism and Global Supervenience," *British Journal for the Philosophy of Science, 35:* 345–58.

French, Steven. (1989). "Individuality, Supervenience and Bell's Theorem," *Philosophical Studies, 55:* 1–22.

Heil, John. (1992). *The Nature of True Minds* (Cambridge University Press).

Hellman, Geoffrey, and Thompson, F. W. (1975). "Physicalism: Ontology, Determination, Reduction," *Journal of Philosophy, 72:* 551–64.

Horgan, Terence. (1982). "Supervenience and Microphysics," *Pacific Philosophical Quarterly, 63:* 29–43.

(1984). "Supervenience and Cosmic Hermeneutics," *Southern Journal of Philosophy, 22,* Supplement: 19–38.

Kim, Jaegwon. (1984). "Concepts of Supervenience," *Philosophy and Phenomenological Research, 45:* 153–76.

(1987). "'Strong' and 'Global' Supervenience Revisited," *Philosophy and Phenomenological Research, 48:* 315–26.

(1989). "The Myth of Nonreductive Materialism," *Proceedings and Addresses of the American Philosophical Association, 33:* 31–47.

(1990). "Supervenience as a Philosophical Concept," *Metaphilosophy, 21:* 1–27.

(1992a). "Multiple Realization and the Metaphysics of Reduction," *Philosophy and Phenomenological Research, 52,* 1–26.

(1992b). "'Downward Causation' in Emergentism and Nonreductive Physicalism," in *Emergence or Reduction? Prospects for Nonreductive Physicalism,* ed. Ansgar Beckermann, Hans Flohr, and Jaegwon Kim (Berlin: De Gruyter), pp. 119–38.

(1993). "The Nonreductivist's Troubles with Mental Causation," in *Mental Causation,* ed. John Heil and Alfred Mele (Oxford University Press), pp. 189–210.

Kincaid, Harold. (1990). "Molecular Biology and the Unity of Science," *Philosophy of Science, 57:* 575–93.

Lewis, David. (1983). "New Work for a Theory of Universals," *Australian Journal of Philosophy, 61:* 343–77.

Macdonald, Cynthia. (1989). *"Mind–Body Identity Theories"* (London: Routledge).

(1990). "Weak Externalism and Mind-Body Identity," *Mind, 99:* 387–404.

(1992). "Weak Externalism and Psychological Reduction," in *Reduction, Explanation, and Realism,* ed. David Charles and Kathleen Lennon (Oxford: Clarendon Press), pp. 133–54.

Millikan, Ruth Garrett. (1984). *Language, Thought and Other Biological Categories* (Cambridge, Mass.: MIT Press).
(1986). "Thoughts without Laws; Cognitive Science without Contents," *Philosophical Review, 95:* 47–80.
(1989). "Biosemantics," *Journal of Philosophy, 86:* 281–97.
(1990). "Truth-Rules, Hoverflies and the Kripke–Wittgenstein Paradox," *Philosophial Review, 99:* 323–53.
(1993). "Explanation in Biopsychology," in *Mental Causation*, ed. John Heil and Alfred Mele (Oxford University Press), pp. 211–32.
Moser, Paul K. (1992). "Physicalism and Global Supervenience," *Southern Journal of Philosophy, 30:* 71–82.
Owens, Joseph. (1993). "Content, Causation, and Psychophysical Supervenience," *Philosophy of Science, 60:* 242–61.
Petrie, Bradford. (1987). "Global Supervenience and Reduction," *Philosophy and Phenomenological Research, 48:* 119–30.
Poland, Jeffrey. (1994). *Physicalism: The Philosophical Foundations* (Oxford University Press).
Post, John F. (1984). "On the Determinacy of Truth and Translation," *Southern Journal of Philosophy, 22,* Supplement: 117–35.
(1987). *The Faces of Existence: An Essay in Nonreductive Metaphysics* (Ithaca, N.Y.: Cornell University Press).
(1991). *Metaphysics: A Contemporary Introduction* (New York: Paragon House).
(forthcoming a). "Versus Asymmetric Supervenient Determination."
(forthcoming b). "Counterexamples and Supervenient Determination."
Rowlands, Mark. (1989). "Property Exemplification and Proliferation," *Analysis, 49:* 194–7.
(forthcoming). "Externalism and Token-Token Identity," *Philosophia, 24* (2).
Teller, Paul. (1984). "A Poor Man's Guide to Supervenience and Determination," *Southern Journal of Philosophy, 22:* 137–62.

Weak Supervenience Supervenes

JOHN BACON

1. Introduction

Confusion Supervenes

Supervenience is a basically useful notion, but 'supervene' has become philosophers' jargon, waved like a wand to dazzle. 'Supervene' and 'supervenience', having been coined in their current philosophical sense around 1950,[1] are now standard philosophical vocabulary. 'Supervene' in this use is purely a term of art, standing for several different concepts, as documented by Teller [p], Kim [cs], and me [s]. Yet the current mode is to take for granted that we all mean the same thing by 'supervenience'. It is treated as though it were an *everyday* word with an ordinary, well-understood meaning we all intuitively grasp. The various technical senses would then be so many proposed *explications* of the assumed ordinary sense. But this common practice gets it upside-down. There *is* no ordinary philosophical sense of 'supervenience'.[2] There are only technical senses; their logical connections are complex. Here I will try once again to disentangle some of them.

A Relation between Families of Properties

A central confusion, or at any rate diversity, in the way 'supervenience' has come to be bandied about concerns the *terms* of the supervenience relation. As originally introduced, supervenience related two *families of properties* of the same type. For example, the mental properties of people might be held to supervene upon their physical properties. If the supervenient family is narrowed down to a single property, that's no problem. Things get odder when the base family[3] is so narrowed (see "Property-on-Property Supervenience," Section 2).

Protosupervenience

Most of the concepts of supervenience that have been seriously proposed can be helpfully organized around a notion I call "protosupervenience." A family of properties S *protosupervenes* on a family B iff there is no S-difference without a B-difference. In other words, if two things are B-indiscernible, then they are S-indiscernible. The properties in S and B make up the *domain* of the particular supervenience relation.[4] While in general S and B contain properties, in the purely extensional context of protosupervenience only the extensions of those properties matter, the corresponding classes (see my [v240]). Work of Kim's [sc, cs] and mine [s] establishes that, given Boolean (in particular, disjunctive) closure of B, protosupervenience entails *coextension:*

$$\forall s \in S \; \exists b \in B \; \forall x(sx \leftrightarrow bx),$$

or every supervenient property (or class) is coextensive with some base property.

Weak Supervenience

Now, if any philosophical sense of 'supervenience' deserves to be treated as basic and prior to all others, it's the *necessitation* of protosupervenience, what Kim called "weak supervenience" [sn152]. In this sense, S-properties supervene on B-properties iff there *can* be no S-difference without a B-difference. In other words, B-indiscernibility *entails* S-indiscernibility. The exact grade of the necessity may be allowed to vary according to application. In my opinion, clarity would have been best served by limiting 'supervenience' as a philosophical term of art to *weak supervenience*. Is it too late to lock the barn door now? (See Lewis [p14].)

Other Superveners?

Weak supervenience, as noted, relates families of properties. But in fact there is talk of all kinds of things supervening: states of affairs, statements, propositions, entities in general. And sometimes not families but individual items are given as supervenience bases. What can that mean?

2. The Relata of Supervenience

Entity-Supervenience: Armstrong

Armstrong has put forward a notion of supervenience relating entities or families of entities:

If there exist possible worlds which contain an entity or entities R, and if in each such world there exists an entity of entities S, then and only then S supervenes on R. [c103]

In symbols,

s supervenes on $b =_{df} \Diamond Eb$ & $(Eb \dashv3 Es)$;

Ss supervenes on $Bs =_{df} \Diamond \exists xBx$ & $(\exists xBx \dashv3 \exists xSx)$.

Of course, the Bs and the Ss here could be properties, as in Armstrong's own illustration (similarities supervening on shared properties). But it appears that, even for properties, Armstrongian supervenience is neither a necessary nor a sufficient condition for weak supervenience.

For example, let B be the set of taxes and S the set of persons. Then S supervenes Armstrongianly on B (there is a world with some taxes, and every such world contains persons). Or let b be the property of being a tax and s be personhood. Or, finally, let B be the set of properties of paying various amounts of tax and S be the set of all individual natures of persons. Again, S supervenes Armstrongianly on B (in any world containing taxpaying properties there exist individual natures of persons, and hence persons).[5] This last example permits a comparison with weak supervenience, for S does *not* weakly supervene on B (two things could pay the same amount of tax without being the same person). Conversely, S will supervene weakly on B, but not Armstrongianly, if '$\Diamond \exists xBx$' is false and S is the same as B (admittedly a degenerate case).

Apart from the possibility clause, Armstrongian supervenience follows logically from 'Only Ss can be Bs' ['$\Box \forall x(Bx \rightarrow Sx)$']. Thus extended objects supervene Armstrongianly on colored ones, and it would appear that extension supervenes on color (for only the extended can be colored). Similarly, rationality supervenes on sexiness (since, presumably, only rational beings can be sexy).

Almost any nonempty nonsymmetric relation R gives rise to an implausible case of Armstrongian supervenience. For

$\exists x\exists yRxy \dashv3 \exists y\exists Rxy$

is a logical truth. If we let 'R' be 'wife of', then '$\exists xRx$' becomes 'husband': husbands supervene on wives. Let 'R' be 'is the tabletop of': then tables supervene on tabletops.

Armstrong likes to say that the supervenient is "nothing over and above" the base, a "free lunch." It sounds very odd indeed to say that husbands are nothing over and above wives, or persons nothing over and above taxes, or rationality a free lunch, given sexiness! All these

counterexamples tend to confirm that Armstrong's definition of supervenience is too broad.

Property-on-Property Supervenience

In the first, singular version of Armstrongian supervenience, one entity is said to supervene on another, rather than one family on another.
If those entities are properties, then we have the claim that one property supervenes on another. Leaving Armstrong's definition to one
side, we do hear such claims fairly often; for example,

> Pain supervenes on C-fiber stimulation

(a contrived example). What can this mean? Not that the family of
pains (or pain tokens) supervenes on the family of C-fiber stimulatings,
for those are families of tropes or events, not properties. It must mean:

> The unit family {being in pain} weakly supervenes on the unit family
> {undergoing C-fiber stimulation},

that is,

$$\Box \forall xy[(Cx \leftrightarrow Cy) \to (Px \leftrightarrow Py)].$$

But this would be true if (necessarily), whenever two subjects' C-fibers
fired, they were pain-free; while whenever their C-fibers rested, they
ached. This can't be what was meant. Rather, in analogy to moral philosophers' "good-making characteristics" (e.g., Hare [180–82]), C-fiber
stimulation is presumably to be a "pain-making characteristic" without
actually *entailing* pain. How is that supposed to work?

Things begin to make more sense if we shift from weak to strong
supervenience (Kim [sc49]):

$$\Box \forall s \in S \; \forall x\{sx \to \exists b \in B[bx \; \& \; \Box \forall y(by \to sy)]\}.^6$$

For now, if S, B are the singletons $\{P\}$, $\{C\}$, this boils down to

$$\Box \forall x\{Px \to [Cx \; \& \; \Box \forall y(Cy \to Py)]\}.$$

Given $\exists x Px$, this in turn yields

$$\Box \forall x(Px \leftrightarrow Cx).$$

This should come as no surprise, given Kim's proof that strong supervenience leads to necessary coextension [sc, cs]. Once again, a supervenience thesis collapses into something very near to reducibility. Thus
we find that property-on-property supervenience doesn't work –
whether we take it to be strong supervenience, weak supervenience,
or Armstrongian supervenience. It's just a bad idea.

Global Supervenience of Propositions

A version of supervenience that has been gaining currency is what Kim (following Teller) calls "global supervenience" [cs22]. *S* supervenes globally on *B* if *B*-indiscernible worlds are also *S*-indiscernible, where *B* and *S* are sets of monadic properties. If we allow these properties to be arbitrarily complex relational properties, then global supervenience is just protosupervenience over a domain of *propositions* (as I argued in [s170]). Coextension accordingly follows, as it does generally from protosupervenience: every supervenient proposition is (necessarily coextensive with) a base proposition. Once again, we have an uncomfortably strong result contrary to the antireductive spirit of supervenience. I report this point here because criticism of [s] may have left the impression that all the reductive results of that essay depend on the controversial principle of closure under resplicing. But that principle is relevant only in model contexts. Notwithstanding the reference to possible worlds here, we have been working with the essentially nonmodal concept of protosupervenience.

3. What Is a Property?

Wrangling over Resplicing

In [s] I showed that, for S4 modalities or stronger, weak supervenience entailed strong supervenience. The proof depended on a principle I called "diagonal closure" or closure under resplicing. According to the principle, if in each possible world you took an extension of a *B* {or *S*} property (not necessarily the same one), the resulting function from worlds to *B*-property extensions would itself be a *B*-property. The effect of this principle was to validate

$$\Box \exists b \in B \, A \rightarrow \exists b \in B \, \Box A,$$

with certain restrictions. The principle seemed natural enough, given the concept of property that, since Kripke, has become standard in modal logic: a function from possible worlds to classes (of individuals). All the same, it is closure under resplicing that several critics pounced on: Van Cleve [s], Currie [s], and Oddie and Tichý [r]. My defense was that to reject resplicing is a desperate move: to save a serviceable version of supervenience by arcane restrictions on property formation gets the cart before the horse. Or so I thought, so long as I continued to think of properties in the Kripkean way. I recognized, to be sure, the desirability of a more satisfactory conception of property: "We need a well-motivated and tested theory of properties" [v242]. I now think I have the rudiments of such a theory.

Tropes

Following Stout [c], Williams [e], Campbell [a], and others, I have come
to take *tropes* as a basic ontological category. A trope is a relation instance or a property instance, conceived as a unitary whole, not as a
structured state of affairs. (The term 'trope', introduced by Williams,
is unfortunate, but it has stuck.) It's natural to refer to tropes by ger-
und or abstract-noun phrases; e.g., Socrates' wisdom, or John's loving
Mary. But such articulated nominalized sentences should not mislead
us into conceiving of Mary or love as separable parts of the trope.
Rather, the tropes are sorted into equivalence and similarity classes
by the higher-level similarity-relations of *concurrence* and *likeness*.
Similarity-relations are defined as reflexive and symmetric. Concurrence is transitive too, making it an equivalence-relation. The concurrence equivalence-classes are the trope bundles that constitute individuals. The likeness similarity-classes are trope bundles constituting
universals, including properties. Unlike individuals, universals may
overlap. Thus, far from Mary's being part of the trope, the trope is
part of Mary. An individual has a property, on this scheme, if they
overlap, that is, share a trope. For example, Socrates is wise if the Socrates bundle and the wisdom bundle share a trope.

Possible Worlds and Localized Properties

A possible world, in trope theory, is any set of tropes (still another kind
of bundle). An individual has a property in a world if the three share
a trope. Thus the tropes making up a given property will very likely be
strewn over several possible worlds. The intersection of the property P
with a particular world w is P_w, P localized to w. Although P_w is not the
extension of P in w, it determines the extension, namely, just those
individuals that overlap P_w.

Resplicing in General

Against this background, resplicing would require at least the following:

(1) $P_w \cup Q_v \subseteq$ some B-property whenever P_w and Q_v each $\subseteq$ some B-
property.

If we first put the more general question of whether

(2) $P_w \cup Q_v \subseteq$ some property whenever P_w and Q_v each $\subseteq$ some
property,

the answer is no. Although properties may overlap, there is no guarantee that P and Q both overlap a common likeness class (property) at all, let alone a superset of $P_w \cup Q_v$. Indeed, (2) is ruled out in the special case where $P_w = P$ and $Q_v \not\subseteq P$. (This would be the not unlikely case in which, in some world w, everything was P.) For it is a general feature of similarity-classes that none can be a proper subset of another (see my [r§130]). Yet in the case at hand, $P \subset P_w \cup Q_v$, which in turn would be a subset of the new property. (If, as in some trope theories, likeness is taken as an *equivalence*-relation rather than just a similarity-relation, then overlapping is ruled out and (2) becomes generally false.) Resplicing is thus untenable for properties in general.

Resplicing of Properties in the Domain

But could it hold specially for supervenience-base properties: the more general (2) might be false but the special case (1) true? Such a view would seem ad hoc in the extreme. We would be saying that (2) is not true of properties in general, but we stipulate base properties (and supervenient properties) to be of the special sort for which (1) holds. A supervenience doctrine on such a basis would lose most of its interest. To get $P_w \cup Q_v$ or its superset as a *compound* property doesn't seem hopeful either. Elsewhere I've developed an account of compound properties in trope theory, but it turns out that only properties localized to the same world lend themselves naturally to compounding [u §3A]. Thus, in the context of trope theory, the set of properties is *not* closed under resplicing. And it doesn't appear in any way natural to stipulate specially that the set of supervenient or base properties is thus closed.

Weak Supervenience Favored

The rejection of resplicing undercuts my earlier derivation of strong supervenience from weak supervenience. This reinstates weak supervenience as a viable alternative. Indeed, I believe that weak supervenience deserves to be recognized as *the* concept of supervenience. In this I concur with Lewis [p14]. Protosupervenience provides a helpful classifying pattern, but is otherwise too weak. Most other concepts of supervenience that have been put forward – strong, global – are too strong, entailing variants of necessary coextensions.[7] So if you want to steer between the Scylla of dualism and the Charybdis of reductive identity, your best bet is supervenience – weak supervenience.

NOTES

I thank Graham Oddie for helpful suggestions.
1. For the history, see Kim's [p] and my [s163, 175n1].
2. Save in headings, I leave the nonphilosophical sense aside; e.g., "Necking, as it was called, supervened in the fullness of time as necking will" – Quine [t43]. (Quine is one of the few writers I know of who use 'supervene' in its ordinary sense.)
3. With R. M. Hare, I eschew the malapropos neologism 'subvenient' for the base properties (personal communication, August 25, 1987).
4. This way of using 'domain' differs somewhat from its use in logic.
5. Since, for Armstrong, properties exist iff they are instantiated. To be sure, Armstrong wouldn't recognize individual natures as properties.
6. Strong supervenience is equivalent to protosupervenience over a domain of thing-world relations. See Kim [sg317].
7. An exception that bears further study is a weakened form of global supervenience used by Jackson [a]: any world B-indiscernible from ours is S-indiscernible from ours.

REFERENCES

Armstrong, David. [c]. *A Combinatorial Theory of Possibility* (Cambridge University Press, 1989).
Bacon, John. [u]. *Universals and Property Instances: The Alphabet of Being*, Aristotelian Society Series (Oxford: Blackwell, 1995).
    [s]. "Supervenience, Necessary Coextension, and Reducibility," *Philosophical Studies 49* (1986) 163–76.
    [v]. "Van Cleve versus Closure," *Philosophical Studies 58* (1990) 239–42.
Campbell, Keith. [a]. *Abstract Particulars* (Oxford: Blackwell, 1990).
Currie, Gregory. [s]. "Supervenience, Essentialism and Aesthetic Properties," *Philosophical Studies 58* (1990) 243–58.
Hare, R. M. [l]. *The Language of Morals* (Oxford: Clarendon Press, 1952).
Jackson, Frank. [a]. "Armchair Metaphysics," Miniconference on Philosophy in Mind (University of New South Wales, Sydney, August 2, 1992).
Kim, Jaegwon. [cs]. "Concepts of Supervenience," *Philosophy and Phenomenological Research 45* (1984) 153–76.
    [p]. "Psychological Supervenience as a Mind-Body Theory," *Cognition and Brain Theory 5* (1982) 129–47.
    [sc]. "Supervenience and Supervenient Causation," *Southern Journal of Philosophy* Supplementary vol. 22 (1984) 45–56.
    [sg]. "'Strong' and 'Global' Supervenience Revisited," *Philosophy and Phenomenological Research 48* (1987) 315–26.
    [sn]. "Supervenience and Nomological Incommensurables," *American Philosophical Quarterly 15* (1978) 149–56.
Lewis, David. [p]. *On the Plurality of Worlds* (Oxford: Blackwell, 1986).

Oddie, Graham, and Tichý, Pavel. [r]. "Resplicing Properties in the Supervenience Base," *Philosophical Studies 58* (1990) 259–69.

Quine, W. W. [t]. *The Time of My Life: An Autobiography* (Cambridge, Mass.: MIT Press, 1985).

Stout, G. F. [c]. "Are the Characteristics of Particular Things Universal or Particular?" (1923) in *The Problem of Universals,* ed. Charles Landesman (New York: Basic, 1971), 178–83.

Teller, Paul. [p]. "A Poor Man's Guide to Supervenience and Determination," *Southern Journal of Philosophy* Supplementary vol. 22 (1984) 137–62.

Van Cleve, James. [s]. "Supervenience and Closure," *Philosophical Studies 55* (1989) 225–38.

Williams, D. C. [e]. "The Elements of Being" (1953), in his *Principles of Empirical Realism* (Springfield, Ill.: Thomas, 1966), 74–109.

The Tweedledum and Tweedledee of Supervenience

THOMAS R. GRIMES

A growing number of philosophers have turned to supervenience in hopes of finding a nonreductive form of determination. The search, however, is complicated by the fact that there is an entire family of supervenience relations, not all of which have the same reductive and determinative capacities. Among these various relations, two have come to receive a considerable amount of attention and interest, namely, strong supervenience and global supervenience.

Strong supervenience is a relation that holds between sets of properties and the individual objects that exemplify these properties. In particular, for two sets of properties A and B:

> **(SS)** *A strongly supervenes* on B just in case, necessarily, for each object x and each property F in A, if x has F, then there is a property G in B such that x has G, and necessarily if any object y has G, it has F.[1]

In contrast to strong supervenience, global supervenience is a holistic relation that applies to entire worlds rather than individual objects:

> **(GS)** *A globally supervenes* on B just in case worlds that are indiscernible with regard to B are also indiscernible with regard to A.[2]

Some philosophers prefer global supervenience over strong, arguing that although strong supervenience might be strong enough to function as a relation of determination, it is not weak enough to be nonreductive. Others prefer strong supervenience over global, arguing that although global supervenience might be weak enough to be nonreductive, it is not strong enough to serve as a relation of determination. I wish to resolve this dispute by showing that the basic objections that are raised against either of these supervenience relations also apply to the other, so that there is no general basis for preferring one relation over the other and that in fact neither succeeds in being either nonreductive or determinative.[3]

1. Strong Supervenience and Reduction

An immediate consequence of strong supervenience is that each supervenient property is necessitated by some subvenient property. That is, (SS) implies

(S$_1$) For each property F in A, there is a property G in B such that necessarily for every object x, if x has G, then x has F.

In light of this consequence, strong supervenience seems well suited for serving as a relation of determination between the supervenient and the subvenient properties. However, it also seems well suited for effecting a form of reduction. For as Jaegwon Kim has shown, if the set of subvenient properties is closed under (infinite) disjunction so that the various subvenient bases that necessitate any given supervenient property can be disjoined to create a complex subvenient property, then strong supervenience yields the result that each supervenient property is *necessarily coextensive* with some subvenient property.[4] That is, with disjunctive closure (SS) implies

(S$_2$) For each property F in A, there is a property G in B such that necessarily for every object x, x has G iff x has F.

And insofar as necessary coextension is sufficient for reduction, strong supervenience turns out to be a reductive relation to the effect that each supervenient property is reducible to some subvenient property.

In an effort to defend strong supervenience against the charge of reduction, some philosophers object that the sorts of disjunctive properties required for (SS) to imply (S$_1$) are rather peculiar. Paul Teller, for example, argues that these disjunctive properties, by virtue of containing widely disparate disjuncts, could never serve as the basis for the type of scientific laws required for reduction.[5] And David Armstrong, though in a different context, makes the stronger claim that properties, by their very nature, cannot be disjunctive.[6] However, if for the sake of discussion these claims are accepted as being true and disjunctive subvenient properties are rejected, this will not be enough to block strong supervenience from functioning as a reductive relation.

The classical source for reduction is Ernest Nagel's *The Structure of Science*.[7] According to Nagel, reduction is essentially a form of explanation that applies to theories and laws. He writes:

> Reduction, in the sense in which the word is here employed, is the explanation of a theory or a set of experimental laws established in one area of inquiry, by a theory usually though not invariably formulated for some other domain.[8]

Since the explanation of a law or theory, on Nagel's view, is based on a logical relation that obtains between the explanans and the explanadum,

> a reduction is effected when the experimental laws of the secondary science (and if it has an adequate theory, its theory as well) are shown to be the logical consequences of the theoretical assumptions (inclusive of the coordinating definitions) of the primary science.[9]

In the case where the secondary science contains terms not found in the primary science, Nagel observes that the reductive derivation requires certain intertheoretic assumptions that link the terms of the two sciences. But Nagel does *not* insist that this link be in the form of a biconditional. That is, for a term '*A*' in the secondary science and a term '*B*' in the primary science, "the linkage between *A* and *B* is not necessarily biconditional in form, and may for example be only a one-way conditional: If *B*, then *A*."[10] Assuming, then, that such a one-way conditional must also be lawlike (a condition that Nagel does not formally impose, but that would follow from his views on explanation), all that is required on this standard conception of reduction to reduce one theory to another is a derivation of the first theory from the second on the basis of lawlike one-way conditionals.

Nagel's account of reduction is explicitly designed for theories, but similar considerations apply to the reduction of properties. Indeed, the main reason that he focuses on the reduction of theories rather than properties is based on a concern that the properties of things can only be specified within the context of a theory. For example,

> whether a given set of "properties" or "behavioral traits" of macroscopic objects can be explained by, or reduced to, the "properties" or "behavioral traits" of atoms and molecules is a function of whatever theory is adopted for specifying the "natures" of these elements. The deduction of the "properties" studied by one science from the "properties" studied by another may be impossible if the latter science postulates these properties in terms of one theory, but the reduction may be quite feasible if a different set of theoretical postulates is adopted.[11]

Thus, Nagel allows for the reduction of one set of properties to another provided these properties are specified in the formal rather than the material mode so as to facilitate the required deduction.

Nowhere, then, does Nagel suggest that reduction, as it applies to theories or properties, requires some kind of necessary coextension between the things being reduced and the things doing the reducing.[12] Instead, a simple derivation of the former from the latter by means of lawlike one-way conditionals will do. Consequently, according to this standard conception of reduction, strong supervenience qualifies as a reductive relation. That is, insofar as strong supervenience implies (S_1), it thereby yields a set of necessary, or lawlike, one-way conditionals that allow for the derivation of (every instantiation of) each supervenient property on the basis of (the instantiation of) some subvenient property. Moreover, this result does not depend in any way upon disjunctive properties. If disjunctive properties are rejected so that the set of subvenient properties is not closed under disjunction, this will suffice to bar strong supervenience from implying (S_2), but not from implying (S_1). Thus, strong supervenience, even without recourse to disjunctive properties, is strong enough to effect a reduction of each supervenient property to some subvenient property.

Philosophers who conceive of reduction as requiring a relation of necessary coextension might not be convinced that strong supervenience is genuinely reductive. However, it seems that there is simply more than one form of reduction and that some of these forms are stronger than others. And though strong supervenience might not satisfy all these forms, it does at least conform to the standard conception of reduction as articulated by Nagel and is thereby sufficiently reductive to be unsuitable for certain important applications. For example, strong supervenience is too reductive for use in any nonreductive theory of mind, such as Donald Davidson's anomalous monism, that asserts that the mental supervenes on the physical while denying any psychophysical laws.[13] And in matters of moral theory, strong supervenience is too reductive for stating the traditional doctrine that the moral supervenes on the nonmoral without any moral property being necessitated by a set of nonmoral properties. Thus, even if strong supervenience fails to imply a relation of necessary coextension, it still remains too reductive to serve as a general vehicle for advancing the nonreductivist agenda.

2. Global Supervenience and Reduction

Based on reductive worries over strong supervenience implying (S_2), some philosophers have opted instead for global supervenience. Indeed, Bradford Petrie has shown that global supervenience, by virtue of its holistic character, fails to imply even (S_1).[14] To see this, consider a world W_1 where x and y both possess G, but only x possesses F; and suppose that in an alternative world W_2, both x and y fail to possess F but that x, unlike y, possesses G. Allowing that F is the only property in A and G is the only property in B, this case is compatible with A globally supervening on B, since the worlds W_1 and W_2 are not indiscernible with regard to B. But given the nature of W_2, where x possesses G but not F, it is not a case that is compatible with (S_1). Thus, global supervenience, unlike strong, is weak enough to avoid being committed to (S_1).

Despite whatever advantage global supervenience might have by not implying (S_1), it should not be concluded that this form of supervenience is sufficiently weak to avoid being reductive. For although global supervenience does not imply (S_1), it does entail that each subvenient property is necessitated by some subvenient basis. That is, global supervenience entails

> **(G_1)** For each property F in A, if F is exemplified by some object x, then there is a condition C that is equivalent to a conjunction of all the exemplifications of properties in B such that necessarily if C obtains, and there is no exemplification of a property in B that is not entailed by C, then x has F.

For a proof of this, suppose that (G_1) is false so that there is a property F in A that is not necessitated by any condition that is equivalent to a conjunction of all the exemplifications of properties in B. Let W_1 be a world where an object x has F, and let C be equivalent to a conjunction of all the exemplifications of B-properties in W_1. Given the assumption that (G_1) is false, it is then not the case that necessarily if C obtains, and there is no exemplification of a property in B that is not entailed by C, then x has F. Consequently, there is another world, say, W_2, where C obtains and is equivalent to a conjunction of all the exemplifications of B-properties in W_2, but x does not possess F. Since W_1 and W_2 are indiscernible with regard to B but are not indiscernible with regard to A, this demonstrates that global supervenience implies (G_1).

What does this show? Aside from two minor differences, global supervenience entails the same type of necessary, or lawlike, conditionals implied by strong supervenience. One minor difference is that the conditionals entailed by global supervenience include a certain qualification as part of the antecedent, namely, that there is no exemplification of a property in B that is not entailed by C. But this qualification is not in any way peculiar or untoward. Instead, it simply functions as a type of ceteris paribus clause, a clause that, as many have emphasized, is essential to almost any genuine law of nature.[15] The other minor difference is that in the case of global supervenience, the types of necessary conditionals implied feature a holistic antecedent that covers the whole range of exemplifications of B-properties. Whether this element of holism inhibits reduction requires further investigation.

Petrie, in arguing that global supervenience is nonreductive, anticipates in a note the entailment of "complex conditionals connecting total specifications of the subvenient properties of a world w and the supervenient properties exemplified in w"[16] but downplays the significance of the matter by suggesting that these conditionals do not form the basis of a "'reduction' of the supervenient properties in any usual sense."[17] By "usual" Petrie presumably has in mind some kind of *local* reduction based on localized property-to-property connections that can be pinned on individual objects. But regardless of whether Petrie is right about this issue of local reduction, it remains the case that the necessary conditionals entailed by global supervenience establish nonlocalized condition-to-property connections that form the basis of an equally unattractive *holistic* reduction. For in matters of reduction, it is the relation of implication that does the reductive work, at least according to Nagel's view, and this relation can obtain between holistic elements just as easily as it can between localized ones.[18] Moreover, the sorts of ordinary properties or objects that are not amenable to any localized reduction – such as *table, door, tall* – seem also to resist any holistic reduction. So the fact that the necessary conditionals implied by global supervenience feature a holistic antecedent seems not to mitigate the reductive force of these conditionals. These conditionals simply provide the basis for a holistic rather than a localized type of reduction.

By virtue, then, of entailing (G_1), global supervenience yields basically the same type of necessary conditionals implied by strong supervenience. Indeed, the two sets of conditionals, despite minor differences, seem equally reductive, with the conditionals implied by global supervenience effecting a kind of holistic rather than localized reduction.

In addition to holistic reduction, global supervenience also promotes a form of localized reduction. That is, global supervenience implies not only (G_1) but also

(G_2) For each property F in A, there is a property G in B such that necessarily for every object x, if x has G, and no other object y has a property in B, then x has F.

The proof proceeds as before. Suppose that (G_2) is false so that there is some F in A that is not necessitated by any property in B. Let W_1 be a world where F is exemplified by an object x, and let G be equivalent to a conjunction of all the properties in B that x possesses. Further suppose that in W_1 no object distinct from x has any property in B. On the assumption that (G_2) is false, there is another world, say, W_2, where x has G and no other object has a property in B, yet x does not have F. Therefore, contrary to what global supervenience requires, W_1 and W_2 are indiscernible with regard to B but are not indiscernible with regard to A, which shows that global supervenience implies (G_2).

Much like strong supervenience, global supervenience, by virtue of implying (G_2), entails necessary conditionals establishing localized property-to-property connections that can be pinned on individual objects. The only difference is that in the case of global supervenience, the conditionals feature a type of ceteris paribus clause that, as noted earlier, is common to genuine laws of nature.[19]

So by implying (G_1) and (G_2), global supervenience lends itself to both holistic and localized forms of reduction. Moreover, global supervenience seems no less reductive than strong supervenience, since both entail one-way conditionals asserting that each supervenient property is necessitated by either some subvenient property or some condition regarding the exemplifications of such properties. Consequently, neither form of supervenience is weak enough to express how the mental could supervene on the physical without there being any psychophysical laws, and neither is adequate for stating how the moral could supervene on the nonmoral without any moral property being necessitated by a set of nonmoral properties. Thus, both strong and global supervenience seem too reductive to function as a general vehicle for articulating the nonreductivist program.

3. Global Supervenience and Determination

Apart from the matter of reduction, some question whether global supervenience is able to yield a genuine form of determination. Kim points out that since global supervenience places no constraints on how the exemplification of supervenient properties can diverge in worlds that are not perfectly indiscernible with respect to the set of subvenient properties, the claim that the mental globally supervenes on the physical is consistent with there being a world exactly like ours except for one trivial difference, such as the rings of Saturn containing one more ammonia molecule, where this other world has some wildly different pattern of mental phenomena or is even devoid of consciousness altogether.[20] And what is even more striking is that due to its holistic character, global supervenience places no constraints on how objects in the same world can differ with respect to their supervenient properties when these objects are *exactly alike* regarding their subvenient properties.[21] Consequently, as demonstrated by Petrie's example, the claim that the mental globally supervenes on the physical allows for two individuals in the same world to have exactly the same physical properties where only one of them has any mental properties. These considerations lead Kim to ask:

> How is it possible to advance a claim of physical dependency of the mental if, as permitted by the global supervenience of the mental on the physical, there should exist a human being physically indistinguishable from you in every respect who has a mental life entirely different from yours or who has no mental life at all?[22]

Thus, global supervenience seems too strong to avoid the threat of reduction yet also too weak to provide an interesting form of determination. Does strong supervenience fare any better?

4. Strong Supervenience and Determination

Whereas global supervenience encounters problems by virtue of being too holistic, some complain that strong supervenience is not holistic enough.[23] In particular, by focusing only on those properties that pertain to individual objects, strong supervenience seems inadequate for accounting for the determination of nonlocal properties. For example, mental properties that feature wide content are determined, at least in part, by properties that extend beyond the makeup of any given individual. Likewise, economic properties of currency owe their existence not simply to the specific characteristics of particular pieces of paper, but to the complex workings of a financial community. Thus, unlike global supervenience, strong supervenience seems too localized to accommodate the determination of nonlocal properties.

In defending strong supervenience against the objection that its focus is too narrow, Kim points out that the objection requires that the subvenient properties be restricted to only the "intrinsic" properties of individual objects. By allowing the set of subvenient properties to include *relational* properties of individuals, properties that extend beyond localized intrinsic characteristics, Kim suggests that the objection no longer applies. For example, among the properties of a particular dollar bill are various relational properties that arise from the bill's relationship to a financial community. Once these relational properties are included in the set of subvenient properties, it is quite plausible to assert that the economic properties of currency strongly supervene on the physical properties of currency.

Kim's appeal to relational properties does seem to overcome the objection that strong supervenience is unable to account for the determination of nonlocal or global properties. Ironically, however, it also renders strong supervenience vulnerable to the same type of objection that Kim raises against global supervenience regarding its failure to express an interesting account of determination. That is, by requiring only that each supervenient property exemplified by an object be necessitated by some subvenient property possessed by that object, strong supervenience allows for one of the object's subvenient properties to necessitate all of its supervenient properties. Consequently, strong supervenience places no constraints on how two individuals can differ with respect to their supervenient properties when each individual has a subvenient property that is not possessed by the other. So if the set of subvenient properties includes both relational and nonrelational properties, the claim that the mental strongly supervenes on the physical is then consistent with there being a world exactly like ours except for two trivial differences, such as the rings of Saturn containing one extra ammonia molecule but one less water molecule, where this other world has some completely different pattern of mental phenomena or perhaps none at all. Or alternatively, this claim of strong supervenience allows for two individuals in the same world to have exactly the same physical properties except for a trivial relational difference regarding, for example, their proximity to the center of a distant star, where one of the individuals is in intense pain while the other is in utter euphoria or has no mental properties whatsoever.

Now, of course, strong supervenience, unlike the situation with global supervenience, at least rules out the possibility that two individuals with the same physical properties will have different mental properties, but it is not clear that this is an important advantage since there will virtually never be a case where two individuals share exactly the same relational and nonrelational physical properties. Instead, each individual will invariably have some relational property, however trivial or mundane, that no other individual has, which then allows, under the constraints of strong supervenience, their mental properties to differ radically despite whatever physical similarities they may have. So although including relational properties within the set of subvenient properties allows strong supervenience to apply to nonlocal properties, it also makes this form of supervenience subject to the same type of objection regarding determination that Kim brings against global supervenience.

It might appear that the problem here facing strong supervenience arises only if the set of subvenient properties is extended to include relational properties. This assessment, however, is only partially right, for essentially the same problem arises even when relational properties are *not* included. That is, even if only intrinsic properties are permitted, then given that strong supervenience imposes no limits on how two individuals can differ with respect to their supervenient properties when each individual has some subvenient property that is not shared by the other, the claim that the mental strongly supervenes on the physical allows for two individuals in the same world to have exactly the same physical properties except for two trivial intrinsic differences, such as one individual having an extra molecule of hair on his left side and the other having an extra molecule of hair on his right side, where one of the individuals is in excruciating pain and the other, who is in exactly the same brain state, is, say, wildly happy or perhaps altogether devoid of consciousness. So regardless of whether the set of subvenient properties includes relational properties, strong supervenience, much like global, seems too holistic to yield an interesting form of determination.

One possible solution to this problem of excessive holism, as it applies to both strong and global supervenience, is to narrow the set of subvenient properties to just the relevant ones so that there could be no trivial subvenient differences. For example, in the case of the mental supervening on the physical, the set of subvenient properties could be identified as the smallest subset of physical properties that still allows for the supervenience of the set of all mental properties.[24] The restricted set of subvenient properties would presumably not include properties involving an extra ammonia or water molecule in the rings of Saturn, the exact distance to the center of a far away star, or the precise amount of hair on one's body, thereby effectively blocking the counterexamples given earlier. This solution, however, does little to overcome the original problem.

In the case of global supervenience, regardless of whether the set of subvenient properties is restricted in a way that eliminates any irrelevant subvenient differences, this form of supervenience still allows for two individuals in the same world to have exactly the same subvenient properties but radically different supervenient properties. Indeed, this much is evident from Petrie's example where there is just one subvenient property. And though strong supervenience prevents individuals with the same subvenient properties from having different supervenient properties, the situation with this form of supervenience is not much better.

If B^* is the smallest subset of physical properties that suffices as a subvenient base for the strong supervenience of all mental properties, there is no guarantee that *all* the properties in B^* are relevant to *each* mental property.[25] Consequently, there could be a certain physical property, such as being exposed to a mild dose of laughing gas, that is relevant to the mental property of feeling relaxed but that is irrelevant to the mental property of being in pain. The claim, then, that the mental strongly supervenes on the physical as restricted to the set B^* is consistent with there being two individuals x and y that have both been struck over the head with a lead pipe and are indiscernible with regard to B^* except for x having the single additional subvenient property of being exposed to a mild dose of laughing gas, where x is in intense pain while y has no mental properties at all. And in the case where y should also have an additional property in B^* that is not possessed by x, a property that is irrelevant to pain such as being mildly tickled on the foot, the claim of strong supervenience places no constraints whatsoever on how the mental states of x and y can differ. The only case that will not be susceptible to this type of problem is where each subvenient property is relevant to each supervenient property, but in this case strong supervenience reduces to the uninteresting claim that the conjunction of all supervenient properties is necessitated by the conjunction of all subvenient properties.

So apart from the special yet uninteresting case just noted, the problem of excessive holism remains for both strong and global supervenience even if the subvenient properties are confined to those relevant properties, relational or otherwise, that form a minimally sufficient set. Consequently, it is difficult to see how either form of supervenience is able to deliver on the promise of providing an interesting relation of determination.[26]

5. Conclusion

Which type of supervenience, then, strong or global, is more suitable for serving as a nonreductive form of determination? The answer seems to be *neither*. Those who claim that strong supervenience is too reductive will do no better by embracing global supervenience, since this other type of supervenience seems equally reductive. And those who claim that global supervenience is too holistic to sustain a suitable form of determination will do no better by adopting strong supervenience, since it is too holistic as well – that is, neither places any constraints on the exemplification of supervenient properties when there are certain trivial differences in the exemplification of the relational or nonrelational subvenient properties. Indeed, despite strong and global supervenience being distinct types of supervenience, the basic objections that are brought against one also apply to the other so that both seem equally inept at furnishing a nonreductive relation of determination. Those philosophers, then, who have turned to strong or global supervenience in search of such a relation appear to be looking in the wrong place.

NOTES

I wish to thank Charles Carr, Ron Endicott, Jim Klagge, and John Post for their helpful advice in preparing this essay.

1. This formulation of strong supervenience is taken from Jaegwon Kim, "Concepts of Supervenience," *Philosophy and Phenomenological Research* 45 (1984): 153–76, but see also Colin McGinn, "Philosophical Materialism," *Synthese* 44 (1980): 173–206. A generic notion of supervenience can arguably be traced back at least to Alexander of Aphrodisias, who taught in Athens in 200 A.D. In rejecting the view that the soul is identical with a certain combination of primary bodies, Alexander suggests that the "soul is more than this simple combination: it is a vital force that comes into being

as an addition to the combination." Athanasios P. Fotinis, *The De Anima of Alexander of Aphrodisias: A Translation and Commentary* (Washington, D.C.: University Press of America, 1979), p. 36. Donatus, in his 1445 Latin translation of Alexander's *De Anima*, uses forms of the verb 'supervenio' to translate certain passages where Alexander describes the relation between the soul and primary bodies. I am grateful to Jacob Adler for bringing these references to Alexander to my attention.

2. For early formulations of global supervenience, see Geoffry Hellman and Frank Thompson, "Physicalism: Ontology, Determination, and Reduction," *Journal of Philosophy* 72 (1975): 551–64; Terence Horgan, "Supervenience and Microphysics," *Pacific Philosophical Quarterly* 63 (1982): 29–43; and John Haugeland, "Weak Supervenience," *American Philosophical Quarterly* 19 (1982): 93–103.

3. Some philosophers regard supervenience as implying a relation of dependency, where dependency is supposed to be the converse of determination. It can be shown, however, that these are distinct relations, not even being converses of each other, such that the generic structure of supervenience provides at best only a form determination, but not dependency. Consequently, my concern will be whether strong or global supervenience is adequate for expressing a relation of determination. For a discussion of the distinction between determination and dependency and their relation to supervenience, see my "Supervenience, Determination, and Dependency," *Philosophical Studies* 62 (1991): 81–92.

4. Kim, "Concepts of Supervenience," pp. 170–1, though Kim himself, based on epistemic considerations, does not regard this result as showing that strong supervenience is reductive. In establishing this result, Kim assumes that the set of subvenient properties is also closed under negation, but this assumption, as James Van Cleve points out, is unnecessary; see Van Cleve's "Supervenience and Closure," *Philosophical Studies* 58 (1990): 225–38.

5. Paul Teller, "Comments on Kim's Paper," *Southern Journal of Philosophy* 22, Supplement (1983): 57–61.

6. David Armstrong, *Universals: An Opinionated Introduction* (Boulder, Colo.: Westview, 1989), chap. 5. For a defense of disjunctive subvenient properties, see Van Cleve, "Supervenience and Closure," and Jaegwon Kim, "Supervenience as a Philosophical Concept," *Metaphilosophy* 21 (1990): 1–27.

7. Ernest Nagel, *The Structure of Science* (New York: Harcourt, Brace, and World, 1961).

8. Ibid., p. 338.

9. Ibid., p. 352.

10. Ibid., p. 355n5.

11. Ibid., p. 365.

12. This point, which Robert C. Richardson emphasizes in his "Functionalism and Reductionism," *Philosophy of Science* 46 (1979): 533–58, is often overlooked in discussions of reduction. For example, Kim writes:

> By *reducibility* we shall understand the Nagel reducibility . . . ; the primary requirement for this type of reduction is that each primitive descriptive

term of the reduced theory be connected by a biconditional bridge law with some predicate of the reducing theory.

Jaegwon Kim, "Supervenience and Nomological Incommensurables," *American Philosophical Quarterly* 15 (1978): 149–56, p. 152.

13. Donald Davidson, "Mental Events," in L. Foster and J. W. Swanson (eds.), *Experience and Theory* (Amherst: University of Massachusetts Press, 1970), pp. 79–101. Davidson does not endorse strong supervenience and instead relies on a weaker form of supervenience for purposes of formulating the doctrine of anomalous monism.

14. Bradford Petrie, "Global Supervenience and Reduction," *Philosophy and Phenomenological Research* 48 (1987): 119–30.

15. See, e.g., Nancy Cartwright, *How the Laws of Physics Lie* (Oxford University Press, 1983).

16. Petrie, "Global Supervenience and Reduction," p. 123n6.

17. Ibid.

18. For an opposing view that recognizes only local reduction, see Harold Kincaid, "Supervenience Doesn't Entail Reducibility," *Southern Journal of Philosophy* 25 (1987): 343–56. Kincaid suggests that reduction, at least as it applies to theories, requires that the explanations of the higher-level theory be replaceable by explanations of the lower-level theory. This may be so, but it is not enough to block global supervenience from being reductive since explanations can apply holistically as well as locally. However, Kincaid also suggests that reduction requires coextension of *individual* predicates in contrast to mere global correlations. Yet this requirement seems not to be satisfied in certain ordinary cases of reduction, such as the reduction of global conservation laws that apply to entire systems.

19. In speaking about global supervenience in his "Supervenience as a Philosophical Concept," p. 22, Kim asserts, "It is known that this covariance relation does not imply property-to-property correlations between supervenient and subvenient properties." But given that global supervenience implies (G_2), Kim's remark needs to be qualified to the effect that this form of supervenience does not imply any *simple* or *non-ceteris-paribus* property-to-property correlations between supervenient and subvenient properties.

20. Jaegwon Kim, "'Strong' and 'Global' Supervenience Revisited," *Philosophy and Phenomenological Research* 48 (1987): 315–26.

21. Though Kim has drawn attention to this fact about global supervenience, W. V. Quine was one of the first to recognize the problem in his "Facts of the Matter," *Southwestern Journal of Philosophy* 9 (1978): 155–69.

22. Kim, "'Strong' and 'Global' Supervenience Revisited," p. 320.

23. See, e.g., Horgan, "Supervenience and Microphysics"; Petrie, "Global Supervenience and Reduction"; and John F. Post, *The Faces of Existence: An Essay in Nonreductive Metaphysics* (Ithaca, N.Y.: Cornell University Press, 1990), chap. 4.

24. This is similar to a solution Post suggests in responding to the different but related charge that global supervenience, or what Post calls "determination," is not localized enough to identify which specific subvenient

properties determine a given supervenient property. See his *Metaphysics: A Contemporary Introduction* (New York: Paragon House, 1991), p. 118.

25. By a single physical property in B^* being relevant to a single mental property F, I mean that the physical property is a member of at least one minimal subset of B^* that provides a subvenient base for the strong supervenience of the unit set containing F.

26. For other nonholistic problems of determination that arise for both strong and global supervenience, see my "The Myth of Supervenience," *Pacific Philosophical Quarterly* 69 (1988): 152–60.

Reduction in the Mind of God

DANIEL BONEVAC

Bertrand Russell (1924) placed at the heart of his logical atomism what he called "the supreme maxim in scientific philosophizing": "Wherever possible, substitute constructions out of known entities for inferences to unknown entities" (p. 326). Rudolf Carnap took this maxim as his motto in explicating the logical structure of the world (1967, p. 5). Twentieth-century metaphysicians have often adopted Russell's maxim tacitly in pursuing reductive strategies.

In an increasing variety of areas, however, a consensus has grown that such strategies face dim prospects. We are still novices at neuroscience, but philosophers of mind no longer have much hope of reducing mental language to physical language. Physics has not yet found a unified theory of basic physical phenomena, much less a theory unifying them with the manifest image of the world, but philosophers of mind have lost faith that our everyday discourse about the world around us will eventually reduce to the language of an ideal physics.

A loss of faith in reduction has not led to a revival of faith in dualism, for its postulation of a realm of immaterial mental entities that have causal powers to affect each other and the material world seems unscientific and without explanatory power. To many, physicalism has remained the only respectable attitude toward the mind–body problem. The challenge has been to find a nonreductive physicalism that resists any commitment to immaterial entities while allowing that psychology and other higher-level theories are autonomous from physics.

Supervenience has seemed a way to express the central insight of physicalism without committing oneself to doing the impossible or, at any rate, the unlikely. Recently, however, Jaegwon Kim (1989, 1990, 1992) has argued that nonreductive physicalism is incoherent. He has urged that the dilemma between reductive physicalism and dualism remains very much alive. Nonreductive physicalists, he argues, face the same problems that emergence theorists such as Samuel Alexander (1920), C. Lloyd Morgan (1923), and C. D. Broad (1925) faced earlier in this century. They are committed to both "upward determination" – the determination of the mental by the physical – and "downward causation" – the capacity of the mental to influence the physical. The for-

124

mer is the claim of supervenience; the latter stems from insisting on the autonomy of psychology. Kim questions their compatibility.

In this essay I shall defend the possibility of nonreductive physicalism. The relation between supervenience and reduction, I shall maintain, is often misunderstood and is properly seen as epistemological. Strong supervenience, sometimes alleged to be equivalent to reduction, is in fact weaker in epistemologically significant ways. But from the ontological perspective of realism, the difference is only epistemological; strong supervenience has precisely the ontological implications of reduction. To an antirealist, in contrast, the difference between supervenience and reduction may have great ontological significance. Whether supervenience suffices for a defense of physicalism thus depends on broad metaphysical issues going far beyond the mind–body problem. Whether downward causation and the autonomy of psychology, moreover, are compatible with strong supervenience depends on a theory of causation and of laws.

In what follows, I outline a nonreductive physicalism that demonstrates the compatibility of upward determination and downward causation, when these are interpreted in certain commonly understood ways. There is nothing new about the position whose coherence I wish to defend: a strong supervenience version of nonreductive physicalism. My defense succeeds only on some conceptions of ontological commitment and causation. But those conceptions strike me as at least plausible. That their denials face one with a dilemma between dualism and reductionism should perhaps count in their favor.

1. Strong Supervenience and Reduction

Supervenience is usually taken to be a relation between kinds of properties; reduction, a relation between theories. These perspectives are different but, fortunately, easily intertranslatable, at least on some theories of properties. I shall represent a kind of property as a set of open formulas of some language: formulas that objects satisfy if and only if they have corresponding properties of the kind in question. I shall often identify the kind with a set of predicates from which the open formulas are generated by standard logical operations. This seems to me harmless, though it does presuppose that kinds of properties are closed under (finite) conjunction, (finite) disjunction, and, most controversially, perhaps, negation (see Bacon 1986, 1990; Van Cleve 1990).

The kind of reduction most directly relevant to the mind–body problem is microreduction, of the kind discussed by Robert Causey (1972a,b, 1977) and Hooker (1981). Beckermann (1992b) uses microreduction to argue, in part against Kim (1978, 1983, 1987) and Bacon

(1986), that strong supervenience is weaker than the kind of reduction relevant to mind–body issues. I am interested in a different distinction between supervenience and reduction, however, one that emerges especially clearly in relation to the more traditional view of reduction as interpretation. It casts ontological issues in an especially clear light. Without denying that microreduction is a better candidate for mind–body relations than the more traditional notion, I shall focus on the latter. This has the additional advantage that it is possible to use arithmetic and other fairly well-understood theories as test cases.

Let L and L' be languages, for the moment without function symbols, and T and T' be theories, that is, sets of sentences in those languages, respectively, closed under logical consequence. Let D be a monadic predicate of L', and let h be a function from n-adic predicates of L to open formulas of L' with n free variables, as well as from individual constants of L to constants of L'. Then $* = <h, D>$ interprets L in L' if and only if

(1) $c^* = h(c)$

(2) $v^* = v$

(3) $R(t_1, \ldots, t_n)^* = h(R)(t_1^*, \ldots, t_n^*)$

(4) $(-A)^* = -A^*$

(5) $(A \mathbin{\&} B)^* = A^* \mathbin{\&} B^*$

(6) $(A \vee B)^* = A^* \vee B^*$

(7) $(A \to B)^* = (A^* \to B^*)$

(8) $((x)A)^* = (x)(Dx \to A^*)$

(9) $((\exists x)A)^* = (\exists x)(Dx \mathbin{\&} A^*)$

The interpretation $*$ interprets T in T' if and only if it maps theorems of T into theorems of T'; if and only if, that is, T^*, the image of T under $*$, is a subset of T'. T is reducible to T' if and only if there is an interpretation of T in T'.

In general, where L and L' contain function symbols, h should map n-ary function symbols f of L into open formulas $h(f)$ of L' in $n + 1$ free variables, such that T' implies $(x_1) \ldots (x_n)((D(x_1) \mathbin{\&} \ldots \mathbin{\&} D(x_n)) \to (\exists y)(A(y) \mathbin{\&} (z)(h(f)(x_1, \ldots, x_n, z) \leftrightarrow z = y)))$. (The definition thus relates a language L to a theory T', not just to its language L'.) Constants, under these circumstances, should be viewed as o-ary function symbols. (3) must change to define the translation of atomic formulas recursively, depending on the number of function symbols. If there are none, then $(Rx_1, \ldots, x_n)^* = h(R)(x_1, \ldots, x_n)$. Otherwise, replace the rightmost function symbol f in the formula A with a new variable, and preface a quantifier on that variable and an antecedent consisting of that function symbol's associated formula $h(f)$ to obtain $(z)(h(f)$ $(x_1, \ldots, x_n, z) \rightarrow A[f(x_1, \ldots, x_n)/z])$.

This conception of reduction has properties that make it extremely useful in formal contexts. Reducibility, so understood, implies relative consistency and, almost, relative decidability and undecidability. If T reduces to T', then the consistency of T' implies the consistency of T; the consistent decidability of T' implies the decidability of a consistent extension of T; and the consistency and essential undecidability of T imply the undecidability of T'. These properties have inspired most twentieth-century mathematical uses of interpretability: the proof of the relative consistency of non-Euclidean geometries, for example, and proofs by Godel and Cohen of the consistency and independence of the axiom of choice and the generalized continuum hypothesis. They have also inspired most logical work on interpretability (e.g., Tarski, Mostowski, and Robinson 1953).

The conception of reduction I have just outlined nevertheless arose in the nineteenth century for somewhat different reasons. Around 1800, a number of mathematical fields were in disarray. Most notable, perhaps, was analysis. The notions of derivative and integral rested on intuitive discussions of infinitesimals. The concept of a continuous function and, indeed, of a function itself, remained intuitive. The convergence of series was not well understood; arguments about infinity were often confused, the nature and legitimacy of negative and complex numbers was disputed, and basic properties of the reals were unappreciated. Analysis and algebra suffered from disputes about particular theorems and about basic principles (see Kline 1972). Cauchy, Dedekind, Weierstrass, Cantor, Peano, and others developed the modern notions of function, limit, real number, and infinity. The rigorization of mathematics culminated in Whitehead and Russell's *Principia Mathematica* (1910–13). Much rigorization work relied implicitly on the conception of reduction I have outlined. Its import, moreover, was clearly ontological. The Weierstrass definition of continuity, for example, showed that the idea did not rest on any commitment to infinitesimals. Cauchy's definition of a function showed that it was nothing mysterious but could be identified with a class of n-tuples. Rigorization in effect brought a reduction of theories of negative and complex numbers to theories without such commitments, hastening the acceptance of such numbers in mathematical practice and the consensus underlying that practice about their properties.

It is fair to say, then, that the central motivation of reduction in the nineteenth century was, at least in part, ontological. Certainly ontological motives have been primary among reductionist twentieth-century philosophers. Russell, for example, employs this conception of reduction in his logicist program to eliminate the need for any Kantian intuition of mathematical entities; mathematics, he argues, commits us to nothing beyond the commitments of logic. The same conception underlies logical atomism and Carnap's construction of the physical from the phenomenalistic.

Because the contrast with supervenience is important for my purposes in this essay, it is worth examining the ontological significance of reduction in greater detail. A reduction has ontological force, in the view of Russell, Carnap, and later philosophers such as Quine, because it shows that certain ways of talking are eliminable. Commitments of a theory that are troublesome for one reason or another can be avoided by showing that the theory translates into another without the same commitments. The troublesome objects thus do not have to be mentioned in giving a complete description of the world (Russell 1918); they do not have to be counted among the ultimate furniture of the universe. This does not mean that a reduction shows that certain objects do not exist, or must be identified with certain other objects. It shows merely that they may be taken not to exist, or, usually, to be identical with certain other objects in the domain of the reducing theory. Reduction thus allows one to avoid a commitment to objects as independently existing.

Strong supervenience, at first glance, appears very different from reduction. Properties of kind J strongly supervene on those of kind K if and only if any two objects with the same K properties also have the same J properties – even if they occupy different possible worlds. To put this in terms somewhat closer to those used earlier for reduction, identify a kind of property with a set of open formulas generated from a set of predicates, or, more simply, with a language. Then language L strongly supervenes on language L' if and only if any two objects indiscernible in L' are also indiscernible in L, even if they occupy different worlds. Unlike other notions of supervenience that lack quantification over both objects and worlds – weak and global supervenience, for example – this is strong enough to support the counterfactuals that seem essential to an idea of dependence or determination.

As Kim (1978, 1983, 1987, 1989) and Bacon (1986) have argued, however, strong supervenience is not as far from reduction as it might seem. If kinds of properties are closed under finite conjunction, disjunction, and negation – and my linguistic representation assumes that they are – then, if L' has a finite number of predicates and no function symbols, strong supervenience is equivalent to reducibility. Given these assumptions about L', if L strongly supervenes on L', every n-adic predicate of L is equivalent to an open formula of L' in n free variables. And this suffices for L to be interpretable in L'.

To see the link with reducibility more directly, note that this definition is equivalent to a more traditional formulation, according to which T is interpretable in T' if and only if there is a recursive set of possible definitions or bridge laws, that is, necessary universalized biconditionals, linking the predicates of L to open formulas of L', which, together with T', imply T. If L' is finite and lacks function symbols, and L strongly supervenes on L', then the truths of L reduce to the truths of L' in precisely this sense.

This result does not dash all hopes for a nonreductive physicalism based on the notion of strong supervenience, for any interesting language has function symbols; certainly the language of physics does, for it includes mathematics, and anything with as much as addition includes function symbols. Any language with operators for forming predicates from predicates – such as English, for example – also lies outside the narrow bounds of this result. So, we must ask about the properties of strong supervenience in a more general setting.

As Kim has shown, if L strongly supervenes on L', then every n-adic predicate of L is equivalent to an open formula of an infinitary extension of L' – a language with the vocabulary of L' that permits infinite conjunctions and disjunctions. There is no way in general to find an equivalent open formula of L' itself. The problem reflects the argument from multiple realizability or compositional plasticity; it may be impossible to specify all possible physical realizations of a given mental state. Reducibility entails strong supervenience, but not vice versa.

It is worth examining strong supervenience more closely to see what it does and does not share with reducibility. Put in terms of translation, strong supervenience entails that the set of true sentences of L translates into a set of true sentences of an infinitary extension of L'. The notion of translation here is somewhat attenuated, however, for it is not recursive. There is no guarantee of a recursive method for finding the translation of a given L-sentence or of determining whether a given sentence of the infinitary version of L' is or is not that translation. It follows that while strong supervenience can still be used to establish relative consistency, it implies nothing about relative decidability or undecidability. It certainly implies nothing about the eliminability in principle of certain kinds of discourse, and thus of certain ontological commitments, for saying what we want to say, from the perspective of L, in an infinitary L' may well be impossible. It is not just that we might have to go on talking forever, though that is bad enough. We might never be able to translate what we want to say in the first place, for the set of disjuncts employed in a definition might not be recursively enumerable.

To return to the mind–body problem, a nonreductive physicalist can coherently maintain that mental language strongly supervenes on physical language without also holding that mental facts reduce to physical facts. Kim (1983) contends that "the strong supervenience of A on B points to a possibility of reducing A to B" (p. 50). Kim (1989) reiterates, "Supervenience of this strength entails the possibility of reducing the supervenient to the subvenient" (p. 46). In isolation, however, this is misleading. As Kim (1983) continues: "If reduction is to provide explanatory understanding, reducibility will crucially depend on the perspicuous describability of the underlying coextensions in B of the properties in A. Supervenience alone does not guarantee that a theory that will supply such descriptions exists or will ever exist" (p. 50). Or, I would add, can even exist at all. Strong supervenience does not imply reducibility in principle, with the problem arising about whether anyone will in practice be able to perform the reduction by devising the proper translation. A translation that a human cognitive agent could use may be impossible in principle. Beckermann (1992b, p. 97) is surely wrong to conclude that "strong supervenience is incompatible with antireductionism."

For example, consider first-order arithmetic, in a language with 0, ' (successor), $+$, and $\times$. Call this language L. L' extends L by adding a truth predicate for L. Tarski's theorem shows that the truths of L' do not reduce to the truths of L; arithmetical truth is not arithmetically definable. (If it were, the liar paradox could be produced within arithmetic.) But truth in L' strongly supervenes on truth in L. A valuation for L determines a valuation for L' in an obvious way. This result is not special to arithmetic; it extends to any theory containing the means for referring to its own sentences (Bonevac 1991). Kim's argument shows that an infinitary definition of arithmetical truth is indeed possible. But that is no surprise: the definition is simply $(x)(\text{True}(x) \leftrightarrow x = n_1 \lor \ldots \lor x = n_m \lor \ldots)$, where $n_1, \ldots, n_m, \ldots$ are the Gödel numbers of the true sentences of arithmetic. This, plainly, is not a helpful definition. We have no way of producing it; the set $\{n_1, \ldots, n_m, \ldots\}$ is not recursively enumerable. Arithmetical truth, then, supervenes on arithmetic but is not arithmetically definable and, thus, not reducible to arithmetic, even in principle.

There is a very clear sense, therefore, in which Kim is wrong to conclude that strong supervenience "gives us dependence but threatens autonomy" (1983, p. 50). For example, if no human agent could possibly perform a reduction of mental language to physical language, then mental language is ineliminable and autonomous. Truth in the mental language may depend completely on truth in the underlying physical language, but the connections may be so complex that they are humanly indecipherable.

2. Dependence and Ontology

Critics have raised two kinds of objections to a strong supervenience version of nonreductive physicalism. First, Grimes (1988) and Kim (1990), echoed by Beckermann (1992a), insist that strong supervenience is too weak to capture the idea of dependence. A variety of authors (Boyd 1980, Fodor 1981, LePore and Loewer 1989, Beckermann 1992a,b) have argued that the notion of realization is more appropriate: mental states depend on physical states in the sense that mental states are realized by physical states. As understood by its advocates, realization is stronger than strong supervenience. A realization account is thus a kind of strong supervenience account. As such, it does not threaten my thesis in this essay. I have no objection to realization theories. I do, however, have objections to some arguments that Kim has used to undermine strong supervenience as representing our intuitive idea of dependence.

Grimes and Kim contend, in essence, that strong supervenience represents only property covariance, not dependence. It is possible, for example, for two kinds of properties – or, in the terms I have been using here, two languages – to strongly supervene on each other. It is possible for L to supervene on L', not because L depends on L', but because both supervene in turn on L''. Consequently, the strong supervenience of the mental on the physical is compatible with dualism, epiphenomenalism, and other nonphysicalist theories of mind. Beckermann, reviewing Kim's arguments, concludes that "the concept of supervenience is not of much help if one wants to formulate a viable version of nonreductive physicalism, since physicalism demands more than just causal or nomological dependence" (1992a, p. 14).

Admittedly, strong supervenience itself does not fully capture the 'because' or 'in virtue of' that people have in mind when they think of dependence. A physicalist thinks that the mental depends on the physical in the sense that something has the mental state it does because or in virtue of its physical state. But what is striking about these arguments is that they can and have been made against reduction. That is, if for these reasons strong supervenience cannot serve the needs of physicalism, then neither can reduction. Reducibility, like strong supervenience, is reflexive and transitive. It is possible for two theories to reduce to each other; indeed, Carnap tried to show that the physical and the phenomenal are mutually reducible. It is also possible for one theory to reduce to another by virtue of the way that they both reduce to some third theory. This, arguably, is precisely the situation with sociology and psychology, or biology and chemistry, from a physicalist point of view. And reducibility is compatible with the independent existence of the objects of both the reduced and the reducing theory. As Russell was careful to point out, a reduction (or, in his terms, an analysis) does not demonstrate the nonexistence of anything: "I want to make clear that I am not denying the existence of anything; I am only refusing to affirm it" (1918, p. 273). For example, Russell sometimes takes the no-class theory as showing that sets are "mere conveniences, not genuine objects," "false abstractions" on a par with "the present King of France" (1910, p. 72; 1906, p. 166). In a more considered mood, however, he stresses that it allows us to be agnostics about the existence of classes, saying, with Laplace, "Je n'ai pas besoin de cette hypothèse" (1919, p. 184).

Reducibility, then, does not entail the nonexistence of the reduced objects or the identity of the reduced and reducing objects; it permits identification but does not require it. Similarly, it does not establish dependence or determination, for theories may reduce to each other. The reduction of the mental to the physical would be perfectly compatible with dualism or epiphenomenalism. Those views would lose their point, however, for the assumption of minds as existing independent of bodies would no longer be necessary; it would carry no explanatory weight and would seem to call for a visit to Occam's styling salon.

The same, I contend, holds for strong supervenience. Strong supervenience does not entail the supervening objects' nonexistence or identity with the objects on which they supervene. It does not by itself entail dependence or determination. Supervenience, like reduction, permits the assumption of dependence or even identification but does not require it. Nevertheless, like reduction, supervenience can have ontological significance because it makes the assumption of an independent realm unnecessary. Kim is right that strong supervenience in itself does not establish ontological conclusions or capture fully our intuitive notion of dependence. But all it needs to accomplish these things is the help of Occam's razor.

This brings me to a second objection, which refines the first. Perhaps supervenience should not be expected to entail ontological conclusions. Is it even compatible with ontological conclusions? Reduction, as conceived by Russell, Carnap, and Quine, accomplishes something ontological because it shows that certain ways of speaking, which bring with them ontological commitments, are avoidable. If the mental reduces to the physical, then we would not need to mention the mental in a complete inventory of the world, for, in cataloging the physical, we would already have given a complete description of reality. Everything we might want to say in mental language can be said, and would have been said, in physical language alone. The same argument, plainly, cannot be used in the case of strong supervenience. As we have seen, strong supervenience implies links between the supervening and base languages of necessary biconditional form. But these may be of a high degree of complexity; they may not be expressible in any available language or, indeed, any humanly learnable language. This is why supervenience allows for the autonomy of the supervening realm. The language of mental states, for example, is autonomous and unavoidable, according to the kind of nonreductive physicalism I have been defending, because the links between that language and the language of physics may be humanly incomprehensible.

We may thus put the second objection in this way: supervenience, unlike reduction, provides no guarantee that the supervening language is eliminable. It consequently has no ontological implications. Supervenience is therefore useless for establishing physicalism.

In Bonevac (1988, 1991), I develop versions of supervenience designed to overcome this problem. Supervenience itself does not guarantee eliminability of the supervening language. From the perspective of a background language, however, we might be able to see that everything the supervening language does, the base language also does. That is, stepping back, it might be possible to see that the work done by the supervening language can be taken over by the base language, even though a direct reduction of the former to the latter may not be possible. Let T be the true sentences of language L, and T', the true sentences of L'. Then we may say that L ontologically supervenes on L' relative to a background theory T'' if and only if there are interpretations * and ** such that * interprets T in T'', ** interprets T' in T'', and $T*$ is a subset of $T'**$. That is, L ontologically supervenes on L' relative to a background theory T'' just in case truth in L and truth in L' both reduce to T'', and the portion of T'' needed for reducing truth in L' includes the portion needed for reducing truth in L. L, in these circumstances, is eliminable not from the point of view of L', but from that of the background theory T''.

From an ontological point of view, the most crucial aspect of ontological supervenience is that, if T ontologically supervenes on T' relative to T'', then every model of the image of T' in T'' is a model of the image of T in T''. On this conception of supervenience, then, the L' facts not only fix the L facts; the domain of L is a subset of the domain of L'. Ontological supervenience, then, not only is compatible with ontological conclusions, but seems, in a particularly direct way, to establish them.

It might seem that ontological supervenience is small comfort, for it requires a background language and reductions to a background theory that seem just as problematic as a reduction of one theory into another. If we despair of reducing psychology to physics, then why should we hope that both will reduce to another theory that will make explicit their connections? Moreover, if we think that the proper background theory for the mind–body problem would simply be the ultimate physics, then ontological supervenience makes no advance over reduction at all, for truth in L ontologically supervenes on truth in L' relative to truth in L' if and only if truth in L reduces to truth in L'.

In some settings, the background theory and reductions are available. Arithmetic with a truth-predicate added, for example, ontologically supervenes on arithmetic; the Tarski, or Kripke, or Gupta/Herzberger, or Koons truth theories give just the background theory required. To take an ontologically more interesting case, truth in a language with λ abstracts ontologically supervenes on truth in the fragment of the language lacking such abstracts (Bonevac 1991). Once again, the background theory is a semantic one. The intensional Russell paradox shows that the language containing abstracts does not reduce to its concrete fragment, but the full language and its concrete portion both reduce to a background theory by way of truth clauses interpreting them. In that semantic theory, it is easy to show that the full language ontologically supervenes on its concrete portion. Ontological supervenience in these cases does not imply reduction, but it does involve an infinitary generalization of reduction; truth for the language as a whole is defined in terms of a transfinite recursion.

The import of ontological supervenience is thus that we may be able to see that a language is eliminable if we step into the right background theory. Recall the objection: One can eliminate ontological commitments only by showing that the kinds of discourse making those commitments are eliminable. Strong supervenience does nothing to show that any kinds of discourse are eliminable. Therefore, strong supervenience cannot eliminate ontological commitments. Ontological supervenience overcomes the objection because it does show that from the perspective of a certain background theory, the supervening discourse is not only eliminable; it speaks of objects to which the base theory is already committed.

Ontological supervenience thus overcomes the objection and can establish ontological conclusions. Unfortunately, despite its utility in semantics and other formal areas, it has little prospect of clarifying the mind–body problem, for the background theory seems unavailable. We cannot merely use set theory, as we can in semantic and mathematical endeavors. We thus seem to face a dilemma. Ontological supervenience can establish ontological conclusions but seems ill-suited to establishing physicalism. Strong supervenience seems well-suited to the case of physicalism but seems unable to establish anything ontological.

Nonreductive physicalists have a way out: deny the first premise. Eliminating a kind of discourse that makes troublesome ontological commitments is one way to eliminate those commitments. But it is not the only way. If nonreductive physicalists were simply to say, "Strong supervenience is another way," we would have nothing more than special pleading. But there is no need to amend ontological principles ad hoc.

The Russell–Carnap–Quine view of ontology underlying the dilemma, and underlying much twentieth-century philosophy, is distinctly linguistic. Quine's well-known criterion of commitment, for example, does not address the question of what there is except by specifying what a theory says that there is. In considering the preceding dilemma, the question of what a theory is becomes crucial. A theory, it is easy to say, is a set of sentences closed under logical consequence. So far, so good. But sentences of what kind of language? One answer would limit us to the kinds of languages that people do and can use. This seems artificially limiting, in some respects, because people have many limitations of memory, computational power, and so on that restrict the class of humanly usable languages quite severely. Another answer, seeking to remove this limitation, would limit us to the kinds of languages that people could in principle learn and use. If people's linguistic abilities are essentially computational, then this would be equivalent to limiting us to languages that computers could learn and use. Sentences of such languages must be finite; grammars must be generated recursively from a finite set of rules from a finite base; the semantics must be compositional; and so on. In the same spirit, we might say that any theory we can consider from an ontological point of view must be a theory that humans and computers could in principle learn and use. This would limit us to recursively enumerable sets of sentences of such a language.

Given this approach, the earlier first premise follows. A person makes an ontological commitment by asserting a recursively enumerable theory in a language recursively generated by a finite number of rules from a finite base. That person can eliminate the commitment either by retracting the assertion or showing it to be eliminable, in the sense that it is equivalent to the assertion of another recursively enumerable theory, or whatever, that makes no such commitment. Strong supervenience does not show this kind of eliminability. It can show that the original assertion is equivalent to the assertion of another theory without the commitment. But that theory may be computationally intractable. It may not be recursively enumerable. Its sentences may be infinite in length; it may not have a finite grammar or a finite base.

The objection asks us to conclude that strong supervenience has no ontological significance. But it seems just as reasonable to conclude that the restrictions on languages and theories on which our dilemma depends are inappropriate. Clearly, they are not unimportant. It matters a great deal whether the languages and theories under discussion are humanly learnable or not. In a sense, however, the issue is epistemological. Strong supervenience allows for the possibility that the connections between the supervening and base languages are so complex that they are humanly incomprehensible. That possibility of incomprehensibility is what makes psychology, for example, autonomous. But it is at root epistemological, a matter of what human beings can and cannot articulate and understand. It is not obvious that such epistemological issues are relevant to ontology. A realist of any stripe is inclined to think that what there is does not depend on what we can articulate, know, or understand. If the realist is right, then to restrict ourselves to computable languages is to blindfold ourselves.

The realist's view of ontology is sub specie aeternitatis. In effect, the realist asks us to consider ontological questions, not from the perspective of a possible human knower, but from the perspective of God. We can continue to speak of languages and theories, but we should have in mind the languages and theories of God. Our own cognitive limitations do not restrict God; neither do they restrict what there is. We are interested not just in our own inventory of the world – what we would have to count as its ultimate constituents – but in God's inventory, in what God would have to so count.

A realist, then, has no trouble avoiding the dilemma or indicating why strong supervenience has ontological implications. Strong supervenience is simply reduction in the mind of God. Recall that strong supervenience implies that for each predicate of the supervening language, there is an equivalent open formula with the same number of free variables in the base language or an infinitary extension of it. That last clause, 'or an infinitary extension of it', distinguishes strong supervenience from reduction. From a human point of view, the distinction is critically important. From God's point of view, however, it is insignificant. Issues of comprehensibility and expressibility do not arise.

The realist, then, can hold that reduction and strong supervenience are on a par in all but epistemological respects. Ontologically, they are similar in showing that commitments are avoidable. Reduction has clear epistemological and explanatory advantages over supervenience, for the connections between realms can be articulated. Ontologically, however, they play the same role.

3. Causation

Kim (1989, 1992) argues that nonreductive physicalists cannot give an adequate account of mental causation. His argument is straightforward: Mental properties are real. To be real is to have causal powers (Alexander's dictum). Therefore, mental properties have causal pow-

ers. Any physical event that has a cause has a physical cause. Therefore, either mental causes make no difference, or they are identical to
physical causes.

"Given that any physical event has a physical cause," Kim asks, "how
is a mental cause also possible?" (1989, p. 44). It makes most sense
to identify physical and mental causes. But this requires identifying a
physical property and a mental property. The reductionist can accept
this, but, Kim argues, the antireductionist cannot. A nonreductive
physicalist, he insists, has no way out. Either mental causes make no
difference, and are always redundant – which, apart from reductionism or eliminativism, would seem hard to defend – or they are
identical to physical causes, and the reductionist is right after all.

Kim himself outlines a way out of the dilemma. We can think of
causal relations among macro events as supervening on causal relations among micro events. Similarly, we can think of mental events as
causing physical events by virtue of supervening on physical events
that cause those events. So the advocate of strong supervenience can
say that mental causes supervene on physical causes. The realist of the
last section can say, moreover, that mental causes are simply physical
causes, without thereby advocating reductionism.

Kim rejects this picture, for it "involves psychophysical laws" and so
"would be enough to give pause to any would-be nonreductive physicalist" (1989, p. 46). Davidson's anomalous monism, after all, was one
of the first attempts at nonreductive physicalism in recent philosophy
and stresses the unavailability of strict psychophysical laws.

A realist, however, need not shy away from the psychophysical laws
that Kim's supervenient causation account demands, for they are psychophysical laws only in the mind of God; they may not be expressible
in any humanly learnable language. Supervenient causation, like
strong supervenience in general, requires necessary biconditionals
linking properties of the supervening level to properties of the base
level. In my terms, they require necessary biconditionals linking predicates of the supervening language and expressions in an infinitary
extension of the base language. Expressing these biconditionals may
require a language with infinitely long sentences; the infinite disjunctions involved, reflecting multiple realizability, among other problems,
may not even be recursively enumerable. The psychophysical laws this
strategy generates, therefore, may not be expressible in any finite, recursively generated language. If we think of laws as relations between
properties, then supervenient causation and strong supervenience in
a general setting, applied to the mind–body problem, yield psychophysical laws. If we think of laws as sentences of a humanly learnable
language, however, they do not yield such laws. Kim (1984, p. 172)
recognizes this but does not take a linguistic view of laws seriously.

If we think of supervenience as reduction in the mind of God, as, I have argued, a realist might, then we can identify mental and physical states without believing that we will ever possess, or could even possess, strict psychophysical laws linking the mental and physical realms. Laws we obtain would typically be either local, pertaining to a restricted context (i.e., some well-defined set of disjuncts), or generic rather than strict. From God's perspective, the mental and physical would be linked by strict biconditional laws, but those laws might be so complex that they are humanly incomprehensible. Mental events, on this view, could have real causal powers. But they would have those causal powers by virtue of their supervenience upon, and thus identity with, physical events.

Does this mean that the existence of the mental would make no difference and that we might as well be eliminativists? The answer, I think, is no. Certainly we would not be able to dispense with talk of mental causation, even if God could. Psychology would be autonomous, for we could not do without it. The connections it would discover – typically local and generic rather than universal and strict – could not be derived from physics or predictable on the basis of physics. Psychology would not be replaceable by physics, even in principle. Moreover, the mental and physical might carve reality in such different ways that certain kinds of causal connections might be far more simply and directly understood as connections among mental events, rather than among the physical events underlying them. That is, even God might find talk of mental causation useful, for it might capture certain kinds of regularities far more efficiently than the language of physics.

REFERENCES

Alexander, S. 1920. *Space, Time and Deity*. London, Macmillan.
Bacon, J. 1986. "Supervenience, Necessary Coextension, and Reducibility," *Philosophical Studies* 49, 163–76.
    1990."Van Cleve versus Closure," *Philosophical Studies* 58, 239–42.
Beckermann, A. 1992a. "Introduction: Reductive and Nonreductive Physicalism," in A. Beckermann, H. Flohr, and J. Kim (eds.), *Emergence or Reduction? Prospects for Nonreductive Physicalism* (pp. 11–21). Berlin: De Gruyter.
    1992b. "Supervenience, Emergence, and Reduction," in A. Beckermann, H. Flohr, and J. Kim (eds.), *Emergence or Reduction? Prospects for Nonreductive Physicalism* (pp. 94–116). Berlin: De Gruyter.
Bonevac, D. 1988. "Supervenience and Ontology," *American Philosophical Quarterly* 25, 37–47.
    1991. "Semantics and Supervenience," *Synthese* 87, 331–61.
Boyd, R. 1980. "Materialism without Reductionism: What Physicalism Does

Not Entail," in N. Block (ed.), *Readings in Philosophy of Psychology*, (vol. 1, pp. 67–106). Cambridge, Mass.: Harvard University Press.

Broad, C. D. 1925. *The Mind and Its Place in Nature*. London: Routledge and Kegan Paul.

Carnap, R. 1967. *The Logical Structure of the World*. Berkeley: University of California Press.

Causey, R. 1972a. "Attribute-Identities and Microreductions," *Journal of Philosophy* 69, 407–22.

1972b. "Uniform Microreductions," *Synthese* 25, 176–218.

1977. *Unity of Science*. Dordrecht: Reidel.

Fodor, J. 1981. *Representations*. Cambridge, Mass.: MIT Press.

Grimes, T. 1988. "The Myth of Supervenience," *Pacific Philosophical Quarterly* 69, 152–60.

Hooker, C. 1981. "Towards a General Theory of Reduction," *Dialogue* 20, 38–60, 201–36, 496–529.

Kim, J. 1978. "Supervenience and Nomological Incommensurables," *American Philosophical Quarterly* 15, 149–56.

1983. "Supervenience and Supervenient Causation," *Southern Journal of Philosophy*, 22 Supplement, 45–56.

1984. "Concepts of Supervenience," *Philosophy and Phenomenological Research* 45, 153–76.

1987. "'Strong' and 'Global' Supervenience Revisited," *Philosophy and Phenomenological Research* 48, 315–26.

1989. "The Myth of Nonreductive Materialism," *Proceedings and Addresses of the American Philosophical Association* 63, 31–47.

1990. "Supervenience as a Philosophical Concept," *Metaphilosophy* 21, 1–27.

1992. "'Downward Causation' in Emergentism and Nonreductive Physicalism," in A. Beckermann, H. Flohr, and J. Kim (eds.), *Emergence or Reduction? Prospects for Nonreductive Physicalism* (pp. 119–38). Berlin: de Gruyter.

Kline, M. 1972. *Mathematical Thought from Ancient to Modern Times*. New York: Oxford University Press.

LePore, E., and Loewer, B. 1989. "More on Making Mind Matter," *Philosophical Topics* 17, 175–91.

Morgan, C. L. 1923. *Emergent Evolution*. London: Williams and Norgate.

Russell, B. 1906. "On the Substitutional Theory of Classes and Relations," in D. Lackey (ed.), *Essays in Analysis* (pp. 175–282). Rpt. New York: George Braziller, 1973.

1918. "The Philosophy of Logical Atomism," in R. Marsh (ed.), *Logic and Knowledge* (pp. 175–218). Rpt. New York: Putnam's, 1956.

1919. *Introduction to Mathematical Philosophy*. London: Allen and Unwin.

1924. "Logical Atomism," in R. Marsh (ed.), *Logic and Knowledge* (pp. 321–43). Rpt. New York: Putnam's, 1956.

Tarski, A., Mostowski, A., and Robinson, J. 1953. *Undecidable Theories*. Amsterdam: North Holland.

Van Cleve, J. 1990. "Supervenience and Closure," *Philosophical Studies* 58, 225–38.

Whitehead, A. N., and Russell, B. 1910–13. *Principia Mathematica*. Cambridge University Press.

Psychophysical Supervenience, Dependency, and Reduction

CYNTHIA MACDONALD

A familiar strategy for nonreductive physicalists of mind to employ in their attempt to reconcile psychophysical event identity with the view that mental and physical properties of events are irreducibly distinct is to appeal to some version of the doctrine of psychophysical supervenience.[1] Many who appeal to this doctrine do so in the belief that psychophysical supervenience not only establishes a covariance relation between mental and physical properties, in the sense that indiscernibility with regard to the latter entails indiscernibility with regard to the former, but establishes an asymmetric relation of *dependency* of mental upon physical properties that falls short of reducibility.[2] Psychophysical supervenience is thus thought to be capable of showing that although mental properties are strictly speaking nonphysical, the ontology of the physical world in some sense both determines and exhausts what there is to the mental domain. I think it fair to say that many nonreductive physicalists of mind, myself included, believe that without supplementation by some version of a supervenience thesis, nonreductive monism is not worthy of the name 'physicalism'.

Recent discussions of psychophysical supervenience have focused primarily on different conceptions of supervenience (strong, weak, global), on the question of which conceptions (if any) are appropriate to the psychophysical case, and on the question of whether those conceptions that may be appropriate to the psychophysical case lead to reducibility. The difficulty faced by nonreductive physicalists is to find a characterization of supervenience that is strong enough to meet the demands of asymmetric dependency without also leading to reducibility. Jaegwon Kim, whose work in this area is seminal, has time and again expressed the view that any doctrine strong enough to meet the demands of dependency will inevitably lead to reducibility.[3] Specifically, his view is that only strong supervenience is strong enough to meet the dependency requirement, and strong supervenience is sufficient for reducibility.

In this essay, I wish to pursue the dependency/reducibility issue, specifically with respect to strong supervenience, since this conception does seem to capture best the relation between intentional mental properties, that is, properties with intentional content, such as the property of believing that Manchester is north of London, and physical properties. My aim is to defend further the consistency of nonreductive monism and strong supervenience with regard to intentional mental properties. In Sections 1 and 2, I outline an antireductionist strategy available to the nonreductive monist that I find plausible, and I defend that strategy against Kim's claim that strong supervenience is sufficient for reducibility. This strategy, unlike many others, focuses on the distinctive nature of intentional mental properties as compared with physical ones, rather than on the questionable nature of the physical properties on which the mental ones are typically thought to supervene.[4] If the strategy is correct, however, the causal powers of intentional mental properties are both determined and exhausted by those of their subvenient bases.

1. Strong Supervenience and the Antireductionist Strategy

Supervenience has been characterized in a number of ways, among these being the following:

(WS) M weakly supervenes on P just in case necessarily for any object x and any property F in M, if x has F, then there exists a property G in P such that x has G, and if any y has G, it has F.

(SS) M strongly supervenes on P just in case necessarily for any object x and any property F in M, if x has F, then there exists a property G in P such that x has G, and necessarily if any y has G, it has F.

(GS) M globally supervenes on P just in case any two worlds with the same distribution of M-properties have the same distribution of P-properties.

M and P are two nonempty families of monadic properties closed under Boolean operations of conjunction and disjunction (perhaps infinite), as well as complementation. (Here we take x and y to range over events.) M is typically referred to as the supervenient (or supervening) family, and P is typically referred to as the supervenience (or subvenient) base. The force of 'necessarily' in (WS) and (SS) is left unspecified.

(SS) is widely thought to capture best the relation of psychophysical supervenience, despite the fact that the relation expressed by (SS) is not asymmetric. What (SS) expresses is a relation of entailment or necessitation between P- and M-properties, and as Kim and others have pointed out, this relation is neither symmetric nor asymmetric, but nonsymmetric.[5] So (SS) expresses a relation that is weaker than asymmetric dependence, one that Kim calls "covariance." Given that psychophysical supervenience is an asymmetric dependency relation, (SS) needs to be supplemented in some way if it is to capture that relation. There are two possible ways of doing this. The first is to strengthen (SS) itself so as to ensure that the relation between M and P is asymmetric. The second is to construe (SS) as expressing a core relation of supervenience that just is covariance, asymmetric dependence being an additional and independent feature possessed by some but not all things that covary, to be justified case by case. The latter seems to be the preferred option for three reasons. First, it is unlikely that (SS) can be strengthened so as to yield necessary *and* sufficient conditions for asymmetric dependence.[6] Second, many who appeal to dependency do so with a view to explaining the covariation relation expressed in (SS). This indicates that dependence is an independent feature of things that covary, rather than a feature of the covariation relation itself. Third, (SS) covers many different types of dependency relations, all of which are plausibly described as ones of supervenience. It covers, for example, the type of dependency relation involved in mereological (part–whole) supervenience, that involved in the relation between determinables and their associated determinates (e.g., being colored, being red), and the functional dependence of mental on physical properties envisaged by functional specification theories of mind. Properties 'constituted' by other properties (from which they are distinct), properties of properties, and properties that objects have in virtue of having other properties all appear to count as cases of higher-order/lower-order property-dependency relations, and all are arguably cases in which the higher-order properties can legitimately be said to supervene on the lower-order ones.

For all of these reasons, dependence is probably best seen as an independent component of psychophysical supervenience, to be justified independently of appeals to supervenience. In the case of nonreductive monism, the dependence of mental on physical properties must have its source in the argument for that position. This argument, which specifically concerns intentional mental events, consists of three premises: first, that there is causal interaction between mental and physical events (the principle of causal interaction, or PCI); second, that where events are causally related, they instantiate a strict causal law (the principle of the nomological character of causality, or PNCC); and third, that there are no strict causal laws governing mental events (the principle of the causal anomalism of the mental, or PAM). The argument moves from the claim that mental and physical events causally interact, the claim that such interactions are governed by strict causal laws, and the claim that there are no strict causal laws governing mental and physical events, to the conclusion that each mental event is a physical event (hence, its causal interactions with physical events are governed by strict physical laws). The asymmetry between intentional mental and physical properties is implicit in the argument from the start and arises from the fact that there are causal laws in which physical properties figure, but there are no causal laws in which intentional mental properties figure. Note that the asymmetry does not concern the causal efficacy of intentional mental and physical *events*. On the familiar view that events just are exemplifyings or instancings of act- or event-properties in objects at times, to say that each intentional mental event is a physical event is to say that each instancing of an intentional mental property is (i.e., is identical with) an instancing of a physical one. So if the physical instancing is causally efficacious, so is the intentional one, and vice versa. The asymmetry concerns the causal powers of mental and physical *properties*. Specifically, the fact that physical properties enter into causal-nomological relations whereas intentional mental ones do not requires, given the PNCC, that intentional properties "discharge" or exercise their causal powers by being co-instanced with physical properties (this just is the argument for nonreductive monism on a reading of it that treats events as property exemplifications), whereas physical properties are not similarly required to exercise any of their causal powers through being jointly instanced with intentional properties.[7] This makes intentional *properties* dependent on physical ones in a way in which physical properties are not dependent on intentional ones.

However, I do not think that this dependence leads to reducibility. The reason, which I develop more fully in Section 2, is that although intentional properties must, in accordance with the PNCC, exercise their causal powers through being jointly instanced with physical properties that figure in causal laws, intentional properties have a contentful nature that is not exhausted by their causal powers. It is in virtue of having this nature that such properties exhibit a rationalistic pattern, or network of relations among themselves. This pattern is not only distinct from that which physical properties display, but irreducible to it for reasons appealed to by the argument for PAM.[8]

To make this claim plausible, some explanation is needed of how, even though intentional mental *events* instantiate a causal-nomological pattern, intentional *properties* exhibit a pattern that is irreducible to the causal-nomological. Nonreductive monists, who appeal to the argument for PAM to establish that there can be no strict causal laws in which mental properties figure, must exploit the considerations in that argument to establish that although psychophysical supervenience may lead to the necessary coextension of intentional mental and physical properties, this does not suffice for reducibility.

How might such a strategy proceed? I believe that a successful argument can be mounted in two stages. First, it needs to be argued that intentional properties exhibit a pattern or network of relations among one another in virtue of having the causal powers they do that is *different* from that exhibited by physical properties. That is to say, nonreductive monists must argue that intentional mental events instantiate two distinct patterns. The first, which they instantiate in virtue of being identical with physical events, is causal-nomological. The second, which is distinctive to intentional mental events alone, is rationalistic. If this stage of the argument is successful, it suggests that the natures of intentional mental properties are not exhausted by the causal powers of any physical property or set of properties on which they supervene. Since the strategy for irreducibility depends crucially on this first stage in the argument, the bulk of Section 2 will be spent developing it.

Of some help in establishing this is an appeal to biological properties. Biology makes use of a species of explanation that exploits properties that are (a) co-instanced with physicochemical properties, (b) supervenient on physicochemical properties in the sense of (SS), but (c) generally acknowledged *not* to be reducible to their physicochemical bases.[9] Biological properties thus seem to present a case of a pattern, or network of relations, in nature that is underwritten by, but is not reducible to, the pattern exhibited by physicochemical properties.

If this stage of the argument works, it establishes a degree of autonomy for mental properties. What the biological example shows is that even if supervenience leads to necessary coextension of properties, this is not sufficient, in some cases at least, for reduction. The interesting question in the biological case is *why*, and here the explanation seems to be that biological properties have a nature that is such as to produce a pattern of relations among themselves that is distinctively different from the causal-nomological pattern produced by physicochemical properties. What makes it distinctively different is that it is functional. The properties are individuated by their biological functions, and the normativity involved in this notion of function has no role to play in physical theory. So the pattern is produced by properties whose individuation conditions are normative. This makes it not only different from, but irreducible to, the causal-nomological pattern exhibited by physical properties.

If this is right, the second stage of the strategy needs to establish that the network of relations produced by intentional mental properties is not only distinctively different from, but irreducible to, that produced by physical properties. In this case, the normative constraints that govern the individuation of intentional mental properties themselves must, as in the biological case, be seen to have no role to play in physical theory.

If both of these stages of the strategy can be successfully completed, then I believe that the case against reducibility, necessary coextensivity notwithstanding, can be established. But everything depends on the biological case and its similarity to the psychophysical case, so the details of the argument need some careful filling out.

2. Developing the Antireductionist Strategy

Because intentional mental properties must, in accordance with the PNCC, discharge their causal powers via being jointly instanced with physical properties, it is difficult to see how there could be any causal work for intentional properties to do, given (SS), that their physical base properties cannot do. It is not that the causal powers of each intentional property can be matched by the causal powers of some one physical base property, since variable realizability prohibits this. On the assumption that intentional properties are variably realizable by their subvenient base properties, the causal powers of any given intentional property and any single base property will not match. Since the causal powers of a property concern possible as well as actual effects its instances may produce, and since distinct physical base properties will have distinct causal powers, the causal powers of a given intentional property will outstrip those possessed by any single physical base property. The problem, rather, is that all of the causal powers that a given intentional property may have seem capable of being exhausted by *all* of the physical base properties, taken together, with which that intentional property with those powers may be jointly co-instanced. It is this thought that fuels the view that causal powers of that property are capable of being matched by powers possessed by a disjunctive physical property formed by Boolean operations on the relevant physical base properties.

It may seem that this threat of causal power matchup is illusory. After all, intentional properties have causal powers to produce *mental* effects, events that are not just instances of physical properties, like that of moving one's arm, but instances of *action* properties, like that of signaling. And action properties, although they may supervene on physical ones, are distinct from them. So whereas the causal powers of physical properties are sensitive to their physical effects (i.e., their effects considered as effects of physical types), the causal powers of intentional properties are sensitive to their mental effects (i.e., their effects considered as effects of mental types).

However, the threat of causal power matchup is unaffected by this observation. For suppose that a given mental property, M, has the causal power to produce instances of mental property M'. Then, given (SS) and the thesis of variable realizability, we can expect that there exists a set of physical properties, P, on which M supervenes, and another set P' on which M' supervenes, such that, necessarily, events indiscernible with regard to $P(P')$ are indiscernible with regard to

$M(M')$. Given nonreductive monism, each instance of $M(M')$ will be an instance of some property in $P(P')$. What motivates the view that the causal powers of M are matched by the causal powers of P is that the causal powers of M are type-effect sensitive to the disjunctive type P^* formed from Boolean operations on members of P' on which M' supervenes. It is true that the type-effect sensitivity of the causal powers of M to P^* can only be established via the type-effect sensitivity of the causal powers of M to M'. For, by hypothesis, it is instances of M' to which the causal powers of M are initially sensitive. So the causal powers of M are type-effect sensitive to P^* in only a derivative sense. However, the derivative nature of the M–P^* connection does not by itself suffice to establish a distinctive role for the causal powers of M to play. One can imagine a reductive-minded physicalist insisting that once one sees that the causal powers of M can be completely discharged by $P\#$, the disjunctive property formed by Boolean operations on members of P (as evidenced by the fact that both M and $P\#$ are type-effect sensitive to P^*), there simply is no more causal work for M to do (even vis-à-vis M') that cannot be done by $P\#$. This theorist will argue that it is the fact that the causal powers can be seen to *match*, not that the causal powers of one are derivative upon the causal powers of the other, that is the crucial factor in the case for or against reduction. For *that* they match will itself be seen to constitute a reason for thinking that reduction is forthcoming.

Of course, one can deny that the causal powers of any intentional property *can* be matched by the causal powers of its disjunctive base property; and this is effectively the path that is pursued by those who argue that properties like $P\#$ and P^* are not bona fide properties, either because they are properties in an extended sense only, or because they are not nomic (perhaps because they do not have bona fide causal powers even though their disjuncts do), or because not every property constructible by means of Boolean operations on physical properties is itself a physical property.[10] However, for reasons that echo Kim's, I do not find the arguments for this view compelling. He does not see why we must be constrained in reduction by such narrow a priori strictures on what counts as a property or on what counts as a nomic property.[11]

> When reduction is at issue, we are talking about theories, theories couched in their distinctive theoretical vocabularies. And it seems that we allow, and ought to allow, freedom to combine and recombine, the basic theoretical predicates and functors by the usual logical and mathematical operations available in the underlying language. (Kim 1990, p. 21)

In general, those who have attempted to block psychophysical reduction have done so by concentrating on the nature of the disjunctive subvenient physical base properties with which intentional properties are deemed necessarily coextensive and arguing that no such property could be of the appropriate kind to serve the theoretical purposes of reduction. However, it seems likely that whether a property is genuine, or whether it is nomic, cannot be settled on a priori grounds alone.

On the other hand, the threat of reduction is real only if (a) the causal powers of intentional properties can be matched by their disjunctive physical base properties, (b) the causal powers of physical properties exhaust their nature, and (c) the causal powers of intentional properties exhaust *their* nature. And whatever nonreductive monists may have to say about (b), no nonreductive monists will concede the truth of (c). They will argue that intentional properties have a nature, due to their possession of intentional content, in virtue of which they enter into broadly logical relations with one another, such relations being grounded in normative constraints that govern the very individuation conditions of those properties. These general relations exhibit a pattern that is not causal-nomological but rationalistic.

This opens up a second antireductionist strategy for nonreductive monists, one where the type-effect sensitivity of properties like M to M' *is* relevant. According to this, the threat of reduction has the force it does only because it assumes that the only pattern, or network of relations, that properties can bear to one another in virtue of having the causal powers they do is a causal-nomological one. If this were true, and if (a), (b), and (c) were true, then there would be no distinctive role for intentional properties to play. But (c) is not true.

This last point can be substantiated by appeal to the case of biological properties. A familiar and plausible view of the nature of such properties is that they arise as a result of natural selection operating on instances of physicochemical properties.[12] The instances of some of these properties have favorable reproductive effects for the organisms that are their subjects. The result is the proliferation of instances of the favored physicochemical properties, which just is the process of natural selection. Such properties are selected in order to produce certain effects, and so organisms that possess them acquire biological functions. These physicochemical properties acquire biological functions – the organisms that have them have them in order that their instances should produce certain effects – as a result of selection. So natural selection produces biological-functional properties.

On this view, biological properties are properties that organisms come to instantiate in virtue of the causal history of some of the instances of certain physicochemical properties. So the process of physical causation operating on instances of physicochemical properties has resulted in a new pattern holding between distinct properties, biological ones. The pattern of relations exhibited by biological properties is different from, though underwritten by, the causal-nomological pattern of relations that holds among the physicochemical properties on which and on whose causal history they can plausibly be said to supervene. That is to say, functional connections are distinct from physical causal-nomological ones and do not replicate them. Suppose, for example, that three organisms all have bottle-green coloring: a chameleon, a butterfly, and a bird. All three, in having bottle-green coloring, can be described from a physicochemical point of view in the same terms, but their descriptions in biological terms will differ radically. The chameleon's bottle-green coloring serves as camouflage, helping it to hide from predators. The butterfly's bottle-green coloring is aposematic, in this case warning putative predators that it is more or less inedible. And the bird has no biological description in virtue of its coloring at all. The pattern of causal relations between physicochemical properties that underwrite the bottle-green coloring possessed by these organisms is undisturbed by the different functional pattern produced at the biological level. The difference between the two patterns shows up, for example, in the different explanations one can give of a chameleon's camouflaging behavior and the behavior of a physicochemical twin who has no biological history. Of each, one can explain the change of coloring (in this case, from brown to green) in terms of the organism's response to changes in light in its immediate environment, but of only the first can one explain the change in coloring as camouflaging behavior. Only a physicochemical property, some of whose instances have a certain causal history, is capable of acquiring a biological function.

As this indicates, biological properties supervene not on the physicochemical properties of a single organism, but on those properties plus their causal history. But supervene on these two factors they do, since, given two organisms indiscernible with regard to the causal history of their (indiscernible) physicochemical properties, their indiscernibility with regard to biological properties is guaranteed.

How relevant is the distinctiveness of the pattern of relations between biological properties vis-à-vis the causal-nomological pattern exhibited by physicochemical properties to the psychophysical case? Highly relevant, I believe. In the biological case, one can see how certain functional properties can arise out of the causal connections holding between instances of physicochemical properties and come to bear relations to one another in a way that does not simply replicate the causal regularities that causal laws exhibit. The connections forged by biological properties depend on these causal regularities but are not exhausted by them. The fertilizing effects of sperm, for instance, are rarely realized, but they are realized often enough for fertilization to be the function of sperm. One cannot explain the function of sperm in statistical-causal terms, since so few sperm perform the function of fertilizing. Fertilization could not emerge as sperm's function on this model.

In other words, the fertilizing function that sperm have they have whether they perform that function or not. They have it in order to fertilize, not because they do all fertilize. The fertilizing function is therefore normative – it is governed by a standard – which very few sperm in fact meet. But that they do not meet this standard (a standard established by the process of natural selection) does not prohibit their having the function. Nevertheless, those sperm that do have fertilizing effects instantiate two patterns: a causal-nomological one, in virtue of causal relations holding between instances of physicochemical properties that govern fertilization, and a biological one, in virtue of relations holding between instances of biological properties. All sperm have the function of fertilization, and so all instantiate a biological pattern, but only those that do fertilize instantiate a physicochemical pattern governing fertilization itself (and all of those that do fertilize instantiate that physicochemical pattern).

What is the relationship between physicochemical properties, biological properties, and their instances? Given that biological properties arise as the result of natural selection operating on instances of physicochemical properties, and given that physicochemical properties acquire biological functions as a result of the process of such selection, the most plausible account of the relationship is that to instance a biological property, say, the property of having aposematic coloring, just is to instance the property of being bottle green in color, given that the latter instance has the causal history it does. It seems, in short, that instances of biological properties just are instances of certain physicochemical properties. In this way, pairs of instances of the physicochemical properties $c–c^*$ (say, ovum penetration [c] and fertilization [c^*]) can come to instantiate two patterns. The first, a causal-nomological one, will connect c-type events causally with c^*-type events. The second, a functional one, will connect the $c–c^*$ instance pair via a functional property possessed by organisms that instance the c-type, a property possessed by them in order that instances of that type should produce instances of c^*.

These two features of biological properties – that they exhibit a pattern of relations that depends on but does not replicate the nomological-causal pattern of relations and that they are co-instanced with physicochemical properties – bear a striking resemblance to the psychophysical case on the model envisaged by the nonreductive monist committed to psychophysical supervenience. That theorist is committed to there being two kinds of patterns or networks of relations between properties, one holding between physical properties, another holding between intentional mental properties, neither of which replicates the other but one of which (the intentional) depends on there being a causal-nomological pattern holding between the other (the physical). For the argument for nonreductive monism to succeed, mental events – instances of mental properties – must be seen to participate in causal-nomological relations; and this they do, as do biological properties, by being co-instanced with instances of other properties that instantiate a causal-nomological pattern. The biological case provides a clear example of how such participation might occur. But this is not all, since, in order to escape reduction, mental properties must be seen to produce another pattern that is not causal-nomological and does not replicate the causal-nomological. And they do, if the argument for PAM is correct. For that argument relies on the distinctive rationalistic functions that intentional properties serve that have no role to play in physical theory, functions that show up in the distinctive explanations peculiar to the mental domain.

Mental properties do the explanatory work they do partly because instances of those properties are seen as having causal efficacy vis-à-vis the behavioral effects that those properties explain. But they do the explanatory work they do also because content properties themselves bear logical relations to one another. It has been thought that if the intentional content of mental properties is to make a causal contribution to the behavior their instances cause, there must be psychophysical laws, and reduction is forthcoming.[13] But this is to suppose that the only contribution that intentional properties can make is causal-nomological. If the argument for PAM is sound, the distinctive rationalistic pattern that intentional properties exhibit itself argues for mental properties having a role to play that is not defined by their participation in causal-nomological relations. And it is this that enables us to say not only that reasons are causes, but that reasons rationalize behavior.

How close is the analogy between psychological properties and biological ones? Both sorts of properties give rise to distinctive types of relations that do not merely reproduce the causal-nomological relations that hold between the physical properties on which they can plausibly be said to supervene. Biological properties, being functional, are by their nature determined by the types of effects their instances have had that have reproductively advantaged the organisms that had them, since this determines the types of effects that they ought to produce. They exist in order that their instances should produce effects of those types, whether or not they actually do produce them. Intentional properties, too, display normativity. An agent who realizes that her finger is being burned by a flame, who wishes to avoid pain, and who believes that, by moving her arm, she can avoid pain, will, if she is rational and other factors do not prevent her doing so, move her arm.

Belief, desire, and other intentional types of state, are by their nature determined in part by the types of effects their instances ought to produce: ought, that is, if the agent instancing them is conforming to, or approaching, various canons of rationality.[14] These canons of rationality set a standard that determines the very nature of intentional properties themselves and so the pattern of relations that holds between them. Being normative, this pattern is no more exhausted by the statistical-cum-causal relations required for causal-nomologicality than is the pattern of relations that holds between biological properties. What matters for *reliable* connections in both the biological and the psychological case is that pairs of such properties are instanced often *enough* to ground the functional/rationalistic connections, and this cannot be determined by a statistical-cum-causal survey alone. People have beliefs and desires whose instances do not in fact have the effects they ideally ought to have: people do not infer what they ought to infer, and they do not act as they ought to act. But this does not prohibit them having those beliefs and desires.

It is the normative nature of functional properties, which is determined by a standard of "normal" set by natural selection, that gives rise to the distinctive pattern of relations between biological properties and shows up in the distinctive type of explanation – functional explanation – in biology. Likewise, I suggest, it is the normative nature of intentional properties, which is determined by a standard of "normal" set by canons of rationality, that gives rise to the distinctive pattern of relations (broadly logical ones) between intentional properties and shows up in the distinctive type of explanation – rationalizing explanation – in intentional psychology. In each case, the distinctive type of explanation is grounded in a distinctive pattern of relations that depends on physical causal-nomological relations. But in neither case does it reproduce those causal-nomological relations. Biological properties can be such that their instances rarely have the effects whose functions those properties are to produce. Yet the functional pattern remains. Intentional properties too are such that their instances can fail to produce effects of types to which they are logically related by the standards set by canons of rationality. Yet the rationalistic pattern is undisturbed by this.

Is the analogy a perfect one? No, since it is doubtful that the kind of normativity that attaches to biological properties is of the same kind as the normativity that attaches to intentional ones.[15] The difference is not that the normative nature of biological properties arises from a standard that, however infrequently met, has in fact been met, whereas the normative nature of intentional properties arises from a standard – of rationality – that serves as an ideal to which subjects only approximate. The standards of functionality that help to determine functional properties are also plausibly viewed as ideals to which organisms only approximate. Nor is the difference that the standards of rationality that establish the normative nature of intentional properties require that such properties bear logical relations to one another in virtue of their intentional contents, whereas the standards of functionality that establish the normative nature of biological properties do not require that those properties bear logical relations to one another. For biological properties, too, are such that their *natures* are in part determined by the types of effect their instances ought to produce, and it is arguable that concepts of such properties bear logical relations to concepts of the types of effects to which their natures are sensitive.[16]

Rather, the difference in the two types of normativity has to do with their respective sources. The normative nature of biological properties is due to a standard of functionality that is fixed by natural selection operating on instances of physicochemical properties. The standard is not agent- (or first-person-)centered. However, the canons of rationality that serve to determine the nature of intentional properties and their relations to one another are essentially agent- (or first-person-), as well as other- (or third-person-)centered. What an agent ought ideally to infer, given certain of her other intentional states, is fixed not only by what it is rational for her to infer, by the lights of others, but, crucially, by what it is rational for her to infer by her own lights. Intentional properties are by their nature both agent-centered and other-centered, which makes the kind of normativity that attaches to them very different from that which attaches to biological properties.[17]

Despite this, the analogy between intentional properties and biological ones is apt. What matters to the antireductionist strategy is that the types of relations biological properties bear to one another and intentional properties bear to one another are different from, and do not merely replicate, the pattern of causal-nomological relations displayed by the physical properties on which they supervene. This is established by way of the claim that the two patterns are not causal-nomological ones because the properties that give rise to them are normative. That the type of normativity that attaches to biological properties is (or is not) different from that which attaches to biological ones is not central to the strategy.

We are now bordering on the second stage of the strategy for reconciling strong supervenience with nonreductive monism, that of arguing for the irreducibility of intentional properties to Boolean properties constructible from their subvenient bases. What the first stage of the antireductionist argument shows is that biological and intentional properties give rise to patterns of relations that are different from that exhibited by physical properties. However, if it works, the bulk of the work of the argument against reducibility is done. The reason is that the first stage, in showing how biological and intentional patterns are different from that exhibited by physical properties, also explains *why* they are different, which is crucial to the second stage of the antireductionist strategy. In both the biological and the intentional cases, the distinctiveness of the network of relations exhibited is traceable to the fact that both kinds of properties are determined to be what they are by a standard or norm that cannot be captured in statistical-causal terms. It is part of the nature of a biological-functional property that its instances ought, if they are doing their normal work, to produce effects of certain types. But "normal" here is not a statistical-cum-causal notion. It is a normative one, fixed by standards of "proper" functioning established by the process of natural selection. It is also part of the concept of an intentional property that its instances ought to produce effects of certain types, if the organisms instancing it are carrying out their normal functions. And here too "normal" is not a statistical-cum-causal notion, but a normative one, fixed by standards of rationality – logical consistency, transitivity of preference, and so on.

It is generally thought that two requirements must be met by a successful reduction. The first is that the laws of the reducing theory must deductively entail the general statements, or theorems, of the reduced theory. The second (which follows from the first) is that the terms of the reducing theory must bear systematic connections to the terms of the reduced theory, in particular, meaning connections, since the first requirement cannot be met otherwise.[18] Alexander Rosenberg (1985) has pointed out that it is an easy matter to meet the second requirement by fashioning terms in the reducing theory for those in the reduced theory and stipulating that these terms have the same meaning or are definitionally equivalent. However, he goes on to say:

> If such artificial changes destroy the character of the theories in which these terms figure, then nothing is proved by successfully deducing one theory from another. For example, if we simply stipulate that 'mass' has the same meaning in Einstein's theory and in Newton's theory, then we can meet the conditions of formal connectibility and logical derivability between the formulae of Newton's theory and Einstein's. But this will not show that Einstein's theory contains Newton's as a special case. For, as noted above, Newton's theory makes appeal to absolute space and time, and absolute, not relative, velocities that are independent of matter, which itself cannot be created, destroyed, or transformed into anything else (such as energy, for instance). Einstein's theory denies all these claims. (Rosenberg 1985, p. 92)

The concept of biological function is significantly different from that of causal function, since the former is purpose- or goal-oriented, whereas the latter is not. The concept of intentional property is similarly significantly different from that of any physical property constructible by means of Boolean operations on subvenient base properties. One can, perhaps, stipulate that terms for such properties are equivalent to terms for intentional ones, or stipulate that intentional properties can be defined in terms of such Boolean properties. But this way of meeting the second requirement for reduction will, if what I have been arguing is correct, destroy the character of the theory – intentional psychology – in which intentional properties figure. Short of this, one can suppose that the second requirement is met only by committing a fallacy of equivocation of which the following is an appropriate example:

> The end of a thing is its goal or purpose.
> Death is the end of life.
> Therefore, death is the goal or purpose of life. (Rosenberg 1985, p. 91)

It is true, as Kim says, that one must not lay down too many a priori strictures on what is to count as a bona fide property, or a nomic property, when it comes to matters pertaining to reducibility. But we can have good reason to think that some fundamental strictures governing reducibility cannot be met in certain cases (and this is a case-by-case matter) without destroying the character of the theories whose reducibility is at issue. Biology and intentional psychology are, I submit, two such cases.

NOTES

I would like to thank Graham Bird, Eve Garrard, and, especially, Graham Macdonald, to whom the views presented in this essay owe much, for comments and advice.

1. The classic example is Davidson (1980). See also Davidson (1993). The position defended in this essay is essentially Davidson's anomalous monism, where the use of 'nonreductive' is intended to emphasize the position's commitment to the view that there are no psychophysical or psychological causal laws while remaining neutral (as anomalous monism is not) on the issue of full mental anomalism.
2. See, e.g., Davidson (1980, 1993), Haugeland (1982), and LePore and Loewer (1989).
3. See Kim (1982, 1984, 1989, 1990, 1993).
4. See, e.g., Teller (1984), Post (1984, 1987, 1991), Macdonald (1989), and Van Cleve (1990).
5. See Kim (1990), Heil (1992), and Lombard (1986). Kim cites the example of a domain of perfect spheres, where the surface area and volume of each sphere mutually depend on one another, and Heil cites the example of the mutual dependence of the length of the sides and area of squares. Both

point out that, for such cases, it is more appropriate to speak not of ontic or metaphysical dependence, but of dependence in the sense of mathematical function.

6. See Kim (1990) and Heil (1992). They point out that two properties could covary asymmetrically because both depend on a third. Kim's example is of the covariation of intelligence with manual dexterity, where both depend on certain environmental and genetic factors. The relation between the two seems to be asymmetric (in the sense that things indiscernible with regard to manual dexterity are indiscernible with regard to intelligence, but not vice versa), but we are disinclined to say that intelligence depends on, or is determined by, manual dexterity. Heil gives a similar example, using the color and texture of objects and their mutual dependence on the molecular configuration of the surfaces of those objects.

7. Note that this is not Davidson's formulation of anomalous monism (see note 1). The property exemplification account of events is a "fine-grained" account (see Goldman 1970, Kim 1976, Lombard 1986, and Heil 1992), and Davidson (1980, 1993) explicitly rejects such an account. The conclusion of anomalous monism for him is that each mental event is a physical event, where events are "unstructured" particulars. So the claim made here is stronger than any claim that Davidson would wish to make. It is stronger even than the claim, to which property exemplification theorists of events who are nonreductive monists are committed, that mental events are identical with physical events in the sense that each event that is the exemplification of a mental property is identical with an event that is the exemplification of a physical property. This latter claim need not commit one to the view, advocated here, that the property *exemplifications* are identical (i.e., that mental properties and physical properties are co-instanced in a *single* instance). The compatibility of nonreductive monism with the property exemplification account of events is defended in Macdonald (1989).

8. The appeal to intentional content and to the normative nature of intentional properties in attempts to establish their irreducibility to physical ones is hardly new: it is the core of the argument for PAM. What I am attempting to do in this essay is to bolster that argument by appeal to another case that is analogous to the psychophysical one and where it is generally recognized that reduction is not forthcoming. A similar strategy is invoked in Macdonald (1992) against reduction in the special sciences generally, and by Macdonald and Macdonald (1994) to defend the causal relevance of mental properties.

9. For a recent defense of a nonreductive conception of biological properties, see Ruth Millikan (1984). See also Neander (1991a,b). Some, such as Rosenberg (1985), concede the antireductionist claim but think it a pragmatic matter only (however, see note 18).

10. See Teller (1984), Post (1984, 1987, 1991), and Macdonald (1989).

11. See also Fodor (1991, esp. pp. 271–2). Of course, this point cuts both ways. Those who think that Boolean properties constructible from physical properties are themselves physical cannot simply assume this a priori.

12. See, e.g., Millikan (1984) and Neander (1991a,b).

13. A classic example of this view is Honderich (1981, 1982, 1988).
14. For example, maximizing logical consistency and inductive rationality among intentional states as a whole, the internal coherence of the agent's system of preferences (e.g., that it conform to the transitivity requirement), etc. See Kim (1985).
15. I depart here from Millikan (1984).
16. See Neander (1991a,b).
17. See Nagel (1979), Davidson (1984), and McDowell (1985).
18. See Nagel (1961), Churchland (1979, 1985), and Rosenberg (1985). Rosenberg considers this to be a reason for relaxing the second requirement on reducibility to something less than meaning equivalence. But if what has been argued here is correct, the point still holds, since the *natures* of both biological and intentional properties are such as to be determined by conditions distinct from those that determine any physical property on which they may be said to supervene. Note that Rosenberg accepts Kim's point that failure of reduction given the necessary coextensitivity of supervenient and subvenient properties is only a pragmatic affair, despite making the point quoted here.

REFERENCES

Brand, M., and Walton, D. (eds.). 1976. *Action Theory*. Dordrecht: D. Reidel.

Charles, D., and Lennon, K. (eds.). 1992. *Reduction, Explanation, and Realism*. Oxford University Press.

Churchland, P. M. 1979. *Scientific Realism and the Plasticity of Mind*. Cambridge University Press.

   1985. "Reduction, Qualia, and the Direct Introspection of Brain States," *Journal of Philosophy*, 82, 8–28.

Davidson, D. 1980. "Mental Events," in *Essays on Actions and Events*. Oxford University Press, 207–24.

   1993. "Thinking Causes," in Heil and Mele (1993), pp. 3–18.

Fodor, J. 1991. "Replies," in B. Loewer and G. Rey (eds.), *Meaning in Mind: Fodor and His Critics*. Oxford: Basil Blackwell, pp. 255–319.

Goldman, A. 1970. *A Theory of Human Action*. Englewood Cliffs, N.J.: Prentice-Hall.

Haugeland, J. 1982. "Weak Supervenience," *American Philosophical Quarterly*, 19, 93–103.

Heil, J. 1992. *The Nature of True Minds*. Cambridge University Press.

Heil, J., and Mele, A. 1993. *Mental Causation*. Oxford University Press.

Honderich, T. 1981. "Psychophysical Lawlike Connections and Their Problem," *Inquiry*, 24, 277–304.

   1982. "The Argument for Anomalous Monism," *Analysis*, 42, 59–64.

   1988. *A Theory of Determinism: The Mind, Neuroscience, and Life-Hopes*. Oxford: Clarendon Press.

Kim, J. 1976. "Events as Property Exemplifications," in Brand and Walton (1976), 159–77.

   1982. "Psychophysical Supervenience," *Philosophical Studies*, 41, 51–70.

1984. "Concepts of Supervenience," *Philosophy and Phenomenological Research,* 45, 153–76.

1985. "Psychophysical Laws," in LePore and McLaughlin (1985), pp. 369–86.

1990. "Supervenience as a Philosophical Concept," *Metaphilosophy,* 12, 1–27.

1993. "The Non-Reductivist's Troubles with Mental Causation," in Heil and Mele (1993), pp. 189–210.

LePore, E., and Loewer, B. 1989. "More on Making Mind Matter," *Philosophical Topics,* 17, 175–91.

LePore, E., and McLaughlin, B. (eds). 1985. *Actions and Events.* Oxford: Basil Blackwell.

Lombard, L. 1986. *Events: A Metaphysical Study.* London: Routledge and Kegan Paul.

Macdonald, C. 1989. *Mind–Body Identity Theories.* London: Routledge.

Macdonald, C., and Macdonald, G. 1994. "How To Be Psychologically Relevant," in *Philosophy of Psychology: Debates on Psychological Explanation.* Vol. 1. Oxford: Basil Blackwell, pp. 60–77.

Macdonald, G. "Reduction in Evolutionary Biology," in Charles and Lennon (1992), pp. 69–96.

McDowell, J. 1985. "Functionalism and Anomalous Monism," in LePore and McLaughlin (1985), pp. 387–98.

Millikan, R. G. 1984. *Language, Thought, and Other Biological Categories.* Cambridge, Mass.: MIT Press.

Nagel, E. 1961. *The Structure of Science.* London: Routledge and Kegan Paul.

1979. "What Is It Like to Be a Bat?" in *Mortal Questions.* Cambridge University Press, pp. 165–80.

Neander, K. 1991a. "Functions as Selected Effects: The Conceptual Analyst's Defense," *Philosophy of Science,* 58, 168–84.

1991b. "The Teleological Notion of 'Function'," *Australasian Journal of Philosophy,* 69, 454–68.

Post, J. 1984. "Comment on Teller," *Southern Journal of Philosophy,* 12, 163–7.

1987. *The Faces of Existence: An Essay in Nonreductive Metaphysics.* Ithaca, N.Y.: Cornell University Press.

1991. *Metaphysics: A Contemporary Introduction.* New York: Paragon House.

Rosenberg, A. 1985. *The Structure of Biological Science.* Cambridge University Press.

Teller, P. 1984. "Comments on Kim's Paper," *Southern Journal of Philosophy,* 12, 57–61.

Van Cleve, J. 1990. "Supervenience and Closure," *Philosophical Studies,* 58, 225–38.

Supervenience Redux

JOHN HEIL

In recent years, philosophers bent on defending physicalism have been attracted to the notion that apparently nonphysical features of our world *supervene* on its physical features. Mental and moral properties, for instance, though not perhaps identifiable with or reducible to physical properties, are thought nevertheless to depend on, and to be determined by, physical properties.[1] More generally, supervenience claims are taken to range over collections or "families" of supervenient properties (A-properties) regarded as depending on distinct families of subvenient B-properties. I shall designate claims of this sort "A/B-supervenience" claims. Sometimes the supervenience relation is distilled into a pair of slogans: "No A-difference without a B-difference"; "Two objects identical with respect to their B-properties must be identical with respect to their A-properties."[2]

According to Richard Miller, appeals to supervenience on behalf of physicalism are empty; it is "trivially" true that "the nonphysical supervenes on the physical."[3] Worse,

> it is equally true that the physical supervenes on the moral, the mental, and the aesthetic. "No difference without a physical difference" is an excellent slogan. The gist of this paper can also be summarized with slogans. "No difference without a moral difference," "no difference without a mental difference," and "no difference without an aesthetic difference," are as (trivially) true as the physicalist slogan. (p. 695)

Miller advances a pair of interesting and important claims. First, the supervenience of the nonphysical on the physical is "trivial." Second, the supervenience relation is invariably *symmetrical:* when As supervene on Bs, the supervenience of Bs on As is "all but guaranteed." Together, these claims yield "the metaphysical insignificance of the supervenience relation" (p. 696). I shall argue that Miller is wrong on both counts. The charge of triviality hinges on an implausibly weak notion of supervenience, and once this notion is replaced by something more apt, the symmetry Miller finds in every supervenience relation evaporates.

Miller characterizes supervenience as follows:

(S₁) For a class of properties [*A*] to supervene on a class of properties *B* is for it to be true for any two things to differ in their [*A*] properties is for them to differ in their *B* properties. (p. 696)

Miller's first claim, that everything "trivially" supervenes on the physical, is a consequence of (S₁) together with what I shall call the "discernibility thesis": every object differs from every other object in some physical detail. If every object differs from every other with respect to its *B*-properties, then, for any *A* at all, there are no *A*-differences without *B*-differences. The supervenience of every property on physical properties is "trivially" assured.

Why should we grant that every object differs from every other in some physical respect? Miller holds that "physical language" possesses the resources to distinguish any two physical objects however similar seeming. Objects so distinguishable, are physically distinguishable, hence physically discernible. The idea is straightforward. Physicalism, the view that every property supervenes on physical properties, must allow for relational and historical properties in the physical supervenience base, along with dispositional and "undetectable" properties. Consider, for instance, the physical supervenience base for moral properties. It is plausible to suppose that this will include relational and dispositional properties of agents. If St. Francis is a good man in part because of deeds done and temptations overcome, a molecular replica of St. Francis constructed last night in a Tijuana laboratory, lacking many of St. Francis's historical properties, would, in consequence, lack many of St. Francis's moral properties. Similar reasoning might be thought to apply in the case of mental properties. Wayne and his twin, Dwayne, are molecular duplicates who inhabit Earth and Twin Earth, respectively. The only physical differences between Wayne, who believes that water is wet, and Dwayne, who believes that twater is wet, are relational, historical, and spatiotemporal differences. If the property of harboring a belief about water is distinct from the property of harboring a belief about twater, and if these properties supervene on physical properties, the physical supervenience base must include nonintrinsic, relational, or historical properties.[4] Thus,

> the base properties upon which moral [and mental] properties supervene include relations, noncontemporaneous properties, and dispositional properties, none of which need be detectable. Moreover, these properties are mathematicized to allow an infinity of distinctions to be drawn.[5] (pp. 697–8)

It is, Miller contends, an immediate consequence of our including relational, dispositional, and undetectable properties in the physical base together with the "mathematization" of physical language that the supervenience of every property on physical properties is "trivialized."

How? Since it will always be possible to draw *some* physical distinction between any two physical objects (this one's origin differs from that one's, this one occupies a different spatial region than that one, this one is composed of fewer molecules than that one, and so on), it follows that every physical object differs physically from every other. Since no two things are physically indistinguishable, there are no differences of any sort without physical differences, and given S_1, everything supervenes on the physical.[6]

> When we consider the complexity of the actual world, plus the fact that the supervenience relation is supported by undetectable differences, relational properties, and dispositional properties, the mathematization of physics ensures supervenience. . . . [I]t is the expressive power of physical language which allows us to assume physical differences where none are detectable. (p. 698)

This brings us to Miller's second contention: supervenience is invariably symmetrical, a "two-way street." If moral properties, for instance, supervene on physical properties, it is no less true that physical properties supervene on moral properties. Again, the idea is straightforward. Suppose we regard A-properties as supervenient on B-properties and regard this as a "trivial" consequence of the B-discernibility of every object. If it turns out that every object differs from every other in some A-respect as well, then, on S_1, every property, including the B-properties, supervenes on A-properties. In the moral case,

> the apparent asymmetry of the supervenience relation . . . is an artifact of certain contingent features of our actual physical and moral languages. Actual physical language is far subtler and closer to an ideal physical language than actual moral language is to an ideal moral language. Actual physical language has incorporated mathematics, while actual moral language, despite the efforts of Jeremy Bentham, has not. (p. 696)

As a result there is a "vast preponderance in the number of physical distinctions we can make in the actual physical language compared to the actual moral language" (p. 696). Comparable "expressive power" should be made available to the moralist, however:

> Just as it is unfair to allow one team to use a different set of rules from another team, it is inappropriate to compare actual moral language to idealized physical language. The illicit comparison of an anemic qualitative moral vocabulary with a robust quantitative physical vocabulary creates the illusion of a metaphysical primacy for the physical. (p. 699)

If we allow both teams to "play by the same rules," however, "the result is a draw" (p. 699). That is, if we permit moralists to "mathematicize" familiar moral distinctions, and if we suppose that the family of moral properties might include "undetectable differences, relational properties, and dispositional properties," it looks as though every object could be said to differ from every other in some moral respect. Why should we imagine that the pencil on my desk or a bit of rock orbiting a distant star possesses distinctive moral properties? Perhaps both have "some slight disposition to affect human flourishing" (p. 700). We can, in this way, concoct a unique assignment of moral properties to every object just as we did in the case of physical properties. But if we can do that, then, since no two things are morally indistinguishable, there are no physical differences without moral differences, and every property (including every physical property) turns out to supervene on the family of moral properties. Furthermore,

> a similar case can be made for the supervenience of the physical on suitably strengthened aesthetic or psychological languages. Give these languages the same resources for generating distinctions as the physical now has, and both will constitute a set of base properties upon which everything may supervene. (pp. 700–1)

Consider just the supervenience of the physical on the mental (no physical difference without a mental difference). If we include undetectable relational, dispositional, and "mathematicized" properties in the mental supervenience base, then it is plausible to imagine that every object differs in some mental respect or other. The tree in the quad differs from a similar tree in the forest, for instance, in having once been observed by Wayne. For its part, the tree in the forest occupies a unique region, R, of space-time relative to the observed tree in virtue of which it possesses an exotic dispositional property: it would be observed by Wayne were Wayne to visit space-time region R. If this mental property seems contrived, it is only because we usually rest content with coarse-grained mental distinctions. An "idealized" psychological language, however, would incorporate resources for the construction of endless mental distinctions. And if this is so, it would seem to follow that every object whatever differs in some mental respect from every other.[7] The supervenience of the mental on the physical and the physical on the mental is thus "all but guaranteed." More generally, it is in the nature of things that whenever As supervene on Bs, Bs will supervene on As. And this, as Miller rightly points out, is not what advocates of physicalism have in mind in appealing to (S_1). (S_1) sanctions "two-way" supervenience relations, but these seem incompatible with the kind of property dependence and determination hankered after by the physicalist.

Now, one might have thought that this shows, at most, that (S_1) is defective. It is certainly an open question whether (S_1) captures the notion of dependence to which physicalists appeal. Miller grants as much: "It is impossible to give a definition of supervenience that will satisfy all participants in the discussion" (p. 696n). Still, Miller's choice of (S_1) is puzzling. (S_1) is distinctively *nonmodal*.[8] Physicalist advocates of supervenience, however, seem on the whole to favor one or another *modal* conception of the notion.[9] Thus, supervenience is typically regarded as a relation holding with necessity, holding *across* some range of possible worlds. Consider, for instance, so-called *strong supervenience*. If As strongly supervene on Bs, then

> (S_2) For any objects x and y and worlds w_i and w_j, if x in w_i is B-indiscernible from y in w_j, then x in w_i is A-indiscernible from y in w_j.

If As strongly supervene on Bs, can we invoke Miller's strategy so as to yield the strong supervenience of Bs on As? Note that, given Miller's insistence that relational and quantitative properties be included in the supervenience base, x in w_i, and y in w_j will be B-indiscernible just in case $x = y$ and $w_i = w_j$. To see why this is so, imagine a world resembling the actual world in every physical respect save for the lack of a single hydrogen atom on the surface of some isolated, dying star. Every object in that world will differ physically from every object in our world. The Washington Monument in our world stands at a certain distance from a star whose surface includes n hydrogen atoms; in that world, the Washington Monument (or its counterpart) has a different relational physical property: it stands at that distance from a star having $n - 1$ hydrogen atoms on its surface. Since no two worlds can contain physically indiscernible objects, then, if every world contains some physical object (and if there are no nonphysical concrete particulars), if every object has some physical property or other, every property strongly supervenes on physical properties.

What of the strong supervenience of physical properties on moral or mental properties? Here Miller's thesis runs into a snag. It is consistent with the strong supervenience of moral properties on physical properties that there are worlds in which no moral properties are instantiated. Worlds consisting entirely of matter in the form assumed by matter in our world at the time of the Big Bang might be of this sort. Such worlds – plasma worlds – would exclude conscious agents as a matter of physical law and so apparently exclude even *dispositional* moral properties: in no nomologically possible world would instances of these physical characteristics "affect human flourishing." Two such worlds might then contain "objects" that differ physically without differing morally.[10] If there are such worlds, then the physical does not strongly supervene on the moral: there are possible objects that differ physically, but not morally.[11] More generally, if it is consistent with the strong supervenience of As on Bs (strong A/B-supervenience) that there are worlds with B-properties but devoid of A-properties, then Miller's strategy will not generate the symmetrical result he claims for it.

Parallel reasoning applies to other conceptions of supervenience. Consider *weak supervenience*. If As weakly supervene on Bs, then

(S_3) No possible world contains objects x and y such that x and y are B-indiscernible, yet A-discernible.

The weak supervenience of As on Bs, however, is consistent with the existence of plasma worlds in which B-properties, but no A-properties, are instantiated. The existence of such worlds, as we have noted already, falsifies strong B/A-supervenience, but it falsifies, as well, *weak* B/A-supervenience. In such worlds, objects differing in respect to their B-properties do not differ in respect to their A-properties.

Consider, finally, a third conception of supervenience, *global supervenience*. If As globally supervene on Bs, then,

(S_4) Worlds that are B-indiscernible are A-indiscernible.

Global supervenience constrains worlds, or world regions, not objects. Yet, just as both strong and weak supervenience are compatible with the existence of A-less plasma worlds, so the global supervenience of As on Bs is consistent with plasma worlds in which B-properties are instantiated but A-properties are not. And if that is so, then global A/B-supervenience fails to guarantee the corresponding global B/A-supervenience. There are worlds that are A-indiscernible, but not B-indiscernible.

Miller's suggestion that the supervenience relation is a de facto symmetrical relation, then, holds, if at all, only for nonmodal conceptions of supervenience like (S_1). Most physicalists, however, embrace not (S_1) but (S_2), (S_3), or (S_4). And Miller's conclusion does not touch these conceptions.[12]

Miller's strategy is a familiar one in philosophy. Take some apparent phenomenon P; provide an account of P and show that this account is defective; then conclude that P is illusory, trivial, or nonexistent.[13] But of course, it is one thing to show that a particular philosophical notion is in some way defective, quite another to show that the object of this notion is nonexistent.

What of Miller's first point, his contention that the supervenience of the moral, the mental, and the aesthetic on the physical is simply a "trivial" consequence of the fact that every physical object is discernible from every other? If we grant the discernibility thesis and accept one of the formulations (S_1)–(S_4) as definitive of supervenience, it follows that every property supervenes on physical properties only if it is also true that every possible object has some physical property (or, in the case of (S_4), global supervenience, only if every world instantiates some physical property). Does this "trivialize" supervenience? There are at least two reasons to think that it does not.

First, suppose we restrict in some way subvenient relational characteristics to those that are *relevant*. Then, although individuals and worlds might invariably differ physically, they need not diverge in physically relevant respects. Wayne, who exists in the actual world, and his counterpart, an inhabitant of a world identical to the actual world save for a single missing molecule, are physically different, though perhaps not in a way that bears on their possession of particular mental, moral, or aesthetic characteristics.

The suggestion has merit, but it faces an immediate difficulty. How, without begging the question, might we specify what is to count as a *relevant* physical characteristic? Perhaps we could take a relevant physical characteristic to be one that figures in the determination of some A-characteristic. This suggestion requires that we have some notion of determination (or dependence) specifiable without reference to a favored conception of supervenience, however, and the point of introducing the notion of supervenience was to articulate this very relation.

Worries of this sort, however, ignore the empirical aspect of supervenience hypotheses. An advocate of mental/physical supervenience, for instance, need not imagine that individuals' physical characteristics are, one and all, relevant to the possession, by those individuals, of particular mental characteristics. In advancing a supervenience claim, one is obliged to identify particular subvenient properties as those responsible for particular supervenient properties. Individuals indiscernible with respect to *these* properties must be indiscernible with respect to the supervenient property in question. A narrowed supervenience claim of this sort would be shown false if it could be shown that there are two individuals, occupants of nomologically or metaphysically possible worlds, with these same subvenient properties but who differed with respect to the supervenient property – their differing in other physical respects would be beside the point. We attempt to discover whether there are such individuals or possible individuals by conducting empirical tests.

We must distinguish, then, generic supervenience hypotheses – the mental supervenes on the physical, for instance – from particular empirically constrained hypotheses. We can do so without rejecting the formulations of supervenience already in play by restricting the domains of A and B to some subset of available subvenient and supervenient characteristics. Thoughts and conscious states might be taken to supervene on agents' neurological characteristics, for instance, or, as is more likely, on some restricted subclass of these. Differences between agents' hair color, weight, or cardiovascular functioning would then be treated as irrelevant. We should suppose that agents indiscernible with respect to these neurological characteristics would be indiscernible with respect to their thoughts.[14] Restrictions of this sort could be motivated by what we know about physiology and psychology, and by some preferred theory of intentionality.

There is a second reason to doubt that supervenience is inherently trivial. It could well be that (S_1)–(S_4) all fail to capture a tolerable notion of supervenience. Consideration of the causal relation in this context is instructive. Causality is, as we suppose, like supervenience, a kind of dependence/determination relation. Just as it is impossible to frame an adequate notion of causality using only material conditionals, so it is unlikely that one could rely exclusively on material conditionals to articulate a credible notion of supervenience. In the case of causality, modalizing the conditionals narrows the gap. If the gap is not closed entirely, however, the moral to draw may just be that dependence relations like causality cannot be captured solely in modal terms.[15] But if that is so, it is at least a good bet that supervenience, considered as a dependence/determination relation, will continue to frustrate attempts at purely modal analyses.

Is there any reason to think that some collections of properties supervene on others in our world? If we stick to characterizations of supervenience like (S_1)–(S_4), the answer seems obviously yes. We need not appeal to Miller's discernibility thesis to support this conclusion, but only to various property-correlations of a sort familiar in everyday life and in our scientific practice. A more interesting question, however, is whether supervenience, regarded as a relation of dependence and determination, is a trait of the deep structure of our world.

The very same question might be, and of course has been, raised concerning the causal relation. In each case, the issue is partly empirical, and in each case, we move toward an affirmative answer in identifying what we take to be instances of the relation in question. As Hume made clear in the case of causality, however, we are limited in any empirical investigation of dependencies to the discovery of patterns of local correlations. The move from correlational evidence to claims about dependence involves additional, nonempirical commitments.

In the case of supervenience, we may be struck by the *layered* appearance of the world. Collections of properties seem not merely to be correlated with, but to rest on, and owe their character to, other collections of properties. Such property relations turn up both in the course of scientific investigation and in ordinary life. Biological features of organisms seem to depend on particular chemical properties, and these, in turn, seem to be determined by still "more basic" physical properties. The cake I bake owes its consistency, flavor, and appearance to less obvious features of the ingredients I have put into it. We find it natural to locate phenomena in this layered picture, to see features of our world as standing in atemporal, noncausal dependence relations, to appeal to "lower-level" properties to explain the possession of "higher-level" characteristics. In so doing, we invoke what might as well as not be called "supervenience."

Of course, it could turn out that supervenience is a "myth," just as it could turn out that causality is a mere "projection." The issues are difficult ones, hinging on answers we are inclined to give to a variety of empirical, conceptual, and metaphysical questions. Whatever one's views on such things, however, it is surely a mistake to conflate philosophical characterizations of supervenience with what is being characterized. The former may, and if history is our guide, probably will, prove inadequate in countless ways. This could be due to some fundamental incoherence in the concept we hope to capture. More likely it is due to our own less dramatic logical or conceptual inadequacies.

NOTES

A version of this essay was presented in a colloquium, "Metaphysics: Identity and Supervenience," at the Pacific Division, American Philosophical Association, meetings in Portland, Oregon, March 25–28, 1991. Jean Kazez provided useful comments. See Heil (1992), chap. 3, for a more detailed discussion of supervenience and further defense of the line advanced here. I am grateful to Jaegwon Kim, Brian P. McLaughlin, and, especially, my colleague Alfred Mele for much helpful discussion.

1. The supervenience relation may be, and has been, formulated in terms of properties, predicates, features, facts, truths, and languages. For simplicity, I shall speak here only of properties.

2. Davidson (1980, p. 214), in a much-quoted passage, after equating supervenience with dependence, suggests that the supervenience of the mental on the physical "might be taken to mean that there cannot be two events alike in all physical respects but differing in some mental respect, or that an object cannot alter in some mental respect without altering in some physical respect."

3. See Miller (1990); citations to this essay appear parenthetically.

4. I am not endorsing this line of reasoning, only echoing Miller.

5. Miller slides back and forth between talk of properties and talk of linguistic "distinctions." His characterization of supervenience makes reference to properties, but his worries about the "metaphysically trivial" character of supervenience are couched in terms of distinctions afforded by actual and ideal "languages." Were there a simple, one-to-one correspondence between properties and "distinctions," this vacillation might be dismissed as a mere stylistic quirk. Without assuming the correspondence – which is, in any case, unlikely – I shall grant it here for the sake of argument.

6. In fact the supervenience of all properties on physical properties does not follow from this result, not if there are nonphysical particulars – Cartesian souls, for instance – that altogether lack physical properties.

7. Or, at any rate, every object in a world in which some object has some mental property. As we shall see, the caveat is important.

8. In consequence, (S_1) would allow that *being a Republican* supervenes on *having an odd number of freckles* if Republicans, but not Democrats, happened as a matter of fact to have an odd number of freckles. (The example is Brian McLaughlin's.)

9. See, e.g., Kim (1984). I know of only two attempts to express the supervenience relation nonmodally: those of Davidson (1985, p. 242; 1993, p. 4).

10. See Hellman (1992). As Hellman points out, worlds like ours, worlds possessing stages causally and epistemically cut off from the advent of conscious agents, might be taken to contain "objects" that differ physically without differing morally.

11. Miller might argue that (i) the complements of moral properties, for instance, are instantiated in such worlds, and (ii) the complement of a moral property is itself a moral property, so (iii) such worlds do contain moral properties after all. Ignoring the question of whether (ii) is plausible, the problem is that in these worlds every object is morally indiscernible, though not physically indiscernible, so physical/moral supervenience fails.

12. It is true, nevertheless, that supervenience, as characterized in (S_2), (S_3), and (S_4) is a nonsymmetrical relation. It is *consistent* with supervenience characterized in any of these ways that *B*s supervene on *A*s when *A*s supervene on *B*s. See Kim (1990) and Grimes (1988).

13. Consider, for instance, Berkeley's proof that material bodies do not exist.

14. The restrictions envisaged might exclude some, but not all, relational features of agents and their neurological components.

15. This point is made by Kim (1990).

REFERENCES

Davidson, D. 1980. "Mental Events," in *Essays in Actions and Events*. Oxford: Clarendon Press, p. 214.

1985. "Replies to Essays X–XII," in Bruce Vermazen and Merrill Hintikka, eds., *Essays on Davidson on Actions and Events*. Oxford: Clarendon Press, pp. 242–52.

Grimes, T. 1988. "The Myth of Supervenience," *Pacific Philosophical Quarterly* 69, 152–60.

Heil, J. 1992. *The Nature of True Minds*. Cambridge University Press.

Hellman, G. 1992. "Supervenience/Determination a Two-Way Street? Yes, but One of the Ways is the Wrong Way!" *Journal of Philosophy* 89, 42–7.

Kim, J. 1984. "Concepts of Supervenience," *Philosophy and Phenomenological Research* 45, 153–76.

1990. "Supervenience as Philosophical Concept," *Metaphilosophy* 12, 1–27.

Miller, R. 1990. "Supervenience is a Two-Way Street," *Journal of Philosophy*
    87, 695–701.
    1993. "Thinking Causes," in John Heil and Alfred Mele, eds., *Mental Causa-
    tion*. Oxford University Press, pp. 41–50.

Nonreducible Supervenient Causation

BERENT ENÇ

Philosophical literature is rich with attempts to identify the different species of the supervenience relation, to work out the logical relations among the different species, and to determine the causal efficacy of supervenient properties. I will here confine my investigation to what has been called strong supervenience.[1] There seem to exist two species of this type of supervenience: local (or mereological) and global. One can illustrate the difference by considering two cases. (i) Many materialists will probably be committed to the view that if an individual of this world and its twin in some possible world differ in some psychological way at a given moment, then these two individuals must also differ in some physical way at that moment. In being so committed, these materialists will be viewing psychological properties as being locally (and strongly) supervenient on physical properties. (ii) A philosopher might think that it is impossible for two individuals, say Oscar and Twinoscar, to have distinct psychological properties at some moment (say, one believes that something is water, and the other believes that it is twater) and yet for the worlds they inhabit, including their own bodily constitution, to be physically identical at that moment. Such a philosopher would be expressing the view that psychological properties are globally (and strongly) supervenient on the physical. One possible definition for strong local supervenience is:

> **(SL)** For any macro property S of an individual, there is a set of some physical property (or a set of some combinations of physical properties) of the parts of the individual such that it is nomologically necessary that any individual instantiating any member of that set at time t instantiates S at t.[2]

And strong global supervenience may be defined as follows:

> **(SG)** For any property S of individuals, any two possible worlds indistinguishable in physical respects at time t will agree in the instantiation of S at t.[3]

The reference to time is introduced to exclude causal relations between base properties and supervenient properties.[4] In these definitions, I have assumed that the base properties are physical properties. (By "physical" I mean properties that appear in the laws of some suitable physical theory.) This assumption diminishes the generality of the definitions, but since I will be concerned mainly with supervenient properties that have only physical bases, the loss of generality will not matter. Finally, these definitions allow the relation of supervenience to be symmetrical. But typically, it is assumed that for any supervenient property *S*, there is a multitude of base properties each of which is sufficient to realize *S*. In what follows, I shall be conforming to this practice. Hence, I will take there to be a tacit understanding that each definition ends with the clause 'but not conversely'.

Global supervenience is the proper relation with which to endorse one version of substance materialism. For if global supervenience holds, there cannot be any change in the world unless there is change in some physical respect. But as it stands, the relation is consistent with a strong form of emergentism. The definition allows, for example, there to be two worlds that differ only with respect to, say, a single atom in Saturn's rings, and to have the first world contain psychological properties, and the second lack them altogether.[5] This result has encouraged attempts to localize the global base to some specifiable region that is still partly outside the individual but that causally interacts with the individual.[6] Examples that conform to these more restricted forms of supervenience can be found in teleologically functional or etiological conceptions of psychological properties.[7] I will attend to specific versions of this more restricted form of the global supervenience relation later.

Returning to local supervenience, we can imagine there to be two kinds of relations between the supervenient property and the base. The first is one that requires that there be what Seager calls a "physical resolution" of the supervenient properties. That is, it is required that there be a mechanism that explains how the possession of the base properties determines, or makes it the case, that the individual possesses the supervenient property. A perfect example for this kind of relation is to be found in the reduction of temperature to the mean kinetic energy of the molecules of a chamber of gas. This relation is constitutive and it is also multiply realizable, for there is a very large number of specifications of mass-velocity assignments to the individual molecules, each of which will constitute one and the same temperature.

In the second kind of relation there will be no such mechanism; that is, it would be impossible to show how the base properties determine the supervenient property. In this second kind, the supervenient property would be viewed as an emergent property.

If we now attend to the causal relations that hold among locally supervenient properties, there emerge several concerns. The first con-

Figure 1

cern is that in the absence of a type–type identification between the supervenient property and the base properties, the causal laws that may be written using the supervenient property will not, in general, be translatable into causal laws that use the vocabulary of the base level. So if such laws are available at the macro level, the type causation that occurs at the macro level will not usually be duplicated by a type causation at the micro level.[8] But type causation in this context is more of an explanatory concern than token causation. Ontological issues emerge much more naturally at the token level. So in what follows, I shall confine myself just to token causation.

The second concern is that of distinguishing between what has been called "event causation" and "causal relevance." When two events, e_1 and e_2 are causally connected, and the two events both have base and supervenient properties, it is clear that e_1 will be the cause of e_2 regardless of which property, supervenient or base, we use in referring to these events. But beyond this platitude, there is an additional question. This question may be formulated in any of the following ways: In virtue of having which property did e_1 cause e_2? What was it about e_1 that made it the case that e_2 occurred?[9] Which properties of e_1 are causally relevant for the occurrence of e_2? Although it is possible to conceive these questions as being concerned with issues about explanation, I will here assume that there is something about the causal structure of the world that determines the correct answers to them.[10] My decision to focus on token causation is motivated by the desire to avoid complications that may arise from purely epistemic concerns.

A brief survey of the literature reveals overwhelming skepticism over the causal relevance of supervenient properties at the token level. One might express this skepticism by setting up a disjunctive dilemma (Figure 1).

Concentrating on local supervenience for the time being, let us first look at the relation in which there is no physical resolution of the supervenient property to its micro base. On the surface, there seems to be good reason to confer causal efficacy on SV_1. A hypothetical example might illustrate this tendency. Suppose that we take psychological properties to be nonresolvable to their base; that is, we accept them as emergent properties. Under this supposition, in a token case where my being in fear of the lion is followed by my running, the natural tendency would be to say that my being in fear was a causally relevant property in the production of my behavior. Although both the fear and the behavior have their respective micro bases, in maintaining that no physical resolution exists, we have denied that there is something determinate about these micro bases in virtue of which they realize the supervenient properties in question; that is, we have assumed that no mechanism exists whereby the base properties physically determine the supervenient property. As a result, we might think that in addition to the causal connection that must obtain between the micro bases, there exists an independent causal relation between the supervenient properties. But further examination of this tendency will give us at least two reasons to move to the opposite conclusion. The first reason is that in each token case of my being in fear that causes my running, there will be determinate micro bases of the fear and the running such that the first of these token micro bases will cause the second. When each token case comes with its explicit micro level causal story, then it will seem unnecessary to invoke the mystery of emergentism and to reify the supervenient properties by conferring on them autonomous causal efficacy. The absence of a physical resolution invites curiosity over the mechanism whereby these supervenient properties cause things. And the absence of a causal mechanism at the supervenient level, coupled with the explicit causal story at the micro level, forces one to start viewing the supervenient properties as being epiphenomenal. But being epiphenomenal is a terminal disease; it ends up razoring the supervenient properties out of our ontology. Such has been the fate of vitalism, and one school of philosophers expects a similar fate to befall our folk psychological properties.[11]

The second reason comes from Jaegwon Kim,[12] who argues that the original tendency to attribute to SV_1 causal efficacy in the production of SV_2 either must end up being untenable or must be purchased at the price of admitting downward causation. His argument is briefly this. If we admit causal efficacy to SV_1, the question, Why is this token of SV_2 instantiated? will have two answers: (i) an instance of SV_1 caused it; and (ii) $m(SV_2)$ physically realizes SV_2, and $m(SV_2)$ is instantiated. These answers cannot both be maintained unless we assume that SV_1 caused $m(SV_2)$. For $m(SV_2)$ is fully sufficient for SV_2 regardless of what antecedent conditions may have obtained. And this fact preempts the causal role of SV_1, unless the way SV_1 causes SV_2 is by its causing $m(SV_2)$. This is as far as Kim takes the argument. But it seems to be clear that when confronted with a choice between getting rid of causal relations between supervenient properties or admitting downward causation, we would naturally opt for the former.

I take either of these two reasons to be good enough to force one into skepticism over causal relations among nonresolvable properties. This completes the first horn of the dilemma.

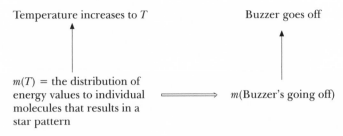

Figure 2

The second horn comes up when we make the assumption that a reductive mechanism does exist by means of which an individual's possessing the base properties it possesses determines, or makes it the case, that that individual instantiates the supervenient properties it instantiates. The literature in which this assumption is pursued is rich. I will only look at one of the many issues discussed because it is one that is directly pertinent to our second horn. There seem to be two categories of cases of supervenience. In one of them the supervenient properties are clearly *not* causally connected. And then there seems to be a second category in which, by contrast, it seems plausible to confer causal efficacy to the supervenient properties.

One of the most elegant and persuasive treatments of this issue is to be found in an unpublished manuscript by Greg Mougin. My discussion here is largely indebted to him. Mougin contrasts several examples with the standard temperature case. One of his examples is this: Suppose a gas chamber has heat introduced to it. Introduction of the heat increases the temperature. The micro base of the new temperature at time t_1 is one specific distribution of kinetic energies to the individual molecules. This specific distribution is unique among other micro bases that will realize the same temperature in that this distribution results in a star pattern among the molecules. There is a star pattern detector in the chamber. The formation of the star pattern causes the micro base of the buzzing of the detector. The detector starts buzzing (Figure 2). It seems intuitively clear that the gas temperature's being what it is at t_1 is not what made it the case that the buzzer went on at t_2. What caused the buzzer was the formation of the star pattern, not the temperature increase.

When we contrast this case with what I have called the "standard temperature case" (Figure 3), it becomes much more plausible to confer causal efficacy to the temperature of the gas when the temperature goes up and the height of the mercury column rises. It should be emphasized that in noting the difference between the standard case and the star pattern example, one does not commit oneself to the claim that the standard case is an instance of genuine causation. The task

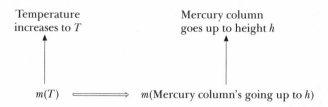

Figure 3

that remains now is to find a set of necessary and sufficient (or perhaps more modestly, a set of just sufficient) conditions that will pry apart cases like the standard temperature example from cases of obvious pseudocausation. The literature presents many worthy attempts at this task.[13] But as Segal and Sober's (1991) examples show, none of these attempts avoids counterexamples.[14]

Greg Mougin's solution, which is distinct from the three I mentioned earlier, is probably the most satisfactory of the lot. He requires there to be a mechanism whereby the base properties determine, or make it the case, that the individuals have the supervenient property in question. In our earlier discussion, we started with an assumption that such a requirement is satisfied. He then imposes a further requirement, which I state very roughly here. It is that the effect-supervenient property not be due to something special about the token micro base of the cause; that is, all other micro base realizations of the cause must be able to cause the same effect-supervenient property.

I will not go into a critical discussion of Mougin's solution. For it seems to me that even after one manages to weed out the pseudocauses from other supervenient causes, still a bitter taste remains in one's mouth. It seems that when, in a token case, the increase in the temperature of the gas causes the rise of the mercury column, what happens is nothing other than that the mean kinetic energy of the molecules causes changes in the micro structure of the liquid mercury. We allow reference to temperature as the cause purely for explanatory considerations. As Putnam once put it with his Peg-Board example, the explanation of the effect by reference to temperature is better than the explanation by reference to the specific kinetic energy assignments to each of the molecules because the former explanation is invariant under changes in the micro base, whereas the latter explanation is not. But assuming that there exists an ontological notion of causal efficacy that is not derived from considerations of explanatory adequacy, the causal efficacy of the temperature seems clearly parasitic on the causal efficacy of the specific kinetic energy distributions to the molecules. The causal drama is being enacted at the micro level, and the macro level is epiphenomenal. We tolerate the macro, to the extent that we do, purely for pragmatic reasons. One of these reasons is the explanatory concern that I mentioned earlier. The other reason is that the macro level is what our senses directly report to us, what most of our crude instruments measure. But as one dear friend once put it, what midsized slow philosophers see is not always a key to the mysteries of ontology.

This completes the second horn of the dilemma. The first horn followed the assumption that the supervenient property was emergent, and the second horn investigated those cases where there existed a reduction of the supervenient property to its physical base. Each horn concluded with a skeptical judgment about the existence of an autonomous, or independent, causal relation between supervenient properties.

In what follows, I propose to investigate a different species of supervenient property. And I propose to argue that in contrast to supervenient properties like temperature or the vital force, which, as I suggested earlier, acquire whatever causal force they might have from the causal efficacy of the micro base, the members of this species have causal efficacy that does not get fully accounted for by the causal role played by the micro base properties.

The properties I have in mind are locally supervenient properties of an individual that are associated with certain globally supervenient properties. These globally supervenient properties will have their base restricted to a region outside the individual in which properties causally interact with the properties of the individual in question. I do not know how to give a general formula that captures all of these globally supervenient properties. But some examples will illustrate the idea. For my purposes, it will turn out that the inability to give such a general formula will not be an important issue.

1. Properties that are defined "causally," for example, being a skin condition that is caused by excessive exposure to sun rays, that is, being a sunburn; or being a limb movement that is caused by a belief–desire pair, that is, being a piece of intentional behavior; or having the function of doing such and such, where functions are understood etiologically.

2. Properties that are defined in terms of what distal propensities they have, for example, fitness in biology, or functions understood in terms of having the disposition to bring about certain distal effects.

3. Properties that are defined in terms of what would have caused them under a set of specifiable conditions, like being a representation of some state of affairs.[15]

These are all examples of properties for which there exists a physical resolution, but in which the physical base given by the resolution includes properties outside the individual or at times other than the time at which the individual instantiates the supervenient property. For each of these properties, there corresponds a locally supervenient property. I will express the relation between such locally supervenient properties and their associated globally supervenient properties by saying that the local supervenient property is "a carrier" of the globally supervenient property. For example, for each sunburn, there is a macro condition of the skin, locally supervening on some micro condition of the cells. This macro condition is not identical with the property of being a sunburn because it is possible for that very same condition to be brought about, for example, by a viral infection. And if it is the result of a viral infection, it will *not* be a *sunburn*. So the token macro condition of the skin, when it is caused by the sun rays, is a "carrier" of the globally supervenient property of being a sunburn.

Again, for example, for each representation of a state of affairs, there will be a structure that embodies the representation and that locally supervenes on some micro structure of the individual. But that supervenient structure will not be identical with the representation. There exist as many views about representation as there are philosophers who have thought about the matter. I will not contribute to the inflation by giving my view here. Instead, I will adopt a simplified version of Dennis Stampe's (1977) account, partly because I think that it is basically the right account, but mainly because what I want to say about the causal role of the supervenient is best expressed by using his account.

Suppose the height of the mercury column in a thermometer represents the room temperature. On Stampe's view this is tantamount to saying that when the thermometer represents the temperature as being, say, 68 degrees Fahrenheit, the height of the mercury column is at a value that would be caused under ideal conditions by the room's being 68 degrees. And the ideal conditions include the thermometer's not malfunctioning, its not being thermally insulated, there being no ice pack near it, and so on. I think it is important here not to equate the property of the mercury column's having a certain height, a property that embodies the representation, with the property of being a representation. The identity conditions for the height of the column can be given by purely internal features of the thermometer. But the identity conditions for being a representation must advert to a subjunctive formulation in which oblique reference is made to factors spatially and temporally outside the thermometer as it is viewed at a given time. Application of this distinction to mental representations invokes the familiar split between, say, a brain structure defined, as Jerry Fodor puts it, "syntactically" and a belief constituted by that structure that is a representation of the world's being a certain way.

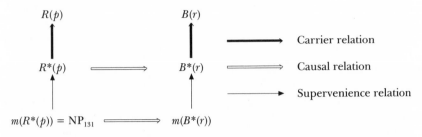

Figure 4

The picture obtained from taking beliefs as representational structures may be illustrated as in Figure 4.

$R(p)$: Belief that there is a tiger.

$R^*(p)$: The "syntactic" structure that codes for the belief that there is a tiger (this structure may be assumed to be functionally defined – that is, in terms of its "narrowly conceived" causal roles).

$B(r)$: Intentionally running away (let us suppose here for the sake of avoiding complications that B will always be a piece of basic behavior).

$B^*(r)$: A pattern of muscular activity that results in fast locomotion such that when it is appropriately caused by a belief, it constitutes intentionally running.

$m(R^*(p))$: A neurophysiological pattern NP_{131} that constitutes the micro base of $R^*(p)$.

$m(B^*(r))$: An event pattern described at the cellular level that constitutes the micro base of B^*r.

The way I have labeled these items in the diagram may mislead. On the cause side, as a Davidsonian would individuate events, I take there to be *one* event, that is, the organism's entering a certain state, which might alternatively be described as its acquiring a belief, as its instantiating a functionally defined property, or as its neurophysiological makeup changing so as to enter into state NP_{131}. Each of these descriptions designates a *property* of the event, and the diagram is to be understood as displaying the supervenience relations among these properties. So when I characterize $R^*(p)$ as a "structure" that supervenes on NP_{131} and is a carrier for $R(p)$, I mean to be referring to a property of the cause event, that is, its having the functionally defined property of being the syntactic structure that embodies the belief. The same set of relations applies mutatis mutandis to the effect side. Applying Stampe's account of representations here, we can say that in a token case when $R^*(p)$ is a representation, it is the structure that *would* be caused by p under a set of specifiable "ideal" conditions. But we cannot say the same thing about NP_{131}. In other words, it is not the case that

NP_{131} is the neurophysiological state that would be caused by p under ideal conditions. This is so because it is only *one* of many neurophysiological states that *might* be caused by p under those conditions. This is not to deny that NP_{131} is a representation of p. However, the full explanation of why NP_{131} is a representation of p must refer to $R^*(p)$. NP_{131} represents p owing to its being a realization of $R^*(p)$. Since the token $R^*(p)$ is assumed to satisfy the counterfactual, $R^*(p)$ is a necessary and sufficient condition for the representation; NP_{131} is only a sufficient condition. In other words, what makes NP_{131} a representation of p is the fact that NP_{131} is a realization of $R^*(p)$ and that $R^*(p)$ represents p.

Still focusing on token cases, let us suppose that at t, p causes $R^*(p)$. Presumably, some micro facts about the setup would explain how NP_{131} gets caused. So given the specifics of the micro structure, we can show that p causes $R^*(p)$ in virtue of the fact that some micro properties that constitute the fact that p, causing NP_{131}. However, what makes $R^*(p)$ a representational structure, what gives it its identity, is *not* the fact that it is determined by NP_{131}. $R^*(p)$ acquires its identity owing to the fact that it is the sort of structure that would under ideal conditions be caused by p – and this, regardless of whether at t what causes it is p or not. What gives $R^*(p)$ *its* identity is distinct from what gives NP_{131} its identity. What gives NP_{131} its identity can be stated in purely neurophysiological terms. NP_{131} is sufficient to determine a structure, which we have called $R^*(p)$, but it is not sufficient to make it the case that the structure it determines constitutes a representation of p. Stars that one "sees" after a blow on the head are not representations of anything. Perhaps a clearer illustration of this point may be given by imagining a newborn baby who is not yet capable of holding any beliefs. Suppose that, in this baby, due to some electrical discharge in the brain, a neurophysiological state type identical to NP_{131} occurs. Even if, four years later, the child is going to acquire the belief that there is a tiger and the micro base of that belief at that moment will be NP_{131}, the NP_{131} that is formed in the brain of the newborn baby is *not* a realization of a representation because that NP_{131} of the baby is not caused in such a way that ideally its cause would be the presence of a tiger.

The double duty that the label $R^*(p)$ is being asked to do here may need some clarification. On the one hand, $R^*(p)$ is a property that is functionally defined and that locally supervenes on the neurophysiological states of the organism. So any one of the many neurophysiological micro bases of $R^*(p)$ is sufficient to determine a tokening of this property. In this sense, the disjunction of all the possible micro bases is perhaps identical with $R^*(p)$. On the other hand, if in a token appearance of $R^*(p)$, it functions as a representation of p, then its identity *as a representational structure* ceases to be fully determinable by the features of its micro base. The $R^*(p)$ that is a carrier for $R(p)$ is no longer definable by the neurophysiological states of the organism. Its identity conditions are now given by the identity conditions for $R(p)$. The distinction that needs to be observed here is perhaps clearer in the sunburn case. On the one hand, the macro condition that may be functionally defined by how it looks and feels, is fully supervenient on the condition of the skin cells. Its identity can be given in purely physiological terms. But if, in a token case, that macro condition (or one of its micro bases) is caused by sun rays, that type of condition is now determined by what sort of skin conditions sun rays will cause under the specific circumstances that surround the token case. What makes the skin condition a sunburn is not that one of the possible micro bases has obtained; it is rather that it was caused by the sun rays.

Now, looking at the effect side, what makes $B^*(r)$ constitute an intentional behavior, that is, $B(r)$, is that it is, among other things, caused by $R^*(p)$. In saying this, I am helping myself to one among several possible conceptions of intentional behavior. I shall take it here that a movement of the limbs constitutes intentional behavior if that movement is caused nondeviantly by the intentional states of the organism, specifically if it is caused by structures that constitute the belief-desire system of the organism. Thus, a rising of the arm in a reflex attempt to regain one's balance while walking on a tightrope will not be intentional behavior. But the very same kind of motion of the arm that is caused by the desire to greet someone will be. I shall not argue for this view here. I will simply assume it to be the correct view of action.

At t, NP_{131} will cause the micro structure of $B^*(r)$, $m(B^*(r))$. The identity conditions for $m(B^*(r))$ come again from pure neurophysiology, from the description of the extension and flexion of specific muscles in a precise pattern and frequency. Of course, just as NP_{131} was a realization of $R^*(p)$, and hence a representation of p, $m(B^*(r))$ is a realization of the intentional behavior *running*, and thereby a micro description of a token of that behavior. But it is not the case that $m(B^*(r))$ is a token of intentional behavior owing to the fact that it was caused by NP_{131}. And this is the *key*. NP_{131} is sufficient to bring about a realization of $B^*(r)$. But just as NP_{131} was *not* sufficient to make it the case that $R^*(p)$ had the property of being a representation, it is also *not* sufficient to bring about a $B^*(r)$ that has the property of being intentional behavior. Recall the example of the newborn baby. When NP_{131} is induced by some haphazard cortical activity, and it causes twitches in the baby's leg muscles that are identical to the movements used in running, the baby would not be running, nor trying to run. In these cases the base is insufficient to determine that the state supervening on it is a structure that constitutes some globally supervenient property. And this is the crucial difference between simple cases of supervenience and cases of supervenience where the locally supervenient properties are the "carriers" of globally supervenient properties.

In other words, the superimposition of a globally supervenient property on a locally supervenient property gives rise to a causal structure that is significantly different from the causal structure we find in examples like the standard temperature case.

The argument I have just given may appear to be fallacious. For I seem to be arguing that just because under certain conditions NP_{131} fails to cause an intentional behavior, when an intentional behavior *is* caused, the cause event's being NP_{131} cannot be its causally effective property. It might be suggested that the following analogy unmasks the fallacy involved: suppose a match is struck, and it lights. Surely its being struck qualifies as a causally effective property, notwithstanding the fact that if there had been no oxygen in the room, the same amount of heat produced in the tip as was produced when the match did light would not have resulted in a flame. I think the putative analogy is dissimilar to the intentional behavior case in an important way, and this dissimilarity reveals that the objection misses the point. The causal structure of the intentional behavior case has an added complexity that fails to obtain in the match striking case. To describe this added element, we need to go back to the token case where, at t, R^*, conceived purely functionally, causes B^*, conceived as limb movements. This causal relation supervenes on the causal relation between NP_{131} and $m(B^*)$, just as the causal relation between a token increase in temperature and the corresponding token rise in the mercury column supervened on (or was said to be parasitic upon) the causal relation between the micro events. But superimposed on this causal story is a different causal story: at t, R^* constitutes a representation of p, and the fact that R^* causes B^* makes it the case that B^* is intentional. As we said, NP_{131}'s causing $m(B^*(r))$, and hence being causally sufficient for $B^*(r)$, is *not* what makes it the case that $B^*(r)$ constitutes intentional behavior. Hence, the causal relation between a token case of $R^*(p)$'s having representational properties and $B^*(r)$'s constituting a piece of intentional behavior does not supervene on (it cannot be said to be parasitic upon) the causal relation between NP_{131} and $m(B^*(r))$. I will label the type of causal relation that exists between locally supervenient properties that function as structures that constitute globally supervenient properties "nonreducible supervenient causation."

Until now, we have been conducting our discussion of causal relevance by focusing our attention on the cause event's properties. However, a moment's reflection will show that whether a property of the cause event is causally relevant or not may, and usually does, depend on which property of the effect event we are focused on.

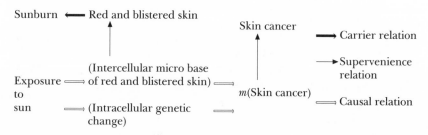

Figure 5

For example, what was causally relevant to Socrates' dying was his drinking the hemlock, not his drinking out of a vial of such and such dimensions. And conversely what made Socrates' drinking hemlock causally relevant to the effect was the fact that the effect had the property of being a death of Socrates. That very same property, that is, the property of being a drinking of hemlock, was not causally relevant to the effect's occurring *in prison*.

Carrying the point to representations, if we take an R^*, focusing on its purely physical (syntactic) properties, and a B^*, focusing on its being a sequence of limb movements, then the causal relevance of R^*'s instantiating those syntactic properties in the production of B^* *qua* limb movement will depend on, or be parasitic upon, the causal ties that exist at the micro level. But R^*'s constituting a representation of something does have causal relevance to the production of a B^*'s being intentional behavior. And this causal connection at the token level is independent of the micro story; it is not parasitic on the causal tie at the micro level.

The contribution made by the effect end of this story cannot be overemphasized. Its role is best seen when we contrast a belief-caused action with a different type of case. Suppose that when the skin is exposed to sun rays for a length of time, sometimes both of the following two things happen: (1) certain changes occur in the intercellular tissue of the epidermis that forms the micro base of the skin's turning red and blistering; (2) certain changes are induced in the intracellular structure of the epidermis whereby the amino acid sequences in the RNA manufacture are altered. Suppose each of these changes is causally necessary and the two together are sufficient for skin cancer. A tokening of these relations is depicted in Figure 5.

Here the skin's being red and blistered is a locally supervenient carrier of the globally supervenient property of being a sunburn. But skin cancer is not a carrier of any such globally supervenient property.

In contrast with the belief-action story, here it seems that the skin's being red and blistered is at most only a partial cause of the skin cancer, and it is so only because the intercellular condition is a partial cause of the micro base of the skin cancer. Here the fact that the skin's being red and blistered is a carrier of its being a sunburn does not do any additional causal work. Even if it may be natural to think that the skin condition's being a sunburn is what causes the cancer, I maintain it is a mistake to think so. Here is the reason. Suppose each of the two necessary causes of cancer can be caused by different things. Say the first can be caused by a viral infection or exposure to the sun and the second can be caused by irradiation by radium isotopes or by exposure to the sun. In the token situation, when both the intercellular condition and the intracellular condition are caused by exposure to sun rays, it is correct to identify that exposure as the cause of cancer. The exposure is also the cause of the red and blistered skin. That is in fact what qualifies that macro skin condition to be a sunburn. But whatever causal relevance the macro skin condition has to the production of cancer is played by the intercellular condition. The fact that the macro skin condition is an effect of the cause of the intercellular condition does not confer any additional causal power to the macro skin condition.

The difference between the sunburn and the belief-action scenarios is the crucial fact that in the latter the effect in question is the individual's possessing some locally supervenient property that is the carrier of a globally supervenient property, whereas in the sunburn scenario, cancer is just a locally supervenient property, period.

In other words, it is essential to the defense of my thesis that both the effect and cause sides have these pairs of properties where one is the carrier for the other. Furthermore, in the intentional behavior case, the globally supervenient properties in the cause and the effect sides are logically (formally) connected. The effect wouldn't have the global property it has (i.e., wouldn't be intentional behavior) unless the cause has the global property *it* has (unless it is a belief or a desire). Recall that when I argued for the thesis that NP_{131} is not a causally efficacious property in the production of the behavior's being an intentional behavior, I entertained an objection to the effect that the argument was fallacious and that if one accepted my argument, one would have to deny that striking a match was causally efficacious in the lighting of the match. I suggested that the match analogy fails to establish a fallacy in the argument because the intentional behavior case has an added complexity. We now have identified this complexity. In the behavior case, for the effect event to be intentional behavior, it is logically necessary that it be caused by a property of the cause event for which being NP_{131} is not sufficient. This is what gives the effect event the three properties depicted in Figure 4 – $m(B(r))$, $B^*(r)$, and $B(r))$ – and makes the property of being a limb movement (i.e., $B^*(r)$) a carrier for the property of being an intentional behavior (i.e., $B(r)$). On the other hand, in the match striking case, the effect event has at most two sets of properties: the physicochemical properties of the micro base and the supervenient property of being a flame. To make the analogy fit, we need to imagine a second gas, say, schmoxygen, which also sustains a flame, and suppose that a match's being "lit" is a causally defined property: a match is "lit" only if its flame is sustained by oxygen (not by schmoxygen). My argument for the intentional behavior case presumes that in our imaginary match case, when the match "lights," the match's being struck is not the causally effective property for its being "lit"; the causally effective property is its being struck *in the presence of oxygen.*

It might appear that in confronting the objection the way I did, I have trivialized my thesis. For I seem to have rested my case for the causal efficacy of a property on the (empirically vacuous) logical necessity of the effect's being caused by that property. I think this appearance is due to the fact that I have been focusing on the contrast between cases where a limb movement is intentional and cases where it is not (e.g., an arm raising that is a greeting and an "identical" arm raising that is a reflex). The difference between the two types of cases does lie just in whether the limb movement is caused by a belief-type representational structure or not. But this logical point does not invalidate the empirical relation between a given piece of behavior and the particular representational structures that cause it. For any behavior, it is an empirical question as to which (if any) of the many possible representational structures was causally relevant to it. So to maintain that the belief that p and the desire that it be the case that r were the causally effective structures in the behavior's being such and such is not to make a vacuous definitional point.

To summarize, then, the nonreducible causal relation between a structure that plays a representational role and an output that constitutes intentional behavior is the source of the irreducibility of the causal role of such supervenient properties. In fact, it is this irreducible causal role, which is derived from the independent identity conditions for these supervenient properties, that saves these properties from death by epiphenomenalism. If this is true, then we have a possible explanation of why folk psychology has been able to hold its own against all attacks aimed at its demise.

I need to issue a disclaimer, and, in doing so, express again my objective in this essay. I have not given any independent arguments for the indispensability of representational structures "broadly" conceived. A skeptic of such structures can quite easily dismiss the main arguments of this essay by insisting that I have given no reason to accept into our ontology the three-tiered property talk implied by Figure

4. The skeptic would maintain that we should dispense with the globally supervenient properties altogether and be content with a structure analogous to the standard temperature case, and that it is just a matter of personal preference, or taste, as to whether we need to accommodate in addition to the micro bases the locally supervenient properties in our ontology. Nothing I have said here was designed to influence this kind of skeptic. My target was more modest. I took myself to be arguing against those skeptics who give *as their reason* for being skeptical of such structures that at the token level *all the causal work that exists* can be described in terms of the causal efficacy of the micro properties, and hence we have no need for the globally supervenient properties. I take myself to have shown that this is *not* a good reason, that if one is willing to embrace these global properties, the causal role they will play is not reducible to the causal role played by micro properties. To put the same point from a different perspective, I can say this. If one is going to talk the language of folk psychology, it just will not do to envisage the ontology of folk psychology to be confined to properties that are locally supervenient. If one did, those properties will have the dubious ontological status that is conferred on properties like temperature, valence, or refraction index: useful in explanation and in other pragmatic concerns, but ultimately dispensable from a hard-nosed inventory of what there is. So if one is going to talk the language of folk psychology, one would be well advised to refer to some globally supervenient properties of the kind I have been discussing. In other words, my thesis has a consequence that seems to be diametrically opposed to the received view, according to which one should not embrace these globally supervenient properties because their causal roles are suspect. So one should confine oneself only to locally supervenient properties. According to my thesis, if one did so confine oneself, one would be depriving oneself of the grounds for maintaining the legitimacy of folk psychological properties. Those grounds emerge only when globally supervenient properties are allowed into our ontology.

NOTES

1. As far as I know, the identification of the different strengths of the supervenience relation was first offered by Kim (1984a). An exhaustive list of the varieties of supervenience and a useful discussion summarizing the literature that investigates the logical relations among them is to be found in Seager (1991). The two definitions I offer are adapted from Seager's definitions.
2. An alternative way of defining (SL) is this: It is nomologically necessary that

if two individuals differ in some macro property S, then those individuals also differ in some physical micro property.

3. In these definitions, the macro properties are said to be the *supervenient properties*, and the micro properties are referred to as the *base properties*.

4. This ploy is used to good effect by Segal and Sober (1991). Seager (1991) introduces the notion of a *constitutive relation* to get around the same problem.

5. Kim (1987).

6. Horgan (1989).

7. Different versions of this approach are to be found in the writings of many philosophers. Stampe (1977), Millikan (1984), and Dretske (1988) are just three examples.

8. Fodor has been betting on this difference between the macro level and the micro level in arguing for the causal efficacy of the macro. See Fodor (1989).

9. See Enç (1986) for an investigation of how one goes about answering this version of the question.

10. For example, if the event that occurred two hours after I left Wisconsin was a tornado, then the following two claims have the same truth value: (1a) the event that occurred two hours after I left Wisconsin caused the destruction; (1b) the tornado caused the destruction. But it seems clear that the first of the following claims is *false*, and the second is true; (2a) the event's being an event that occurred two hours after I left Wisconsin is what caused the destruction; (2b) the event's being a tornado is what caused the destruction. It is in virtue of the difference between (2a) and (2b) that one takes *being a tornado* as a "causally relevant" property of the event and *occurring two hours after I left Wisconsin* not to be a causally relevant property.

11. It is no accident that most philosophers who are nonrealists about folk psychology are convinced about the nonexistence of a physical resolution for psychological properties.

12. See Kim (1993, p. 205).

13. Dong Ryul Choo, who in an unpublished manuscript has provided an encyclopedic survey of some 75 articles on this issue, classifies the different types of attempts into three categories: (i) the counterfactual solution, (ii) the nomological solution, and (iii) the epiphenomenal solution. Roughly, the counterfactual solution amounts to observing that in cases of real causal efficacy, it is true that if the supervenient property$_1$ had not been instantiated, then the supervenient property$_2$ would not have been instantiated, but that it is false that if the micro base of the supervenient property$_1$ had not been instantiated, then the supervenient property$_2$ would not have been instantiated (see, e.g., LePore and Loewer 1987, and Horgan 1991). The nomological solution merely requires there to be a law that holds between supervenient property$_1$ and supervenient property$_2$ (see, e.g., Fodor 1989). And finally the epiphenomenal solution admits that the causal efficacy of the supervenient property is owing to the causal efficacy of the micro base when the micro and the macro levels

are related in a certain way and the conditions of the nomological solution hold (see, e.g., Kim 1984b and Segal and Sober 1991).
14. Mougin's example shoots down all of these except for the nomological solution. But it is not hard to find counterexamples to that, too.
15. See Dennis Stampe (1977).

REFERENCES

Dretske, Fred. (1988). *Explanation of Behavior: Reasons in a World of Causes*. Cambridge, Mass.: MIT Press.
Enç, Berent. (1986). "Essentialism without Individual Essences: Causation, Kinds, Supervenience, and Restricted Identities," in *Midwest Studies in Philosophy*, vol. 11, pp. 403–26, Peter A. French, Theodore E. Uehling, and Howard K. Wettstein, eds., Minneapolis: University of Minnesota Press.
Fodor, Jerry. (1989). "Making Mind Matter More," reprinted in his *A Theory of Content and Other Essays*. Cambridge Mass.: MIT Press, 1990, pp. 59–79
Horgan, Terrence. (1989). "Mental Quausation," *Philosophical Perspectives*, 3, 47–76.
  (1991). "Actions, Reasons and the Explanatory Role of Content," in *Dretske and His Critics*, Brian McLaughlin, ed., Oxford: Basil Blackwell, pp. 73–101
Kim, Jaegwon. (1984a). "Concepts of Supervenience," *Philosophy and Phenomenological Research*, 45, 153–76.
  (1984b). "Epiphenomenal and Supervenient Causation" in *Midwest Studies in Philosophy*, vol. 9, 257–78. Peter A. French, Theodore E. Uehling, and Howard K. Wettstein, eds., Minneapolis: University of Minnesota Press.
  (1987). "'Strong' and 'Global' Supervenience Revisited," *Philosophy and Phenomenological Research*, 48, 315–26.
  (1993). "The Non-Reductivist's Troubles with Mental Causation," in *Mental Causation*, John Heil and Alfred Mele, eds., Oxford: Clarendon Press, pp. 189–210.
LePore, Ernest, and Loewer, Barry. (1987). "Mind Matters," *Journal of Philosophy*, 84, 630–42.
Millikan, Ruth. (1984). *Language, Thought, and Other Biological Categories: New Foundations for Realism*. Cambridge, Mass.: MIT Press.
Seager, William. (1991). *Metaphysics of Consciousness*. London: Routledge.
Segal, Gabriel, and Sober, Elliot. (1991). "The Causal Efficacy of Content," *Philosophical Studies*, 62: 155–84.
Stampe, Dennis. (1977). "Toward a Causal Theory of Linguistic Representation," in *Midwest Studies in Philosophy*, vol 2, pp. 42–63. Peter A. French, Theodore E. Uehling, and Howard K. Wettstein, eds., Minneapolis: University of Minnesota Press.

Physicalism, Supervenience, and Dependence

PAUL K. MOSER AND J. D. TROUT

Contemporary physicalists typically reject two opposing positions concerning the relation between physical and psychological properties: Cartesian dualism and reductive physicalism. In doing so, they embrace some kind of *nonreductive* physicalism entailing that psychological properties depend on, but are irreducible to, physical properties. This essay assesses the viability of such nonreductive physicalism. In particular, it examines whether nonreductive physicalism can, with help from certain nonreductive supervenience relations, steer a clear course between Cartesian dualism and reductive physicalism. We shall see that the course is far from clear, owing to complications facing a physicalist account of the pertinent notion of dependence. Physicalist psychofunctionalism in particular, we shall contend, raises serious problems for current conceptions of nonreductive mind–body supervenience relations, owing to its requiring relatively local causal mechanisms for the occurrence of psychological properties. Let us begin with sketches of the two positions nonreductive physicalists aim to avoid: dualism and reductionism.

1. Dualism and Independence

Cartesian dualism affirms the ontological independence of the psychological from the physical, in a sense to be specified. Cartesian *substance* dualism implies that psychological substances (e.g., thinking *individuals*) do not depend ontologically on physical substances or properties. Cartesian *property* dualism implies that psychological properties – psychological features that can be exemplified by individuals – do not depend ontologically on physical substances or properties. Cartesians, following Aristotle, might distinguish substances and properties roughly as follows: properties are predicable of things and are multiply realizable, but substances are individuals that are not thus predicable or realizable. Cartesian dualism needs clarification of the kind of ontological dependence relevant to those two species of dualism.

The ontological dependence of something, X, on another thing, Y, is not captured by the claim that X depends for its existence on Y. X

might depend for its existence on Y owing to the causal dependence of X on Y given the actual laws of nature. In that case, Y is a causal prerequisite for the existence of X under the actual laws of nature. Such causal dependence is allowable by Cartesians denying ontological dependence of the mental on the physical. In particular, Cartesians can grant that under the actual laws of nature, certain bodily events are causal preconditions for certain of our mental events. Descartes himself evidently held that mental substances necessarily lack physical features; but one need not regard the ontological independence of the mental from the physical as entailing that view. The rejection of that view, according to many philosophers, would facilitate an account of causal interaction between the mental and the physical.

Cartesians endorse the following kind of independence of the mental from the physical: it is coherently conceivable that mental substances, properties, states, or events exist without physical substances, properties, states, or events (see Descartes 1637, p. 101; 1641a, p. 190). Coherent conceivability, we may assume, is just conceivability without contradiction. If it is coherently conceivable that something, X, exists without something, Y, then, on the Cartesian view, X is ontologically independent of Y. In particular, since it is coherently conceivable that thinking exists without a body, according to the Cartesian view, thinking is ontologically independent of a body. We can put this point in terms of concepts: the concept of thinking does not depend, for its semantic determinacy, on the concept of body (see Descartes 1641c, p. 101). Descartes drew controversial ontological lessons from conceptual points of that sort, offering conceivability arguments for his ontological dualism (see 1637, p. 101; 1641b, p. 23).[1] Many philosophers resist Descartes's inference of an actual ontological distinction regarding mind and body from a coherently conceivable distinction between the two.

Let us continue, for the sake of familiar taxonomy, with a Cartesian understanding of ontological dependence wherein X depends ontologically on Y if and only if it is not coherently conceivable that X exists without Y. Ontological independence of X from Y, on this view, permits causal dependence of X on Y. Even if it is coherently conceivable that X exists without Y, it can still be that, owing to the actual laws of nature, Y is a causal precondition of X. While endorsing the ontological independence of the mind from the body, Descartes held that the mind is "substantially united to the body" (1641c, p. 102). Dualist interactionists can regard such "substantial unity" as involving (perhaps among other things) extensive causal interaction between mind and body.

A Cartesian view of the ontological independence of the mental from the physical threatens the view that physicalism, construed as entailing a mind–body identity thesis, is conceptually or analytically true. A Cartesian view of ontological independence also challenges those versions of physicalism implying that certain psychological concepts are *defined* (if only partly) in terms of the typical physical causes of the relevant psychological states identified by those concepts. (On such versions of physicalism, see Lewis 1966; Armstrong 1968; Lewis and Armstrong nonetheless regard their mind–body identity theses as contingently true.)[2] If we define 'pain', for instance, in terms of the typical bodily causes of pain, we shall have to reject the coherent conceivability of pain without bodies. (See Lewis 1980 for an attempt to handle this problem.) Proponents of physicalism as a contingently true thesis can, however, accommodate ontological independence of a Cartesian sort, as long as they grant the coherent conceivability of mental phenomena without physical phenomena.

Physicalists of any stripe, whether reductive or nonreductive, reject a certain Cartesian position regarding composition: namely, the implication of Cartesian substance dualism that one's mind (regarded as a temporal individual) is composed, or made up, of a nonphysical substance different in kind from one's body. They likewise reject the Cartesian view that some mental properties are actually instantiated by nonphysical entities, entities not spatially extended. Physicalists are uniformly monistic in their view that all actual entities that instantiate mental properties are physical. They divide, however, over some theses about mental properties, including that all mental properties are equivalent or identical to some conjunction of physical properties. Nonreductive physicalists (e.g., Boyd 1980; Post 1987) reject that thesis, allowing that mental properties can be instantiated in a nonphysical world. Such physicalists include functionalists holding that mental properties differ from physical properties in virtue of certain causal or functional roles the former have. The causal or functional roles that determine mental properties, according to many physicalists, are specified by the taxonomies of our best psychological theories. The pertinent causal or functional roles can depend on systemic relational considerations independent of considerations of the composition of what instantiates mental properties. Mental properties can thus be multiply realizable in compositionally different systems.

Some philosophers express physicalist supervenience with the slogan, "No mental difference without a physical difference."[3] The consequences of this claim are not clear, however, in the absence of some principle specifying what constitutes a permissible difference. There are elucidations of this slogan that many physicalist supervenience theorists would reject. For example, although many supervenience theorists would allow that some relational properties are real, most contemporary physicalists hold that the world is not relational all the way down; in particular, they hold that the (or, at least, certain) properties of physics (in particular, regarding ultimate constituents of the physical world) are nonrelational, or intrinsic. (One might hold that a property of an object is nonrelational if and only if that property's identity does not depend on its relations to other properties or individuals.) The physicalists in question can hold nonetheless that at least some psychologically taxonomic properties are relational. A physicalist might reject, accordingly, the claim that the intrinsic properties of a person's body determine the type-properties of a psychological state.

Imagine, for example, the same token physical state in two different possible worlds, W_1 and W_2.[4] If we assume that the identity of the physical state is completely determined by its intrinsic properties (and the intrinsic properties of its parts), then the same token-state can be contingently identical with two type-distinct psychological states. This is possible if psychological states are identified relationally. If (but perhaps not only if) W_1 and W_2 have different physical laws, then different psychological laws could hold concerning the bearer of a certain state in W_1 and the bearer of the physically identical state in W_2. (We shall return to an analogous case in Section 3.) Consequently, the same physical state, nonrelationally (and thus nonintentionally) individuated, could be implicated in type-distinct psychological processes, as long as the psychological states with which the physical state are contingently identical have had type-distinct causes. On such a scenario, it would be false that there is "no difference without a physical difference," when that difference concerns the nonrelational physical properties of the body.

Nonreductive physicalists oppose familiar theses about reducing mental properties to physical properties. Let us briefly consider those theses. After doing so, we shall ask whether certain versions of nonreductive physicalism relying on supervenience relations can maintain the dependence of the mental on the physical without commitment to reduction of some sort.

2. Reduction: Definitional and Nomic

Physicalists favoring supervenience accounts of mind–body relations often seek to avoid reductive versions of physicalism. There is, however, considerable disagreement about how to characterize the relation of reduction and about various other basic issues concerning reduction. For some, the objects of reduction are syntactic (Nagel 1961; Carnap 1966; Causey 1977). For others, the objects of reduction are ontological (Oppenheim and Putnam 1958; Hooker 1981). According to traditional, formal accounts of reduction, theories, laws, and terms can be objects of reduction. Reduction concerning laws and terms, involving nomic and definitional reduction, is of special interest in this section. One law, for instance, is reducible to another if the law targeted for reduction is logically derivable from laws in the reducing domain.

Reduction is a relation between two theoretically characterized domains of entities, whether postulated objects, properties, processes, states, events, laws, or terms. (A postulated entity need not be an actual entity.) A primary goal of reduction is ontological unification, at least regarding ontological postulates. Reduction has taken a variety of forms in the history of science, too many to document here. It is, moreover, still unclear, after persistent attempts to clarify, what the exact criteria are for the success of a reduction. Because identities involving different theoretically characterized domains are so seldom established, judgments of degree of reduction require judgments of theoretical similarity. There is still some dispute, however, about the relevant dimensions of similarity. Relevant proposed criteria are ontological, explanatory, and semantic. Perhaps the satisfaction of more than one condition is required. We would not regard a reduction as successful, for example, unless the reducing theory can replace – without loss of explanatory power – all the *explanations* of the reduced theory, including its ontological postulates. Even so, how should similarity of ontology, explanation, and meaning be assessed? The most commonly employed measure is causal, treating ontology, explanation, and meaning as having been successfully reduced (a "retentive" reduction) when the postulated objects of the higher-level domain have been replaced with those of similarly assigned causal role.

The ontology of psychology is connected to the ontology of the physical by means of identity statements, alternatively referred to as correspondence rules, bridge laws, and coordinating definitions. Since identity is a symmetrical relation but reduction is not, typically we advert to some nonformal, theoretical assumptions to specify direction of dependence. Reduction can be a relation between older and newer theories (we might call this "old–new reduction"), or it can be a relation between a higher-level theory, such as psychology, and a lower-level one, such as physics (this has been called "interlevel reduction," a kind of reduction from the "bottom up"). We shall be mainly concerned with bottom-up reduction.

In the case of interlevel, or bottom-up, reduction, bridge laws or identity statements typically, though not necessarily, link macroscopic properties of the higher level to microscopic properties within the reducing theory. This relation is often thought to have epistemic significance, because the macroscopic properties, such as temperature, are observable, but the reducing properties are theoretical, or unobservable. Reduction, in any case, grades from smooth to radical, from ontologically retentive to ontologically eliminative. The reduction of thermodynamics to statistical mechanics is deemed smooth, while the reduction of the theory of vital spirits by physical accounts of animacy and locomotion is radical, or eliminative. Reductions are normally as uneven as the theories involved. For example, alchemy postulated personal, projective mechanisms of bonding that were eliminated by modern accounts, but nevertheless endorsed practices and vocabulary that sometimes isolated elements recognized by modern taxonomy, such as lead. When a theory's ontological postulates have been reduced or eliminated, its laws are not long to follow.

Nomic Reduction

Psychophysical laws express counterfactual supporting relations between mental states and physical states. In a successful nomic reduction, one condition that must be satisfied is *correlation* of a minimal sort: the holding of psychological laws is accompanied by the holding of physical laws. According to nomic reduction, therefore, there is no instantiation of a particular psychological law that does not co-occur with the instantiation of a particular physical law.

On the correlational interpretation of psychophysical laws, the bridge statement links the instantiation of the psychological law with the instantiation of the physical law. The bridge statement, in fact, just is the psychophysical law. This general kind of correlation is compatible, however, with the independence of the mental from the physical. It is conceivable that the psychological laws in question could be instantiated by relations among nonphysical kinds, instantiations that co-occur with actual physical-object relations complying with relevant physical laws.

Psychophysical reduction is thought to involve more than just type–type co-occurrence in nearby regions of space; it requires the *dependence*, in a certain sense, of the mental on the physical. It is only by acknowledging such dependence, according to many physicalists, that we maintain the ontological primacy of the physical. The relevant sort of dependence, it is arguable, can be captured only in counterfactual form. In accord with this line, the second necessary condition on a successful nomic reduction is that of *counterfactual dependence:* true counterfactual-supporting psychological generalizations hold *because of, or in virtue of,* counterfactual-supporting physical generalizations.

Nomic reduction, as the name suggests, concerns the reduction of laws from one domain to another – from those of thermodynamics to those of statistical mechanics, Newtonian mechanics to special relativity, and so on. Because the fundamental elements of nomic reduction are laws, the generalizations of the higher-level theory must be higher-level laws, and those laws must be characterized in terms of generalizations that are laws in the more basic, reducing theory. A successful nomic reduction must therefore state appropriate correspondence relations among generalizations that are *taxonomic* in the home discipline. Nomic reduction is thus thought to preclude liberal strategies of reduction, according to which a higher-level law is putatively reduced to a disjunction of numerous and diverse lower-level laws. Even if each generalization of the basic domain is a law, the corresponding disjunction may not be. There is a moral here for accounts of mind–body relations that employ this liberal strategy to accommodate the benefits of multiple-realizability arguments: namely, reduction to a disjunction is not necessarily reduction to a theoretically taxonomic category or property.

When the higher-level law is linked biconditionally to a lower-level law, we have a type–type nomic reduction. Although bridge laws are understood to state identities between two types, reductions are seldom that smooth. Typically, a higher-level (e.g., macroscopic) law is reduced by a restricted class of lower-level laws. Snell's law, for example, can be explained by a class of laws about electromagnetic radiation, of which light is a certain sort, and laws concerning features of diffraction. Reductions are directional, moving from higher-level, macroscopic objects to those more basic. Mere correlations between high-level and lower-level laws are therefore insufficient to represent the direction of, and thus to effect, a reduction. To capture the direction of causal dependence, bridge statements must support counterfactuals.[5] The resulting prospects for nomic reduction will be assessed in Section 4.

Definitional Reduction

One way to achieve the relevant identities – without attention to the history of science – is to make reduction a *semantic* relation between the vocabulary of the higher-level and lower-level theory. This effort took a variety of forms in philosophy of science, first in the operationalist movement, and later in law-cluster accounts of theoretical definition of a sort found in Carnap (1966). Given definitional reduction, what we *mean* by some higher-level (e.g., macro) predicate is what is meant by predicates at a lower level. One such definitional reduction comes from the claim that 'temperature' just means 'mean kinetic motion'. Such definitions are called conventions, coordinating definitions, bridge statements, or meaning postulates, though they execute the same function under these diverse titles: they semantically link theoretical terms of the reducing theory to those of the reduced theory.

Definitional approaches to reduction raise a couple of noteworthy difficulties in connection with our current concerns about mind–body relations. First, because the reduced term (e.g., 'temperature') is *se-*

mantically identified with whatever is meant by the reducing term (e.g., 'mean kinetic motion'), definitional reduction entails that children, pre-kinetic-theory scientists, and modern novices must be said to mean whatever occurs on the other side of the identity sign. Because, moreover, definitional reductionism is a semantic rather than an ontological thesis, definitional reductionists cannot take refuge in the claim (as central state-type-reductionists had) that they are only committed to the position that mean kinetic motion is what temperature *is*, not what 'temperature' *means*. This consequence seems to violate a perfectly innocent semantic assumption that separates meaning and reference. The current problem bears directly on any attempt to define mental terms by physical terms.

The second difficulty arising from definitional reduction – a difficulty central to our current purposes – is that such reduction is obviously too demanding for nonreductive physicalist supervenience. Because definitional reduction identifies the psychological term with whatever is meant by the reducing physical (e.g., biological) term, it supplies a chauvinistic interpretation of the meanings of psychological terms. It rules out as semantically incoherent the possibility of psychological states having an atypical cause or basis, and thus rules out the sort of multiple realizability of psychological states characteristically permitted by (nonreductive) physicalist functional definitions. Definitional reduction, then, rules out the kind of multiple realizability endorsed by typical nonreductive supervenience theories of psychological phenomena.[6]

3. Supervenience and Dependence

Nonreductive physicalists reject definitional and nomic reduction of mental properties to physical properties, but nonetheless endorse monism about what instantiates mental properties. Current versions of nonreductive physicalism typically take their lead from Donald Davidson's following remarks:

> Although the position I describe denies there are psychophysical laws, it is consistent with the view that mental characteristics are in some sense dependent, or supervenient, on physical characteristics. Such supervenience might be taken to mean that there cannot be two events alike in all physical respects but differing in some mental respect, or that an object cannot alter in some mental respect without altering in some physical respect. Dependence or supervenience of this kind does not entail reducibility through law or definition. (1970, p. 215)

Davidson recommends a brand of physicalism wherein (a) all events, including psychological events, are physical events, (b) psychological events somehow supervene on physical events, and (c) no definitional or nomic reduction (at least via strict laws) holds between the psychological and the physical.

Davidson sometimes puts his thesis of supervenience as indicating a relation between predicates rather than events:

> The notion of supervenience, as I have used it, is best thought of as a relation between a predicate and a set of predicates in a language: a predicate *p* is supervenient to a set of predicates *S* if for every pair of objects such that *p* is true of one and not of the other there is a predicate of *S* that is true of one and not of the other. All the individual entities that can be distinguished using the supervenient predicate can be distinguished using the subvenient predicates. (1985, p. 242)

Davidson relies on supervenience to avoid the troublesome views that mental properties are physical properties and that there are strict laws connecting mental properties and physical properties. (A "strict" law, according to Davidson [1993, p. 8], is "free from caveats and *ceteris paribus* clauses.") He wants supervenience to allow him to shun the reductive view that if mental events are identical to physical events, then the properties of mental events are just physical properties or at least are reducible to some conjunction of physical properties (1985, p. 243).

Davidson's characterization of supervenience in terms of predicates does not accommodate his earlier talk of mental characteristics as "in some sense dependent, or supervenient, on physical characteristics." Consider a case where, for every pair of objects, if a predicate, *p*, is true of one but not of the other, then a predicate from a set of predicates, *S*, is true of the one but not of the other. Such a case does not necessarily involve the *dependence* of the properties identified or expressed by *p* on properties identified or expressed by predicates from *S*. The properties identified or expressed by *p* may simply be constantly conjoined, in a suitably coincidental Humean fashion, with properties identified or expressed by predicates from *S*. Davidson's 1985 characterization of supervenience fails, then, to capture his idea, in "Mental Events," that "mental characteristics are in some sense dependent, or supervenient, on physical characteristics."[7] We shall presently consider some approaches to the kind of dependence pertinent to mind–body supervenience.

Mental–physical dependence of some sort, as indicated by Davidson, seems essential to any kind of mental–physical supervenience appropriate to physicalism. David Lewis notes:

> A supervenience thesis is a denial of independent variation. . . . To say that so-and-so supervenes on such-and-such is to say that there can be no difference in respect of so-and-so without difference in respect of such-and-such. Beauty of statues supervenes on their shape, size, and colour, for instance, if no two statues, in the same or different worlds, ever differ in beauty without also differing in shape or size or colour. (1983, p. 358)

Lewis explicitly accommodates a dependence thesis with his view that "supervenience means that there *could* be no difference of the one sort without difference of the other sort," adding that "without the modality [indicated by 'could'] we have nothing of interest" (1986, p. 15).

Given a dependence thesis, we can acknowledge supervenience as precluding independent variation of mental events relative to physical events. Supervenience, on this approach, is essentially a relation of *dependent variation*. This characterization is compatible with Jaegwon Kim's conclusion that "it is best to separate the covariation element from the dependency element in the relation of supervenience" (1990, p. 16). Mental–physical covariation, we have noted, does not entail mental–physical dependence. The relevant kind of dependence is, moreover, ontic and not (merely) epistemic; after all, supervenience theses are not (merely) epistemic.

What about *necessary* mental–physical covariation? Suppose it is necessarily the case that for every pair of objects, if a predicate, *p*, is true of one but not of the other, then a predicate from a set of predicates, *S*, is true of the one but not of the other. Does such a case involve the relevant kind of dependence of the properties identified or expressed by *p* on properties identified or expressed by predicates from *S*? The properties identified or expressed by *p* would not in that case be coincidentally conjoined with properties identified or expressed by predicates from *S*, with respect to their being instantiated by the objects in question. The operator 'necessarily' blocks such coincidental conjunction, while permitting a kind of (possibly unexplained) covariation between ontologically distinct domains, even between the mental and the physical.

Let us grant, if only for the sake of argument, that necessary covariation entails *some* kind of dependence, even if not the kind pertinent to nonreductive supervenience. If 'necessarily' connotes *conceptual* necessity, or analyticity, *p* stands in a relation of semantic (e.g., definitional) dependence toward predicates in *S*. We might characterize such dependence as follows: one's understanding *p* (or some synonymous predicate) requires one's understanding a predicate in *S* (or some synonymous predicate). If, in contrast, merely logical necessity obtains, then *p* logically depends on predicates in *S;* that is, *p*'s being true of something logically requires that a predicate of *S* be true of it too. If, however, causal necessity obtains, then *p* depends causally on predicates in *S;* in other words, *p*'s being true of something causally requires, at least in worlds causally similar to the actual world, that a predicate of *S* also be true of that thing. In addition, one might introduce a special kind of metaphysical necessity concerning all worlds where certain kinds of objects exist; but let us not digress.

Nonreductive physicalists do not characterize the kind of dependence appropriate to supervenience in terms of conceptually or logically necessary covariation. Those sorts of covariation are too demanding for their nonreductive aims. Proponents of nonreductive supervenience typically seek a kind of covariation that requires neither semantic nor logical dependence of mental predicates on physical predicates. They seek a kind of logically contingent covariation that entails, nonetheless, dependence of the mental on the physical. We shall consider whether a certain kind of necessary covariation can serve the purposes of nonreductive physicalism.

The commitment by Davidson and other supervenience theorists to mental–physical dependence, of a sort exceeding mere covariation, involves a basic tenet of physicalism: the ontological primacy of the physical. This primacy entails, at least by the lights of many physicalists, that physical entities are contingently a subvenient ontological base for mental properties. A typical way of characterizing the relevant subvenience appeals to dependent covariation that is logically contingent. The denial of any such dependence, on this approach, undermines the ontological primacy of the physical and constitutes a rejection of physicalism. We shall contend that the kind of supervenience-dependence relevant to psychofunctionalist physicalism involves not just necessary mental–physical covariation, but also support of counterfactuals involving suitable (relatively local) causal mechanisms.

How exactly can physicalists capture the pertinent kind of mental–physical dependence? Nonreductive physicalists characteristically endorse Davidson's rejection of definitional and nomic reduction of psychological properties to physical properties. They divide in various ways, however, over the preferred supervenience relation between psychological and physical phenomena.[8] One general point of division is noteworthy. Proponents of *nonglobal* supervenience rely on property-to-property relations (involving the psychological and the physical, e.g.) between individuals in just *one* possible world, such as the actual world. Proponents of *global* supervenience, in contrast, talk of various possible worlds to identify pertinent supervenience relations between psychological and physical phenomena; they thus use whole worlds as the items being compared for indiscernibility. In doing so, they compare phenomena from different possible worlds, seeking to achieve a nonreductive supervenience connection between the psychological and the physical that does not rest on particular property-to-property relations.[9] We shall consider a species of global supervenience prominent among nonreductive physicalists.

Here is a representative principle of global supervenience, offered by John Post:

(GS) Given any two physically possible worlds W_1 and W_2, if the same physical conditions obtain in both, the same nonphysical conditions obtain in both. (1991, p. 118; cf. Post 1987, p. 185)

Post recommends (GS) on the ground that it accommodates cases where something's nonphysical properties are not determined by that thing's own physical properties and physical relations or even by physical phenomena in the spatiotemporal vicinity of that thing. (GS) is designed to allow for nonphysical truths that hold only in virtue of (because they are about) the totality of physical phenomena, not in virtue of some proper part of that totality (cf. Post 1987, p. 188).

One problem with (GS) (elaborated in Moser 1993, chap. 5) is that it fails to account for physically possible worlds with atypical psychological laws. Imagine two physically possible worlds, W_1 and W_2, where (a) the same physical conditions obtain, (b) the proximate nonphysical effects of the physical conditions in W_1 and W_2 are the same, but (c) sameness lapses for the nonphysical effects of the former proximate nonphysical effects. Let us call the relevant proximate nonphysical effects "first-level psychological phenomena" and their nonphysical effects "secondary psychological phenomena."

The physical facts in W_1 and W_2 are the same and determine the same first-level psychological phenomena. Given differing laws of *psychological causation* in W_1 and W_2, however, the same first-level psychological phenomena in W_1 and W_2 do not determine the same secondary psychological phenomena. In one of many possible scenarios, psychological events of assenting generate *dispositional,* or habit-like, belief-states and intention-states in W_1 but not in W_2. W_2, by hypothesis, does not share W_1's laws of psychological causation, notably with respect to assenting. This seems imaginable with only a mild exercise of imagination. The imagined situation is *psychologically uniform* at the first level but *psychologically divergent* at a secondary level. (GS), however, implies that such divergence in the case of W_1 and W_2, where the same physical conditions obtain, is not physically possible.

Since the denial of (GS) is, as just indicated, conceptually coherent, proponents must explain what sort of ground (if any) we have for thinking it true of all physically possible worlds with the same physical conditions. What sort of evidence, empirical or a priori, enables us to generalize, as in (GS), to *any* two such worlds? What sort of inference pattern, in addition, can secure such a universal generalization as (GS) on the basis of the evidence in question? Apart from cogent answers, (GS) will not belong to a warranted account of psychological phenomena.

The imagined case of psychological divergence is not necessarily a case of *actual* physical and nonphysical conditions. To falsify (GS), the foregoing example need only provide two *physically possible* worlds with psychological divergence under the same physical conditions; for (GS) concerns *any* two physically possible worlds with the same physical conditions. The case of divergence appears to be one of physically possible worlds with the same physical conditions. It seems not to violate any (known) physical law. In the absence of contrary evidence, then, we may proceed with the assumption of its being physically possible.

Friends of (GS) might claim that in all physically possible worlds with the same physical conditions and physical laws, the same laws of *psychological* causation always obtain. This claim proposes, in effect, that laws of psychological causation supervene on relevant physical conditions and physical laws. However agreeable this proposal is to physicalists, it seems not to resolve the real problem at hand. We have no compelling reason to hold that in *all* physically possible worlds with the same physical conditions and physical laws, the same laws of psychological causation always obtain. It seems quite plausible to suppose, after all, that the aforementioned case of psychological divergence at a secondary level involves physically possible worlds. The anticipated proposal is simply question begging.

Given cases of divergence, we might introduce a principle of supervenience that requires sameness of laws of *psychological* as well as physical causation. We shall then have departed significantly, however, from the sort of supervenience favored by proponents of (GS). Physicalists will be uneasy about including psychological laws in the subvenient base.

Can (GS) account for the kind of dependence, or dependent variation, invoked previously by Davidson? Following Lewis (1983), Post seeks to accommodate "what physicalists have in mind when they say that there being a nonphysical difference depends on there being a physical difference" (1987, p. 176). In fact, he recommends talk of "determination" over talk of supervenience, owing to the failure of the latter to convey, at least in ordinary language, "the dependence intended" (1987, p. 182; cf. p. 186). A general commitment to determination or supervenience as requiring dependent variation does not, however, validate (GS) as yielding a kind of dependence appropriate to physicalism.

Physicalists inclined to functionalism about mental properties (as developed in Turing machine and non–Turing machine versions by, e.g., Fodor 1981, 1987, Sober 1985) will find (GS) inadequate to yield mental–physical dependence of an appropriate sort. (This, incidentally, probably includes most contemporary physicalists.) We can make do now with the following minimal thesis offered by Ned Block:

> One characterization of functionalism that is probably vague enough to be acceptable to most functionalists is: each type of mental state is a state consisting of a disposition to act in certain ways *and to have certain mental states*, given certain sensory inputs and certain mental states. . . . Functionalists want to individuate mental states causally, and since mental states have mental causes and effects as well as sensory causes and behavioral effects, functionalists individuate mental states partly in terms of causal relations to other mental states. (1978, p. 262; cf. Fodor 1981, p. 245)

If, in accord with such generic psychofunctionalism, mental processes are causal sequences of tokens and are individuated by their causal roles in a system of tokens, then (GS) must preserve the dependence of mental states on pertinent causal roles. Does it actually do so?

Jerry Fodor has identified a constraint on psychofunctionalism that merits attention in connection with (GS) and, for that matter, in connection with any principle of mental–physical dependence. He notes that functionalism seems too easy to some philosophers, owing to the following: "Since functionalism licenses the individuation of states by reference to their causal role, it appears to allow a trivial explanation of any observed event, E, that is, it appears to postulate an E-causer" (1981, p. 247). The problem is that such talk of E-causers can be vacuous, or otherwise explanatorily mysterious, and thus ill suited for the demands of psychological explanation. Fodor recommends that a functionalist avoid this problem "by allowing functionally defined theoretical constructs only where mechanisms exist that can carry out the function and only where he has some notion of what such mechanisms might be like" (1981, p. 247). Functional characterization of mental states, on this plausible recommendation, requires specification of *causal mechanisms* suitable to the production of such states. In the absence of such specification, psychofunctionalism offers causal mystery. The pertinent relation here is (possibly atemporal) between an object's micro structure and its macro structure. If talk of "production" unavoidably connotes the causal propagation of effects *over time*, then read 'realize' instead of 'produce'; for realization of X in Y is a relation of co-occurrence between X and Y. Causal mechanisms of the relevant sort are, moreover, relatively local by nature. At least, they are more local than a whole world or even the totality of physical phenomena in a physically possible world. (Note that commitment to such relative locality of causal mechanisms does not entail psychological individualism.)

Consider, for example, the psychological processes of thinking (including their instantiated mental properties) involved in your reading this essay with understanding. This includes your discerning and remembering the truth conditions for many of this essay's claims. Given psychofunctionalism, you thereby instantiate a nexus of causal properties wherein various causal relations hold between tokens of the functional system you are. In such a case involving causally complex psychological processes, the causal relations among tokens of your functional system must be correspondingly complex. In fact, the psychological processes in question are, given psychofunctionalism, individuated by the causal relations in question. Accommodating Fodor's recommendation, we must acknowledge that the pertinent causal relations depend on suitable (relatively local) causal mechanisms, mechanisms causally adequate to yield the complex causal relations at issue. In particular, causally complex psychological processes require correspondingly complex causal relations among tokens, which in turn depend on causal mechanisms adequate to produce such causal relations.

Causal systems whose tokens have only minimal causal powers will sustain only minimal causal relations and will not sustain causally complex psychological processes. In fact, this is a causally necessary truth on any version of psychofunctionalism consistent with Fodor's recommendation about the necessity of suitable causal mechanisms. A physical system consisting of only two copper pennies, for example, is causally inadequate to yield the psychologically complex causal relations essential (on psychofunctionalism) to the psychological process of thinking about this essay. The latter psychological process causally depends on a mechanism (or a cluster of mechanisms) sufficiently powerful to generate complex causal relations of the sort essential to thinking. Absence of a causal mechanism of that sort precludes a causally viable scenario manifesting causal relations appropriate to thinking. The kind of causal relations crucial to thinking, given psychofunctionalism, become altogether mysterious, if not outright unintelligible, in the absence of a suitably powerful (relatively local) causal mechanism for such relations. This is a key motivation for Fodor's aforementioned recommendation about suitable causal mechanisms.

(GS) fails to accommodate Fodor's recommendation; for it does not require that complex psychological processes depend causally on suitably powerful (relatively local) causal mechanisms. As far as (GS) goes, a physically possible world that is physically type-identical to the actual world except for its including two more copper pennies in causal interaction could yield a psychological process wherein its pennies think about this paper. (GS) allows this because it does not make psychological processes depend on suitably powerful (relatively local) causal mechanisms instantiated by relevant tokens, tokens such as the pennies in the alternative physically possible world. It makes a claim only about physically possible worlds with the same physical conditions: namely, that the same nonphysical conditions obtain in them. The physically possible world with two additional pennies does not have the same physical conditions as the actual world; so (GS) does not preclude that the pennies in that alternative world think about this essay. (GS) thus fails to accommodate the kind of dependence appropriate to psychofunctionalism, in particular, the kind of psychofunctionalism complying with Fodor's recommendation about suitable causal mechanisms.[10]

Fodor's recommendation is compatible with the multiple realizability of mental properties. It does not require that a causal mechanism consist of any particular kind of stuff: for example, carbon-based as opposed to silicon-based stuff. In this respect, Fodor's recommendation fits with a key motivation for psychofunctionalism. Principles of global supervenience compare worlds as wholes and thus neglect strictures on relatively local causal mechanisms within worlds. On this score, global supervenience is insufficiently sensitive to the kinds of relatively local causal mechanisms crucial to psychofunctional causal relations. Witness the case of the physically possible world with two additional pennies.[11]

We need, then, an account of supervenience-dependence that captures the relevant dependence of mental properties on suitable causal mechanisms. In particular, we need to answer whether nonreductive physicalism has any hope of offering such an account. If nonreductive physicalism, in accord with Davidson's aforementioned view, is to avoid nomic as well as definitional reduction, it must offer an account of mental–physical dependence that avoids both species of reduction.

The prospects for nonreductive physicalism look bleak because a common understanding of dependence raises a serious problem. Mental–physical dependence of the sort pertinent to physicalism, including psychofunctionalist physicalism, supports counterfactual and subjunctive conditionals, in particular, such conditionals involving suitable underlying causal mechanisms. Given physicalism and psychofunctionalism, for example, if one's thinking about this essay depends on one's having a physical causal mechanism that is functionally brainlike, then if one were to lack such a causal mechanism, one would not be thinking about this essay. Barring analytical functionalism, the conditional consequent of the previous conditional is not an analytically true thesis, but is rather a thesis whose truth is causally necessary: necessary given the actual laws of nature. The relevant support of counterfactual and subjunctive conditionals here is inherently nomic, even if it is difficult in some cases to specify the pertinent law.[12]

A denial that mental–physical dependence is nomic leaves only mystery in its train. In the absence of nomic connections between mental properties and physical properties, it is altogether unclear what a claim to dependence of the mental on the physical involves. The point is not just that an absence of nomic connections precludes a cogent explanation of dependent mental–physical variation (although that point is quite plausible); the point is rather that a notion of nomic connection is crucial to an understanding of dependent mental–physical covariation. The pertinent talk of dependence is inherently nomic in that it supports counterfactual and subjunctive conditionals. Such talk, we have noted, is not just talk of coincidental covariation (contrary to a previously noted implication of Davidson's 1985 characterization of supervenience). Nomic connections make supervenience more than mere Humean covariation; and nomic connections involving suitable causal mechanisms make mental–physical supervenience-dependence, of the sort relevant to physicalist psychofunctionalism, more than global supervenience or merely necessary covariation.

One might seek a way around nomic connections and suitable causal mechanisms by claiming that supervenience-dependence is sui generis and unexplainable. This, however, would be an odd view for a physicalist, because an understanding of nonreductive supervenience-physicalism requires an account of supervenience-dependence. We can regard supervenience-dependence as unexplainable only at the expense of leaving nonreductive physicalism itself unexplainable. If physicalists are going to fault Cartesian dualism for promoting mystery instead of explanation, they are themselves well advised to offer explanation instead of mystery, especially when it comes to their thesis of mental–physical dependent variation. Physicalism, after all, is at bottom an explanatory thesis; and the convergence of diverse explanatory postulates on the same causal mechanisms is definitive of the kind of comprehensiveness and unification that constrains physicalist explanation and makes it scientifically valuable. Pockets of causal mystery allowed by physicalism can only impede the main, explanatory interests of physicalism; for causal mystery is no substitute for specification of explanatory causal mechanisms. Let us briefly consider some relevant treatments of dependence.

4. Approaches to Dependence

Nonreductive physicalists, we have indicated, must steer a treacherous course in attempting to fashion a notion of dependence that honors both the primacy of the physical and the autonomy of the mental. There are various species of dependence a supervenience theorist might invoke to characterize mind–body relations. One is *deterministic dependence;* another is *probabilistic dependence,* the latter offering at least two interpretations – frequency and propensity interpretations. We shall consider these approaches in turn.

Deterministic Dependence

Some laws are deterministic, such as those of Newtonian systems. In such systems, generalizations implicating some process, state, or event indicate whether the causal factor C completely determines the presence (or absence) of some factor E. The fact that presence and absence are dichotomous variables should not be taken to suggest that deterministic laws are strict (see Hempel 1988; cf. Kim 1993). Theoretical generalizations concerning deterministic phenomena contain implicit assumptions, or "provisos," specifying the parameters wherein the generalizations hold. For instance, laws of magnetic interaction, as

Hempel (1988) notes, typically assume that the relevant objects are free from mutual gravitational influences. The most important feature of these generalizations is not that they are strict, but rather (strict or not) that they support counterfactuals of a certain sort.

A deterministic statement of a mind–body relation standardly takes this form:

> The presence of a member of a particular set of physical states p completely determines the presence of mental state m.

When cast as a law about an individual, X, such a deterministic psychophysical statement supports a counterfactual of the following form:

> If X were not in a member of a particular set of physical states p, X would not be in mental state m.

We have suggested that on any plausible physicalist version of psychofunctionalism, the relevant counterfactuals will involve suitable physical causal mechanisms for psychological phenomena. When a psychophysical statement supports counterfactuals, the dependence relation represented in the relation between the antecedent and the consequent can be elucidated (at least in principle) by reference to lawful relations between the two domains: the physical and the psychological. As a result, the prospects exist for a nomic reduction of at least modest retention. Kim notes accordingly that "once we begin talking about correlations and dependencies between specific psychological and physical properties, we are in effect talking about psychophysical laws, and these laws raise the specter of unwanted physical reductionism" (1989, p. 42). There is a close relation, then, between counterfactual dependence and the possibility of nomic reduction. Although this relation is especially clear in the case of deterministic laws, it emerges in the case of stochastic laws too.

Probabilistic Dependence

THE FREQUENCY INTERPRETATION. One might formulate the relevant notion of dependence by analogy with circumstances for which probabilistic or statistical *in*dependence does not hold. According to this probabilistic rule, two events (or processes, properties, or states) are independent if a change in the probability of (the occurrence of) the one event has no effect, either positively or negatively, on the probability of the other event. More formally, event A is independent of event B if $p(A/B) = p(A/B') = p(A)$. This relation of independence is symmetrical: if A is independent of B, then B is independent of A.

As a relation between supervenient mental states and subvenient physical states, purely probabilistic dependence fails to honor the ontological primacy of the physical, at least as that primacy is rendered by physicalist psychofunctionalism. It is conceivable that being in a certain physical state affects the probability that one is in a particular mental state, but this is compatible with mere Humean constant conjunction. Such conjunction does not amount to ontic dependence.

In identifying probabilities with long-run frequencies, the frequency interpretation is confronted by two general difficulties. First, it is unable by itself to provide criteria of relevance that distinguish causation from mere (Humean) correlation. Second, it is unable to determine – even make sense of – so-called single-case probabilities. Some events are unique, such as Elvis Presley's death, a 1992 Olympic victory in the women's 100-meter dash, or the election of the twentieth U.S. president. It is not clear, however, that the probability of any of these events can be given by the frequency with which these events occur in the long run; it is not even clear what that means. (On related problems, see Earman and Salmon 1992, pp. 77–81.) In recent years, the propensity interpretation has been introduced to offer some relief.

THE PROPENSITY INTERPRETATION. Given the problem of the single case and widely held views concerning probabilistic causation, a propensity interpretation evolved, according to which probabilities are *tendencies* to produce long-run frequencies. Because the source of the frequency distribution is a tendency or disposition, probabilistic dispositional predicates, like other dispositional predicates, support certain counterfactual and subjunctive conditionals. This is one important difference between frequency and propensity interpretations. Propensities are theoretical in a way that frequencies are not.[13]

An appropriate notion of interlevel dependence must capture the sense in which the mental is counterfactually related to the physical. In the lifetime of an individual, X, we might propose:

> If X had not been in a member of a particular set of physical states p, the probability that X would not have been in mental state m is greater than (say) .96.

The probability could, of course, be higher or lower than .96; and it could vary relative to varying nomic features of situations or worlds. Some worlds are, of course, nomically different from the actual world and, as a result, support correspondingly different probabilities. The central point is that being in a member of a set of physical states p increases the probability of being in mental state m. The physical characteristics of p have a propensity or tendency to produce m. This claim need not be interpreted temporally. States of p can co-occur with m. The relevant language is used to capture the relation of dependence, not the time elapsed during the propagation of the effects. One might find a nontemporal use of 'produce' jarring; for on one reading of 'produce', X could not have produced m unless X had preceded m. The relation we are attempting to capture, however, is (possibly atemporal) between an object's micro structure and its macro structure. Physical features of a micro state can contribute to the causal powers of its (macro state) functional realization. It is in this sense that m causally depends on X. (If, as we suggested previously, the vocabulary of production implies the causal propagation of effects over time, then substitute 'realize' for 'produce'.)

Two points about stochastic conditionals merit comment. First, supervenience theorists should not rest content with a merely epistemic interpretation of the relevant probabilities; for, as noted previously, supervenience-dependence serves as an ontic relation, not a merely epistemic relation. Second, although the relevant conditionals have associated with their consequents a certain probability, each such entire conditional can itself have a degree of confirmation or disconfirmation.

Nonreductive physicalists seeking to accommodate dependent variation between the mental and the physical must now face this consideration: all the *relevant* approaches to dependence face at least the threat of nomic reduction. Merely statistical or frequency dependence is an irrelevant approach to mental–physical dependence, compatible as it is with mere Humean correlation of the mental and physical. Any relevant approach to mental–physical dependence, whether for deterministic or stochastic processes, employs the notion of a law, complete with counterfactual and subjunctive support; in particular, if we endorse physicalist psychofunctionalism compatible with Fodor's recommendation, we shall have to posit suitable causal mechanisms that entail counterfactual and subjunctive support. Whether a nomic reduction can actually be effected between psychological and physical laws turns on how numerous and diverse the physical laws are on which the relevant psychological laws depend.

We cannot now rest content with an unexplicated notion of propensity, a feature of the universe that physicalists have not typically counted among its fundamental parts. More important for current purposes, a propensity account of mind–body dependence commits us to the existence of theoretical entities (propensities) about which there are (psychophysical) laws – counterfactual supporting taxonomic generalizations. To accommodate dependence of the mental on the physical, physicalists must seriously face the prospect of nomic reduction. Nonreductive physicalism does not sit well with this lesson; and complications only multiply when such physicalism aims to be agreeable with a kind of psychofunctionalism that satisfies Fodor's recommendation about suitable causal mechanisms.

5. Composition and Dependence

Inasmuch as a notion of ontic dependence serves to explain the primacy of the physical, one version of nonreductive physicalism is noteworthy for its freedom from talk of dependence. This version favors instead a notion of material composition. We shall briefly consider this version to determine if worries about dependent mental–physical variation are actually beside the point.

According to Richard Boyd's compositional materialism,

> what materialists should claim is that mental states are *in fact* central-nervous-system states but that their having a central nervous system is not essential to them. Such an account is exactly like the one defended here: that mental states are identical to contingently physical states. (1980, p. 105)

The most distinctive feature of compositional materialism is its rejection of a certain kind of token-identity as an unduly strong version of physicalism. On this view, physical (and thus, for the physicalist, psychological) events are not typically identical to their smaller constituent features. There is, according to compositional materialism, plasticity (or multiple realizability) even within a single physical token, just as there is within a type susceptible to instantiation by different physical tokens.

Boyd recruits support from our ordinary criteria of identity for physical objects:

> A car remains the same car in the actual world if its generator (a constituent part) is replaced, and it is hard to see why the same plasticity should not obtain across possible worlds. (1980, p. 100)

The same car accident, on Boyd's view, could have occurred even if the car involved had had a different generator. A difference in molecular constituents of the accident in two possible worlds does not preclude, on this view, sameness of accident.

If the introduction of transworld criteria of identity is not for the purpose of representing the instantiation of different tokens, then the function of the car's occurrence in different possible worlds is not clear; the same point might have been made about two different stages in the lifetime of the car. (In accord with such considerations, David Lewis restricts the occurrence of an individual to a single world.) In arguing that the very same token could be variously composed in different possible worlds, we must therefore be explicit about taxonomy.

If the taxonomic question about some token is whether, *qua car,* the specific composition it has is essential to its identity (as a car), then the compositional materialist's point is well taken. Compositional materialism was designed, however, to explicate the sense in which mental events, states, and processes could be said to have a (perhaps contingent) physical basis. *Qua* physical items, the token cars instantiated in different possible worlds are *different tokens,* because they have different physical compositions.

Boyd takes a predictable line on familiar historical events:

> The historian who says, "World War II would have ended earlier had the Allied powers not adopted the 'Unconditional surrender' slogan," certainly seems to be talking about a possible outcome for the very same war which, in the actual world, ended in August 1945. It would be absurd to insist that the materialist should resist this conclusion on the ground that World War II, like all other events, is entirely physical and therefore must have *exactly the same* physical realization in each possible world. Instead, the materialist should maintain that many kinds of physical events are like physical objects in displaying transworld plasticity. (1980, p. 100)

Ordinary language is no arbiter in a case such as this, even by Boyd's standards; so it is scant recommendation of a view that it comports with our ordinary use of 'war'. Perhaps it is true that we use 'war' in a way that characterizes individuals as a lot like types, but such considerations are not decisive against a stricter understanding of physical tokens. 'War', as used in ordinary discourse or historical sciences, signifies a type, and individual wars are tokens; but time slices of wars are not tokens of wars. Intuitions of plasticity here arise from a categorical intuition that World War II would have been *the same war* even if there had been fewer soldiers involved or one of the guns had been different.

We should not infer that ordinary talk of individual wars connotes tokens of the sort appropriate to an explanation of a war as physical concreta, or a series of physical events; for tokens of the latter sort do not admit of multiple realizability. On the traditional physicalist conception, physical tokens are not multiply realizable, nor do they have various exemplifications. If one needs a special notion of a physical token, different from that of the traditional conception, one could introduce such a notion suitable to one's special taxonomic purposes. In that case, one will be left with two different conceptions of tokenhood – one involving multiple realizability for higher-level phenomena, another for the more basic phenomena of physics.

A token electron, for instance, lacks multiple exemplifications. We grant that the *essential* features of a token electron might be accompanied in different worlds by different contingent features – for example, by slightly different levels of energy. This consideration does not, however, threaten our point about tokenhood. Token electrons with different contingent features are different *tokens*, even if they share essential features. Such distinct tokens can still be of the same type (for some relevant type), and can even share the same token essential features (in different possible worlds). Sameness of token essential features does not, of course, entail sameness of constituent features (as not all constituents need be essential), and hence does not entail sameness of token. Any notion of token giving due attention to compositional features in tokenhood will accommodate the token-determining role of constituent features.

Compositional materialism, in giving due weight to compositionality, should lead one to hold that compositional differences entail differences in tokens. Such materialism would then acknowledge that composition determines strict token-identity. The best way to account for compositional differences, given materialism, is via a notion of token wherein physical compositional differences constitute differences in physical tokens. An alternative view will risk preventing physicalists from explaining compositional differences as differences in physical *things*, where things are tokens rather than types. Physicalists must account for compositional differences as differences in physical things. If the relevant compositional differences are not simply type-differences, they are token-differences, that is, differences in physical tokens. Physical differences are either type-differences or token-differences, and therefore when they are not just type-differences, they are token-differences. Our approach to tokenhood, being sensitive to changes in physical composition, enables physicalists to handle such considerations with ease. It also permits the same token to exist in alternative worlds as long as that token maintains the same composition; and it permits that the same token can exist over time as long as sameness of composition persists.

Unless we hold that a change in physical thing follows *any* change in physical composition, we face the view that the basic physical constituents of the world themselves have a variety of exemplifications, at least across possible worlds. On that view, only property-like, multiply-exemplifiable entities constitute the basic ontological inventory of the physical universe; the physical universe is, then, property-like throughout, from top to bottom. By contrast, our proposed conception of tokenhood allows us to honor the doctrine, widely embraced by physicalists, that the basic constituents of the physical universe are physical things; it does so by counting any physical change in composition as constituting a change in physical thing.

In contrast to the view of tokenhood just proposed, Boyd motivates his compositional materialism as follows:

The same set of molecular motions may realize several different token events, states, or processes, as well as several different types of events, states, or processes. For example, suppose that the set of molecular motions that realizes Jim's pain at t constitute the firing of a particular C-fiber f. Then these motions realize at least three different token states: Jim's pain at t, the firing at t of f, and the token that satisfies the description "the motion of m_1 along t_1, and the motion of m_2 along t_2, and the motion . . ." where the enumeration describes the precise trajectory for each of the molecules involved in the actual world of Jim's pain at t. These token states are not identical (as one can easily see by reflecting on the fact that, for any pair of them, there is a possible world in which only one is manifested), so they could hardly all be identical to the particular set of molecular motions in question (the third token state is, of course, identical to just that set of motions). (1980, p. 102)

A distinctive feature of Boyd's materialism is thus its talk of various *token*-states being realized by a set of molecular motions. If "being realized" amounts to "being instantiated," then Boyd's "tokens" look a lot like types. If, however, types are at issue, then talk of physical composition becomes misplaced. Spatiotemporal concreta can be composed, or made up, of physical constituents, but types, being multiply-realizable universals (with variable degrees of abstractness), are not properly regarded as composed of physical constituents.

Boyd shows some awareness of his shift to type-like "tokens" as follows:

These considerations have the effect of making token events, states, and processes seem less like stereotypical "individuals" and more like type events, states, processes – more like "universals" – in that a token event, for example, may have more than one instance (although in different possible worlds), to none of which it would need be identical. This would be worrisome were it not for the fact that consideration of reidentification of individuals (physical things, for example, and people) over time shows that individuals are not very much like the convenient philosophical stereotype of individuals either. (1980, p. 102)

Boyd thus appears to hold that ordinary usage treats the concept of an individual person, for example, as a token whose identity nevertheless admits of compositional changes.

Appeal to ordinary usage of the term 'individuals' is not decisive, even on Boyd's account. If it were, however, there are typical applications of the term, in ordinary psychological contexts and elsewhere, requiring that the tokens be temporal stages of a person and thus that an individual person is a type rather than a token. When we praise or blame, or punish someone for a criminal act, our assessment of responsibility is typically sensitive to the psychological proximity of the person's present state to the person's earlier state by whose hand the crime was committed. This is why juries are usually moved by remorse (or lack of it), and by conversions from criminal character. Such treatment of a person as capable of substantial change – perhaps involving as much difference between earlier and later stages of the same embodied person as there are routine differences between contemporaneous states of different embodied persons – can be given a rationale only if the relevant tokens are temporally indexed states of a person. If we were to count these temporal stages as compositionally different stages of the same *token*-person, we would be left with the peculiar twofold view that (a) a token of a person *qua* person has saliently different intrinsic causal powers over time that do not matter to its type-identity, and (b) there is no necessary connection between salient changes in intrinsic causal powers and changes in the token's composition.

Our operative assumption is that relevant changes in intrinsic causal powers entail changes in tokens, even if a certain ordinary notion of "individual" violates this assumption. Relevant changes in intrinsic causal powers, on any explanatorily adequate version of physicalism, involve changes in intrinsic physical features of whatever has the causal powers in question; denial of this assumption makes a mystery of intrinsic causal powers: in particular, a mystery of what brings about differences in potential effects. Notions of individuals conflicting with this stricture on tokens – including notions of personal individuals as "tokens" in Boyd's sense – fail to offer the kind of fine-grained account of constituents suitable to physicalism; specifically, they abstract from underlying local causal mechanisms to which physical taxonomy is irredeemably sensitive. This harks back to our point, at the end of Section 3, about the nature of physicalist explanation, namely, its natural intolerance toward causal mystery.

Appeal to the taxonomy of scientific psychology to settle issues of tokenhood serves the explanatory aims of physicalist psychologists but leaves unanswered questions about the subvenient physical causal factors yielding psychological phenomena. The latter questions have occupied center stage throughout the history of physicalist approaches to the mind–body problem, at least from Hobbes to contemporary theorists. Evasion of traditional issues about underlying physical causal mechanisms marks a striking departure from typical physicalist methodology, a departure needing independent support. This stress on the explanatory importance of underlying causal mechanisms does not entail reductionism, at least no more than does stress on the explanatory importance of the genetic basis of heredity to evolutionary biology. It was, in fact, the focus of evolutionary biology and genetics on physical causal mechanisms realizing supervenient properties that enabled an explanatorily superior alternative to vitalist accounts. Directly analogous points about the explanatory importance of causal mechanisms apply to various similar developments in the physical sciences.

In connection with scientific taxonomy, we should note that some purposes of psychological explanation require us to treat different temporal stages of a single person as different tokens. The phenomena of concept acquisition and perceptual learning are explained in terms of the child's current store of information plus its interaction with contingent features of its social and physical environment. Were we to treat this child as a token, we would be forced to hold that despite the remarkable physical and psychological changes that this "individual" undergoes – changes that could easily influence this individual's position on taxonomic dimensions of a variety of diagnostic scales – this person is nonetheless a single token, from incontinence to conceptual and locomotor complexity and finally to incontinence again.

It seems, then, that the compositional plasticity Boyd attributes to tokens is actually the natural variation found among tokens of *the same type*. Witness, for example, that no actual science has only one type – one natural kind – in its proprietary domain. As a result, our treatment of the psychology of a person over time as a type need not commit us to the view that psychology, as a science of psychological kinds, can only generalize about an individual person. There can be as much generalization-permitting similarity among types (and thus persons) in psychology as there is among types in biology. A similar point holds for Boyd's car examples.

One might propose that the relation of composition is an appropriate dependence relation, and thus that it is adequate for physicalists to hold, regarding mental–physical dependence, that every mental event is exhaustively composed of physical events in all nomologically relevant worlds. The main problem with such a proposal is its explanatory narrowness, especially in connection with Fodor's recommendation about the specification of suitable causal mechanisms. Physicalists inclined to psychofunctionalism need not just the thesis that all events are physically composed, but also an explanation of how, or in virtue of what, mental properties depend on physical properties – in particular, how mental properties depend for their occurrence on suitable physical causal mechanisms. In the absence of such an explanation, we risk having an excessively liberal attitude toward relations between mental and physical properties; this was illustrated by the previous case involving the two copper pennies.

The compositional differences permitted in transworld-identical "tokens" by Boyd's view make compositional materialism unfit as an account of mental-physical *dependence*. Although a "token" car may be differently composed in different possible worlds on Boyd's view, *qua physical concreta*, the differently composed tokens are actually distinct tokens, strictly speaking. If, as we suggested, Boyd has misidentified the admitted variability of instantiations of types as the compositional plasticity of transworld variants of the same "token," then the phenomena Boyd describes are really types and, as such, are not physically composed concreta. Only tokens, strictly speaking, have physical composition. If, therefore, compositional materialism is to be a thesis about composition pertinent to physicalism, it had better be about tokens. It appears, then, that compositional materialism must surrender either the primacy of the physical or a consistent taxonomy of states, events, and processes.

Compositional materialism opposes definitional and nomic reduction but provides no alternative account of dependence relations between mental types and the physical entities realizing those types. Lacking an account of mental–physical dependence, compositional materialism offers no unmysterious account of the psychophysical mechanisms crucial to physicalist psychofunctionalism. For nonreductive physicalists, then, compositional materialism offers no advantage over traditional token-identity theory and is burdened with the price of a shifting conception of tokenhood.

Does our demand for specific causal mechanisms entail type-identity, the identification of psychological types with physical types? Our demand is, of course, quite compatible with token-identity. Indeed, we hold that any adequate version of physicalism must accommodate the view that all tokens are physical: physicalism without token-identity is really no physicalism at all. Our demand can, furthermore, avoid the kind of chauvinistic type-identity whose rejection is a key motivation for psychofunctionalism. The need for suitable causal mechanisms in mental-physical dependence does not entail the restriction of mental phenomena to any *particular* kind of physical base – say, a carbon base as opposed to a silicon base. Suitable causal mechanisms can occur, at least characteristically, in a range of physical causal bases. It is, on our view, an *empirical* issue how plastic a physical causal base can be for the occurrence of mental phenomena. We hold, accordingly, that empirical investigations must answer how chauvinistic or liberal physicalist psychofunctionalism should be. The relevant degree of chauvinism or freedom will depend on the sorts of physical causal mechanisms that can subserve a certain psychological phenomenon. This fits well with our view that physicalist psychofunctionalism is a logically contingent thesis.

6. Conclusion

Overall, then, the prospects for nonreductive supervenience-physicalism seem bleak. We have identified the crucial role of mental–physical dependent variation in supervenience accounts of mind–body relations and have argued that the relevant kind of dependent variation, in supporting counterfactuals, harbors the real threat of nomic reduction. Our argument acknowledges the central role of suitable (relatively local) causal mechanisms in any adequate psychofunctionalist approach to mind–body dependence. On this basis, we have faulted standard approaches to global supervenience, noting that they fail to preserve the relevant kind of mind–body dependence. Failing thus, those approaches to supervenience fail likewise to accommodate the ontological primacy of the physical. Whatever the ultimate fate of nonreductive physicalism, standard global supervenience and compositional approaches do not capture the acknowledged mental–physical dependence in need of explanation.

NOTES

We thank Richard Boyd, Suzanne Cunningham, John Heil, Al Mele, John Post, and Alan Sidelle for comments.

1. See Michael Hooker (1978) for a statement and assessment of Descartes's conceivability argument. Richard Swinburne (1986) has defended a variation on Descartes's conceivability argument for dualism. For criticism of Swinburne's Cartesian argument, see Moser and vander Nat (1993).

2. Lewis holds that a finite set of conditions specifying the typical causes (e.g., bodily causes) of an experience are true of the experience "by analytic necessity" (1966, p. 165; cf. p. 163). Armstrong (1977) speaks of the relevant causal conditions as deriving from "conceptual analysis."

3. For discussions bearing on this slogan, see Putnam (1975, pp. 223–7; 1979, pp. 165–6; 1988, chap. 2), Burge (1986), Fodor (1987, chap. 2), and Post (1987, pp. 174–80).

4. This assumption violates David Lewis's stricture that one individual cannot exist in more than one possible world (see Lewis 1986, p. 213). Whatever one's view about Lewis's stricture, Boyd's (1980) version of compositional materialism (described in Section 5, this chapter) does not satisfy it.

5. Even so, physicalists typically hold that expressions of mind–body causal sequences should be extensional, that transitivity and substitutivity should hold.

6. For a more detailed discussion of the problems associated with reductionist efforts in twentieth-century philosophy of science, see the introductory essay on reductionism by Trout in Boyd, Gasper, and Trout (1991, pp. 387–92).

7. Kim (1990, p. 11) says of Davidson's 1985 characterization that "we can

easily verify that this is equivalent to weak covariance" of the following sort: Necessarily, if anything has property *F* in (supervenient set of properties) *A*, there exists a property, *G*, in (subvenient set of properties) *B* such that the thing has *G*, and everything that has *G* has *F*. Kim's claim is false, because Davidson does not use the modal term 'necessarily' or any equivalent terms.

8. See Teller (1984) and Kim (1984, 1990) for useful taxonomy.

9. Proponents of global supervenience of one species or another include Hellman and Thompson (1975), Horgan (1982), Lewis (1983), Post (1987, 1991), and Papineau (1990).

10. For criticisms of global supervenience regarding dependence that are independent of the place of causal mechanisms in psychofunctionalism, see Kim (1989, pp. 40–2; 1990, pp. 22–3) and Heil (1992, chap. 3). An appeal to the significance of (relatively local) causal mechanisms in psychological processes can add cogency to some of Kim's criticisms of global supervenience, although Kim does not note that significance.

11. Even if we acknowledge Post's observation that "functional and intentional states are defined without regard to their physical or other realizations" (1987, p. 161), we can still acknowledge the indispensability of relatively local causal mechanisms in psychological processes.

12. The current point fits with Davidson's remark that "lawlike statements are general statements that support counterfactual and subjunctive claims, and are supported by their instances" (1970, p. 217).

13. The propensity interpretation is thus an inadmissible interpretation of the probability calculus. This is not especially surprising. The propensity interpretation was introduced not as an analysis of probability, but in order to capture the dependence of causal claims; and it does rather well with probabilistic causation. Although it would have been nice to have an account of probabilistic causation that also honored the canons of probability theory, the propensity interpretation can restrict its purview to complex and integrated stochastic systems, leaving the frequency interpretation to address those domains in which the probability calculus's idealizing assumptions hold, such as that of independence.

REFERENCES

Armstrong, D. M. 1968. *A Materialist Theory of the Mind.* London: Routledge and Kegan Paul.

1977. "The Causal Theory of the Mind," *Neue Heft für Philosophie* 11, 82–95. Reprinted in Armstrong, *The Nature of Mind,* pp. 16–31. St. Lucia: University of Queensland Press, 1980.

Block, Ned. 1978. "Troubles with Functionalism." In C. W. Savage, ed., *Minnesota Studies in the Philosophy of Science, Volume 9: Perception and Cognition: Issues in the Foundations of Psychology,* pp. 261–325. Minneapolis: University of Minnesota Press.

Boyd, Richard. 1980. "Materialism without Reductionism: What Physicalism

Does Not Entail." In Ned Block, ed., *Readings in Philosophy of Psychology, Volume 1*, pp. 67–106. Cambridge, Mass.: Harvard University Press.

Boyd, Richard, Philip Gasper, and J. D. Trout, eds. 1991. *The Philosophy of Science*. Cambridge, Mass.: MIT Press.

Burge, Tyler. 1986. "Individualism and Psychology," *Philosophical Review* 95, 3–45.

Carnap, Rudolf. 1966. *Philosophical Foundations of Physics*. New York: Basic.

Causey, Robert. 1977. *The Unity of Science*. Dordrecht: Reidel.

Davidson, Donald. 1970. "Mental Events." In Davidson, *Essays on Actions and Events*, pp. 207–25. New York: Oxford University Press, 1980.

　　1985. "Reply to Harry Lewis." In Bruce Vermazen and Merrill Hintikka, eds., *Essays on Davidson*, pp. 242–4. New York: Oxford University Press.

　　1993. "Thinking Causes." In John Heil and Alfred Mele, eds., *Mental Causation*, pp. 3–18. New York: Oxford University Press.

Descartes, René. 1637. *Discourse on the Method*. In E. S. Haldane and G. R. T. Ross, eds., *The Philosophical Works of Descartes, Volume 1*. Cambridge University Press, 1911.

　　1641a. *Meditations on First Philosophy*. In E. S. Haldane and G. R. T. Ross, eds., *The Philosophical Works of Descartes, Volume 1*. Cambridge University Press, 1911.

　　1641b."Reply to the First Objections." In E. S. Haldane and G. R. T. Ross, eds., *The Philosophical Works of Descartes, Volume 2*. Cambridge University Press, 1912.

　　1641c. "Reply to Fourth Objections." In E. S. Haldane and G. R. T. Ross, eds., *The Philosophical Works of Descartes, Volume 2*. Cambridge University Press, 1912.

Earman, John, and Wesley Salmon. 1992. "The Confirmation of Scientific Hypotheses." In M. H. Salmon et al., *Introduction to the Philosophy of Science*, pp. 42–103. Englewood Cliffs, N.J.: Prentice-Hall.

Fodor, Jerry. 1981. "The Mind–Body Problem." *Scientific American* 244, 114–23. Reprinted in Paul Moser, ed., *Reality in Focus*, pp. 240–52. Englewood Cliffs, N.J.: Prentice-Hall, 1990. Reference is to this reprint.

　　1987. *Psychosemantics*. Cambridge, Mass.: MIT Press.

Heil, John. 1992. *The Nature of True Minds*. Cambridge University Press.

Hellman, Geoffrey, and F. W. Thompson. 1975. "Physicalism: Ontology, Determination, Reduction," *Journal of Philosophy* 72, 551–64.

Hempel, Carl. 1988. "Provisos: A Problem Concerning the Inferential Function of Scientific Theories." In Adolf Grünbaum and Wesley Salmon, eds., *The Limitations of Deductivism*, pp. 19–36. Berkeley and Los Angeles: University of California Press.

Hooker, C. A. 1981. "Towards a General Theory of Reduction," *Dialogue* 20, 38–59, 201–36, 496–529.

Hooker, Michael. 1978. "Descartes's Denial of Mind–Body Identity." In Michael Hooker, ed., *Descartes: Critical and Interpretive Essays*, pp. 171–85. Baltimore: Johns Hopkins University Press.

Horgan, Terence. 1982. "Supervenience and Microphysics," *Pacific Philosophical Quarterly* 63, 29–43.

Kim, Jaegwon. 1984. "Concepts of Supervenience," *Philosophy and Phenomenological Research* 45, 153–76.
  1989. "The Myth of Nonreductive Materialism." *Proceedings and Addresses of the American Philosophical Association* 63, 31–47.
  1990. "Supervenience as a Philosophical Concept," *Metaphilosophy* 21, 1–27.
  1993. "Can Supervenience and 'Non-Strict Laws' Save Anomalous Monism?" in John Heil and Alfred Mele, eds., *Mental Causation*, pp. 19–26. New York: Oxford University Press.
Lewis, David. 1966. "An Argument for the Identity Theory," *Journal of Philosophy* 63, 17–25. Reprinted in David Rosenthal, ed., *Materialism and the Mind–Body Problem*, pp. 162–71. Englewood Cliffs, N.J.: Prentice-Hall, 1971. Reference is to this reprint.
  1980. "Mad Pain and Martian Pain." In Ned Block, ed., *Readings in Philosophy of Psychology, Volume 1*, pp. 216–22. Cambridge, Mass.: Harvard University Press.
  1983. "New Work for a Theory of Universals," *Australasian Journal of Philosophy* 61, 343–77.
  1986. *On the Plurality of Worlds*. Oxford: Basil Blackwell.
Moser, Paul. 1993. *Philosophy after Objectivity*. New York: Oxford University Press.
Moser, Paul, and Arnold vander Nat. 1993. "Surviving Souls," *Canadian Journal of Philosophy* 23, 101–6.
Nagel, Ernest. 1961. *The Structure of Science*. New York: Harcourt, Brace, and World.
Oppenheim, Paul, and Hilary Putnam. 1958. "The Unity of Science as a Working Hypothesis." In Herbert Feigl, Michael Scriven, and Grover Maxwell, eds., *Minnesota Studies in the Philosophy of Science, Volume 2: Concepts, Theories, and the Mind–Body Problem*, pp. 3–36. Minneapolis: University of Minnesota Press.
Papineau, David. 1990. "Why Supervenience?" *Analysis* 50, 66–71.
Post, John. 1987. *The Faces of Existence*. Ithaca, N.Y.: Cornell University Press.
  1991. *Metaphysics*. New York: Paragon.
Putnam, Hilary. 1975. "The Meaning of 'Meaning'." In Putnam, *Mind, Language, and Reality: Philosophical Papers, Volume 2*, pp. 215–71. Cambridge University Press.
  1979. "Reflections on Goodman's *Ways of Worldmaking*." In Putnam, *Realism and Reason: Philosophical Papers, Volume 3*, pp. 155–69. Cambridge University Press.
  1988. *Representation and Reality*. Cambridge, Mass.: MIT Press.
Sober, Elliott. 1985. "Panglossian Functionalism and the Philosophy of Mind," *Synthese* 64, 165–93.
Suppes, Patrick. 1984. *Probabilistic Metaphysics*. Oxford: Basil Blackwell.
Swinburne, Richard. 1986. *The Evolution of the Soul*. New York: Oxford University Press.
Teller, Paul. 1984. "A Poor Man's Guide to Supervenience and Determination," *Southern Journal of Philosophy* 22, Supplement, 137–62.

An Argument for Strong Supervenience

BARRY LOEWER

Jerry Fodor enunciates the physicalist credo thus:

> I suppose that sooner or later physicists will complete the catalogue that
> they have been compiling of the ultimate and irreducible properties of
> things. When they do, the likes of spin, charm, and charge will perhaps
> appear on their list. But aboutness surely won't. Intentionality simply
> doesn't go that deep. It is hard to see in the face of this consideration, how
> one can be a Realist about intentionality without also being, to some extent
> or other, a Reductionist. If the semantic and the intentional are real prop-
> erties of things, it must be in virtue of their identity (or perhaps super-
> venience on?) properties that are themselves neither intentional nor se-
> mantic.[1]

Fodor is claiming that if intentional predicates – for example, 'believes
that tigers have stripes' and 'desires to see a tiger' – express genuine
properties, then these properties must either be identical to or supervene on the properties of basic physics; that is, the properties in the
physicists' completed catalogue or complexes composed of such properties. A thoroughgoing physicalist holds that *all* genuine properties,
or at least all properties that play a role in science, are identical to or
supervene on physical properties. Of course, most philosophers nowa-
days do not think that psychological properties (intentional properties
among them) are identical to physical properties (or complexes of
physical properties). Their view, which it is fair to say is now the received view, is that psychological properties either are not real or supervene on basic physical properties.

But why should we believe that the only real properties are identical
to or supervene on physical properties? Paul Boghossian, commenting
on Fodor, raises this question and says, "There is, I think, no obvious
answer."[2] He continues:

> And what the naturalist needs is an argument why, in general it is a condi-
> tion on a property's being real that it supervenes on the properties recog-
> nized by physics. There are, to be sure, specific local areas in which some
> sort of supervenience thesis seems correct. For example, mere reflection on
> the *concept* of a moral property reveals that moral properties weakly super-

vene on non-moral properties. . . . But this sort of deliverance – which it is worth emphasizing is, in any case only of a *weak* supervenience thesis – does not appear to be forthcoming in general. It is simply not true that mere reflection on the concept of an arbitrary property discloses that property's supervenience – however weak – on the physical. . . . If any of this is right we are owed an explanation why we ought to believe in the supervenience thesis.

In this essay I will provide the argument Boghossian asks for and thus an explanation of why we ought to believe in the supervenience thesis. Let's begin with a general definition of supervenience:

A property M (the supervenient property) supervenes on properties and relations $\{P, \ldots, R, \ldots\}$ (the base properties) iff given a class of possible worlds W, for every w and u belonging to W and individuals x and y that exist respectively in w and u, if x and y differ with respect to M (i.e., one has M while the other doesn't), then x and y are parts of physical systems that differ with respect to some of the properties and relations in $\{P, \ldots, R, \ldots\}$.

I will assume (as in this definition) that the individuals that exemplify the supervenient properties are composed of physical entities ("systems") that exemplify (or have parts that exemplify) the base properties. By "system" I mean any collection of particles or fields or whatever entities basic physics posits. The strength of a supervenience thesis varies with the size and nature of the base properties, the class W of possible worlds, and the properties that are claimed to supervene. I will be arguing for a supervenience thesis in which the base properties are properties of fundamental physics, the class of possible worlds is the class of worlds in which the laws are the fundamental laws of physics, and the supervenient properties are properties that satisfy a condition of "physical detectability," which I will explain later.

In formulating a supervenience thesis that expresses physicalism, I need to say which properties are basic physical properties and which laws are fundamental laws of physics. According to current physics, the basic properties are quantum mechanical observables (e.g., position, energy, spin, particle number) whose values are determined by a system's quantum mechanical state (which is characterized by a vector in an appropriate Hilbert space). The fundamental laws are dynamic laws that describe the evolution of the quantum state. There are well-known problems in the foundations of quantum theory, so it is fortunate that I don't have to assume its correctness.[3] However, my argument is committed to two features of current physical theory and to the view that these features will survive in future physics (when the list is completed). One is that physics is closed and complete. Roughly (details later), this means that the evolution of the physical state is ac-

counted for to the extent that it can be accounted for solely in terms
of prior physical states. The second is that there are some properties or
putative properties that are not physical properties – more specifically,
that psychological and intentional properties are not physical properties and so won't appear in the physicists' completed list.[4] As Fodor
says, "Intentionality simply doesn't go that deep."

With these preliminaries out of the way, I can state the thesis of
this essay:

> **(SPS)** For every physically detectable property M and physically pos-
> sible worlds w and u and individuals x and y that exist respectively in w
> and u, if x and y differ with respect to M at time t, then x and y are parts
> of systems X and Y, and there is a basic physical property P (or relation
> R) such that X and Y differ with respect to P (or contain parts that differ
> with respect to R) at t at worlds w and u.

(SPS) is a very strong supervenience claim. It is, for example,
stronger than the weak supervenience doctrine mentioned by Boghossian, stronger than global supervenience, and stronger than a thesis
that is sometimes called "nomological supervenience." The first says
that there can be no two individuals in the same world that agree on
all their P properties but disagree with respect to M. In contrast to
(SPS), this allows for individuals in different worlds to possess the same
P properties while disagreeing with respect to M.[5] Global supervenience says, roughly, that two worlds that differ on their distribution
of supervening properties also differ on their distribution of base
properties. This allows, in contrast to (SPS), worlds that are identical
at t, but that differ in the distant past on their base properties, to differ
on their supervening properties at t. The definition of nomological
supervenience restricts the class of possible worlds to those that conform to all the natural laws. If this class is properly included in the
class of physically possible worlds (i.e., if there are laws that don't follow from the laws of physics), then the resulting thesis is weaker than
(SPS).[6]

Physical detectability is, roughly, the requirement that whether or
not M is exemplified by an individual at space-time region $\langle t, X \rangle$ is
detectable by the value of some physical quantity. Here is a more precise characterization: an M-detector is a system @ and physical quantity Q pertaining to @ with two values, x and y. The idea is that if an
M-detector is suitably situated with respect to $\langle t, X \rangle$ in a region $\langle t, X' \rangle$
(disjoint from $\langle t, X \rangle$), then the probability of the values of Q at a specified time t' after t will differ depending on whether or not F is exemplified in X at t. A property is detectable just in case for every physically
possible world w and region X in w there is an M-detector. It may be
that in many worlds there are no M-detectors suitably located with

respect to R so the presence or absence of F is undetected. The point is that it would have consequences (concerning the chances of the values of Q) if an M-detector were present. Note that detectability is a counterfactual notion. In evaluating the counterfactual "If an M detector were present at $\langle X, t' \rangle$ and F were present at $\langle t, X \rangle$, then the probability at t that $Q = x$ at t' is p" at world w, we look at worlds that are physically indistinguishable from w with respect to R (and its backward lightcone) but that contain a detector at $\langle t, R' \rangle$.[7]

I am not offering physical detectability as a conceptually or metaphysically necessary condition for the existence of a property. There are dualist and epiphenomenalist views that as far as I can see, are conceptually possible but on which mental properties are not physically detectable. But I do claim that properties invoked in scientific theories and explanations are physically detectable. For example, the property of electron spin can be detected by the behavior of an electron in an appropriately oriented magnetic field; and being acidic is detectable by litmus paper under appropriate conditions. If intentional predicates express properties, then it is plausible that these too are detectable, though if currently popular accounts of intentional content are correct, a detector for them may need to interact with a big chunk of environment.[8]

The main premise from which I will derive (SPS) says that physics is closed and complete. Here is a formulation of this idea:

(CCP) For any physical quantity Q, the probability at t that $Q = q$ at a later time t^* is completely determined by the physical state of the world at t and the fundamental laws of physics.

(CCP) says that the physical state of the world at t accounts – to the extent there is an account – for the values of physical quantities at later times. My argument for (SPS) also requires an assumption concerning the evaluation of counterfactuals.

(Count) If $P(t) \to Q(t')$ is a counterfactual whose antecedent and consequent make reference only to physical properties and w is physically possible, then the truth value of $P(t) \to Q(t')$ at w is determined by the physical state of w at t and the physical laws.

(Count) says that the physical facts suffice for the evaluation of physical counterfactuals.[9] It doesn't strictly follow from (CCP), but anyone who accepts (CCP) should accept (Count) as well.

The argument for (SPS) is now straightforward. Suppose that w and u are physically possible worlds that are physically identical at t and that M is exemplified in R by \$ at t in w, but not in u. Suppose that M is a physically detectable property and that @ is an M-detector for w

and u at a region, R. Then there is a p such that the following counterfactual is true at w but false at u.

(1) If @ were suitably situated with respect to \$, then the probability that $Q = x$ would be p.

But (1) is a physical counterfactual, so its truth value is determined by the physical state at a world at t. Since w and u have the same physical state at t, it follows that (1) has the same truth value at both worlds. Hence, there cannot be physically possible worlds that share physical states at t but differ with respect to M. This establishes (SPS).

The argument for (SPS) actually establishes something a little stronger than (SPS). It is that a property, M, supervenes on those physical properties (or states) that are sufficient for determining the values of Q (the detecting property) at t' (the time the detection is complete) in the detector. These may be something less than the state of the world at t. If, for example, causal influences propagate at no more than the speed of light, then the state of the world restricted to a slice at t of the backward lightcone of the detector at t' will suffice.

How important is this result? For starters, it shows that anyone who accepts (CCP) either ought also to accept (SPS) for, say, intentional properties, or deny that these properties are physically detectable. If physical detectability is a condition on a property's being real (or being scientific), then it follows that a property either supervenes on physical properties or is not real (or not scientific). This throws some interesting light on Donald Davidson's position that he calls "anomalous monism."[10] Davidson seems to endorse (CCP). However, he claims that intentional properties *weakly* supervene on physical properties while denying that they *strongly* supervene on physical properties. Many commentators have suspected that this combination of views involves irrealism concerning intentional properties or at least the view that intentional properties are epiphenomenal.[11] If detectability is a condition on a property being real or being causal, then the argument for (SPS) shows that these suspicions are justified.[12]

A second interesting consequence concerns Jaegwon Kim's "explanatory exclusion principle."[13] According to Kim, there cannot be two *independent* causes of the same event (or property exemplification) unless the event is literally causally overdetermined. It follows that if physics is causally complete, then a nonphysical event or the exemplification of a nonphysical property can be the cause of a physical event only if the former is dependent on physical events. For example, the exemplification of a mental property can cause a bodily movement only if the exemplification of the mental event *depends* on the exemplifications of physical properties. If we assume that every causal property is detectable, then Kim's exclusionary principle follows from

(SPS). Further, (SPS) spells out the way higher-level causal properties must depend on physical properties.[14]

A last consequence concerns the naturalization project expressed by the quote from Fodor at the beginning of this essay. Fodor thinks that intentional properties are real and figure in scientific laws and therefore supervene on physical properties. The argument of this essay shows that his inference is correct. Fodor also appreciates that strong supervenience claims are in need of explanation. If intentional properties are physical properties or logical constructs out of physical properties, then that explains their supervenience on the physical. But Fodor has argued (and most philosophers of mind agree) that intentional properties are not identical to physical properties or constructs out of physical properties. A suggestion that has sometimes been made is that supervenience is attributable to the existence of fundamental laws connecting physical and intentional properties. But this won't account for (SPS). Aside from the implausibility of there being such laws, they don't explain (SPS), which, as I pointed out earlier, is stronger than nomological supervenience.

The only way I know of accounting for how a nonphysical property strongly supervenes on physical properties is to show that the property is a functional property that can be realized by physical properties. A functional property, F, is a property that is exemplified by x just in case x has, or is part of a system that has, certain physical properties (or lower-level functional properties with physical properties at the lowest level) that are related to each other in certain ways – for example, by law or causation. If the relevant laws or causal relations are themselves physical, then it follows that functional properties strongly supervene on physical properties. Fodor's proposed account of intentional properties is a functionalist account under this characterization.[15] Whether or not that account is correct, we can appreciate the significance of discovering such an account. Without one, the supervenience of intentional properties is mysterious. And while the existence of such a mystery may not be sufficient reason to adopt irrealism about the intentional, it should make a realist very uncomfortable.[16]

NOTES

Earlier versions of this essay were read to the philosophy departments at Illinois State University, Washington University, and Brown University. I would like to thank David Albert, Kati Balog, Gary Gates, Brian McLaughlin, and Fritz Warfield for comments and discussion.

1. Fodor (1987, p. 97).
2. "Naturalizing Content" in Loewer and Rey (1991, p. 65). In a footnote,

Boghossian suggests that it may be possible in certain cases to argue for supervenience on the basis of considerations of causality. This seems correct and is the basis of the argument that I give in this essay.

3. These difficulties include the problem of squaring quantum and relativity theory, quantum gravity, and the measurement problem in quantum mechanics. For a discussion of the last of these, see Albert and Loewer (1991). In view of these problems, a physicalist should be cautious about aligning himself too closely to current physics.

4. Not every philosopher and physicist would agree with this. Descartes thought that the values of certain physical quantities (e.g., the direction of motion of a particle) may be determined by mental factors. More recently, physicists have entertained the proposal that the evolution of the wave function may depend on a conscious observer interacting with it.

5. If the "cannot" in a weak supervenience claim is a metaphysical or conceptual impossibility, then it is one respect stronger than (SPS), since the latter says nothing about worlds that are not physically possible. See Kim (1990a).

6. The difference between physical and nomological supervenience is important since the latter but not the former is compatible with the existence of fundamental (i.e., nonreducible) laws connecting, for example, mental and physical properties. For this reason, nomological supervenience isn't necessarily a reductive or even a dependency relation.

7. I am assuming a version of the Lewis–Stalnaker account of counterfactuals on which the counterfactual "$A > B$" is true at w just in case all the worlds most similar to w in which A is true, B is true.

8. What I have in mind is the view that content properties are individuated, at least in part in terms of causal relations. A *refers-to-water* detector may need to include a water detector and a detector of causal relations and a good deal else. If reference is a real relation, there are conditions under which whether some thought refers to water or not makes a difference to the value of a physical variable.

9. I am not claiming that the similarity metric is determined by the physical facts but that, given a similarity metric, the value of a physical counterfactual at w depends only on the physical facts at w. The similarity metric used to evaluate these counterfactuals is the one described in note 7.

10. See Davidson (1980).

11. See, e.g., Blackburn (1985) and Antony (1990), who accuse Davidson of irrealism for different reasons.

12. I think that Davidson ought to respond to my argument by granting that the mental strongly supervenes on the physical. He might worry that this conflicts with his view that there are no psychological laws, but this conflict is far from obvious. While the supervenient connections between physical properties and psychological properties that hold if (SPS) is true have the force of physical necessity, they are quite unlike laws; and their existence, as far as I can see, does not compromise the autonomy of the intentional that Davidson emphasizes.

13. See Kim (1990b).

14. An exemplification of M's causing an event requires more than M super-

vening on physical properties. For example, it may require a causal law involving M or the truth of certain counterfactuals involving M.

15. See Fodor (1987), "A Theory of Content, Part II." Fodor says that his account of mental content is nonfunctionalist. By this he means that causal relations among mental expressions do not constitute its content. His account is functionalist on my broader construal.

16. After completing this essay, I learned of work by David Papineau in which he develops a similar argument for strong supervenience. See Papineau (1990, 1993).

REFERENCES

Albert, David, and Loewer, Barry. 1991. "The Measurement Problem: Some Solutions," *Synthese*, 86: 87–98.
Antony, Louise. 1990. "Davidson's Anomalous Monism," *Philosophical Review*, 100: 33–52.
Blackburn, Simon. 1985. *Spreading the Word*. Oxford University Press.
Davidson, Donald. 1980. "Mental Events," in *Essays in Actions and Events*, Oxford: Clarendon Press, pp. 207–27.
Fodor, Jerry. 1987. *Psychosemantics*. Cambridge, Mass.: MIT Press.
Kim, Jaegwon. 1990a. "Supervenience as a Philosophical Concept," in *Supervenience and Mind*. Cambridge University Press, pp. 131–60.
    1990b. "Mechanism, Purpose, and Explanatory Exclusion," in *Supervenience and Mind*. Cambridge University Press, pp. 237–64.
Loewer, Barry, and Rey, Georges. 1991. *Meaning in Mind*. Oxford: Blackwell.
Papineau, David. 1990. "Why Supervenience," *Analysis 50:* 66–71.
    1993. *Philosophical Naturalism*. Oxford: Blackwell.

Arguments for Supervenience and Physical Realization

DAVID PAPINEAU

1. Introduction

In this essay my primary focus will be on the *why* of supervenience, rather than the *what*. That is, I shall be more concerned with the *arguments* for supervenience, in particular for the supervenience of the mental on the physical, than with questions of precisely how to *formulate* the doctrine. Much has been written on the latter topic, but relatively little on the former. I think this is a pity, for it has encouraged the view that the supervenience of the mental on the physical depends on some kind of basic intuition and that those who find physicalism unappealing are therefore free to reject it. I will show that, on the contrary, the doctrine of supervenience is a simple consequence of some evident truths. (Of course, the "why" of supervenience is not entirely irrelevant to the "what": once we understand the argument for the doctrine, we will be better able to see which versions of it are defensible.)

Once I have laid out the argument for supervenience, it will be helpful to compare it with a related argument for the thesis of *physical realization* (i.e., in the mind–brain case, the thesis that mental states are always realized by physical states). The relationship between the doctrine of supervenience and the doctrine of physical realization is not always well understood. Distinguishing the reasons for believing these two doctrines will help to clarify their relationship.[1]

It will be convenient in what follows to focus on the relationship between mental and physical phenomena. But the structure of my arguments will make it clear that many of my points apply equally to other subjects, such as meteorology, biology, or economics.

2. Supervenience: Initial Points

Although, as I said, I am not primarily concerned with questions of how to define supervenience, it will be useful to start with a brief account of how I understand this doctrine. I take supervenience to be a relatively "local" matter, relating the properties of individual systems

226

(like organisms), rather than whole worlds. So, in the first instance, the supervenience of one set of phenomena – the *M*s, say – on another – the *P*s – requires that two *systems* cannot differ in respect of their *M*-properties without differing in their *P*-properties; or, to put it the other way around, if two systems are qualitatively *P*-identical, then they must also be qualitatively *M*-identical. Clearly, on any intuitive understanding of "system," this is a stronger doctrine than the merely "global" claim that two *worlds* that differ anywhere in their *M*-properties must differ somewhere in their *P*-properties.

However, there is an obvious respect in which this local version of supervenience is too strong. Consider the property of *being the outermost electron in an atom*, say. Intuitively, two electrons can be physically identical, yet differ in that one can be outermost in an atom and the other not. Yet we wouldn't on this account want to deny that being the outermost electron in an atom supervenes on physical properties. This property is fixed by the physical facts if anything is.

The obvious response to this problem is to note that being the outermost electron in an atom is a *relational* property of electrons, depending not only on the intrinsic features of the electron, but also on the features of other entities, namely, a nearby nucleus and the other electrons bound by it. Accordingly, we should modify the requirement of supervenience for relational properties so as to demand that such properties should be fixed not only by the intrinsic physical characteristics of the system at issue, but also by the physical characteristics of any relevantly related systems. On this account, being the outermost electron in an atom supervenes on physical facts once more. For this property is obviously fixed by the intrinsic physics of the electron plus the physics of any nearby nucleus and the other electrons bound by it. (Equivalently, if less naturally, we could say that the relational properties of a system were not really properties of that system as such, but only of some larger system incorporating the relevant related systems, and then require that such relational properties be fixed by the intrinsic physical properties of the larger system.)

Note that this strategy for dealing with relational properties need not collapse into "global" supervenience. For we are only widening the "supervenience base" beyond the intrinsic physical features of the system at issue when we have some independent reason to do so, namely, when we have independent reason to regard the putatively supervening property as relational.

It will be important in what follows that supervenience, as I am thinking of it, allows that *M*-properties and *P*-properties can be *ontologically distinct*. *M*-properties can supervene on *P*-properties without being identical with or even physically realized by them. To see this, consider the version of dualism known as "epiphenomenalism." According to epiphenomenalism, mental states "float above" the brain as distinct phenomena, not responsible for any physical effects themselves, but nevertheless causally determined by the physics of the brain and so incapable of varying without physical variation. Epiphenomenalism satisfies supervenience, since it rules out the possibility of mental variation without physical variation. But it doesn't involve any ontological dependence of the mental on the physical, since it explicitly specifies that mental properties are quite distinct from physical ones.[2]

One last point about the formulation of supervenience. Supervenience is a modal doctrine. It says that two systems *cannot* differ mentally without differing physically. But what is the modal force of the "cannot" here? Different ways of reading this term give us different versions of supervenience. The literature standardly distinguishes a strong from a weak version. The weak version says that, within any possible world, two systems cannot differ mentally without differing physically. The strong version says that two physically identical systems will be mentally identical even if they are in different possible worlds.[3] The argument for supervenience I offer will support the strong version of supervenience, at least to the extent that it will show that physical identity implies mental identity for any systems from any *physically* possible worlds.

3. The Completeness of Physics

The arguments for supervenience and for physical realization that follow share one premise, which I call "the completeness of physics." It is convenient to explain this premise at this point.

I take it that physics, unlike other sciences, is *complete* in the sense that all physical events are either determined, or have their chances determined, by prior *physical* events according to *physical* laws. In other words, we never need to look beyond the realm of the physical to identify a set of antecedents that fixes the chances of any subsequent physical occurrence. A purely physical specification, plus physical laws, will always suffice to tell us what is physically going to happen, insofar as that can be foretold at all.

Note that not all subject areas are complete in this way. For instance, meteorology is not complete. Some weather phenomena arise from antecedents that are not themselves weather phenomena. The beat of a butterfly's wing, students of chaos tell us, can play a part in determining next week's cyclone. Less exotically, psychology is obviously not complete, given that plenty of mental events result from nonmental ones, as when I sit on a drawing pin and feel a pain. But physics is special in this respect. If we take any physical result and look back in time to see what gave rise to it, then, I say, prior *physical* factors will always suffice to give us as full an explanation of that result as is possible.[4]

I expect the completeness of physics to recommend itself as intrinsically plausible to most readers. Even so, the doctrine is not as straightforward as it seems. In particular, there are difficulties about how best to understand "physics" in this context. If we tie the notion too closely to *current* physics, then this threatens to make the completeness claim false, for there are surely some uncontroversially physical effects that current physics cannot yet explain. On the other hand, if we take "physics" to refer to some *future* descendant of current physics, then the completeness thesis is open to charges of emptiness or unsupportability. However, it would take us too far afield to pursue these issues here. For one account of how to make the completeness thesis both precise and beliefworthy, see Papineau (1990, 1991), Crane (1991).

4. The Manifestability Argument for Supervenience

Consider the following argument for the supervenience of psychology on physics:

Premise (1). According to the completeness of physics, the chances of physical consequences are fixed, once physical antecedents are given. So if two systems are physically identical and in the same physical contexts, they will issue in the same physical consequences or chances thereof.

Premise (2). Now add in the assumption, which I call the "manifestability of the mental," that if two systems are mentally different, then there must be some physical contexts in which this difference will display itself in differential physical consequences, or at least in differential chances for such consequences.

Conclusion. It follows that mental differences without physical differences are impossible. (1) tells us that physical identity guarantees identity of physical consequences or chances thereof. And (2) tells us that mental difference requires the possibility of different physical consequences or chances thereof. So physical identity rules out mental difference.[5]

The crucial idea is that the completeness of physics leaves *no room* for mental differences to make a difference to physical consequences, once physical antecedents are given. Physical categories by themselves always suffice to fix the chances of physical consequences, without the help of mental categories. So the only way for mental differences to be manifestable is for them to have different physical bases.

Note that the argument does not work in reverse. We cannot argue similarly that all physical differences must depend on mental differences. The essential reason is that the mental, unlike the physical, is not complete. Suppose we assume, as is not entirely implausible, the "mental manifestability of the physical" ("if two systems are physically different, there must be contexts in which this will produce differential mental effects" – think of the mental effects produced in observers). This then gives us the second premise necessary for a "reversed version" of the preceding argument. But we still won't be able to conclude that these differential mental effects that manifest physical differences must always be produced by prior mental differences, for we will lack the other premise about completeness. It simply isn't true, as observed earlier, that mental effects are always fixed by mental antecedents. So there is still plenty of room left for mentally identical systems to be physically different and to show this (as required by the "mental manifestability of the physical") in differential mental effects.

5. Strong Supervenience Upheld

We can note immediately that, if this argument is sound, then it will support a version of strong supervenience. As I said earlier, the supervenience thesis has a weak and a strong reading, depending on whether we read the "cannot" in "cannot be mentally different without being physically different" as constraining mental variation only within worlds, or across worlds as well. This argument entails the strong form, at least to the extent of showing that physical identity implies mental identity across all physically possible worlds. For, as long as we hold the laws of physics fixed, then, by the completeness of physics, two systems with the same physical nature will display the same physical consequences in any given physical circumstances, even if those systems are in different possible worlds. And so, assuming still that mental differences must manifest themselves physically in some physical circumstances, it follows that those two systems will be mentally identical.

6. Supervenience on Brain States

Premise (1) rests on nothing more than the completeness of physics. But what about the premise (2), the manifestability of the mental? This may seem initially plausible, but it deserves closer scrutiny.

The most obvious argument for this principle would be that mental differences must always be capable of showing themselves in differential *behavior*. There certainly seems something initially odd about the idea of two people who are mentally different, yet behave in the same way in all physical contexts. (In this connection, note that the manifestability principle is not the strong requirement that every *token* mental difference *actually* manifests itself in differential physical consequences; just the weaker assumption that, for any *type* of mental difference, there is *some* type of physical context in which that difference would be physically manifested.)

If this behavioral interpretation of the manifestability principle were acceptable, then a highly local version of the supervenience of the psychological on the physical would follow, namely, the supervenience of psychological states on *brain states*. The argument could run as follows. Mental differences require behavioral differences. But behavioral differences are fixed entirely by prior brain states. So there cannot be mental differences without brain state differences.[6]

7. Broad Supervenience

Recent work in the philosophy of mind, however, makes it clear that this behavioral version of the manifestability requirement is too strong. For there is a wide range of mental states, namely, broad propositional attitudes, which do not supervene on brain states. The distinguishing characteristic of broad attitudes is precisely that individuals with identical brains can fail to share them. For example, Hilary Putnam has shown that the possession of natural kind beliefs depends on what kinds are actually present in the believer's world, as well as on the state of the believer's head (1975); and Tyler Burge has argued for a similar dependence of various kinds of theoretical beliefs on the believer's social context (1979, 1982).

Given that broad mental states do not supervene on brain states, it follows (by contraposition from the "narrow" version of the supervenience argument outlined in the previous section) that a manifestability requirement in terms of behavioral displays is too strong a requirement for broad attitudes. And this is, of course, what we do find: differences in broad attitude don't automatically display themselves in behavioral differences. To take a familiar example, consider Carl, who wants a glass of H_2O, and Lrac, his physically identical Twin Earth counterpart, who wants a glass of XYZ. They have different broad attitudes. But their behavior, in the sense of the physical movements of their bodies, will be the same in all physical contexts.[7]

However, the failure of broad attitudes to supervene on *brain* states should not make us reject the supervenience of mental on the physical tout court. For broad attitudes are *relational* states: when broad thinkers represent the world, they do so in virtue of their location in a historical or social context. So, in line with the discussion of relational states in Section 2, the appropriate requirement for the supervenience of broad mental attitudes is that broad attitudes should supervene on the physics of the individual thinker and the relevant context, even if not on the physics of the individual thinker alone.

It remains possible that the general manifestability argument for supervenience might still establish this weaker kind of supervenience for broad beliefs, even if not supervenience on brain states. All we need is a weaker manifestability premise to the effect that differences in broad beliefs are *somewhere* manifested in physical effects, even if they are not manifested in behavioral effects.

In defense of this weaker version of the manifestability premise, note that a mental difference that was not physically manifestable in any way would be radically undetectable. We know that our sense organs work by physical interaction with the environment, as do the instruments and other aids by which we extend the power of our sense organs. So if two different mental states yielded exactly the same physical manifestations in all contexts, then there would be no possibility whatsoever of our ever finding out about their difference. Yet surely any real mental difference ought to be somehow detectable, even if not behaviorally.

To illustrate this point, note that even the broad mental difference between Carl and his identical doppelganger Lrac will be distinguished by some differential physical consequences. For this broad mental difference depends on the relational difference that Carl is surrounded by H_2O, whereas Lrac is surrounded by XYZ. And this difference in their environments will obviously produce *some* differential physical effects by which we can distinguish the two cases.

I admit that this defense of the manifestability requirement is less than fully principled. Still, it would not be unreasonable to rest the case for supervenience at this point. For the argument for supervenience I have now given can be denied only by postulating mental differences that are completely undetectable by human beings, or at least that are not detectable by any normal physical means. The only possibility would seem to be introspectible private differences that are unconstrained by the physics of the brain, as in the radical "inverted spectrum" hypothesis that allows one person to introspect *green* where a physical identical introspects *red*. I suspect that most contemporary philosophers would be persuaded by an argument for supervenience that can be avoided only by accepting this extreme inverted spectrum hypothesis.

However, I think we can do even better. A variant of the argument we have been considering can be used to rule out all forms of dualism, including the inverted spectrum hypothesis. This is the argument for physical realization that I alluded to earlier and that I will explain in the next three sections.

The argument for physical realization won't in itself guarantee supervenience, for as we shall see physical realization is in one respect weaker than supervenience. But once we have established physical realization, and thereby ruled out dualism, it will be doubtful that any acceptable view of the mental can continue to deny the manifestability requirement on which supervenience rests. I shall return to these points in Section 13.

8. The Overdetermination Argument for Mind–Brain Coincidence

I have just pointed out that a radical form of dualism that is prepared to allow "inverted spectra" in physical identicals will escape the argument for supervenience. It is worth noting, however, that there are less radical forms of dualism, which do not wish to deny the premises of the supervenience argument and which therefore accept that there cannot be mental variation without physical variation. Epiphenomenalism of the kind mentioned earlier would be a case in point. We can think of epiphenomenalists as dualists who accept that mental differences must have physical symptoms and who therefore conclude, in light of the completeness of physics and in line with the argument we have been examining, that there cannot be mental differences without underlying physical differences.

Note, however, that to understand the manifestability argument as applying to epiphenomenalism in this way, it is clearly necessary that the manifestability premise be read *noncausally*. For epiphenomenalism denies that mental events ever *cause* any physical effects, and so in particular will deny the physical manifestability of the mental, if this is understood as the claim that mental differences *cause* differential physical *effects*. Still, we don't have to understand the manifestability requirement in this causal way. Instead of formulating it in terms of physical effects, we can simply say, as I did in the preceding section, that mental differences must be able to show themselves in differential physical "consequences." If we read premise (2) in this causally neutral way, as specifying only that mental differences be *followed* by physical differences, then it will be acceptable to epiphenomenalists. And this will then enable it to account for the epiphenomenalist commitment to supervenience, in the way just outlined.

But suppose that we do replace the manifestability premise by an explicitly causal premise that specifies that mental events do have physical effects. If we combine this alternative premise with the completeness of physics, then we will be in a position to mount an argument against epiphenomenalism in particular and dualist views of the mind in general. The thrust of this argument, in broad terms, won't be that the completeness of physics leaves no room for a nonphysical mind to manifest itself, but rather that it leaves no room for a nonphysical mind to exert a causal influence on the physical world. (Of course, this argument will be dialectically impotent against those specific forms of dualism, like epiphenomenalism, that explicitly deny that mental events have physical effects. But let us examine the argument first and come back to this point later.)

For the argument I want to consider, we will need the following corollary of the completeness of physics:

Premise (3). All physical effects have complete physical causes.

"Complete" here means that these causes on their own suffice to fix the chances of those effects. I originally formulated the completeness of physics in terms of "determination" rather than causation. But premise (3) will follow immediately from this formulation, on just about any account of causation.

Now I add the following explicitly causal requirement, in place of the earlier manifestability requirement:

Premise (4). Every mental occurrence causes some physical effect. (I shall call this the "assumption of mental influence.")

Consider some mental occurrence and one of the physical effects that are required by (4). For example, suppose you decide to lift your arm and, as a result, your arm rises.[8] By (3), this physical effect will also have a complete physical cause, which will presumably involve the neuronal and other physical antecedents of your arm rising. So it follows that your arm rising has two causes: a mental cause, your decision, and also a physical cause, your neurones firing.

Does this mean that such physical effects are always overdetermined, like the death of the man who is shot and simultaneously struck by a random bolt of lightning? This doesn't seem right. After all, when an effect is overdetermined by two causes, it follows that it would still have occurred if either one of the causes had been absent: the man would still have been killed by the lightning bolt even if he hadn't been shot, and vice versa. But we don't similarly want to say that your arm would still have gone up even if you hadn't wanted to lift it or, alternatively, even if different neurones had fired in your brain.

Given this last point, we can add another premise to (3) and (4):

Premise (5). The physical effects of mental states are not always overdetermined by independent mental and physical causes.

It follows from premises (3)–(5) that when your desire and your neurones cause your arm to move, these are not generally two independent causes, like the shot and the lightning bolt, but are somehow ontologically dependent. The mental cause must in some sense coincide with the physical cause if we are to avoid the conclusion that the movement of your arm was overdetermined.[9]

Note how this argument differs from the earlier argument for supervenience. There the aim was to show that the physical always *covaries* with the mental, and the argument was that physical variation is needed to produce the external evidence for mental variation. In this section, the aim has been to show that the mental is ontologically *inseparable* from the physical, and the argument has been that such a separation would imply an absurd proliferation of causal overdetermination.

9. Events and Facts

The argument of the preceding section shows that mental causes must somehow coincide with physical causes. Exactly how we understand this conclusion, however, depends on how we think about causation.

Some philosophers, most prominently Donald Davidson (1967), think that causation is a relation between events construed as "bare particulars" shorn of any general attributes. If you adopt this Davidsonian view of causation, then the natural way to make mental causes coincide with physical causes is to hold that such pairs of causes are both literally identical with some event, construed as a bare particular, which happens to have both mental and physical attributes. This is, of course, what Davidson himself does.

However, there are good arguments for being dissatisfied with this anemic view of causation and for preferring to view causal relata as *facts* rather than as Davidsonian bare particulars.[10] Accordingly, I shall assume the factual view of causal relata in what follows. This will then require a more full-blooded sense of mind–brain coincidence than Davidsonian event identity.

It is worth pointing out, however, that you could well feel a desire for such a more full-blooded version of mind–brain coincidence even if you agree with Davidson on the somewhat technical issue of the relata of causation. For this desire will arise for anyone who is inclined to accept any version of premise (4) that includes the idea that mental occurrences cause physical occurrences in *virtue of their mental properties*. This idea may seem independently plausible, even if you agree with Davidson about the causal relation itself. (When the pain makes me pull my arm away, isn't this in virtue of the cause being *painful?*) Any such version of premise (4) will lead to the conclusion that instantiations of mental properties must in some sense be ontologically intertwined with instantiations of physical properties, when conjoined with suitably adjusted versions of premise (3) (all physical effects result from physical causes in *virtue of nothing but the latter's physical properties*) and premise (5) (the physical effects of mental causes aren't always caused *both by virtue of their causes' physical properties and by virtue of their mental properties*).

It is no doubt some such line of thought that has led a number of commentators to complain that a Davidsonian view of the mind–brain relation involves an "epiphenomenalism of properties." For insofar as Davidsonians deny any more substantial relation between mental and physical properties than that they are co-instantiated in the same particular events,[11] then the line of argument just sketched shows that they need to reject any version of premise (4) according to which mental occurrences cause physical occurrences in virtue of their mental properties.

10. Physical Realization

As I said, I take the relata of causation to be facts, not events. So I take the overdetermination argument for physical realizability to show that *mental facts* are in some sense coincident with *physical facts*, not just that mental events are also physical events.

It is implausible, however, to uphold this conclusion as the strong claim that mental facts are strictly *identical* with physical facts. Consider the two facts, that I want to eat an ice cream, and that such and such neurons are firing in my brain. Since these two facts, respectively, involve the properties *wanting to eat an ice cream* and *having such and such neurons firing in one's brain*, their identity would require the identity of these properties. But there are strong arguments against identifying these properties, not least being the implausibility of supposing that there is a physically specifiable arrangement of neurons that is common to all and only those beings who want an ice cream. (Apart from anything else, consider all the Martians, or dogs, or people with brain prostheses who might want an ice cream.)

However, there is another way in which two facts can be ontologically dependent without being identical. The notion we need is *realization*. We can say that the fact that certain neurons are firing in my brain *realizes* the fact that I want an ice cream, even though the two properties involved are not identical. This will give us enough ontological dependence to satisfy the overdetermination argument but will fall short of strict identity.

Somewhat surprisingly, there is no agreed philosophical analysis of the notion of realization. Philosophers tend to use this notion much more freely than they explain it. Still, for present purposes we need an explicit account, so that we can check that the notion is adequate to the theoretical task that we want it to perform. In particular, we need to check that when some mental cause M is realized by some physical cause P, then the common effects of M and P are not overdetermined.

I propose that we adopt the following account of realization. The mental fact that person X has mental property M is realized by the physical fact that X has physical property P if and only if M is a higher-level property – a property of instantiating some lower-level property with certain features R – and P's instantiation in X has these character-istics R. In such a case, we can say that X satisfies M *in virtue of* satis-fying P.

By way of illustration, consider how the fact that *a painting is defaced* may be realized by the fact that *it has black ink marks on it*. We can take the property of being defaced to be the higher-level property of having some (any) physical feature that (a) is produced by an agent other than the original artist and (b) detracts from the appearance of the painting. In a particular case, some black ink marks may satisfy these require-ments. Then the painting will be defaced *in virtue of* having the marks; its having the marks will *realize* its being defaced.

Some philosophers might want to query whether all cases of realiza-tion fit this characterization. My response would be that it certainly fits most of the familiar cases in which philosophers deploy the notion,[12] and it is hard to think of any clear counterexamples.[13] So, short of attempting an exhaustive survey of existing philosophical usage, let me simply propose that we understand the notion of realization in this manner henceforth.

When P realizes M in this sense, it is clear that any common effects of M and P are not overdetermined. For, when P (being marked with black ink) realizes M (being defaced), it is not true that X (the painting) would still have been M (defaced) even if it hadn't been P (marked), nor is it true that X would still have been P (marked) even if it hadn't been M (defaced).[14] So if these two facts have a common effect, E (such as making the painting darker), it won't be true that the effect E would still have occurred if X hadn't been M (defaced) or, alternatively, if X hadn't been P (marked).

Some readers might wonder whether the thesis that mental effects are realized by physical facts is strong enough to satisfy premise (4), which claimed, remember, that *every mental occurrence causes some physical effect*. The worry would be that when some physical P realizes mental M, it is only P that, strictly speaking, causes any physical effects, and not M. However, this worry is irrelevant to my argument. Let us adopt the terminology of Frank Jackson and Philip Pettit (1988, 1990, 1992), who, in such cases, distinguish the causal "efficacy" of P from the causal "relevance" of M. There are philosophical contexts in which this is a distinction worth making. But it is not a distinction to which much regard is paid by the everyday notion of cause. (It seems just as true that the defacement made the painting darker as that the ink marks did.) I intend premise (4) in the way it is understood in everyday discourse, that is, as allowing that realiz*ed* states can be causes, as well as realiz*ing* states. This is why this premise, along with the completeness and overdetermination premises, implies that if mental causes aren't type-identical with the physical causes of their physical effects (which they generally aren't), then they must at least be realized by them.

11. Varieties of Realization

The notion of realization is most commonly deployed in connection with the functionalist view that mental properties can be characterized as the property of having some property that causally mediates in a certain way between perception and behavior.[15] If we add to this functionalist idea the assumption that those causal roles are in fact played by physical properties, then it follows immediately from the account of realization given in the preceding section that functionalist mental properties are realized by physical properties.

It is worth pointing out, however, that a wide range of views of the mind apart from functionalism are also consistent with the thesis that mental facts are realized by physical facts in the sense I have defined. To take an example that is somewhat removed from functionalism, consider Donald Davidson's (1980) view of the mental. Though the aspect of Davidson's views I want to consider is standardly presented in harness with his view of causation mentioned earlier, we can separate his view of causation from the further thesis that to be in a given mental state M is to be in some state that causes behavior that would warrant the attribution of M to you. The point I want to make about this thesis is that while it is clearly quite different from functionalism, since it makes essential appeal to the nonscientific canons of interpretation that Davidson takes to govern our attributions of mental states to others, it equally accepts the idea that the mental may be realized by the physical. For if it is physical fact P that causes the behavior that warrants the attribution of M to person X, then X is in M in virtue of being in P, and consequently M is realized by P.

12. The Rejection of Dualism

I have argued that we need to accept that mental facts are realized by physical facts in order to avoid the conclusion that the physical effects of mental causes are overdetermined. This still leaves open, as I have just observed, a wide range of positions in the philosophy of mind. But it does rule out dualism.

Dualists standardly defend their position by maintaining that the distinctively conscious features of mind could not possibly be possessed by merely physical states. Let us take it that this is the defining thesis of dualism. That is, let us understand dualism as the view that the mental properties essentially involve certain conscious characteristics *C* that cannot possibly be features of physical properties. Then it follows from my account of realization that dualists must deny that mental facts can be realized by physical facts. For, by dualist hypothesis, it cannot be in virtue of having any physical property *P* that you are in a state with such conscious characteristics *C*.

So the overdetermination argument for physical realization amounts to an argument against dualism. Of course, as I observed earlier, this will cut no dialectical ice against those epiphenomenalist forms of dualism that are prepared to deny that mental occurrences have any effects, for such epiphenomenalists simply escape the overdetermination argument by denying its premise (4).

Even so, the overdetermination argument does still tell us something important about dualism. It shows that epiphenomenalism isn't an *optional* form of dualism, but a conclusion that all dualists are forced into. Dualists need to deny some premise in the overdetermination argument for physical realization, and the obvious candidate is premise (4), the principle of mental influence. (Alternatives would be to deny the completeness of physics or to accept that all behavior is overdetermined; but as far as I know, no contemporary dualists have taken these options.)

I have no further argument to give in this essay for this principle of mental influence, apart from the fact that it flies in the face of normal thinking to deny it. But we might well ask *why* epiphenomenalists want to adopt the curious view that mental occurrences are causally impotent, especially given the availability of physicalist alternatives that avoid this. The answer, of course, has to do with various intuitions about the radically nonphysical nature of consciousness. I myself think these intuitions are ill-founded, but it would take us too far afield to pursue this issue here.[16]

13. Realization without Supervenience

Compare the argument for physical realization with the argument for supervenience once more. The argument for supervenience, remember, rested on the "principle of the manifestability of the mental," the principle that any mental difference must be capable of showing itself in differential physical consequences. The argument for physical realization, by contrast, did not refer to this manifestability requirement as such, but rather to the "principle of mental influence," which required that each mental state must have some physical effect.

Some readers might have noted that this requirement of mental influence is in one respect weaker than that of manifestability, in that it requires only that each mental state must have *some* physical effect, not necessarily that different mental states always have *different* effects. This suggests the possibility that the mental may conform to the weaker principle of mental influence, but violate the stronger requirement of manifestability, and for this reason display physical realization, but not supervenience.

This relates to the question, left hanging at the end of Section 7, concerning the status of the principle of mental manifestability. In a moment I will make a few further comments on this question. But first it will be interesting to note that there is a partial illustration of the possibility of influence without manifestability, and hence realization without supervenience. This is the example of broad attitudes and their relation to brain states. As I observed in Section 7, broad attitudes do not supervene on brain states, in line with the fact that they do not satisfy a narrow manifestability requirement framed in terms of strictly behavioral effects. Nevertheless, broad beliefs do arguably satisfy a narrow requirement of mental influence, in that they arguably do all have *some* behavioral effects, and so they ought at least to be realized by brain states.

Consider once more Carl and his physically identical doppelganger Lrac. When Carl believes that a glass contains H_2O, Lrac believes that a glass contains XYZ. These differing beliefs don't manifest themselves in behavioral *differences*. But this doesn't mean that they aren't causally influential on behavior. For this requires only that Carl's belief, and Lrac's, each have *some* behavioral effects, maybe the same effects, like moving an arm, and there is no reason to deny this. And then, given this influence on behavioral effects, plus the fact that those behavioral effects will also be caused by brain states, we can argue, as before, that these beliefs must each be realized by some brain state.

There is nothing puzzling about the idea of a state that fails to supervene on the physics of the brain, but is nevertheless realized by some physical feature of the brain. The failure of supervenience on brain states for broad attitudes arises because these particular mental properties are not only higher level but *relational:* they are properties of having some property that bears some relation to features of the individual's environment and history. So one individual can have a brain property with the relevant relational features (Carl is in a world with H_2O), and so instantiate the relevant mental state, while another individual (Lrac) can have just the same brain property, but without its having the relevant relational features, and so be mentally different. Yet in both cases it is still an internal brain property that has or lacks the relevant relational features, and so it is still a brain property that realizes the broad belief.

Now, as I said earlier, the fact that broad attitudes don't supervene on brain states does not show that they don't supervene on the physical properties of the thinker *and* the relevant context. Moreover, as I also observed earlier, we would be able to argue that they *must* so supervene if we could assume that differences in broad attitudes must *somewhere* be manifested in physical effects, even if these are only effects of aspects of the relevant context rather than of the thinker.

The question left hanging at the end of Section 7 was whether any further argument can be given for this broad manifestability requirement. We saw that dualists who believe in inverted spectra will deny this requirement. But we have now ruled out dualism, via the overdetermination argument, and more generally established that if mental properties aren't themselves identical with physical properties, then they must be higher-order properties involving some role R (like a functionalist causal role or a Davidsonian interpretational role), and these higher-order properties must be realized by physical properties that in fact play those roles R. This now gives us a further reason, I believe, to suppose that differences in mental states must be manifested by difference in physical effects. For if mental differences require different roles, and these roles must be realized by physical states, it is difficult to see how such differences could fail to produce differential physical consequences somewhere.

NOTES

1. I first put forward this argument for supervenience in Papineau (1990). For a similar line of argument, see Barry Loewer's contribution to this volume. I make the distinction between this argument and the argument for physical realization in Papineau (1993, chap. 1). Much of the other material in this chapter also derives from Papineau (1993, chap. 1).

2. The compatibility of supervenience with ontological independence is emphasized in Horgan (1993, sec. 1).

3. See Kim (1984).

4. Some readers might object to my use of "explanation" here, on the grounds that a full physical specification of the antecedents of some large-scale physical outcome won't necessarily be *illuminating* to humans, in the way that an explanation using chemical or biological or psychological terminology might be (cf. Putnam 1978, p. 42). No matter. My argument only requires that the physical antecedents *fix* or *cause* the physical outcome, not that they illuminate it. David Owens (1992) is even more particular and would object to this last use of "cause," on the grounds that causes aren't causes unless they illuminate. Again no matter. My arguments need only whatever is left in the notion of cause after we take away the anthropocentric factor of illumination.

5. A version of this argument is found in McGinn (1982, p. 29) and further discussed by McFetridge (1990, p. 86).

6. This is the version of the argument articulated by McGinn. He does, however, observe that it may not apply to all mental states.

7. It is true that Carl will pick up a glass of H_2O, where Lrac will pick up a glass of XYZ. But let us simplify the exposition by understanding 'behavior' to stand for the kind of strictly bodily movement that Carl and Lrac share.

8. Are bodily movements, like arms raising, mouths moving, and so on, properly counted as *physical* effects? Strictly, no. "Arm" and "mouth" are biological terms, not physical ones, and it is doubtful that they can be *reduced* to physical notions. So for complete accuracy, we ought to take the physical effects of mental causes to be the motion of bits of matter, which happen to be in arms, mouths, and so on. However, it will smooth the exposition if I can be less than strict on this point.

9. This form of argument for physical realization is to be found in Peacocke (1979, sec. 3.3). David Lewis has also used the completeness of physics to argue for a version of mind–brain identity (1966). But his second premise is much stronger than the "assumption of mental influence." Where I, following Peacocke, need only the uncontentious claim that each *particular* mental occurrence has *some* physical effect, Lewis invokes the far stronger functionalist thesis that mental *types* can be *defined* in terms of their characteristic roles in mediating between physical causes and effects.

10. For a defense of this view, see Mellor (1987). Another alternative to Davidson's view of causation is to allow that causes are events but insist that events are instantiations of properties, rather than Davidsonian bare particulars (Kim 1973). However, Mellor (1987) argues that "events" of this kind are simply a subspecies of facts. My terminology will follow Mellor rather than Kim.

11. It is a moot point whether Davidsonians *have* to reject a substantial ontological relation between mental and physical properties. After all, Davidson holds that mental truths supervene on physical truths. True, supervenience doesn't itself require any ontological dependence of mental and physical properties, as I have stressed. But as I shall show later, Davidson also has a rationale for the different claim that mental properties are *realized* by physical properties, and so are ontologically intertwined with them. This seems to me to allow a reasonable Davidsonian defense against the charge of epiphenomenalism.

12. I have only characterized realization, it is true, for facts of the form *Fa*. But the idea can easily enough be extended to cover more complicated cases.

13. What about a specific disjunct "realizing" a disjunction? My reaction is that if there is no principle that ties all the different possible disjuncts together, then it is unnatural to think of any one disjunct as realizing anything; whereas, if there is such a principle, then to realize the disjunct is in effect to realize a higher-level property, namely, the property of having the property specified by the principle in question.

14. Note that these are counterfactuals, not general claims of necessity. Of course, it is in general true that paintings can be defaced without having black ink marks, as well as have black ink marks without being defaced. But, in the actual circumstances, *this* painting wouldn't be defaced if it

didn't have these black ink marks, and wouldn't have these black ink marks if it wasn't defaced.

15. I am here assuming the "functional state identity" rather than the "functional specification" version of functionalism. See Block (1980).

16. For a discussion of these intuitions, and a defense of a physicalist view of consciousness, see Papineau (1993, chap. 4).

REFERENCES

Block, N. (1980). "What Is Functionalism?" in N. Block (ed.), *Readings in the Philosophy of Psychology*, Vol. 1, pp. 171–84. London: Methuen.

Burge, T. (1979). "Individualism and the Mental," in P. French et al. (eds.), *Midwest Studies in Philosophy*, Vol. 4, pp. 73–121.

Burge, T. (1982). "Other Bodies," in A. Woodfield (ed.), *Thought and Object*, pp. 97–120. Oxford: Clarendon Press.

Crane, T. (1991). "Why Indeed?" *Analysis*, 51, 32–7.

Davidson, D. (1967). "Causal Relations," *Journal of Philosophy*, 64, 691–703.

(1980). *Essays on Actions and Events*. Oxford: Clarendon Press.

Horgan, T. (1993). "From Supervenience to Superdupervenience: Meeting the Demands of the Material World," *Mind*, 102, 555–86.

Jackson, F., and Pettit, P. (1988). "Functionalism and Broad Content," *Mind*, 97, 381–400.

(1990). "Program Explanation: A General Perspective," *Analysis*, 107–17.

(1992). "Structural Explanation in Social Theory," in D. Charles and K. Lennon (eds.), *Reduction, Explanation and Realism* (pp. 97–131). Oxford: Clarendon Press.

Kim, J. (1973). "Causation, Nomic Subsumption, and the Concept of Event." *Journal of Philosophy*, 70, 217–36.

(1984). "Supervenience and Supervenient Causation." *Southern Journal of Philosophy*, 70, 45–56.

Lewis, D. (1966). "An Argument for the Identity Theory." *Journal of Philosophy*, 63, 17–25.

McFetridge, I. (1990). *Logical Necessity*. London: Aristotelian Society.

McGinn, C. (1982). *The Character of Mind*. Oxford University Press.

Mellor, D. (1987). "The Singularly Affecting Facts of Causation," in P. Pettit et al. (eds.), *Metaphysics and Morality* (pp. 111–33). Oxford: Basil Blackwell.

Owens, D. (1992). *Causes and Coincidences*. Cambridge University Press.

Papineau, D. (1990). "Why Supervenience?" *Analysis*, 50, 66–71.

(1991). "The Reason Why," *Analysis*, 51, 37–40.

(1993). *Philosophical Naturalism*. Oxford: Basil Blackwell.

Peacocke, C. (1979). *Holistic Explanation*. Oxford: Clarendon Press.

Putnam, H. (1975). "The Meaning of 'Meaning'," in his *Mind, Language and Reality*, 215–71. Cambridge University Press.

(1978). *Meaning and the Moral Sciences*. London: Routledge and Kegan Paul.

Supervenience and the Essences of Events

ELIAS E. SAVELLOS

1. Introduction

It is no secret that where A and B denote distinct types of properties, entities, or what have you, philosophers disagree as to what is precisely implied by the assertion that As *supervene* on Bs. On the other hand, there is general philosophical agreement that at the very core of this assertion is the idea of nonreducibility-cum-dependence: As' covariation with and dependence on Bs is consistent with their irreducibility to Bs.[1] It is precisely this core feature of supervenience that looks attractive when we discuss the ontic status of events. It is well known that Donald Davidson formidably pioneered, and many after him pursued, the idea that events are best thought of as ontologically distinct, irreducible entities.[2] The case for the dependence of events, on the other hand, may be easier to make. It suffices, for example, to go along with the currently popular view of events as instances of properties.[3] If events are exemplifyings, as this account has it, then, clearly, there must be something that exemplifies, something on which events are, to some degree or other, dependent. The upshot of the combination of these ideas is that events and supervenience seem to be made for each other.

The issue of the supervenience of events has received its first, and to date only, systematic examination in Lawrence Lombard's *Events: A Metaphysical Study*.[4] The account of event-supervenience of *Events* is important in many ways. As a pioneering work, it invaluably maps the logical territory of the case and provides a focus for the discussion. Moreover, it is metaphysically novel and interesting. Following Jaegwon Kim's original formulation of principles of supervenience, such principles are usually formulated in the literature in terms of a set of properties supervening on a different set of properties. In *Events*, however, we find a principle of "ontological supervenience," one that purports to capture the supervenience of events as a distinct type of entity on entities of quite a different ontic type. Finally, it should be noticed that Lombard's own view of events is at the very center of the account of events as instances of properties. It should not be surprising if Lombard's discussion of event-supervenience has important ramifications for other forms of this account.

In the course of the argument in this essay, I will show that, despite its merits, the account of supervenience in *Events* is seriously flawed nonetheless. *Events* prompts us to seek a connection between the proposed principle of event-supervenience and the avowance of essentialism. Yet when we do so, we find that the principle of event-supervenience neither supports, nor is supported by, the view that events have essences, and it is at conflict with the view that events have individual essences (haecceities). In fact, it turns out that if event-haecceitism is what we want to hold on to, we might as well abandon hope that any substantive event-supervenience thesis can be formulated.

2. Main Tenets of Lombard's View

Three tenets of *Events* are of concern here. In an initial and rough formulation, these are (a) events are changes, (b) events have essences as well as individual essences, and (c) events are supervenient entities. On pain of injustice to Lombard's thoughtful and thorough discussion, let me briefly amplify these tenets to the extent necessary for the present inquiry.

According to Lombard, the true theory of events will view these entities as ontologically unique particulars and will construe them, roughly, as nonrelational changes in/of objects. Now, a change, Lombard argues, is to be understood as a "movement" from the having of one to the having of another "static" property by an object through some portion of a "quality space" during an interval of time. A "static" property is to be understood as the kind of property that does not imply change, and the notion of a "quality space" is the notion of a space of static properties closed under scientific empirical theories. Finally, in its moving (in a quality space) from having the one to having the other static property, an object is said to have a "dynamic" property.[5] Given that much, the first main tenet of Lombard's position can be rewritten more informatively as

(MT) Events are the exemplifyings of dynamic properties by objects at times.[6]

The second central feature of Lombard's account of events is the avowance of essentialism.[7] Lombard is convinced that events have essences (essential properties), and he engages in detailed argument to establish each of the following. First, events are essentially changes in the object they are in fact changes in; if an event occurred at all, it could not have been a change in an object other than the one it was in fact a change in. Second, the time of occurrence of an event is essential to it; events occur at the same times in every possible world in which they occur. Third, events are essentially the exemplifyings, or havings, of *certain* of the dynamic properties of which they are in fact the havings. And this last sort of essentialism needs some clarification. Some dynamic properties are what we may call "sortal" properties, that is, properties that divide or individuate events into kinds or types. Lombard argues that if an event e is in fact an instance of the type Fing, where Fing is such a "sortal" dynamic property, then e would be an instance of Fing in all possible worlds in which it exists. That is, e's being an exemplifying of the "sortal" dynamic property Fing that e is in fact an exemplifying is an essence of e.[8] With this, we can now informally summarize the essentialism that Lombard argues for as follows:

> **(LESS)** The object that is in fact the subject of the event, the dynamic event-type Fing of which the event is in fact an exemplifying, and the time at which the exemplifying of Fing by the object in fact occurs, are essential to the event having them.[9]

In *Events* we find essentialism carried a step further. In addition to essences, events, we are told, have *individual essences,* or *haecceities,* that is, essences that an event x has in all possible worlds in which it exists and that no event y other than x can share. The individual essences of events, Lombard claims, are rather peculiar "compounds" of three different types of entity: objects, properties, and times. Let us take Lombard on his word and talk of these haecceities from now on by employing a *canonical description,* a singular term of the form '$[o_i, \text{Fing}_i, t_i]$', where '$o_i$' is the name (or any singularly referring term) of an object capable of change and such that it is essential to an event e, 'Fing_i' is the name of an essential dynamic property-type of which event e is in fact an exemplifying, and 't_i' is the name of an essential to e interval of time during which the object o_i in fact exemplifies Fing_i.[10] The attribution of haecceities to Lombard-style events can now be articulated more perspicuously as

> **(LHCT)** $\Box(e)(e$ is an event & e "has" $[o_i, \text{Fing}_i, t_i] \supset \Box(e')(e = e' \equiv e'$ "has" $[o_i, \text{Fing}_i, t_i])$.[11]

The minimal reading of the sort of haecceitism expressed by (LHCT) yields a principle that makes individual essences necessary for the existence of an event:

> **(PE)** If some event e exists in some world w, then some $[o_i, \text{Fing}_i, t_i]$ occurs in w.

A much stronger principle that can also be "read off" the haecceitist doctrine expressed by (LHCT) is the converse of (PE), a principle that engenders event-existence from the existence of some $[o_i, \text{Fing}_i, t_i]$ in a world:

(CPE) If some $[o_i, \text{Fing}_i, t_i]$ occurs in some world w, then some event e occurs in w.

Whether we are entitled to this preceding principle is at the heart of the argument of this inquiry, and so its discussion will have to wait.[12] Presuming the truth of the rest of Lombard's tenets thus far, we can move on to the final issue of concern here, the claim that events are supervenient entities. Events, Lombard believes, covary with, depend on, and are not reducible to, objects, dynamic properties, and times. The specific articulation of event-supervenience, Lombard claims, takes the form of a principle that I denominate here as (GSL) and that goes as follows:[13]

(GSL) Possible worlds cannot be alike with respect to the truth and falsity of propositions concerning the existence of objects capable of non-relational change, the possession and non-possession of static properties by those objects, and the times at which those objects possess and fail to possess those properties, and alike with respect to the truth or falsity of the proposition that there are events, and yet unalike with respect to the truth and falsity of propositions concerning which events occur. (*Events*, p. 221)

3. (GSL) and Essences: Principle (LESS)

We cannot fail to notice that (GSL) exhibits a striking similarity of both conceptual content and function with Lombard's essentialist tenets, principles (LESS) and (LHCT). The conceptual resources employed in the formulation of all of these principles are the same. Furthermore, (GSL) purports to express the cross-world supervenience of events on other kinds of entities, namely, objects, *dynamic* properties,[14] and times. As formulated, (GSL) informs us that *specific* events ("*which* events occur") are transworld fixed by the way things are with the latter entities ("subvenient base," or "base" for short). (LESS) and (LHCT), on the other hand, also provide (each to some degree or other) for specific one-to-one cross-world correlations between specific events and specific objects, dynamic properties, and times.

These similarities should make us suspect that there is a close connection among these principles. And there is a further consideration that reinforces this suspicion. (GSL) expresses the determination of *specific* events. Yet it would be quite a mystery if this determination were to obtain in a "holistic" or "global" manner, that is, in a manner such that the total set of entities of the base fixes *as a whole* the occurrence of individual events.[15] Given that events are understood as objects exemplifying dynamic properties at times, and given that (GSL) expresses the determination of specific events, if true at all, (GSL) must be "read off" as implying, *minimally*, a strict, one-to-one determination of specific events by specific (base) *subsets* of objects, dynamic properties, and times. Let us call this latter determination implied by (GSL) the "singular association" requirement. It must be obvious that a further mystery remains, namely, how this "singular association" requirement is satisfied at all. If we are to dispel this latter mystery and understand how each supervenient event is necessitated by the base, we must minimally suppose that both of the following obtain. First, (GSL) (as formulated) requires that the cross-world indiscernibility of the base is understood as the indiscernibility of specific subsets of the base whose members are particular objects, dynamic properties, and times. Second, the determination of specific events by these subsets is related to *principles* that are such that they are either sufficient, necessary, or both to mediate the singular association between specific subsets of the base and specific events that are determined by those. But what could be a better candidate for this job than the essentialist principles (LESS) and/or (LHCT)?[16]

It seems then that a close connection between (GSL) and either or both (LESS) and (LHCT) is intended by Lombard. Yet Lombard is not clear about this, and the reader may complain at this point that I have forced the upholder of (GSL) to a result that is already setting up a trap for his position. So never mind, nothing is lost if we go about this in a hypothetico-deductive manner and ask, What, if any, is the relation between the supervenience thesis (GSL) and the essentialist principles for events that Lombard proposes? The remainder of this essay will take up this question.

As a start, let me demonstrate that there could be no connection between (GSL) and the essentialist principle (LESS). Suppose that both (GSL) and (LESS) are true, and suppose further that the transworld indiscernibility of the subvenient base is in terms of essential properties of events. (Of course, at this point we must also suppose that the dynamic properties involved are restricted to Fings, i.e., "sortal" dynamic properties.) We can now see that the claim that events have essential properties could not yield the supervenience thesis. (LESS) assures us that where F^* is an essence of an event e, in every possible world in which e exists, e will have that essence.[17] But (LESS) does not guarantee that no event other than e will share F^* with e. Essences are shareable, and this means that the existence of two worlds w and w^* indiscernible in respects of the essences of the events in them, does not guarantee that w, w^* will contain the same number of events, much less the same number of the very same events, as (GSL) would have it. Thus, the truth of (LESS) is quite compatible with the existence of a world w^* where e exists and has F^*, *and* an infinite number of events distinct from e also exist in w^* and also have F^*. But this is to say that (LESS) is compatible with the falsity of (GSL). (LESS) does *not* imply (GSL).

Could it be that, in the converse direction, it is the supervenience thesis that implies the claim that events have essences? Again it is not hard to see that the answer to this must be negative. Where F is an essential property and a is an event, it suffices to consider the pair of worlds w, w^* that are such that, in w, a exists and has F, and in w^*, a exists and lacks F. This is a minimal model that falsifies (LESS), but it is consistent with the truth of (GSL). (GSL) does *not* imply (LESS).[18]

(LESS) neither implies nor is implied by (GSL).[19] If there is a connection between (GSL) and the avowance of event-essentialism, it must be sought in a principle stronger than the one that tells us that events have essences. Let us turn to the principle that assures us that events have *individual* essences, the haecceitist principle (LHCT).

4. (GSL) and Individual Essences: Principle (LHCT)

Let us suppose that principle (LHCT) is true and furthermore that the indiscernibility of (GSL)'s base is the intraworld indiscernibility of $[o_1,$ $\text{Fing}_1, t_1] \ldots [o_n, \text{Fing}_n, t_n]$, that is, of individual essences (haecceities) of events. What exactly could the connection between (GSL) and (LHCT) be? Now it seems to be the case that Lombard himself wants to establish a connection. Yet Lombard's discussion of this is not clear, and besides we have agreed to go about this in a hypothetical manner.[20] We had best attempt to untangle the possible connection between (GSL) and (LHCT) by taking one issue at a time.

It can be shown quickly first that (GSL) does *not* imply that events have the individual essences that we are assured they have by principle (LHCT): (A) We know that (GSL) does not imply (LESS) (from the argument of the previous section). (B) Assume now that (GSL) implies (LHCT). (C) We know that (LHCT) implies (LESS) (from the definition of (LHCT)). (D) Thus, (GSL) implies (LESS), which contradicts (A). (GSL) does not imply (LHCT).[21]

If we combine this last result with those reached in the preceding section, we have thus far that the truth of (GSL) does not support either Lombard's claim that events have essences or his claim that events have individual essences. And this means that if there is a connection between the supervenience principle (GSL) and Lombard-style haecceitism, this must be sought in the direction of the presumed truth of (LHCT) implying the truth of (GSL). Although (LHCT) is not necessary for the truth of (GSL), it may well be that it is sufficient. Let us turn then to the question of whether (LHCT) implies (GSL).[22]

At first glance, the upholder of both (LHCT) and (GSL) seems to be on good ground here, for it can be demonstrated that our adherence to (LHCT) goes a long way toward ensuring the truth of (GSL). To see this, let us, for simplicity, use H_i as a shorthand name of a haecceity [o_i, $Fing_i$, t_i], and let a, b, c, d be events. We can see that the following models of worlds are precluded by our adherence to (LHCT):

(A)	(B)	(C)	(D)
w_1: H_1, a	w_1: H_1, a	w_1: H_1, a, b	w_1: H_1, H_2, a, b
w_2: H_1, b	w_2: H_1, b, c	w_2: H_1, c	w_2: H_1, H_2, c, d

In (A) we have a minimal model of worlds indiscernible in haecceities and containing the same number of events, yet we suppose that these are different events from world to world. But how can this be? By (PE), both a and b must have an essence, and so both have H_1. But then by (LHCT), they are the same event, which contradicts the hypothesis that they are different events. In (B) we suppose that we have worlds indiscernible in haecceities yet differing both as to which particular events occur in them and as to the number of these events. But again, this is not possible: each of the existing events a, b, c, must have a haecceity. So H_1 is had by a in w_1, while in w_2 it is "split" to be had by both b and c. But then by (LHCT), $a = b = c$, which contradicts the assumption. Similar considerations will show that model (C), where H_1 is "split" over a and b in w_1 yet "fused" back over c in w_2, is also impossible.

The upshot so far is that our adherence to (LHCT) prohibits "switching," "fusion," and "fission" in the "distribution" of haecceities over events in and across worlds and imposes a very strict one-to-one "association" between the former and the latter. (For reasons that will become immediately obvious I avoid "instantiation" and its cognates.) We should not think, moreover, that these results are due to the "minimalism" in the number of haecceities in the models we have examined. As long as the same number of events occurs across worlds, "richer" models like (D) will also be rendered impossible by the one-to-one association imposed by (LHCT). For suppose (D) is understood as follows:

$$w_1: a \char`^ H_1, b \char`^ H_2 \quad (\text{"}\char`^\text{": "}x \text{ is one-to-one associated to } y\text{")}$$
$$w_2: c \char`^ H_1, d \char`^ H_2$$

By (LHCT), $a = c$ and $b = d$. Thus w_1, w_2, which are indiscernible in haecceities, contain again exactly the same events.

So far, so good. On the basis of our acceptance of the truth of (LHCT), it appears that we can grant the truth of (GSL) every step of the way. Is this to say that (LHCT) makes (GSL) immune to all counterexamples? The answer depends crucially on how we respond to the possibility of the following model:

(E)
w_1: H_1, H_2, a, b
w_2: H_1, H_2, c

We assume that, like (D), the worlds w_1, w_2 are "rich" in haecceities that are cross-world indiscernible, yet unlike (D), the number of events differs from world to world.[23] Two observations about (E) are in order before we go on. First, if (E) is a possible (cogent) model, then (E) suffices to demonstrate that (GSL) is false, in which case, in turn, (LHCT) does not imply (GSL). And this is to say that if (LHCT) is true, (E) is possible only if (GSL) is false. Second, we must take notice that in having assumed the truth of (LHCT), (E) is the only model left that could pose a threat to (GSL). For (E) has been arrived at by the previous elimination of other sparser models, and (E) itself is the minimal case of the sort of worlds that could falsify (GSL). If (E) succeeds in falsifying (GSL), there is no need to consider yet richer models, and if (E) fails in its task, it will fail, as we shall see, for reasons that carry over to richer models. Thus, given (LHCT), (GSL) is false only if (E) is possible. From the conjunction of these observations, we can conclude that, given (LHCT), (GSL) is true if and only if (E) is not possible.

Is (E) a possible model? To be sure, if we think that (E) is possible it must be that we think along the following lines: by principle (PE), every occurring event must have some individual essence, and so event c in w_2 either has both H_1 and H_2 or it has only one of them. Now, the assumption that c has both H_1 and H_2 leads once again to the impossibility of (E). For by parity of reasoning, we must allow that the events of w_1 can have both H_1 and H_2, and since H_1, H_2 exhaust the haecceities occurring in both worlds, by (LHCT), $b = a = c$. On the other hand, why should we assume that both H_1 and H_2 in w_2 are had by c? For we can suppose instead that only one of the haecceities in w_2 is correlated with c while *the other exists in w_2 and yet it remains associated with no event whatsoever (in w_2)*. Given this supposition, we can now conclude, model (E) appears to be perfectly cogent.

Can we accept this line of thinking as to the cogency of (E)? Clearly, the answer to this depends crucially on whether or not we can accept the hypothesis that a haecceity of an event can exist in a world w_i and *not* be "associated" with any event in w_i. Let us call this latter assumption "hypothesis h." Let us be clear about a couple of things as to h. The first is obvious: if h is true, then (E) shows that worlds w_1, w_2, which are indiscernible in terms of the haecceities occurring in them, differ as to which events occur in them. Thus, the supervenience thesis (GSL) is false, and it is not implied by (LHCT). What may not be immediately obvious, however, is, second, that h is the *only* assumption that could make (E) possible given our assumption that (LHCT) is true. The one-to-one association of events and haecceities that, as we have seen, is imposed on us from our adherence to (LHCT), recurs in (E) and renders it an impossible model. The only way we can avoid this is to postulate h. From both of these remarks, we have in the end that, given (LHCT), (E) is possible if and only if h holds. Thus, the crucial question appears to be the acceptability of h.

5. The Debate about h

What reason could we have to hold h? In this section I will first suggest some reasons that may prompt the foe of (GSL) to think that h holds. Then I will suggest how the friend of (GSL) may respond to the challenge. I must say, nonetheless, that I will not attempt to make a conclusive case for either the foe or the friend of (GSL). And why I say this will soon become obvious.

The foe of GSL can insist that the truth of h yields the possibility of (E) and thus, in turn, the falsity of (GSL). Let us see some reasons the foe of (GSL) may have to uphold h. He may say: (A) Haecceities are individual properties of events, yet they are properties nevertheless. But properties are "necessary beings"; they exist in all possible worlds regardless of whether they are instantiated by an event. So the existence in a world of some haecceity does not imply the existence of the event that is its would-be bearer of its instantiation. Hypothesis h holds. (B) Let us assume that haecceities of events exist only *qua* instantiated properties. Why should they be instantiated only by their would-be bearer event? Perhaps they exist in some world w_i *qua* being instantiated by something else, say, a spatiotemporal zone z. Then, again, h holds. (C) Let us not forget that we are dealing with very special haecceities – haecceities construed Lombard-style as compounds of objects, "sortal" dynamic properties (Fings), and times. Surely, both objects and times, two of the component parts of *these* haecceities, can exist in a world without events. As for the dynamic properties, the last component of the haecceities, these are either "necessary beings" existing uninstantiated in every world, or if we insist that they exist only *qua* being instantiated, they *are* after all instantiated: they are instantiated by the objects that have them. But if every part of the compound haecceity $[o_i, \text{Fing}_i, t_i]$ exists, why not accept that the whole haecceity exists? So, why do we need to assume the existence of some event in a world in order for it to be the bearer of the instantiation and thus of the existence of that haecceity in that world? We must conclude that h holds.

Let me turn now to the friend of (GSL) and make a few suggestions concerning how he might respond to these challenges. Clearly, challenge (A) can prove to be troublesome for his position. Perhaps the defender of (GSL) can point out that theses of supervenience are important tools that we should not easily abandon. But the proposed hypothesis that properties can exist unexemplified in all possible worlds would be unpalatable not only to the advocate of the supervenience involved here, but to the advocates of a garden variety of supervenience theses that are formulated in terms of indiscernibility of properties. For any such thesis, the effect of this hypothesis is that now all worlds are indiscernible in terms of the properties in them, and thus their indiscernibility is now trivially assured. Supervenience theses that construe the indiscernibility of the base as the indiscernibility of properties will now make little or no sense of the determination of anything by that base. Of course, these issues are complicated, and I have already said earlier that for reasons soon to be seen, I will refrain from getting too involved. So, never mind, let us move on to (B).

When it comes to challenger's argument (B), the defender of (GSL) is on better ground. For, on the assumption that he has won the day on (A), he can now point out that a haecceity of the sort we are concerned with is an individual *property* of an event, and if it exists at all in some world w, it must be instantiated either by something other than an event or by an event. Yet the first hypothesis, that proposed by his challenger in (B), yields absurd results for the envisaged model (E): suppose that H_2 is instantiated by an event in w_1, and it exists *qua* being instantiated by something else, say, a spatiotemporal zone z, in w_2. Then by (LHCT), the event of w_1 equals the zone of w_2, which is absurd. Alternatively, suppose that in *both* worlds w_1 and w_2 of the model (E), H_2 is instantiated by a zone. But the case in point is (GSL), and we have agreed that (GSL) is now to be understood as being formulated in terms of individual properties *of events*. If H_2 is an individual essence *of an event*, then by (LHCT) as before, the zone is the event. And if it is not, we are not talking about the same thing. Thus, we must say that H_2 is itself instantiated by an event if it is instantiated at all. Moreover, a haecceity of an event is an *individual* property of an event. As we already know, as such it has a strict "exclusivity" or "incommunicability" in its association with an event. And this means in the end that if a haecceity of an event is to be thought of as existing in some world, it must be thought as existing *qua* being instantiated by and only by the particular event that is its would-be bearer. Challenge (B) will not establish h, and will not thus pose a threat to GSL.

Finally, the defender of (GSL) can point out to his challenger that argument (C) seems to rest on a confusion arising from the "nested instantiations" present here. Never mind whether the dynamic property Fing exists uninstantiated or it exists *qua* being instantiated by an object, the dynamic property is only a component part of *another* property, the whole compound individual *property* (haecceity) [o_i, Fing$_i$, t_i]. But it is this *latter* property that is the individual essence *of an event*, and it is this latter property that we want to know as a whole how and by what it is instantiated. Now since the whole compound [o_i, Fing$_i$, t_i] is itself a property, it exists (*qua* property) by being instantiated either by something other than an event or by an event . . . We are back to the previous argument.

If the friend of (GSL) has been successful in his responses, then he has shown that h has been held for dubious reasons and must be rejected. Moreover, as goes the rejection of h, so goes the rejection of the cogency of (E), and with the latter rejection, in turn, so goes the possibility of a counterexample to the truth of (GSL). Has the friend of (GSL) been successful? Perhaps, but it does not matter. He has lost already, as I will now show.

6. What Price Victory?

The friend of (GSL) should be, obviously, wary of being *unsuccessful* in his attempt to show that hypothesis h is false. For if h is accepted as true, (E) remains a possible model that demonstrates that the supervenience thesis (GSL) is false. On the other hand, the friend of (GSL) should be equally wary of being *successful* in his attempt to rescue (GSL) by showing that h is false – at least if he also wants to hold on to his haecceitist thesis (LHCT). Let me explain.

Suppose that the friend of (GSL) has been successful in his arguments against h and has shown us that h should be rejected. But now to argue for the negation of h is exactly to argue for the acceptance of the thesis that if a haecceity of an event [o_i, Fing$_i$, t_i] occurs in some possible world, then the event whose haecceity [o_i, Fing$_i$, t_i] is does not fail to exist in that world. Yet this, in turn, is exactly to accept (CPE), the principle that engenders the existence of a particular event in a world from the existence of that event's haecceity in that world. But to admit that much when we also adhere to (PE) (the minimal implication of (LHCT)), is to accept that an event exists if and only if its haecceity exists, which is to say that an event exists if and only if an appropriate combination of a material object, a certain property had by the object, and a time at which that property is had by that object exists. And this is when it begins to look like something has gone wrong. For now there is very little, if nothing, to stop the foe of events from unleashing a systematic program for the reduction of events to these other entities. Yet, on the other hand, Lombard has been at pains to establish that events are ontologically autonomous entities that *supervene* on, and are *not* reducible to, objects, properties, and times.[24]

There is indeed a problem for the objector to h who wants to uphold both (GSL) and (LHCT), and it goes beyond Lombard's favorite views as to supervenience and reduction. It can be put more perspicuously as follows. In Section 4, I have shown that, given (LHCT), model (E) is possible if and only if hypothesis h is true, as well as that (LHCT) implies (GSL) if and only if (E) is rejected. In his attempt to save (GSL), its friend has argued against his challenger that h is false. Let us suppose that he has successfully shown us that h is indeed false. Then he has shown us that principle (CPE) is true. The intermediate conclusion to be drawn is that, if h has been successfully rejected, the friend of GSL has established that (LHCT) implies (GSL) only if (LHCT) implies (CPE). But if we have also accepted (LHCT), we have minimally accepted (PE). With our current additional acceptance of (CPE), we embrace the reduction of events. It follows so far that, if h is false, (LHCT) implies (GSL) only if (LHCT) implies the reduction of events. On the other hand, (GSL) purports to be a supervenience thesis. As such, on anyone's view on supervenience, it ought to be nonreductive; that is, it ought not imply the reducibility of the supervenient events to their subvenient basis.[25] The valid conclusion to be drawn is that (LHCT) implies (GSL) only if (LHCT) is false. And this means that the price of the successful rejection of h is that the event-haecceitism expressed by (LHCT) implies the event-supervenience expressed by (GSL) only on pain of event-haecceitism (i.e., (LHCT)) being false.

It is worth noting that the same conclusion can be reached via an alternative route. Suppose again that the rejection of h has been successful, model (E) is not possible, and (GSL) is demonstrably true on the strength of (LHCT). Clearly, (GSL) is neither a definition nor an identity. If true, (GSL) purports to express a supervenience claim and so purports to capture the one-way, *asymmetrical dependence* of events on their individual essences. But this one-way, "nonconvertibility" of dependence arising out of the supervenience character of (GSL) *implies*, in turn, the possibility of a pair of worlds indiscernible in the events occurring in them and yet discernible as to the haecceities existing in them. Yet this, in turn, amounts to saying that the truth of (GSL) *qua supervenience* thesis implies the rejection of (PE), the principle that asserts the existence of a haecceity $[o_i,\, \text{Fing}_i,\, t_i]$ in a world from the existence of the event whose haecceity $[o_i,\, \text{Fing}_i,\, t_i]$ is. Clearly, we now have a problem if, along with (GSL), we also want to uphold the haecceitist thesis (LHCT). For (PE) is, surely, a minimal implication of (LHCT). The conclusion to be drawn is, once again, that (LHCT) implies (GSL) only if (LHCT) is false.

From either or both of these considerations, that is, from either or both limbs of the results of the "success" in rejecting h, we get that the truth of the supervenience thesis (GSL) is implied by the haecceitist position (LHCT) only if (LHCT) expresses a false doctrine. And this means that if h is successfully rejected, the haecceitist doctrine (LHCT) cannot be held together with the supervenience thesis (GSL). On the other hand, we have seen earlier that the result of the failure to reject h yields the falsity of (GSL). Thus, if h is not successfully defeated, the supervenience thesis (GSL) cannot be held together with the haecceitist thesis (LHCT). In the end, the upholder of both (GSL) and (LHCT), as either winner or loser of the debate as to the acceptability of h, must accept that one of his positions is false and must be abandoned.

7. Results

It is time to take stock of our results. I have sought the connection between the event-supervenience thesis (GSL) and the event-essentialist claims expressed by theses (LESS) and (LHCT). In Section 3, I have shown that (GSL) neither implies nor is implied by the claim that events have essences as expressed by thesis (LESS). A consequence of this, I have further shown in Section 4, is that the stronger haecceitist doctrine expressed by thesis (LHCT) cannot be the result of our upholding the supervenience thesis (GSL) either. Finally, in pursuing in the converse direction the question of whether (LHCT) implies (GSL), it turned out that this is so only on the assumption that (LHCT) is a false doctrine. (LHCT) and (GSL) express incompatible positions.

Given that much, we are now in the position to see that if, in following Lombard, we insist that events have individual essences, even graver results obtain. To begin with, when we recall that the haecceities that Lombard attributes to events are composites of objects, properties, and times, we may be inclined to think that the conflict with (GSL) is due to the peculiar nature of these haecceities. Yet this would be wrong. The nature of the haecceities attributed to events is not the issue. (GSL) will be false under *any* view of event-haecceitism.[26] It is easy to see this. Let (GSL*) and (CPE*) be the principles that invoke event-haecceities of a type other than the one favored by Lombard and that parallel in their formulation principles (GSL) and (CPE) as before. Either the haecceities at hand occur unexemplified or they do not (i.e., either model (E) of Section 4 holds or it does not). The argument of Section 4 can now be repeated. In the former case, (GSL*) fails, and in the latter case the acceptance of (CPE*) will yield the incompatibility of (GSL*) and the present form of haecceitism, which, on the assumption of the truth of haecceitism, yields, again, the falsity of (GSL*).

Adhering thus to event-haecceitism, we preclude not only the truth of (GSL), but also the truth of any principle (GSL*) that, like (GSL), involves individual essences of events in its subvenient base. And we can take this result a step further. (GSL) and/or (GSL*) make explicit intraworld comparisons to assure us that events (i.e., the supervenient) are completely fixed or determined across worlds when these worlds are indiscernible in event-haecceities (the subvenient base). As such, they are forms of "global" supervenience, a principle that in just one formulation due to Kim says,

(GS) Worlds alike in features x are alike in features y,

or equivalently,

(GS*) No differences of kind A between worlds w and w^* without differences of kind B.

Global supervenience characteristically invokes whole "worlds" as the units of comparison, and it asserts that the indiscernibility of these worlds in terms of the subvenient base "fixes" the indiscernibility of these worlds in terms of the supervenient. It is an attractive way of expressing supervenience claims, since global supervenience stands modestly between principles strong enough to threaten with reduction and weak enough to express anything interesting. But now it looks as though our adherence to event-haecceitism diminishes the hope of formulating a substantive global event-supervenience principle.[27]

The rejection of global supervenience in favor of individual essences for events leads to worse consequences in turn. To express the supervenience of events, we must now opt for one of the remaining forms or patterns of supervenience, namely, either "strong" or "weak" supervenience. Where A is the set of supervenient properties, and B is the set of "base" or subvenient properties, Kim formulates these principles (in one way) as follows:

Weak Supervenience Necessarily, if anything has property F in A, there exists a property G in B such that the thing has G, and everything with G has F.

Strong Supervenience Necessarily, if anything has property F in A, there exists a property G in B such that the thing has G, and *necessarily* everything with G has F.[28]

However, neither strong nor weak supervenience will do. The problem with strong supervenience is twofold. First, as Kim has repeatedly emphasized, strong supervenience allows for "bridge principles" that open the door to reduction. Opting for a principle that has such reductive implications ought to be unpalatable to anyone advocating the ontic autonomy of events.[29] Second, and more important, pursuant to Kim's demonstration, it is now known that strong supervenience *implies* global supervenience.[30] Since, as we have seen, event-haecceitism falsifies global supervenience, it follows that in maintaining the view that events have individual essences, we are committed to the rejection of a principle of strong event-supervenience also. Thus, we are left with only the weakest form of supervenience claims, claims like the preceding Weak Supervenience. But weak supervenience claims are claims about a *single* world with no modal force for correlations *across* possible worlds. Haecceitist claims, on the other hand, are par excellence claims about cross-world matters. I just do not see how these diverse claims could be combined to generate anything true (or even interesting) about the supervenience of events.

Thus, we exhaust the available options. To insist on the supervenience of events, we would have to resort to some such "generic" pronouncement like "no difference of events without difference of event-essences." But in view of the preceding remarks, the substantive character of such pronouncements would be in want of some explanation. In the end, the friend of event-haecceitism might as well abandon the hope of formulating an event-supervenience thesis.

NOTES

A first draft of this essay took shape during Jaegwon Kim's 1990 NEH Summer Seminar entitled "Supervenience and Its Philosophical Applications." I am grateful to NEH for its support, as well as to Jaegwon Kim and the seminar participants for many valuable comments. I am particularly indebted to Ümit Yalçın for many hours of helpful discussion that resulted in significant improvements in this essay.

1. Covariance, dependence, and nonreducibility are integral to the concept of supervenience. For a discussion of this matter and an overview of many of the central issues that have emerged, see Jaegwon Kim, "Supervenience as a Philosophical Concept," *Metaphilosophy* 21 (1990): 1–27.

2. Davidson has made his case in a variety of ways. A representative sample of his views is to be found in his *Essays on Action and Events* (Oxford: Clarendon Press, 1985).

3. This account has its origins in the works of Jaegwon Kim. See, e.g., "Events as Property Exemplifications" in M. Brand and D. Walton (eds.), *Action Theory* (Dordrecht: Reidel, 1980), pp. 158–77. It is further developed in Lawrence Lombard, *Events: A Metaphysical Study* (London: Routledge, 1986). A more recent version is presented in Jonathan Bennett, *Events and Their Names* (Indianapolis, Ind.: Hackett, 1980). The differences among the versions of the account need not concern us here.

4. This is not quite right. Both Kim and Bennett have also dealt with the supervenience of events. However, Kim's discussion is confined to the issue of the relation to each other of two subcategories of events, mental and physical. Kim does not deal with the issue that concerns Lombard, the possible supervenience of events *as an ontic category* on other ontic categories.

Bennett, on the other hand, accepts event-supervenience rather grudgingly and neither endorses nor defends any particular supervenience principle. Lombard's *Events: A Metaphysical Study* will hereafter be referred to as *Events*.

5. A bit more precisely, a dynamic property is such that if *x* is an object, '*x* exemplifies a dynamic property *F* at time *t*' implies 'at *t*, *x* exemplifies the property of *first* having F_i *and then* having the property F_j', where F_i, F_j is a pair of *static* properties, and *t* must be understood as an *interval* of time.

6. Thesis (MT) is intricately related to a key element of Lombard's theory, his criterion of identity for events, a principle we can denominate here as (CIL) and that can be roughly formulated for present purposes as follows:

(CIL) *Necessarily* event *e* is event *e'* iff *e, e'* are the same exemplifyings of the same dynamic properties by the same objects at the same times.

We can see that (CIL) mirrors (MT). Objects, dynamic properties, and times – the conceptual resources embodied in the conception of what it is to be an event – are the same as those employed in the interpretation of the identity conditions for events. This is no accident. Lombard insists that the criterion of identity for events has the central ontological function of revealing what it is to be an event according to some theory.

7. Essentialism, as the principle attributing to individuals of ontic type *K* a property *F* possessed by any *K* having it in all possible worlds in which that *K* exists, is standardly expressed as a principle having the form

(ESS) $\Box(x)(x$ is a $K \ \& \ Fx \supset \Box(y) \ (x = y \supset Fy))$.

(ESS) should be distinguished from the principle that says of an essential property *F* that it is an *individual essence* of a *K*. This latter principle has the form

(HCT) $\Box(x)(x$ is a $K \ \& \ Fx \supset \Box((y) \ (y = x \equiv Fy))$.

(HCT) is a much stronger principle. It says that there is no possible world *w* in which *x* exists and lacks *F, and* there can be no individual *y* other than *x* in *w* that also has *F.*

8. The property of an event to belong to the kind it in fact belongs to is called by Lombard a "property essence." Events, Lombard emphasizes, can have more than one property essence, and distinct events can share a property essence (*Events*, pp. 176–8).

9. I must emphasize that the "Fings," the dynamic properties involved in (LESS), are of the "sortal" kind that, as explained in the main text, divide events into kinds. From now on, to the degree that my discussion makes reference to Fings, these should be understood as being the sort of dynamic property-types that I have called "sortal."

10. I must guard against a possible confusion. My explication of a canonical description agrees with that of Lombard's, but my usage of it is different from Lombard's own (see *Events*, pp. 173–4). I use canonical descriptions as singular terms for haecceities of events, while Lombard uses them to name events. A bit more perspicuously, my canonical description involves relational singular terms that are such that each of them names a part of the compound haecceity, and each of them involves the event *e* itself as

one relatum. Lombard's canonical description of events involves, again, relational singular terms, but those terms are only related to each other and in toto name an event.

11. Let me briefly clarify a couple of points. First, the reader in need of more details with regard to Lombard's haecceitist doctrine will best look at chapter 8 of *Events*. I can do no better here than to offer the following remarks of Lombard's:

> Events are changes, they are the havings of dynamic properties by objects at times; and to be this or that event is just to be a having of this or that (essential) dynamic property by this or that (essentially involved) object at this or that particular minimal interval of time. There just does not seem to be anything more that is needed to pin down the 'individuality' of a particular event. And this suggests that events do have individual essences that are articulated in terms of events' essential subjects, dynamic properties, and times, and that events are *completely determined by* their minimal subjects, the dynamic properties of which they are essentially the havings, and their minimal times of occurrence. (*Events*, pp. 221–2; my emphasis)

Second, the exact way in which haecceities are related or associated to events is central to the argument here. Thus, the principle (LHCT) is purposefully formulated with the vague expression "has" for now.

12. We should not think that because the names involved in the canonical description of a haecceity are, in part, rigidly attached to a specific event (see note 10) there is something we can ipso facto infer about the existence of an event from the existence of a haecceity. Think of the one and only creator of Sherlock Holmes.

13. I have used "supervenience" and its cognates instead of Lombard's own preference for "covariance." The choice between these two, Kim has pointed out, is mainly a terminological one. I prefer "supervenience" to signify the broader relation whose one implication is covariance. This should not be disagreeable to Lombard. His discussion of (GSL) shows that he views this "covariance" principle in my sense of "supervenience."

14. We should not be fooled by the mention of *static* properties and the expression "objects possess and fail to possess those properties" that occur in (GSL). Lombard intends (GSL) to involve the relations of a pair of static properties to a specific object (at a time interval), and this expression to be read as "objects possess *and then* fail to possess those properties." That is, Lombard wants (GSL) to involve *dynamic* properties:

> (GSL) insists that for possible worlds to match with respect to events, they must not only be alike in containing just the same changeable objects, static properties, and times, they must also be alike in that the objects, properties and times are related to each other in the same way. That is, the same objects must *have and then lack* the same properties at the same times. (*Events*, p. 223 – slightly modified to preserve continuity; my emphasis)

The indiscernibility of *dynamic* properties involved in (GSL)'s base is as it should be. Events are the exemplifyings of *dynamic* properties, and their determination by merely static properties would be a mystery.

15. This would amount to a very weak determination that is not determina-

tion at all. The weakness of the "global" or "holistic" determination is a point that Kim has often emphasized (see, e.g., "Supervenience as a Philosophical Concept," p. 5).

16. Well, not exactly. To be sure, a prima facie alternative candidate that par excellence correlates specific events to specific objects, dynamic properties, and times is the criterion of identity, principle (CIL) (see note 6). Yet this candidate must be immediately excluded. (GSL), obviously, asks for comparisons of *particular* events *across* worlds. And how would (CIL) stand up to the task? Taking Lombard on his own word, (CIL) is a principle that tells what it is to be *an* event. It is not a principle of counting events or of telling us what it is to be *this* rather than *that* event. And even if Lombard is wrong in this, (CIL) clearly lacks the appropriate modal force to perform the demanding task of relating events *across* possible worlds. Thus, if there is at all a connection, this must be sought in the essentialist principles (LESS) and/or (LHCT). Of course, it could be that (CIL) *in conjunction* with either (LESS) or (LHCT) or both could yield just what is needed. There will be a tripartite proof that this is not the case (see notes 19, 21, and 22).

17. The alternative understanding of an essential property of x is the understanding of a property F without possessing which x could not exist. That is, F is essential if and only if for every possible world w, if x exists in w, x has F in w. Indeed, (ESS) (see note 7) is sometimes expressed as "$\Box(x)(x$ is a K & $Fx \supset \Box(x$ exists $\supset Fx)$)."

18. This result should be particularly disturbing to Lombard, who argues that the time of occurrence of an event is essential to the event on the basis of the truth of (GSL) (see *Events*, pp. 206–17).

19. Since (GSL) neither implies nor is implied by (LESS), and since (CIL) does not imply (GSL), it follows that the conjunction of (CIL) and (LESS) neither implies nor is implied by (GSL). We can thus see the first part of the proof I promised in note 16.

20. Lombard himself surely appears to want to connect (GSL) with his avowal of haecceitism, yet how exactly the connection obtains is not at all clear from his discussion. On one hand, Lombard seems to want to make (GSL) *demonstrate* that events have individual essences that are articulated in terms of objects, properties, and times – to show, that is, that (LHCT) is true. On the other hand, we also get the impression that (GSL) is the *consequence* of his acceptance of (LHCT). However, it would be impossible to substantiate these remarks and still remain with a single essay. I leave it to the reader to confirm or disconfirm my impression. The relevant material appears on pp. 206–33 of *Events*.

21. Since (GSL) does not imply (LHCT) and, as we know, (CIL) does not imply (GSL), it follows that the conjunction of (CIL) and (LHCT) does not imply (GSL). We have, thus, the second part of the proof I promised in note 16.

22. At this point we can finish up with the business of the possible relevancy of (CIL): either (HCT) implies (GSL), or (LHCT) does not imply (GSL). If the former, (CIL) is not relevant to yielding (GSL), and we should stop worrying about the role of (CIL). If the latter, given that, as we know,

(CIL) does not by itself imply (GSL), it follows that the conjunction of (CIL) and (LHCT) does not imply the truth of (GSL) either. This is the last part of the proof I promised in note 16. To be sure, it could well be that the conjunction of (CIL) with some principle other than (LESS) or (LHCT) yields the truth of (GSL). But showing what that other principle could be is a burden that hardly falls on me.

23. Of course, it would not make a difference if we had a model (E*), where the occurrence of events was interchanged so that it was w_2 that had more events than w_1. Whatever can be said about (E) can be said mutatis mutandis about (E*).

24. Lombard should not disagree with this. He works hard in *Events* to make a strong case for the ontic autonomy of events. But he sees that (CPE) opens the door to reduction, and he is at pains to denounce it with such remarks as the following:

> The existence of no event follows from the mere existence of an appropriate object, *dynamic* property, and time, even given that there are, in general, events. (*Events*, p. 223; my emphasis)

> Events do have individual essences that are articulated in terms of events' essential subjects, dynamic properties, and times, and . . . events are completely determined by their minimal subjects, the dynamic properties of which they are essentially the havings, and their minimal times of occurrence. But this, again, does not imply that events are reducible to or are nothing but these other entities; for the occurrence of no event follows from the existence of those other entities. It is just that if there is an event which is an exemplifying of a certain (essential) dynamic property by a certain (essential) object at a certain (essential) time, then all the crucial and important facts about that event are determined by the facts about that object, property, and time. (*Events*, pp. 221–2)

25. Lombard seems to believe that supervenience implies *irreducibility*. There may be good reasons to accept this, but never mind. For the present purposes, the weaker position, namely, that supervenience is *nonreductive*, i.e., consistent with irreducibility, will do. The nonreducibility component of supervenience is standardly accepted in the literature. See, e.g., Kim, "Supervenience as a Philosophical Concept," p. 8.

26. A Lombard-type event-haecceity is one that R. M. Adams calls a "nonqualitative essence" of x – an individual essence of x expressible with the aid of nonpurely qualitative properties of x. If we follow Adams, we can distinguish at least two more kinds: a "thisness" of an individual x – the property of being this very individual x, or of being identical with x – and a "qualitative essence" of x – a conjunction of purely qualitative properties, i.e., properties expressible without the aid of "uniquely referring devices," which are possessed only by x. See R. M. Adams, "Actualism and Thisness," *Synthese* 49 (1981), pp. 3–41.

27. To the degree that the haecceities of events are involved in a principle of global event-supervenience either as the supervenience base *or as the supervenient*, the conflict of that principle with haecceitism is bound to occur. To see this, let (CGSL) be the principle that in a manner *converse* to

that of (GSL)'s, expresses the global supervenience of haecceities on events. In parallel fashion to (GSL), such principle would say:

(CGSL) Possible worlds cannot be alike with respect to the truth and falsity of propositions concerning which events occur and yet unlike with respect to the truth and falsity of propositions concerning the existence of objects capable of nonrelational change, the possession and nonpossession of static properties by those objects, and the times at which those objects possess and fail to possess those properties.

The argument of the text as to the conflict of (GSL) and (LHCT) can now be recast for the present case: from the truth of (LHCT) and the "incommunicability" of haecceities we have seen in Section 4, we have it that (CGSL) is true if and only if we reject the possibility of a pair of worlds, w_1 and w_2, indiscernible with regard to events yet differing with regard to the haecceities occurring in them. Where a, b are events and H_i denotes a haecceity, such pair of worlds would be represented in model (E**):

(E**)
w_1: a, b, H_1, H_2
w_2: a, b, H_1, H_2, H_3

Yet for reasons already mentioned in the text, we can accept the cogency of (E**) if and only if we can accept the hypothesis that a haecceity of an event can exist in a world w_1 and *not* be "associated" with any event in w_1 ("hypothesis *h*" of the main text) . . . We can now continue as in the main text.

28. The principles are Kim's "Weak Covariance II" and "Strong Covariance I" (see his "Supervenience as a Philosophical Concept," p. 10). Global, weak, and strong formulations of supervenience are the standard ones in the literature. Alternative and more unusual options are, of course, available; see, e.g., Thomas Grimes, "Supervenience, Determination, and Dependency," *Philosophical Studies* 62 (1991): 81–92. Obviously, Kim's principles hold between *properties* (of distinct kinds), while Lombard's basis of comparison is one between different kinds of *entity* (indeed, Lombard views (GSL) as a subspecies of a more general principle of "ontological supervenience" capable of expressing covariance also for the ontic categories of sets and of material objects – see *Events*, p. 223). But this is a difference that does not affect the issues here.

29. For the reductive character of strong supervenience, see Kim, inter alia, "Supervenience as a Philosophical Concept," p. 19.

30. See Kim, "Concepts of Supervenience," *Philosophy and Phenomenological Research* 45 (1984): 153–76.

How Does Ontology Supervene on What There Is?

FELICIA ACKERMAN

This essay's title may seem paradoxical. Ontology *is* what there is; so how can there be a question about the relation between the "former" and the "latter"? The answer lies in distinguishing two types of ontological questions. Consider a philosophy professor who is wondering

(1) Will any of the students in my seminar have brown eyes?

This sentence can be taken in more than one way. The first way is to take it as

(2) Will any of the students in my seminar be brown-eyed?

where (2) is indifferent to the ontological status of eyes but is to be answered affirmatively just in case not every student in question is either eyeless, or blue-eyed, green-eyed, hazel-eyed, etc. On the second construal (which is the type this essay will give to sentences of this sort), however, (1) asks a question that is different from (2) and receives an affirmative answer iff the empirical conditions necessary for an affirmative answer to (2) are satisfied *and* eyes have the ontological status of being entities. I will call questions of the sort expressed by (2) "ontological-basics questions" and questions of the sort expressed by (1), on the second construal, "ontological-status questions."

This distinction must be distinguished from several other distinctions. It might be tempting to say ontological-basics questions are empirical, while ontological-status questions deal with matters that go beyond empirical facts. But this would be a mistake. The interrogative sentence 'Are there any primes between 15 and 25?' has an ontological-basics interpretation (where an affirmative answer does not commit one to the existence of numbers as entities), but this ontological-basics question is not empirical. It would also be an error to say that ontological-status questions are philosophical, while ontological-basics questions, even if they deal with nonempirical matters such as mathematics, are not. The question of whether the mental is reducible to the physical is clearly philosophical, even in its ontological-basics form, which concerns itself not with whether there exist mental *entities* (such as thoughts or sense-data), but with whether, for example, that J is in pain can be analyzed in purely behavioristic terms.[1]

Finally, the distinction at issue should not be conflated with Carnap's distinction between two kinds of questions of existence – internal and external – which it may superficially seem to resemble. As Carnap puts it, internal questions are "questions of the existence of certain entities . . . *within the framework*"[2] and external questions are "questions concerning the existence or reality *of the system of entities as a whole.*"[3] The present distinction, however, holds neither that ontological-basics questions must be relativized to a framework nor that ontological-status questions apply only to a system as a whole.

Although ontological-basics questions may be empirical or necessary, philosophical or nonphilosophical, depending on the particular ontological-basics question at hand, ontological-status questions over and above ontological-basics questions are always philosophical. In fact, ontological-status questions are generally considered very important philosophically, which is why philosophers have spent enormous amounts of time and energy arguing over such matters as whether there are abstract objects or whether there are sense-data. But I will now give an argument for the *triviality* of ontological-status questions over and above ontological-basics questions. Consider the sentence

(3) John and Mary are talking,

where (3) is taken to name two entities and say how they are related. But just as (1) can be replaced with (2) with no change in what is expressed except the ontological-status aspect of the question, (3) can be replaced with

(4) John Mary-talks-with,

where (4) is taken not to name two entities and say how they are related but rather, like

(5) John is dark-haired,

to pick out only one entity and ascribe a property to it. This technique can be applied generally to make whatever entity one likes the only entity in the world and turn "everything else" into properties of it.[4] For example, consider

(6) Talking John-Mary's,

where John and Mary's conversation is now a property of the state of talking, or consider even

(7) The number 3 John-Mary-talks,

that is, the number 3 is such that John and Mary are talking, and neither John, Mary, nor the conversation is construed as an entity. But if transformations of this sort are so easy to make, why not make them?[5] And what would this show about ontological-status questions over and above ontological-basics questions – that they are trivial? Meaningless? Undecidable? I will consider several possibilities.

First, the following argument might be given to show that the transformations in question are not universally available. Consider

(8) John is not riding on Pegasus,

where (8) is construed as picking out just one entity, John, and denying a property of (or ascribing a negative property to) him. Sentence (8) clearly cannot be transformed into

(9) Pegasus is not John-ridden,

where (9) is construed as picking out just one entity, Pegasus, and denying a property of (or ascribing a negative property to) it. The reason is that the truth of (8) would not be sufficient to guarantee the ontological-basics conditions for the truth of (9), that is, to guarantee that if winged horses are admissible sorts of entities, there will in fact be anything in the world for 'Pegasus' to pick out. But this qualification still leaves us with the question of the triviality of ontological-status questions over and above ontological-basics questions.

One possibility would be to give an argument that denying that John and Mary are both entities and affirming (4), (6), or (7) but rejecting (3) is simply wrong. For example, Bennett asks:

> What are the criteria for the distinction between something's being an object or objective substance and its being a property of an object or a process which objects undergo?[6]

He suggests that the answer is a matter of whether

> the facts we can report by means of [the substantival expression for the putative(?) entity under consideration] can also be expressed in statements [lacking a substantival for that putative(?) entity]. . . . On this criterion . . . a house is [an entity] while a fight is not, because what we say with the substantive 'fight' can easily be said without it. We can replace 'The fight was a fierce one' by something like 'The men fought fiercely,' and so on; whereas no such replacements seem to be available for everything we might say using 'the house'.[7]

The foregoing examples (3), (4), (6), and (7) show that this is wrong, however, as the technique behind these examples can be used with 'the house' as well – for example, by replacing 'The house is on fire' with 'A fire burns the-housily'. The fact that English happens to have the locution 'brown-eyed' but not 'burns-the-housily' is surely irrelevant to ontological-status questions.

Defenders of intensional abstract objects have also used arguments that recourse to such entities is necessary for a complete picture of the world. One such argument is that we cannot account for such matters as that John believes something Mary does not or that John and Mary agree on exactly three things. Quine has attempted to get around this by saying that such locutions "seem queer to begin with,"[8] and even "are expendable, for [they] tend . . . to be pretty trivial in what they affirm, and useful only in heralding more tangible information."[9] But the present standpoint offers another way of handling these examples. This is just to offer such sentences as

(10) John and Mary agree threely,

where this is understood as bearing the same relation to

(11) John and Mary agree on exactly three things

as (2) bears to (1). Quine would presumably grant the irrelevance of the fact that English lacks the locution 'agree threely', since he allows such neologisms as 'pegasizes'.[10]

Quine's attitude toward nonintensional abstract objects is much more favorable, for he claims that "classical mathematics, as the example [that there are] primes larger than a million clearly illustrates, is up to its neck in commitments to an ontology of abstract entities,"[11] a view that arises from his famous dictum that to be is to be the value of a variable.[12] But this claim also falls prey to the strategy presently under consideration. For example, if John is the sole entity whose existence is countenanced, the preceding statement about primes can be replaced by 'John primes larger than a million' and similarly for other statements of classical mathematics that allegedly require quantification over abstract objects.

The foregoing remarks also undercut Quine's view that all ontological questions should be decided on pragmatic grounds.[13] The ontological transformations I have suggested are so easily available that they undermine the view that there is any particular sort of entity that pragmatic considerations ever call for, that is, that pragmatic considerations ever point to any particular answer to ontological-status questions over and above ontological-basics questions. So what sort of consideration could help settle questions of the former sort? An obvious candidate is Occam's razor. But its application is problematic in light of the argument of this essay. I have mentioned that the suggested technique of ontological transformation allows the possibility of reducing the number of entities to one and making "everything else" a property of it.

But there seems to be no philosophical gain in doing this. As Armstrong points out in another context:

> Theoretical economy about entities is not like being economical with money. To be economical with money is to spend as little quantity of money as is consistent with one's purposes. But theoretical economy with entities is a matter of postulating the smallest number of *sorts* of entities that will explain the phenomena.[14]

Such considerations of economy when combined with the ontological transformations indicated earlier suggest that we should allow only (or at most) one type of entity. But these considerations do not tell us whether this type should be physical, mental, or abstract.[15] Moreover, the very ease of making the ontological transformations raises questions about the fundamental merits of Occam's razor at all. Presumably, the most attractive motivation for Occam's razor involves the blocking of such suppositions as what "enforces" the law of gravity is that each physical object has its own invisible gravity-gremlin whose will pulls it down. In fact, however, the objectionability of such a supposition seems unmitigated when it is transformed into property form – by saying each physical object is gremlin-will-pulled-down (where this is understood to have no ontological implication that gremlins or gremlins' wills are *entities*). The intuitive motivation for supposing that entities must be justified either by observation or by theoretical efficacy seems paralleled by a similar caveat against ascribing superfluous "positive" properties to entities. (The qualifier "positive" is to allow for the fact that lacking the property of being gremlin-will-pulled-down entails having the property of not being gremlin-will-pulled-down.) The parallel, combined with the preceding argument about the ease of making ontological-status transformations, leaves it obscure just why minimizing even types of entities is a desirable goal if the answers to ontological-basics questions are unchanged.

If there are no good arguments favoring certain answers to ontological-status questions over and above ontological-basics questions, what sorts of considerations might be relevant? One possibility is an appeal to intuition, where 'intuition' means not some special and mysterious faculty, but simply the means by which some things just seem obviously true in their own right, rather than needing justification by means of something else. James Van Cleve has suggested in conversation that some of our commonsense beliefs about ontological-status issues have this sort of intuitive justification. For example, it just seems obvious to him that he has a cat (i.e., that he and his cat are two entities standing in a certain relation to each other), rather than that he is "catted" (where 'I am catted' bears the same relation to 'I have a cat' as (2) bears to (1) and hence does not imply the existence of an entity that is one's cat). But the intuition that there is an entity that is Van Cleve's cat seems to dwindle severely in light of such possible alternatives as his being catted. I have argued elsewhere that it is surely true that once we have weighed the relevant arguments, we must ultimately rely on our judgment ("intuition") about whether, in light of these arguments it just seems reasonable to accept a given philosophical view. But this does not entail that our considered philosophical judgments – about ontological-status questions or anything else – must not conflict with our commonsense *pre*philosophical views.[16]

The difficulty of settling ontological-status questions gives rise to an obvious possibility: perhaps there is really no fact of the matter when it comes to ontological-status questions over and above ontological-basics questions; for example, perhaps (3), (4), and (6) are all different ways of saying the same thing. This approach might be expected to appeal to a behaviorist, since there are no behavioral correlates of having apples or sense-data in one's ontology rather than holding that the tree is two-appled or that John is appeared to redly.[17] But although Quine holds the behaviorist view that "semantics is vitiated by a pernicious mentalism as long as we regard a man's semantics as somehow determinate in his mind beyond what might be implicit in his dispositions to overt behavior . . . there are no meanings, nor likenesses nor distinctions of meaning, beyond what are implicit in people's dispositions to overt behavior,"[18] he rejects the consequence that there is no difference between talking about rabbits, talking about rabbit stages, and talking about instantiations of the universal rabbithood, and so presumably would reject as well the view that (3), (4), and (6) all say the same thing. His reasoning is problematic, though. He claims the objectionable consequence of indeterminacy of reference is avoided because

> it is meaningless to ask whether, in general, our terms "rabbit," "rabbit part," "number," etc., really refer respectively to rabbits, rabbit parts, numbers, etc., rather than to some ingeniously permuted denotations. It is meaningless to ask this absolutely; we can meaningfully ask it only relative to some background language.[19]

He gives an affirmative answer to the question of whether we are now involved in an infinite regress.

But although Quine regards this regress as benign, it actually defeats his aim of providing determinacy for reference, since a reference that is determinate only relative to another language that is determinate only relative to another, ad infinitum, is not determinate at all, any more than you will ever get the answer to a question if you can get it only by consulting a person who will direct you to another person who will direct you to another, ad infinitum. And if the question of whether 'rabbit' refers absolutely to rabbits is truly "meaningless," how can it even be debated? Just what does Quine mean by "meaningless" here? Quine may be right that "querying reference in any more absolute way . . . is very much like asking whether our neighbor may not systematically see everything upside down, or in complementary colors, forever undetectably,"[20] but this will count as a point in favor of the "meaninglessness" of the former query only to someone whose views include strong elements of verificationism, ordinary language philosophy, or similar approaches.[21] In fact, there is a good reason for granting the meaningfulness of ontological-status questions over and above ontological-basics questions, and hence for granting that (3), (4), and (6) do not all say the same thing: one can argue in favor of or against different answers to ontological-status questions, even if we hold answers to ontological-basics questions constant.[22]

But if such sentences as (3), (4), and (6) say different things, and no one can be shown to be better than the others, how is the situation to be resolved? Considering alternative ways of dividing the color spectrum provides a useful analogy.

```
    red      orange     yellow    green    blue    indigo    violet
   |   :   |      :     |    :    |   :    |   :   |    :    |   :   |
   |   :   |      :     |    :    |   :    |   :   |    :    |   :   |
   |   :   |   : qrs |  t : u  | v : w |  x :     |  y : z  |   :   |
   |   :   |      :     |    :    |   :    |   :   |    :    |   :   |
   |   :   |      :     |    :    |   :    |   :   |    :    |   :   |
   der  rorange    yorange  grellow   breen brindigo  vindigo    tev
```

The dashed lines and top labels of the diagram represent our way of dividing the spectrum (with the idealization of ignoring the fuzzy boundaries of our color categories). The dotted lines and bottom labels of the diagram represent the division of a hypothetical alternative society A (with the same idealization).

The members of A would give different answers from ours to questions about colors. For example, if people were shown samples of colors at points s, t, and u along the spectrum, 'What color is s?' would receive the answer 'orange' in our society and 'yorange' in A, and 'Are t and u different shades of the same color?' would get an affirmative answer from us and a negative answer from members of A. Yet it seems obvious that our way of dividing the spectrum and A's are equally correct. So I suggest that there is no uniquely correct answer to the question of what color s is. s is both orange and yorange, as well as an infinite number of other colors corresponding to the infinitely many possible ways of dividing the spectrum, although, of course, there are wrong answers as well, such as 'red' and 'vindigo'. But the question 'Are t and u different shades of the same color?' has an answer only relative to a particular way of dividing the spectrum, just as the question 'Is J bigger?' has an answer only relative to some object of comparison. Finally, the fact that there are an infinite number of equally correct ways of dividing the spectrum does not require us to say there are no wrong ways; perhaps a way that classified colors with the appearance of our q, s, and y as the same color and a color with the appearance of our r as a different one would be wrong. I will not try to settle this question here, but calling this classification wrong is certainly compatible with the approach I am advocating.

The parallels with ontological-status questions are close at hand. Answers to ontological-status questions supervene on answers to ontological-basics questions in fundamentally the same way that divisions of the color spectrum supervene on the spectrum itself. Thus, Bill Clinton, the number 3, and cupidity all "exist" in both entity and property form, and it is acceptable to count Bill Clinton, or the number 3, or cupidity in one's conceptual scheme either in only entity form, in only property form, or in both, just as it is acceptable to include yellow but not grellow, grellow but not yellow, or both yellow and grellow in one's conceptual scheme. Similarly, just as my account of the color spectrum allows but does not require that some divisions are so bizarre as to be incorrect, the present account of ontology allows that some oddities, such as "Crinton," the putative(?) entity that is Bill Clinton on Wednesdays and Ronald Reagan the rest of the week (see note 5), would also be so bizarre as to be impermissible either as entities or in a form that allows that, for example, anyone ever Crinton-talks-with. This sort of restriction would be independent of the thesis of this essay.

NOTES

I thank Ernest Sosa and James Van Cleve for helpful discussion of the material in this essay.

1. Thus, the debate over dualism can take either an ontological-basics form (is the mental reducible to the physical or vice versa?) or an ontological-status form (can we make do with either only mental or only physical *entities?*), depending on precisely what question is under consideration.
2. R. Carnap, "Empiricism, Semantics, and Ontology," in *The Linguistic Turn,* ed. R. Rorty (Chicago: University of Chicago Press, 1967), p. 73.
3. Ibid.
4. Or perhaps, as Ernest Sosa has suggested in conversation, we can even manage with *no* entities, construing everything on the model of 'It is raining'.
5. This point also applies when we are considering such oddities as "Crinton," i.e., the putative(?) entity that is Bill Clinton on Wednesdays and Ronald

Reagan the rest of the week. Whether Crinton is an entity is an ontological-status question, but whether it is true either that Crinton is an entity
or that, e.g., anyone ever-Crinton-talks-with (in a sense parallel to (4)) is
an ontological-basics question.

6. J. Bennett, *Locke, Berkeley, Hume* (Oxford: Clarendon Press, 1971), p. 84.

7. Ibid.

8. W. V. Quine, *Word and Object* (Cambridge, Mass.: MIT Press, 1960), p. 211.

9. Ibid., p. 215.

10. See W. V. Quine, *From a Logical Point of View* (Cambridge, Mass.: Harvard
University Press, 1963), pp. 8 and 167.

11. Ibid., p. 13.

12. See ibid., pp. 13, 15, 103.

13. See ibid., chap. 1, and pp. 78–9.

14. D. M. Armstrong, *A Materialist Theory of the Mind* (London: Routledge and
Kegan Paul, 1968), p. 81.

15. On the failure of Occam's razor to favor a particular type of entity, see
W. P. Alston, "Ontological Commitments," in P. Benacerraf and H. Putnam (eds.), *Philosophy of Mathematics: Selected Readings*, 2nd ed. (Cambridge, Mass.: Harvard University Press, 1983), p. 255.

16. See F. Ackerman, "Philosophical Knowledge," in J. Dancy and E. Sosa
(eds.), *A Companion to Epistemology* (Oxford: Blackwell, 1992), pp. 342–5.

17. Of course, the fact that believers in different answers to ontological-status
questions are apt to differ in "verbal behavior," i.e., in what sentences they
assert, is beside the point, since the problem reappears in the form of the
question of what determines how these different sentences are to be interpreted.

18. W. V. Quine, "Ontological Relativity," in *Ontological Relativity and Other Essays* (New York: Columbia University Press, 1968), pp. 27, 29.

19. Ibid., p. 48.

20. Ibid., p. 49.

21. For some criticisms of such approaches, see my "Does Philosophy Only
State What Everyone Admits? A Discussion of the Method of Witt-
genstein's *Philosophical Investigations*," in P. French (ed.), *Midwest Studies in
Philosophy*, vol. 17: *The Wittgenstein Legacy* (Notre Dame, Ind.: University
of Notre Dame Press, 1992), pp. 246–54, and also my "Philosophical
Knowledge."

22. James Van Cleve made this point in conversation.

Supervenience and Intentionality

EARL CONEE

1. Meanings

An attractive semantic view invokes abstract entities as the meanings of predicate expressions. According to this sort of view, people who use predicates enter into a three-term meaning relation in which a person associates a predicate with an entity that is the predicate's meaning. These entities may be Fregean senses, Platonistic properties, or some other sort of universal. The role they will have in the present inquiry is so schematic that differences among them do not matter. The idea will become clear enough from the sort of work that is supposed to be done by these 'Meanings,' as they will be called here.

A semantic approach that appeals to Meanings as the meanings of predicates is familiar. Let us briefly review a few important aspects of it. If it is said, for instance, that some object 'has a spherical shape', then this predication attributes to the object the Meaning *being spherically shaped*. This particular abstract entity is what is meant by the predicate, because it is the entity with which English speakers enter into the mental relation of meaning, or intending, by the predicate. Quite similarly, when someone asserts in English, 'The Loch Ness monster is a dragon', this is an attempt to predicate *being a dragon* of something that lives in Loch Ness, because that Meaning is what is intended by English speakers who predicate the expression 'is a dragon'.

There are no dragons. The Meaning view of predicate meaning has it that the portion of reality that accounts for this truth is the fact that the Meaning *being a dragon* is unexemplified (or it applies to nothing, or it has no instances, or nothing falls under it, etc.). Two important apparent facts about unexemplified Meanings are that they do not exist in space and they have no effects. The reason that the first appears to be a fact is that abstract Meanings appear to be located, if anywhere, where their instances are. Likewise, their causal role, if any, appears to depend on their instances. The meaning of a predicate is something in virtue of which the predicate does, or would, apply. For instance, predicates that attribute the having of mass apply in virtue of the massiveness of things. Massiveness appears to be located only in occupied

273

spatial regions, and it appears to account for only effects of events involving things that have mass. If a Meaning's location and effects thus derive from the locations and effects of what exemplifies it, then unexemplified Meanings have no location and no effects.

The importance of these apparent facts is the mystery that they appear to generate for the Meaning view of predicate meaning. It seems mysterious that we are able to enter into any relation of explanatory significance that is neither spatial nor spatially mediated.[1] Yet according to the semantic view that we are considering, we enter into some such cognitive relation to a Meaning whenever one of our meaningful predicates is not true of anything. How do we manage thus to address our attention to an entity without our having any spatial or causal connection to it? Part of the purpose of the present essay is to eliminate this mystery. But first we should have before us some reason to work on the problem, some reason to defend the Meaning view of predicate meaning.

One main attraction of this semantic view is its straightforward explanation of many familiar semantic facts, for example:

(F$_1$) English speakers mean the same thing by 'dog' that French speakers mean by 'chien'.

(F$_2$) English speakers mean the same thing by 'dragon' that French speakers mean by 'dragon'.

The Meaning view allows us to say that there is a thing that is meant in predicating 'dog', and it is identical to the thing that is meant in predicating 'chien'. This thing is the Meaning *being a dog,* because that entity is something that both English and French speakers mean in their respective predicative uses of the terms 'dog' and 'chien'.

As a first point of comparison we can note that a nominalistic approach to meaning that invokes only linguistic entities and speakers has no straightforward explanation available for the truth of facts like (F$_1$). There need not be any linguistic entity that is accessible in some way both to an English 'dog' user and to a French 'chien' user.

Some non-Platonistic semantic views can match this advantage. Various nominalistic views have some mutually accessible thing – for example the fusion of all actual dogs – to be the one thing that is meant in predicating the two expressions 'dog' and 'chien'. In fact, if we consider only familiar predicates that apply to actual things, there is some initial appeal to a view of meaning according to which meanings are the things to which the predicates apply, the things meant. By 'dog' we mean the dogs themselves. Indeed, it should not be denied that the word 'dog' is meant to apply to the dogs themselves (one at a time), nor should it be denied that this makes the dogs themselves a legitimate candidate for "what is meant by 'dog'," when dogs exist.

It takes further reflection to observe that the word 'dog' is meant to apply to dogs on a certain basis. This basis is a particular way that we take dogs to be, namely, *being a dog*. This basis of intended application is sufficient for the meaningful use of 'dog' in English. After such reflection we can see that this basis of application provides a sense of "what is meant by 'dog'" concerning which the actual existence of dogs is not required. This is a more fundamental sense of 'meaning' in that it is a meaning of a predicate whether or not there is also something that is a 'meaning' in the sense of an application of the expression. As long as a given expression is supposed to apply to something in virtue of its being a dog, the expression means what 'dog' means, regardless of whether or not there are any dogs. This sort of fact favors an abstract candidate for the role of the more basic sense of 'meaning'. The Meaning *being a dog* exists even without the dogs themselves, their fusion, and all kindred contingent material entities.

This permanent availability of Meanings is not a confirming vindication of the Meaning view of meaning. We have not made the prior discovery that Meanings exist necessarily in some independent investigation of them. Rather, it has turned out that noncontingency is a desirable attribute for Meanings to have in order to account for the semantic data, and we lack any reason to deny that Meanings necessarily exist if they exist at all.

Another asset of the Meaning view of meaning is that facts like (F_2) are accounted for in exactly the same way as are facts like (F_1). The single Meaning *being a dragon* is meant by both the English and the French speakers in their respective predicative uses of 'dragon'. This uniformity in the account of these facts is a virtue not to be sneezed at. The inference from (F_2) to the following explicitly existential conclusion seems clearly to be sound:

> **(C_2)** There is something that is meant by both the English 'dragon' and the French 'dragon'.

(C_2) seems clearly to be true, just as clearly true as the corresponding existential implication of (F_1):

> **(C_1)** There is something that is meant by both the English 'dog' and the French 'chien'.

These existential facts are compatible with the possibility that the English and French speakers exist in a pervasive mutual causal isolation. Speakers of the two languages could have separately concocted the idea of a dragon in telling fabulous tales with no common origin. The

English usage might have been derived from exaggerations of actual reptiles, while the French usage might have arisen from fanciful imaginings based on knurled trees and forest shadows. Given the possibility of such causally isolated conceptual sources, no ordinary spatiotemporally located object, property, or state of affairs is a promising candidate for being what is meant by both the English 'dragon' and the French 'dragon'. An abstract entity has the relative advantage here of at least not being in some definitely unsuitable spatiotemporal position to be a meaning that is shared by such speakers.

Again it should be acknowledged that we are not here confirming something that it was antecedently reasonable to believe about the entities that we are counting as Meanings in semantic theory. We are called on to locate Meanings nowhere in the external world by data such as the possibility of substantially independent causal origins of uses of terms that have the same meaning. In general, we identify characteristics of Meanings by attributing to them features that seem best to fit them for the roles that they are to serve in those philosophical theories in which they are invoked. This is not a novel or objectionable methodology. Indeed, it will be urged later that we do more of the same. It will be helpful later to note now that the Meanings of semantic theory are not supposed to be certain familiar, necessarily existing, nonspatial entities that we had kicking around in our ontology anyway, recruited for a semantic purpose. Our purely role-driven characterization renders Meanings vulnerable to complete refutation by a better theory that fills all semantic roles without them. But it also renders them completely revisable to suit our best conception of what might serve their role, guided by both the semantic desiderata and whatever other access to their nature is allowed to us by our theory.

Finally on behalf of Meanings in semantic theory, let us remind ourselves that other semantic facts are also well accounted for by postulating relations to Meanings, and not readily accounted for otherwise. For instance:

(F3) As predicates, 'brillig' has no meaning, 'aluminum' has just one meaning, and 'boring' has just two meanings.

The three predicate expressions mentioned in (F₃), 'brillig', 'aluminum', and 'boring', are all used in some ways by English speakers. There is thus no simple, obvious way to construct a use theory of meaning that implies the (F₃) quantities of meanings from some natural general principle of meaning individuation. 'Aluminum' and 'boring' each has a variety of roles in English speakers' inferences. So no simple, obvious inferential role theory of meaning shows promise of getting the count right either. The Meaning view of predicate meaning, on the other hand, readily accounts for the (F₃) quantities. Clear introspectable differences exist among the psychological states associated with English speakers' uses of the three expressions. The Meaning view has it that these differing psychological states are cases of intending no Meaning for 'brillig', uniformly intending one and the same Meaning for 'aluminum', and at various times intending one or the other of exactly two Meanings for 'boring'.

2. Problems

Such explanatory virtues of the Meaning view of predicate meaning might be widely conceded. But many philosophers would contend that these virtues are overwhelmingly overridden by mysteries about Meanings, especially unexemplified Meanings. There is the mystery that has already been described of how it is possible to gain access to unexemplified Meanings in order to use them, in light of their apparent spatial and causal detachment from us. There is also a mystery for all putative Meanings, including those that are exemplified, which arises from the plausibility of mental supervenience claims. Settled empirical facts are the evidence here, prominently including facts about the relation of differences in central neural structure to differences in cognitive capacities and the relation of brain damage to cognitive damage. Such facts strongly support the thesis that all mental states are entirely dependent on purely physical states and processes. It is highly plausible that states identified by properties that figure in basic physical laws, principally brain states (and according to externalists, certain environmental conditions as well), at least uniquely determine all mental states. Thus, it is highly plausible that if someone is thinking that there are dragons, then there is some purely physical condition of that person (and perhaps portions of the person's environment) that is at least nomologically sufficient for the person to be thinking that there are dragons. Details of this empirically based intuitive supervenience thesis are worth clarifying and studying. But let us see how, even without further refinement, the idea poses a threat to the Meaning view of predicate meaning.

The problem derives from an argument by Jaegwon Kim.[2] Any state consisting in an irreducible relation to a Meaning would seem to be unacceptably epiphenomenal. It is thoroughly plausible that basic physical laws suffice to account for every physical change that has any explanation. So no property not mentioned in any physical law is needed to account for any physical effect. Something that supervenes on a physical effect seems to be fully explained by the physical explanation of that effect plus the relevant fact of supervenience. Properties not mentioned in physical laws thus seem not to be needed to account for anything that supervenes on physical effects. But all plausible candidates for effects that are attributable to mental states seem to be physical states, events, processes, and the like, or entities that are supervenient on such purely physical things. So the mental states seem to be causally inert, unless they are identical to something physical. Yet it is quite doubtful that intentional states are epiphenomenal. How could a state such as that of meaning a certain thing by a predicate turn out to be wholly inconsequential? Such states seem clearly to be causal factors – for example, in the assertive use of predicates.

Moreover, it seems that no unexemplified Meaning could help to constitute any purely physical state. For one thing, spatiotemporal location seems to be a necessary condition for being physical, and as has been discussed, it seems that uninstantiated Meanings do not exist in space. For another thing, an adequate physical characterization of a thing seems to consist in a specification of the fundamental physical magnitudes and relations that the thing exemplifies at each time of its existence. Mental relations to unexemplified Meanings seem to have neither the location nor the role in fundamental laws that appear to be requisite for being among these magnitudes and relations, nor do they seem to be logical constructions out of the physical properties. Even in the case of Meanings that are true of something, no relation of thinking of one of them appears likely to figure in a basic physical law or to be a construction out of any such law-constituting materials. Mental states consisting in such relations too thus seem to lack any effect.

3. Nonsolutions from Elsewhere

The considerations that create this threat of an implausible epiphenomenality are not unique to invocations of Meanings in semantics. Unfortunately, solutions to the problem seem not to have been provided elsewhere.

Moral Properties

Warren Quinn discusses much the same problem as it affects a nonreductive realist view of moral properties.[3] These properties, such as *being a good person,* seem at least to supervene on psychological characteristics, such as *being honest* and *having benevolent intentions* (which seem in turn to supervene on basic physical properties). The psychological properties seem to better explain any causal outcome that might at first appear to be due to some moral property (and the underlying physical properties seem in principle capable of doing yet better). For instance, the claim that Smith is a good person seems not to explain why she helps others and forgoes her own enjoyment as well as do claims to the effect that she has certain intentions that are thereby enacted. Reflection on a variety of such contrasts defends the conclusion that moral properties are never involved in the best explanation of any effect.

Quinn seeks to ally these moral properties to certain ordinary and seemingly uncontroversially exemplified nonmoral properties, such as *being a chair.* Such properties appear to supervene on more basic physical properties of shape and composition, even though the latter physical properties seem to provide for better explanations of any effect that might be thought to involve the ordinary properties.[4] For example, perhaps at first it appears that my body's being at rest relative to the floor is accounted for partly by the fact that beneath me is something that exemplifies the property of *being a chair.* But on reflection it seems clear that this fact about my body's state of motion and configuration is better accounted for by the physical states of basic physical entities: those constituting the chair and its underpinnings, and those constituting my body.

In spite of this, Quinn appeals in Moorean fashion to his confidence in the existence of chairs. He asserts that he is more certain of the reality of the chair beneath him than he is of any philosophical requirement that is not met by the fact that it is a chair.[5]

Whatever the merit of a Moorean response to the specific explanatory requirement that Quinn is discussing, confidence based on common sense is not a good basis for replying to Kim's argument for the epiphenomenality of nonphysical properties. A central assumption in that argument can be formulated as the claim that all mental states and events have subvenient physical bases that are causally sufficient for at least subvenient bases of every effect that it might be tempting to attribute to a mental state or event. This premise is not offered as an item of overriding common sense. It is defended principally by the extensive and ever-mounting success of physical science in providing thorough causal explanations of all events involving those microconstituents that turn out exhaustively to constitute human organisms and their environments.

The same sort of considerations argue for the epiphenomenality of any irreducible property of *being a chair,* our confidence in its explanatory significance to the contrary notwithstanding. However certain we are that my seated posture can be best accounted for by a causal explanation that invokes the property of *being a chair,* the fact turns out to be that the state of motion of my body is fully attributable to physical properties of microconstituents of my body, my chair, and the rest of my environment. The property of *being a chair* is superfluous to the causal account. If such commonsensical properties are exemplified in spite of their causal superfluousness, then their exemplification is explained by adding the pertinent facts about their supervenience on the underlying physical states. So this sort of analogy does not help us to see how to avoid the threat of an implausible epiphenomenality. Rather, it shares the problem.

We cannot define our way out of trouble here. We can define a sense of 'cause' in which supervening properties are "causes." We can give a definition of 'cause' according to which whatever supervenes on some effect is "caused" by whatever supervenes on a (genuine) cause of the effect.[6] To avoid confusion, let us express this defined sense of 'cause' with the coinage 'supercause'. Brian McLaughlin has effectively shown that this is an insufficiently demanding definition to capture the intended relation.[7] But even if the definition were refined to match the contours of our commonsense judgments of causes and effects, it would not identify a sense of our commonsense causal judgments in which they were already true. Supercauses often present initial appearances of being causes because they are relatively readily discerned and at least partial correlates of efficacious factors. The gross solidity of a wooden chair is a more conspicuous apparent factor in supporting weight than are the subatomic properties and processes in terms of which basic mechanics ultimately accounts for every explicable state of relative motion. This appearance does not turn supercauses into real causes, and we have no other reason for thinking that they are.

Analogously, we can define a sense of 'friend' in which anyone who is detected only dimly, at a distance, in a fog, and is some friend's identical twin, is a "friend." This sense turns some sentences containing 'friend' that assert errors based on sensory limitations into sentences that now have a true sense too. But in making statements with those sentences we were making pure errors (except when we were friends of both twins). We were classifying as friends people who were dimly detected identical twins of friends. There is no good reason to think that beyond this understandable and fully explicable error, we were also getting something right with these sentences in such cases. So there is no good reason to provide for a true sense of such sentences.

Iron pyrite offers a closer analogy to supercauses. Iron pyrite is not gold, despite thousands of excited initial judgments that it is. Veins of iron pyrite are sufficiently similar in appearance to veins of gold to have earned the designation 'fool's gold'. Few are fooled for long. But it would not be gold if it fooled most of the people most of the time. And it would not be gold if it usually had the same full-blown practical role as that of genuine gold, though in the last event distinguishing iron pyrite from genuine gold might only rarely be worth doing.

Likewise, if we count as a cause some property that we predicate on an evidential basis that is comparatively manifest to us, and strongly correlated with underlying causes, there is no good reason to suppose that we are nonetheless right that what we have identified using our more or less reliable basis really is also a cause. Being intimately related to a cause, even being so closely associated that the difference usually makes no practical difference, is no way not to be epiphenomenal.

Liquid Properties

In another effort that shows some promise of helping us to deny the epiphenomenality of putative mental states relating us to Meanings, John Searle defends a causal role for unreduced mental states by analogy with a causal role that he finds for "liquid properties"[8] of water. As evidence of the causal efficacy of these liquid properties, Searle writes: "Furthermore, the surface features of water themselves function causally. In its liquid state water is wet, pours, you can drink it, you can wash in it, etc."[9] Searle does not make it clear what is to be caused by water's "liquid properties" or, as he calls them here, its "surface properties." Perhaps the best example that Searle offers is that of washing. Presumably the idea is that it is partly as a result of liquid or surface properties of water that it cleanses the skin of dirt.

Let us assume that water's *being liquid* is a surface property that is supposed to play a causal role in its cleansing. Our understanding of this role is intended by Searle to help us understand by analogy the causal function of mental states, such as that of intending to walk, in producing behavior, such as walking, in spite of the causal sufficiency of various internal biochemical events for microevents constitutive of any bodily motion.[10]

Rather than providing us with an analogous case in which a supervening property clearly has its own causal role, the intended analog to a mental state is no less clearly causally eclipsed by its subvenient base. If certain relations of cohesion obtain among H_2O molecules, then the water that the molecules compose is in a liquid state. The liquidity supervenes on the intermolecular relations of the constituent H_2O molecules. These same cohesive relations affect the motion of H_2O molecules in proximity to skin when they move so as to dislodge and dissolve dirt particles on the skin. A cleansing of the skin supervenes on these motions of dirt particles away from it. An exhaustive causal account of the motions would not mention liquidity in addition to the molecular relations on which it supervenes. Water does have a capacity to cleanse in its liquid state, as Searle says. But the subvenient molecular base of the liquidity seems to possess the causal power and to do all of the relevant causing when the process occurs, just as the biochemical states of the brain seem to do in the case of an intention and subsequent action. In both cases, once the microprocesses and the laws that govern them are appreciated, any irreducible supervening properties seem to be along just for the ride. Thus, Searle does not help us to see how a supervening mental state can have its own effects.

Numbers and Propositions

Robert Stalnaker attempts to "dispel the mystery"[11] of how any abstract object can be related to any physical object. This attempt is intended to be a step toward a naturalistic theory of intentionality.[12] Unfortunately, the attempt is of no assistance to the Meaning view of meaning. At a crucial point, it relies on an unexplained and problematic relation to an abstract object. Stalnaker writes:

> What is it about such physical properties as having a certain height or weight that makes it correct to represent them as relations between the thing to which the property is ascribed and a number? The reason that we can understand such properties – physical quantities – in this way is that they belong to families of properties which have a structure in common with the real numbers. Because the family of properties which are *weights* of physical objects has this structure, we can (given a unit, fixed by a standard object) use a number to pick a particular one of the properties out of the family. That, I think, is all there is to the fact that weights and other physical quantities are, or can be understood as, relations between physical objects and numbers.[13]

Real numbers have a structure in common with a relation among weights. But to exploit this common structure we have to be able to "use" numbers in a certain way. This use requires referring to a number in order to specify a weight. How do we manage to relate to any number so as to refer to it? What we most need for a defense of the Meaning view of meaning is to see how some cognitive relation to a nonspatial object such as reference to the object is established in the first place. Stalnaker's work does not explain this. It is not difficult to see how, if we already have one way of singling out an abstract object, that relation can be used to bring about other links to the object. If we already understand how we manage to enter into, for example, the mental relation of thinking of a number, then we can see how we might exploit that mental relation to associate a numeral with that number to use in referring to it. But Stalnaker has explicitly abjured any approach that employs some primitive mental relation to abstracta.[14] Thinking of a number is the sort of intentional relation that he hopes to explain naturalistically rather than to take for granted. His explanation is supposed to be partly based on the preceding discussion of weight. More to the point of our semantic concerns, it would not be helpful for our own purposes to start with an unanalyzed relation, *thinking of,* which can relate a person to an unlocated causally inert entity that is a number. For we are seeking an understanding of how we are able to enter into just such a relation to those apparently unlocated causally inert entities that are Meanings, and it is their seeming lack of location and effect that presents the problem.

Stalnaker also offers examples that are designed to show how people can enter into various relations to propositions, relations that he intends to be unproblematic from a naturalistic point of view. Like numbers, propositions are abstract objects according to Stalnaker.[15] So his examples may help us to understand how we are able to associate abstract Meanings with predicates. Here is the simplest of Stalnaker's examples, followed by his statement of its point:

> Consider a concept of *need* defined as follows: an organism *needs it to be the case that P (at a certain time)* if and only if the organism would survive beyond that time only if P. . . . [T]his simple relation does have some of the properties that philosophers have found puzzling about intentional relations. One can need food (strictly, given my artificial definition, need it to be the case that one eats food) without there being any particular food that one needs. And an unfortunate organism may need something (may need it to be the case that it has something) which does not exist. I take the fact that the simple need relation has such properties to show, not that this relation is intentional, but rather that these properties are not restricted to intentional relations and are not, in themselves, problematic from a naturalistic point of view.[16]

Stalnaker's definition of a "need" for something to be the case explains the relation in terms of a primitive subjunctive construction of the form "*a* would phi only if *Y*" (omitting temporal reference). This expresses a relation that is at least necessarily equivalent to the relation expressed by "if not-*Y* were to be the case, then *a* would not phi." As is well known, Stalnaker is an originator and proponent of the following sort of truth conditions for such subjunctive conditionals:

> "If not-*Y* were to be the case, then *a* would not phi" is true iff it is not the case that *a* phi's in the possible world in which not-*Y* is the case that is most similar to the actual world.

Thus, the definiens in the definition of *a*'s *need* in effect attributes to *a* entrance into a relation of the form: not phi-ing in the *w* that is most similar to the actual *w* among those *w*'s in which not-*Y* is the case.

This complex relation does not help us understand how a person might be related to an abstract Meaning. In those cases where the *need* in question is met, being in the relation entails lacking a certain property – namely, phi – in some world that is not actual. Our puzzlement about relations to Meanings concerns the apparently nonspatial and ineffectual nature of at least the unexemplified Meanings. This obscurity is not removed by an analogy that makes primitive appeal to a relation of failing to instantiate a property "in" something else that is apparently ineffectual and to which we seem to have no spatial relation – a nonactual possible world.[17]

4. Potential Solutions

The two problems about Meanings have more promising solutions. We can take advantage of how little we really know about Meanings, minds, and material states. We are in a position to concede virtually everything to the various pressures of the semantic data, our understanding of relations, and the apparent facts of supervenience and causation. A coherent and attractive Meaning theory remains available.

The first problem is that of how we are able to enter into a nonspatial relation to some unexemplified Meaning in order to intend it by some predicate. The best solution is to admit that this cannot be done and to locate the Meaning wherever the state of intending it exists. We saw two initial problems with this idea. The first is that instantiable entities such as those that we are calling Meanings seem to get their locations from their instances. We can agree about this source of location, while denying its exclusivity. We can acknowledge that Meanings do get a location from any instance, while adding that they also get a location by entering into the cognitive relation of being a topic of some intentional state. After all, what do we know that gives us reason to believe that Meanings can be located *only* in things that exemplify them? A state of contemplating the Meaning *being a dog* seems on introspective grounds somehow to include the contemplated Meaning. Suppose that the state of contemplation is located. Why not add that the Meaning is there, wherever it is contemplated, helping to constitute the contemplative state? We are urged in this direction by the semantic data in combination with our understanding of how relations are possible, and nothing that we have yet seen requires that we resist.

This locating hypothesis, together with the sort of use of Meanings in semantic theory that was suggested earlier, may lead to empirically refutable consequences. The Meaning view of meaning has it that whenever two language users, however mutually isolated, mean the same thing by some predicate, those individuals bear a cognitive relation to one and the same Meaning. If these Meanings are, as we are now supposing, spatial constituents of cognitive states, then it may be feasible to observe these states and discover whether or not they have something distinctive in common, something also constitutive of other thoughts on the topic of the same Meaning. The feasibility and the particular means by which we might make such observations depends on how we are able to detect cognitive states. And that in turn depends on their nature. This issue is best discussed in connection with the second problem about Meanings, the threat of an implausible epiphenomenality.

Kim's argument is powerful. States involving Meanings either merely derive from states that have effects, or they are identical to physical states. Moreover, intentional states give every ordinary appearance of having effects.

It is best to conclude that intentional states are identical to certain physical states. The clearest and leanest identity theory is type-identity theory. Each mental property is identical to some physical property,[18] and each state consisting in exemplifying a mental property is identical to some state consisting in exemplifying a physical property. For instance, any possible being who is in a state that is identical to contemplating the Meaning *being a dragon* is in a physical state that all actual thinkers are in exactly when they contemplate the Meaning *being a dragon*. Since they are physical states, such intentional mental states in all likelihood do have effects. They have the effects of the physical states to which they are identical, presumably at least largely including the apparent effects of intentional states on reasoning, speaking, and so on. Ordinary conceptions of intentional states do not make them seem to be identical to states conceived of in physical terms. But this is not a weakness in type-identity theory. The identities are not supposed to be a priori truths.

The alleged multiple physical realizability of mental state types is widely thought to be fatal to this type-identity view.[19] But this sort of objection turns out to be far from fatal. Jerry Fodor and Ned Block present the classic elaboration of this sort of objection against the mental state/physical state type-identity thesis (which they call "physicalism"). They begin as follows:

> The argument against physicalism rests on the empirical likelihood that creatures of different composition and structure, which are in no interesting sense in identical physical states, can nevertheless be in identical psychological states. . . . First, the Lashleyan doctrine of neurological equipotentiality holds that any of a wide variety of psychological functions can be served by any of a wide variety of brain structures. . . . [I]t does seem clear that the central nervous system is highly labile. . . . For example, though linguistic functions are normally represented in the left hemisphere of right handed persons, insult to the left hemisphere can lead to the establishment of these functions in the *right* hemisphere. (Of course, this point is not *conclusive*, since there may be some relevant neurological property in common to the structures involved.)[20]

The parenthetical acknowledgment at the end of this citation is overly mild. Given the far-reaching symmetry between the two brain hemispheres, it is more reasonable to wonder whether there is any neurological property that is *not* in common between brain structures in the left hemisphere and those in the right that serve the same linguistic function.

Even if the empirical fact is that linguistic function, or some other psychological capacity, is served by brain structures that are palpably different in physical properties such as shape, size, and number and pattern of neural connections, there are numerous other purely physical properties that they may share. Temperature is a simple example offered by Kim.[21] More plausible candidates exist for being the sort of physical state to which intentional states are identical. There are, for instance, the various patterns of energy transmissions, patterns including configuration, duration, and intensity of the electrical discharges that occur during neural activity, as well as dispositions to induce such patterns. The same propensity to induce variations in the rate of electrical discharges through the same numbers and combinations of synaptic connections may be present, in spite of large differences in the visible anatomy of two brain structures.

This is an entirely speculative example of a sort of physical state that may correlate exactly with some psychological state. The example does not have to be anywhere near right to make the critical point: there is no quick and easy way to get good reason to conclude from gross physical differences that two physical structures lack every shared physical state that might be identical to some psychological state. The sheer fact of the psychological equipotentiality of some brain regions by itself raises no serious doubt about the type-identity thesis. This equipotentiality just indicates a line of empirical research that could eventually turn out to find sufficiently sweeping physical differences that, if accompanied by sufficiently compelling evidence of identical intentional states, would refute the asserted identities. Such a combination of evidence remains to be seen.

Fodor and Block continue their objections:

> The second consideration depends on the assumption that the Darwinian doctrine of convergence applies to the phylogeny of psychology as well as to the phylogeny of morphology and of behavior. . . . Psychological similarities across species may often reflect convergent environmental selection rather than underlying physiological similarities. For example, we have no particular reason to suppose that the physiology of pain in man must have much in common with the physiology of pain in phylogenetically remote organisms. But if there are organisms whose psychology is homologous with ours but whose physiology is quite different, such organisms may provide counterexamples to the psychophysical correlations physicalism requires.[22]

This line of criticism offers no more than a suggestion of a locale for possible counterexamples. It is doubtful that any such counterexample will be forthcoming. The idea is that evolutionary developments may, for all we know, have produced different mechanisms for the same psychology. But the evolutionary case for intentional state convergence is not strong. Fitness to survive is the test. Psychology seems more independent of survival adaptations than is morphology. And the psychological states at stake here, intentional states, seem to be relatively unconstrained by survival forces even among psychological states. Various psychological organisms might construct diverse external world ontologies from sensory states delivered by morphologically identical mechanisms. Assorted ideologies and rationalizations can produce behavior of identical survival value. In any event, there is no reason to suppose that the survival function of apparently more directly involved psychological states, such as Fodor and Block's example of pain, would be served by the identical state in physiologically differing organisms. This survival function appears to be that of producing a strong aversive and protective response. As Hume pointed out, it seems that even a mere diminution in pleasure might have prompted the same aversive and protective responses.[23] Many psychological mechanisms employing other states that together would produce the same survival-related results can be envisaged in our armchairs. We have no evolutionary reason to suppose that convergent psychology must, or would be likely to, lie behind convergent adaptive behavior. Since, as we have seen, we also lack conceptual grounds to attribute identical psychological states on the basis of the same evolutionary forces and behavioral adaptations, if we were presented with really drastic physiological differences, such as the difference between the presence and the absence of a central nervous system, this could be accommodated quite reasonably by attributing different psychological states that accomplish the same evolutionary result. And as before, any less than sweeping physiological differences allow numerous and diverse physical states to be shared.

Fodor and Block conclude their multiple-realizability objections as follows:

> Finally, if we allow the conceptual possibility that psychological predicates could apply to artifacts, then it seems likely that physicalism will prove empirically false. For it seems very likely that given any psychophysical correlation that holds for an organism, it is possible to build a machine which is similar to the organism psychologically, but physiologically sufficiently different from the organism that the psychophysical correlation does not hold for the machine.[24]

This objection is not carefully targeted, though the idea seems clear. Making the idea explicit, however, highlights the weakness of the objection. Type-identity theory is not threatened by the possibility that psychological "predicates" apply to machines, nor by the possibility of a machine that is psychologically "similar" to an organism. Psychological predicates may apply to machines in senses that differ from their senses when they are strictly literally applicable to conscious human beings.[25] And the type-identity thesis does not also assert that any possible state that is *similar* to some actual psychological state is identical to some actual physical state.

A threat to physicalism would arise from a likely possibility that something physically different enough from an organism not to be in any physical correlate of the organism's psychological states is in some identical psychological state. But Fodor and Block do not give good grounds for regarding this as a likely possibility. The first weakness is now familiar. The difference in material composition between an organism's nervous system and a machine's hardware leaves open a variety of physical states that have some plausibility as being those identical to the organism's intentional psychological states. There will be, for example, various physical properties of the energy transactions within any machine (and any extraterrestrial, to mention another frequently cited sort of possible bearer of psychological states) that provides output that is on balance indicative of being in psychological states.[26]

Again, maybe in the final analysis no common physical property can be found to be had by all of the organisms and machines that are in a certain intentional state. But imagined differences in material structure and composition between an organism and some hypothesized psychologically identical machine are not at all telling. Forceful counterevidence would arise only from a thorough empirical search that was fully informed about the wide range of physical states that might be shared.

Second, psychological states in a machine (or an extraterrestrial) that are not identical to those of a given organism may function like those of the organism in all of the ways that yield the behavioral evidence that argues for psychological attributions. Block himself would agree in the case of pain.[27] The qualitative character of pain, which is essential to it, need not be present for a state to play the behavioral role and the causal role among other mental states that is played by pain. If we consider the matter carefully, we can observe that the same goes for intentional states, and for substantially the same reason. Attentively meaning a certain thing by a certain predicate has no palpable introspective character. In this way it differs from qualitative mental states like pain. But like qualitative mental states, meaning a certain thing is accessible to reflective awareness. We can tell that we are doing this simply by taking note of what we have in mind while we do it. Call what is thus revealed to introspection "the phenomenal character of meaning something." It is plausible that the phenomenal character of meaning something is essential to intentional states. It is impossible to conceive of, say, meaning *being a dragon* by predicating 'dragon' while nothing is introspectable as what is meant. That is the essential point. But distinctive meanings also seem accessible. It seems impossible to conceive of meaning *being a dragon* while introspection appears to reveal that one means *being a potato*, or anything else other than *being a dragon*. We do not have to pay close attention to what we mean in order to mean it. But we could not mean anything if meaning were unavailable to reflective attention.

If the phenomenal character of meaning something is essential to such states, then one type of evidence against physicalism is harder to come by than otherwise might have been thought. Except in autopsychological experimentation, we are barred in a certain way from having any decisive evidence that something which functions as an intentional state really is one. We have to reckon with a rival hypothesis that cannot be excluded by any externally detectable causal consequence: the hypothesis that the state in question functions the same ways with other states in producing behavior as does an intentional state, while it lacks the phenomenal character of meaning something that is essential to our intentional states. This is not to say that these rival views cannot be empirically adjudicated. Potentially externally observable physical differences are decisive if the type-identity thesis is correct. But if this thesis is at issue and cannot be relied on, then we lack any means to exclude the rival hypothesis. Any candidate for being an intentional state of a machine (or of an extraterrestrial, or even a previous state of oneself) might be a mere causal replica of an intentional state. The case for a physically different realization of the same intentional state will always have this hole in it.

Thus, the three multiple-realizability considerations presented by Fodor and Block do not give us good reason to believe that any intentional mental state really is multiply physically realized. One other purported mode of realization of psychological states should be mentioned: What about the apparent possibility of wholly disembodied minds?

This possibility is not actually apparent. It is clear that we can form thoughts about the exemplification of certain intentional states, without forming the thought that something material exists, or while forming the thought that nothing material exists, and while not perceptually imagining anything material. But this is no reason to think that intentional states might have been exemplified while nothing material existed. It is a familiar fact that we can think and imagine so selectively that we are able to ignore some necessary accompaniments of what we consider. We are able, after all, to think of one mathematical fact without thinking of all others. Perceptual facts illustrate the same point. We can imagine the visual appearance of the front side of a mask without imagining or forming any thought about the back. But this is no good reason to think that there might have been a mask with a front and no back. It is reason only to think that vision can be so selective that we need not visually experience all that necessarily accompanies what we see. It is not apparent how we might do anything better toward conceiving of, or otherwise defending, the alleged possibility of a disembodied mind.[28]

5. Conclusion

There is a place for Meanings in a purely physical world. Exemplified or not, Meanings can be where they are meant. Objections based on multiple realization do not refute a type-identity thesis for intentional states, at least as far as the criticism has been developed in the classic statement of the objection. These potential solutions to the problems serve to remove the threats that we have reviewed to the Meaning view of predicate meaning. Reverting to our standard example of an unexemplified Meaning, if the Meaning *being a dragon* is a constituent of some physical state, then it is a physical entity that is located wherever that state is. The threat of a mysterious nonspatial relation to Meanings is gone. And continuing with our standard example, if the intentional state of meaning *being a dragon* by predicating 'dragon' is identical to some efficacious physical state, then the threat of an implausible epiphenomenality of intentional states is gone.

When the Meaning view is so defended, a healthy threat of empirical refutation remains. There does have to be some one physical state that every possible thinker is in exactly when he or she brings to mind *being a dragon,* and this state must have a physical constituent that is that Meaning. We might discover otherwise. In any attempt to make this discovery, we should be mindful of the diversity of physical states that can be shared by physically differing entities, and we should be mindful of the possibility of mere causal simulations of genuine intentional states. But some clearly specifiable empirical matters definitely and decisively matter here. The Meaning view is thus viable and vulnerable.

NOTES

1. We unproblematically enter into various uninteresting relations to any entity that exists, inescapable relations such as existing in the same world with the entity and even contingent transitory singular relations such as existing

on a Tuesday while the entity is the only even prime number. But such vacuously entered relations are not essential to any explanation, unlike cognitive relations such as thinking of some Meaning. Intuitively, that such vacuously entered relations hold is wholly determined by the separate facts about the jointly existing relata, while cognitively significant relations require some connection to be forged between the relata. So there would appear to be no way to enter into any cognitive relation to a Meaning, without being in any spatial proximity either to it or to something else that is spatially linked so as to mediate a causal connection to it.

2. The problem is raised by Jaegwon Kim in "The Myth of Nonreductive Materialism," *American Philosophical Association Proceedings* 63 (1989), 31–47, especially in sec. 5. The argument in the present paragraph does not report Kim's exact reasoning, but his work is the direct inspiration here.

3. Warren Quinn, "Truth in Ethics," *Ethics* 96 (1986), 524–44.

4. Ibid., pp. 537–9.

5. Ibid., p. 539.

6. Jaegwon Kim has developed and applied this sort of notion of causation in a number of papers. See, e.g., sec. 2 of his, "Supervenience and Supervenient Causation," *Southern Journal of Philosophy*, 22, Supplement (1983), 45–56.

7. Brian McLaughlin, "Event Supervenience and Supervenient Causation," *Southern Journal of Philosophy*, 22, Supplement (1988), 83–4.

8. John Searle, *Intentionality* (Cambridge University Press, 1983), pp. 265–6.

9. Ibid., p. 266.

10. Ibid., pp. 264–6.

11. Robert Stalnaker, *Inquiry* (Cambridge, Mass.: MIT Press, 1987), p. 9.

12. Ibid., p. 6.

13. Ibid., p. 9.

14. Ibid., p. 8.

15. In particular, he thinks that they are functions from possible worlds to truth values (ibid., p. 2).

16. Ibid., pp. 11–12.

17. Stalnaker's own view of the nature of possible worlds of *Inquiry* is difficult to discern. It is not entirely clear that he would agree they are things that are not spatially related to us. In some parts of the "Possible Worlds" chapter of *Inquiry* (e.g., on p. 46), he seems to defend a moderate realism about possible worlds according to which they are unexemplified properties and presumably unlocated. But he also says in that chapter things such as this: "A possible world is not a particular kind of thing or place. . . . A possible world is what truth is relative to, what people distinguish among in their rational activities. To believe in possible worlds is to believe only that those activities have a certain structure, the structure which possible worlds theory helps to bring out" (p. 57). These latter comments seem to allude to a sort of logical construction view of possible worlds. Absent the details of the construction, we cannot see if a proposal like his definition of 'need', when fully spelled out, would help us to understand how mental relations to Meanings are possible (or perhaps would rather help us to understand how they are unnecessary to account for the semantic phenomena).

18. For an illuminating though inconclusive discussion of "physical property" as it is intended here, see Ned Block, "Troubles with Functionalism," reprinted in Ned Block, ed., *Readings in Philosophy of Psychology*, vol. 1 (Cambridge, Mass.: Harvard University Press, 1980), pp. 268–305, note 4.

19. The objection is traced to Hilary Putnam, "The Nature of Mental States," reprinted in *Readings in Philosophy of Psychology*, pp. 223–31.

20. Jerry Fodor and Ned Block, "What Psychological States Are Not," reprinted in *Readings in Philosophy of Psychology*, pp. 237, 238.

21. Jaegwon Kim, "Physicalism and the Multiple Realizability of Mental States," reprinted in *Readings in Philosophy of Psychology*, p. 235.

22. Fodor and Block, "What Psychological States Are Not," p. 238.

23. David Hume, "Dialogs Concerning Natural Religion," from R. P. Wolff, ed., *The Essential David Hume* (New York: Mentor Books, 1969), p. 346.

24. Fodor and Block, "What Psychological States Are Not," p. 238.

25. In fact they plainly do, as when we say that a car is "trying" to start although its battery is weak.

26. The qualification "on balance" is added to exclude the prima facie case made by the derivative apparent psychologies of televisions and the like.

27. Block, "Troubles with Functionalism," pp. 275–80.

28. Stephen Yablo helpfully discusses conceivability and possibility in "Is Conceivability a Guide to Possibility?" *Philosophy and Phenomenological Research*, 53 (1993), 1–42. The notion of P's being conceivable to S that Yablo defends there is equated with S's being able to imagine a possible world that S takes to verify P (p. 29). The application of this notion is notably sensitive to new thoughts by S. For instance, perhaps until we thought about the points just mentioned we could have imagined a possible world that we would have taken to verify that disembodied minds exist. Perhaps now we have doubts about what we can succeed in imagining, and we can no longer take any imagined world to verify that proposition. Then Yablo's account has it that the proposition that disembodied minds exist was conceivable to us, but it is no longer conceivable to us. We are therefore no longer in a position to argue from conceivability for the possibility of disembodied minds, even if conceivability is a reliable guide to possibility. And the thought dependency of this sort of conceivability argues that it is not reliable.

Supervenience, Coherence, and Trustworthiness

KEITH LEHRER

In this essay, I shall explore the relationship between supervenience and epistemology. There are many theories of supervenience and many theories of epistemology, and that means that it will be extremely difficult to say anything definitive. It is not my aim to explore this subject in a definitive way. My interest in the subject of supervenience and epistemology was aroused by the work of Alston, Van Cleve, and Sosa.[1] They have argued that if epistemic terms supervene on nonepistemic ones, then one argument in favor of coherence theories over foundation theories of justification is undermined. The argument is one to the effect that if the supervenience thesis is correct, then the coherence theorist must sacrifice her primary alleged advantage over any foundation theorist. That advantage is that the coherence theorist can explain why our most fundamental beliefs are justified, namely, because they cohere with some system of beliefs, while the foundation theorist is limited to saying that our basic beliefs are justified without giving any explanation of why. Any explanation of why our basic beliefs are justified would become the basis of an argument to the conclusion that they are justified, and such an argument would render the justification of the beliefs in question nonbasic. The coherence theorist thus claims that the foundation theorist is left with a kind of explanatory surd that the coherence theorist can avoid by explaining justification in terms of coherence. That issue is the one that interests me and, in fact, convinces me that the coherence theorist should resist the supervenience thesis. I intend to resist and exhibit my resistance herein.

What, however, is the thesis I shall resist? The basic idea behind supervenience can be refined in many different ways, but it is basically a modal thesis. Suppose that S is the supervening property and that B is the base property on which it supervenes. The idea is that for any supervening property S, there is some base property such that, if something is B, then necessarily it is S. The idea can be modified and weakened to allow for the possibility of there being nothing that is S, even though some things are B, by affirming that, if anything is S, then, if something is B, it is necessarily S.[2] I shall focus on the simpler and stronger thesis which says that S supervenes on B just in case, if anything is *B*, then necessarily it is *S*, but I shall comment on the weaker thesis as well. It is unnecessary to my epistemic purposes to concern myself with any kind of necessity other than metaphysical necessity or something stronger – in short, with forms of necessity that hold across possible worlds and are noncontingent. The reason for restricting myself to metaphysical necessity is that a form of necessity that does not hold across all possible worlds will make supervenience a factual relation and one that, therefore, calls for explanation in a way that a metaphysical relation does not. Of course, one might argue that basic laws of nature, though contingent, do not call for explanation or that some metaphysical principles, though noncontingent, do call for explanation. I shall, however, restrict myself to considering and arguing that metaphysical supervenience, which has been embraced by a leading foundation theorist, must, in fact, be denied by the coherence theorist to retain the explanatory advantage of the coherence theory. I shall, moreover, argue that there are good reasons for a coherence theorist to reject metaphysical supervenience of the standard variety. I leave open the question of whether supervenience based on some form of contingent necessity – characteristic of laws of nature, for example – might hold between epistemic properties and nonepistemic ones. I have argued that the foundationalist must simply assume some principle of the form

   (F) If *NBp*, then *Jp*,

where *NB* is a naturalistic property of basic beliefs and *J* is a property of justification. To the question of why we are justified in accepting that *P* if *NB* of *p*, the answer is that we just are. I have juxtaposed this position to a coherence theory that rather than just positing some such principle, offers an explanation as to why we are justified in accepting that *p* if *NB* of *p*, namely, that if *NB* of *p*, then *p* coheres with the appropriate background system and corrected versions thereof.[3]

Van Cleve has objected that the coherence theory itself commits us to a principle that plays the same role as (F) does in the foundations theory. Let *NCp* say that *p* coheres with some system in some naturalistic manner required for justification by the coherence theory. Van Cleve's point would be that the coherentist must accept some principle having the same form as (F), where *NC* is now a coherence property as follows:

   (C) If *NCp*, then *Jp*.

And the coherence theorist can no more answer the question of why we are justified in accepting that *p* if *NC* of *p* than the foundationalist is capable of answering the question directed at (F). Thus, the coherence theory does not have any advantage over the foundations theory. In essence, this argument is that both theories assume that justification supervenes on some nonepistemic property. Both (F) and (C) are claimed to be principles of supervenience, and given that epistemic properties supervene on nonepistemic ones, whether the sort that a foundationalist defends or the sort that a coherence theorist defends, the principle of supervenience is basic. Thus, if some supervenience principle holds, it will, in a sense, be a first principle of justification, and as a result, there will be no answer to the question of why it is true other than "It just is!" It is a kind of epistemic surd. Of course, the principle might generate justified acceptance of claims that could be used to justify the principle itself. It might yield justified premises adequate to conclude that the property of being *NB* or *NC* is a reliable indicator of truth. But again, that does not distinguish the foundations theory from the coherence theory.

This is a formidable argument that Van Cleve has presented in a completely convincing way.[4] The crux is a dilemma. Either justification supervenes on a nonepistemic property or it does not. If it does, then we can obtain justified premises as a result of supervenience and use them to justify the principle of supervenience on either kind of theory. If justification does not supervene on a nonepistemic property, then we cannot obtain justified premises on either theory.

I wish to take the second horn of the dilemma. In my most recent work, I define 'coherence' in terms of a comparative notion of reasonableness, to wit, that it is more reasonable for a person to accept one thing rather than another on the basis of a system of the person, and therefore, I am not committed to holding that justification supervenes on any nonepistemic property.[5] The notion of comparative reasonableness on a system is an epistemic notion, not a naturalistic one. In short, it is open to a coherence theorist to argue that coherence is itself an epistemic notion and, therefore, to reject any principle of the form of (C) as metaphysically necessary. There is, he might argue, no principle of the supervenience of the epistemic on the nonepistemic. There is no exit from the epistemic circle.

One central motive for defending a coherence theory is precisely the rejection of the supervenience thesis. It is not the case that the coherence theorist rejects the supervenience thesis after noticing that acceptance of it leaves her with a principle that is as basic as the principles of basic belief on the foundations theory. It is, rather, that the coherence theorist notes that either we must accept some principle of supervenience without explanation, or we shall ultimately appeal to a system of beliefs for the justification of any belief and, thus, finally argue in a circle. The coherence theorist chooses the second alternative. The claim of the coherence theorist, though not only the coherence theorist, is that the principles connecting the nonepistemic with the epistemic are not necessary but contingent. To borrow a term from Sosa, the epistemic is "autonomous" from the nonepistemic and does not supervene thereupon.[6] It is the great merit of Van Cleve, Alston, and Sosa that they showed us why a coherence theorist should accept the thesis of autonomy.

First, I will present some remarks about the consequences for a coherence theory of accepting that (C) is necessary and that justification supervenes on nonepistemic properties of coherence. The only difference between the supervenient coherence theory and the supervenient foundations theory would be that the former maintains that justification supervenes on a coherence relation to a system of nonepistemic things rather than supervening on any single nonepistemic item, as a foundations theory might hold. This is not a trivial difference. A coherence theorist might hold that the system which generates justification contains a nonepistemic relationship to principle (C) itself. He might claim, for example, that something like the following is true:

(CSR) If S has an acceptance system A that contains (CSR) and p n-coheres with A, then S is justified in accepting that p.

If "n-coheres" were defined nonepistemically, perhaps in terms of probability relations, this principle could be construed as a principle of supervenience assuming that all statements of the form "S accepts that . . ." are nonepistemic. The assumption that all statements of the form "S accepts that . . ." are nonepistemic seems reasonable even if what fills in for ". . ." is epistemic. The statement that a person accepts that God exists is a naturalistic psychological statement about the person, rather than a supernaturalistic statement about God. Acceptance, even of epistemic or supernatural content, is a nonepistemic natural state. So (CSR) might articulate a principle of supervenience for a naturalistic coherence theorist of some sort. However, (CSR) will only yield justification for a person who accepts that it does. This is all naturalistic enough, but it is nonfoundational in character. Part of the explanation for why any person is justified in accepting anything is that he accepts a principle of justification that yields the result that he is justified in accepting it.

Let us call this a naturalized coherence theory. Notice that if (CSR) n-coheres with A, then S is justified in accepting that (CSR). Whether this is the case might depend on what A contains, but it would be an account where we would not be driven to the epistemic surd. We can answer the question of why a person is justified in accepting something that n-coheres with her acceptance system. The answer is that (CSR) says so. The foundationalist can make a similar remark when asked why we are justified in accepting something that has NB, to wit, that is what (F) tells us. But the foundationalist is committed to the surd when asked why we are justified in accepting what (F) tells us. On the other hand, when the naturalized coherence theorist is asked why we are justified in accepting the things that (CSR) tells us we are justified in accepting, she can reply that we are justified in accepting that (CSR) because (CSR) n-coheres with our acceptance system and is contained therein. The coherence theory loops around the surd. The principle of justification together with other things we accept – for example, that n-coherence with an acceptance system yields truth – loops back to the result that we are justified in accepting the principle itself. One might complain of the circularity of this, but it seems to me a virtue of a theory of justification that it should vouch for itself in a justificatory loop tying it together with other things that we accept. The naturalized coherence theorist may favor the loop over the surd and the regress.

Is this observation enough of a defense of the coherence theorist over the foundationalist even granted the supervenience thesis? No! The reason is that the foundationalist may employ a similar strategy by amending principle (F) so that it is self-justifying by simply picking the property *NB* in such a way that (F) has that property or by adding reference to the principle within it as follows:

(FSR) *S* is justified in accepting that *p* if either *p* has *NB* or *p* is identical to (FSR).

To be sure, the way in which this principle justifies itself lacks the subtlety of having it turn out that the principle justifies itself as a result of cohering with an acceptance system. (FSR) justifies itself immediately rather than as a result of coherence, but that would hardly be a fair objection to a foundationalist advocating a doctrine of self-justifying basic beliefs. The foundationalist advocating (FSR) is in a position to avoid the surd by answering the question of why we are justified in accepting that *p* by saying that (FSR) tells us so and to answer why we are justified in accepting what (FSR) tells us by saying that (FSR) tells us that we are. We are hardly entitled to complain against a theory built on self-justification on the grounds that it justifies itself, especially if we take it to be a virtue of the competing coherence theory that it tells us that justification results from coherence with a system.

If we are interested, therefore, in arguing that the coherence theory has an advantage in explaining why things are justified that the foundations theory must lack, we must reject the thesis of supervenience and argue for a coherence theory that makes justification autonomous. Moreover, we must do this in such a way as to show why coherence leads to the doctrine of autonomy and the foundations theory does not. But how can we accomplish this? What is there about coherence that yields autonomy? The answer, in brief, is that an adequate account of coherence must involve epistemic notions. I have argued that the sort of justification required for knowledge is undefeated personal justification based on an acceptance system of the person in question.[7] The intuitive idea I wish to capture is that a person is justified in accepting something just in case he can meet the objections to what he accepts in terms of what he accepts without relying on any falsehoods. More technically, a person is personally justified in accepting something if and only if competitors to it are beaten or neutralized in terms of the acceptance system of the person. The justification is undefeated if and only if correction of errors in the acceptance system preserves the justification. But the critical point is that the notions of competition, beating, or neutralizing are defined in terms of the comparative reasonableness of things on the basis of the acceptance system. Competitors are things that, if assumed, make it less reasonable to accept the things with which they compete. Competitors are beaten if they are less reasonable than the things with which they compete; competitors are neutralized by considerations that, if conjoined, eliminate the competition without loss of reasonableness. I will not elaborate these ideas here, for they have appeared often elsewhere.[8] The point is that coherence, which is analyzed in terms of beating or neutralizing competition to resolve conflict, is itself analyzed in terms of a comparative epistemic primitive.

One might, of course, define the notion differently, but I continue to think that any definition of coherence that is adequate will involve epistemic terms irreducibly and autonomously. These two claims are different. Autonomy implies irreducibility, though not vice versa, because autonomy is the denial of supervenience and, hence, of the thesis that nonepistemic properties are sufficient, with a kind of metaphysical necessity, for epistemic ones. I shall, therefore, explain why the assumptions behind the coherence theory I defend are incompatible with supervenience. The crux of the matter is that coherence is based on a system of what one accepts, and such a system, in order to yield undefeated justification, must contain epistemic truths. A person who accepts nothing about evidence, knows nothing as a result. To know anything, one must accept a minimal epistemic theory and be correct in doing so.

What does a person have to accept about evidence to be justified in what she accepts? Take a standard example. I know that I see a hand. That is something that I am justified in accepting, and my justification is not defeated by error. I can meet objections, all of them, in fact, and the way I meet them does not depend on error. Now one obvious objection is that my evidence that I see a hand is deceptive. I must deny this; that is, I must accept that the evidence that I see a hand is not deceptive. Another obvious objection is that I do not have any trustworthy way of telling whether the evidence is deceptive. I deny this too. I accept I am trustworthy in what I accept about the evidence as well as about what I see, to wit, my hand.

Notice, however, that it is not sufficient for me to know that I see a hand, that I accept that the evidence is not deceptive, and that I accept that I am trustworthy in what I accept about the evidence, and even that I accept that I am trustworthy in what I accept about what I see. These things that I accept must also be true or my justification will be defeated. Corrections of my errors must not destroy my justification, and if the things I accept are errors, my justification will be defeated. What I accept about my trustworthiness in these matters must be correct or my justification will not suffice for knowledge. The notion of trustworthiness is, however, an epistemic notion. I am trustworthy in accepting that p if and only if p is more worthy of my trust than nonacceptance. This comparative notion of the worthiness of my trust connects us again with the notion of comparative reasonableness. If acceptance of p is more worthy of my trust than nonacceptance, then it is more reasonable for me to accept that p than not to accept that p. Coherence with an acceptance system, if it is to yield undefeated justification and, hence, knowledge, must involve coherence with what we accept about our trustworthiness, and what we accept about it must also be true. Thus, coherence presupposes the truth of epistemic claims.

I shall assume, without further argument, that a person does not know something unless he accepts that his evidence is nondeceptive and is trustworthy in so doing. I recognize that some externalists have offered analyses that run contrary to this claim, and I have attempted elsewhere to counter these. My basic comment on them is that merely receiving information in some reliable manner does not suffice for the person receiving the information to know. The reason is that the person might have no idea that he has received information that is correct or that he has received it in a trustworthy way. If he receives the information that p but does not know that the information that p is trustworthy or correct, then he does not know that p. To know that the information is trustworthy and correct, he must know that his evidence is not deceptive, that he is trustworthy in accepting what he does. This claim might seem to lead to regress. It might seem that to know that the information he has received is trustworthy and correct, he must know that his evidence is not deceptive, and to know this he must know something else that gives him this knowledge, and so forth ad infinitum. The brief answer to this is that my acceptance that I am trustworthy in what I accept is something that I also accept and justifies acceptance of it in conjunction with other things I accept. The acceptance of my trustworthiness is a make-or-break epistemic principle, and though it does not justify itself, it does play a role in the justification of itself together with the other things that I accept. In short, there is a minimal theory about my trustworthiness, about where and when I am and am not trustworthy, the acceptance of which, if correct, converts the raw doxastic stuff of acceptance into the constructive materials of knowledge.

Let us formulate the argument a bit more precisely. Consider the following principle:

(A) I am trustworthy in what I accept.

Let us suppose that by "accept" we refer to a cautious doxastic state representing a conscientious effort to avoid error without totally sacrificing the goal of obtaining truth. Thus, let us assume that in those areas in which I cannot distinguish truth from error in a trustworthy manner, I withhold acceptance, and, therefore, (A) becomes true. From (A) and

I accept that p,

we may conclude

(W) Acceptance of p is more worthy of my trust (for the purpose of obtaining truth and avoiding error in what I accept) than the nonacceptance of p.

From (W) we may infer

(M) Acceptance of p is more reasonable for me (for the purpose of obtaining truth and avoiding error in what I accept) than the nonacceptance of p,

and finally,

(R) It is reasonable (for the purpose of obtaining truth and avoiding error in what I accept) for me to accept that p.

Now, this argument might appear to simply generate a principle of supervenience, rather than supporting autonomy, namely, the principle

(S) If I accept that p, then it is reasonable for me to accept that p.

This is not a principle of supervenience, however. The first reason is that (S) is a contingent, not a necessary truth. Whether it is true depends on what I am like, and there is no necessity in that. Nevertheless, a defender of supervenience might insist that if we add the general features G about me that would make (S) true, then we would obtain a necessary truth, namely:

(SG) If I accept that p and I have G, then it is reasonable for me to accept that p.

Put in this way, however, it is apparent that the supervenience claim depends on whether G can be filled in without using epistemic notions. I claim that it cannot be. To see why not, let me return to

(A) I am trustworthy in what I accept,

which drives the argument to the conclusion

(R) It is reasonable for me to accept that p.

The first thing to notice is that principle (A) contains an epistemic term, namely, 'trustworthy'. In fact, it is equivalent to

(AW) If I accept something, then acceptance of it is more worthy of my trust than nonacceptance of it;

and since the latter says that acceptance has greater worth than nonacceptance, it is normative and epistemic. That observation does not by itself defeat the supervenience claim, for we have yet to show that my trustworthiness does not supervene on nonepistemic properties. How can we show that?

Notice that principle (A) has the interesting feature of applying to itself and thus is capable of bootstrapping. Simply substitute principle (A) for the variable p in the preceding premises and you derive the conclusion, first, that I am trustworthy in accepting that (A), and, finally, that it is reasonable for me to accept that (A). Thus, a necessary condition of my being trustworthy in what I accept is that if I accept that I am trustworthy in what I accept, then I am trustworthy in accepting that. My acceptance that I am trustworthy in what I accept is, of course, a naturalistic state. It is, however, something that I must accept if I am trustworthy in what I accept. The reason is that I am trustworthy in what I accept only if I can tell whether I am trustworthy or not. I must be able to tell whether I am trustworthy or not about something in order to be trustworthy about it. I must accept that I am trustworthy when I am and not accept that I am trustworthy when I am not, at least a trustworthy amount of the time. I must, for example, accept that I am trustworthy in certain kinds of memory beliefs, clear and confident ones, and not trustworthy in others, uncertain and obscure ones, in order to be trustworthy in what I accept about what I remember. The same is true of perception. If I cannot tell when I am trustworthy in what I recall and when not, if I cannot tell when I am trustworthy in what I perceive and when not, then I am not trustworthy in these matters.

The foregoing observations may be reinforced with a very simple argument. Let us assume, for the purpose of reducing the assumption to absurdity, that justification results from some naturalized coherence relation, n-coherence, to a background acceptance system. Assume that something n-coheres with the things that I accept. Could it follow from such coherence that I am justified in accepting something? Suppose that even I do not think the things I accept are worth accepting. Why should n-coherence with things that I accept but do not think are worth accepting justify me in accepting anything? Suppose that I accept that the things I accept are worth accepting. Would it follow from n-coherence with such a system that I am justified in accepting something? Some kind of justification might result from such n-coherence, but it would be a subjective justification based entirely on what *I* accept about epistemic and factual matters.[9] If I am wrong in what I accept about either of these matters, the subjective justification might not survive the correction of my errors and, therefore, be defeated by them. Thus, undefeated justification, the stuff of which knowledge is made, requires not only that I accept that the things I accept are worth accepting, but that they really are worth accepting. The worth of their acceptance is an epistemic matter that transcends the natural state of acceptance. Coherence that converts into undefeated justification, the refined stuff of knowledge, depends on our correct acceptance of the worth of what we accept.

The crux of the matter is that it is the trustworthiness of my acceptance, which includes the acceptance of it, that is required for the sort of justification that yields knowledge, to wit, undefeated justification. That is why supervenience fails. There is nothing about me, short of my being trustworthy in what I accept, that necessitates that I am trustworthy in what I accept. I might be successful in the pursuit of truth, or it might even be a consequence of a law of nature that I am successful, but success, even nomologically backed, does not metaphysically necessitate that I am trustworthy in what I accept. My success might be luck, even if it is a consequence of a law of nature, for such successes might result even though acceptance of my trustworthiness is no more worthy of my trust than nonacceptance. Success may lead us to accept that we and others are worthy of trust, but that is not necessitated. Unerring success, even that which is a consequence of a law of nature, might fail to reveal to me and others that I or they are worthy of trust. If natural success in attaining truth could vouch for itself, could reveal that it is worthy of our trust, then supervenience would result. But about what is worthy or reasonable, nature tells us nothing. Nature tells us what will be, not what is worthy of being or of being trusted. Nature tells us what will be, but about what is worthy of being it is as silent as a stone.

Can we imagine two worlds that are the same except that in one what people accept is worthy of their acceptance but in the other not? A person in one world will be right about the course of nature exactly when her naturally identical correlate in the other world is right about the course of nature. So how can the one be ignorant when the other knows? That is what autonomy, the denial of supervenience, implies. How can it be true? Of course, if only one person has any idea that her evidence is trustworthy and that she is trustworthy in what she accepts upon it, there is an important difference between the two people. One understands the epistemic merits of her position, and the other does not. With such a distinction, where one person takes her evidence to be worthy of her trust, and the other has no idea of the worth of it, the reason for ascribing knowledge to the one and not to the other is clear enough. But what ideas people have depends on their nature, so two creatures identical to each other in every natural way cannot differ in their ideas. They can, however, differ in the truth of their ideas when those ideas refer to something beyond natural phenomena. Suppose both people believed in supernatural beings, and one world contained such beings but the other not. One person would have true beliefs and the other not, though nature was the same in both worlds. If there is no supernatural, then witch-making properties do not a witch make, even though, in a world with the supernatural, such properties do make someone a witch.

Let us consider properties less controversial than supernatural ones to argue for the autonomy of the epistemic. Let us consider truth. Does truth supervene on naturalistic properties? If the answer is negative, then it becomes plausible to suppose that the answer is negative in the case of epistemic properties as well. Truth is, after all, an objective of justification. How might one argue for the autonomy of truth? Suppose someone argues that T supervenes on B, where B is the base property and T is truth. This amounts to the claim that

(X) If something is B, then it is T

and, moreover, that this is a necessary truth.
But suppose that (X) is B. Then

(XT) If (X) is B, then (X) is T.

Thus, a necessary condition of (X) is the truth of (X). The point is that (X) says of itself that it is true, though perhaps only indirectly. Does this show that (X) is not necessarily true? Not necessarily, but it allows for an argument against the necessity of (X). It seems that there might be two worlds – one in which (X) is true, one in which it is not – that are otherwise (i.e., nonsemantically) identical. The reason that (X) is true in one world and not in the other is that there is no truth in the one world but there is in the other. There is nothing absurd in denying the necessary truth of such an (X) or, therefore, of supposing that worlds identical nonsemantically might differ semantically.

What about weak supervenience, that is, the thesis that if anything is true, then truth supervenes on some base property? If there is any truth in a world, then some proposition of the form of (X) is necessarily true. Is that true? It is not obvious.

Consider the claim

(E) Everything that is true is true.

That seems obviously true to some but not to others because it violates restrictions regarding language levels. Maybe (E) is true in some possible worlds but not in others that are otherwise the same but restrict the application of the truth predicate differently. Consider again

(L) This sentence refers to itself.

Maybe there are possible worlds that are otherwise identical such that this sentence is true in one and not the others. In some possible worlds, semantically self-referential sentences are neither true nor false; but in others, ones that are less restrictive about truth, it is true. Thus, (E) and (R) are sentences that might or might not be true in a world depending on the semantics of those worlds. Two worlds identical nonsemantically might have different semantics and different truth restrictions, and that explains why the sentences are true in one and not true in the other.

There are some simple connections between worlds without truth and worlds without justification, at least undefeated justification, if truth be the goal of justification. In a truthless world, one might accept things about truth and about trustworthy ways of arriving at truth that would yield subjective justification based on one's acceptance system. But the system would contain errors pertaining to truth, and when they were eliminated, the justification would be defeated. Two worlds that were naturalistically identical but semantically different might, therefore, differ with respect to what a person was justified in accepting, at least in an undefeated way. Even two naturalistically identical worlds that both contained truth but differed semantically with the result that (L) was true in one and not the other might, as a result, yield undefeated justification for the acceptance of (L) in the one world but not in the other.

Does all this have anything to do with coherence? Only this – the coherence theory, at least as I conceive of it, tells us that justification and knowledge result from coherence with a system of acceptance that resolves epistemic conflict to obtain coherence. The system of acceptance articulates the connections between the epistemic and nonepistemic conditions that together yield coherence, justification, and knowledge. That system represents a world of epistemic value and a world of natural fact. Those two worlds must be coherently joined in a true and trustworthy way to yield the world of knowledge. Knowledge does not supervene on the natural world. Coherence is the glue that bonds the natural world, as we conceive of it, to the world of epistemic value, as we conceive of that. The glue of coherence requires matching surfaces of acceptance and truth to hold fast, but it does not bond across possible worlds. Coherence suffices for our knowledge of our actual world and explains how it suffices. The autonomy of coherence transcends the epistemic surd.

NOTES

I am indebted to J. Van Cleve and J. Bender, as well as J. Pollock, T. Price, and other students and colleagues at the University of Arizona, for valuable criticism.

1. W. P. Alston, "Two Types of Foundationalism," *Journal of Philosophy,* 73 (1976), 165–85; J. Van Cleve, "Foundationalism, Epistemic Principles and the Cartesian Circle," *Philosophical Review,* 88 (1979), 55–91; and E. Sosa, *Knowledge in Perspective* (Cambridge University Press, 1991).
2. Cf. J. Kim, "Concepts of Supervenience," *Philosophy and Phenomenological Research,* 44 (1984), 153–76.
3. K. Lehrer, *Theory of Knowledge* (Boulder, Colo.: Westview; and London: Routledge, 1990).
4. Van Cleve, "Foundationalism."
5. Lehrer, *Theory of Knowledge.*
6. Sosa, *Knowledge in Perspective.*
7. K. Lehrer, "Metaknowledge: Undefeated Justification," originally published in 1988, reprinted in K. Lehrer, *Metamind* (Oxford: Clarendon Press, 1990), chap. 11.
8. Ibid.
9. This naturalized and subjectivized notion of justification is not the same notion as that of personal justification incorporated in the accounts of undefeated justification I have used elsewhere. The notion of personal justification is defined in terms of a primitive epistemic notion of comparative reasonableness on the basis of an acceptance system, and that epistemic notion is not reducible even if extensionally equivalent to some naturalized relation.

Does Truth Supervene on Evidence?

JAMES VAN CLEVE

A characteristic principle of much contemporary antirealism is this: truth supervenes on evidence, in the sense that there can be no difference in truth value (between two statements, theories, worldviews, etc.) unless there is also a difference in epistemic value. In the first part of this essay, I will demonstrate this principle at work in the writings of two leading antirealists, Hilary Putnam and Nelson Goodman. In the remainder of the essay, I will argue that the principle is self-refuting in much the same way as the logical positivists' criterion of meaningfulness is: it fails to satisfy the requirements it seeks to impose on other views. There are ways of construing the principle to save it from self-refutation, but they all have the effect of undermining its intended applications.

1. The Principle Exposed

Though never explicitly formulated, the supervenience principle plays a critical role in the arguments of Putnam and Goodman. Both writers make much of the fact that there are theories or descriptions of the world that are logically incompatible if taken at face value but that, at the same time, are in some sense equivalent. The equivalence in question is clearly supposed to be some sort of *epistemic* equivalence. It is not, however, to be understood in narrow empiricist fashion; it involves not merely covering equally well any relevant empirical data, but also fulfilling to the same degree any further constraints that reason may impose. In Putnam's terms, epistemically equivalent theories meet equally well not only all "operational constraints," but also all "theoretical constraints," including such desiderata as simplicity. Putnam cites the following as cases in point:

> Field theory versus action-at-a-distance theory[1]
> Theories that treat points as primitive entities versus theories that treat points as Whiteheadian constructions[2]
> Carnapian ontology (only atoms exist) versus Lesniewskian ontology (in addition, all sums of atoms exist)[3]

There is room for debate over whether these examples really fill the bill. Perhaps Carnap and Lesniewski, rightly understood, are not inconsistent with each other; perhaps action-at-a-distance theory is epistemically preferable on grounds of parsimony to field theory.[4] I shall sidestep these issues here, asking the reader simply to pretend that we have got before us two theories that are logically at odds but epistemically on a par.[5] What should we make of such a situation?

One possible response is *hard-core realism:* one of the theories is true and the other false, even if we could never know which is which.[6] Here is what Putnam says about this response:

> A 'hard-core' realist might claim that there is a fact of the matter as to which is true, story 1 or story 2. . . . [T]his gives up the discovery that this whole article is about: the discovery that there can be incompatible but equivalent versions of the world.[7]

In rejecting hard-core realism, Putnam is implicitly relying on the supervenience principle. He is assuming that if two stories are epistemically equivalent, it cannot be the case that one of them is true and the other false – that there cannot be a difference in truth value between them if there is no difference in epistemic value. Indeed, this principle is so entrenched in Putnam's thinking that he cannot help attributing it to others. In the passage just quoted, he represents the realist as having to *deny the phenomenon* of equivalent but incompatible versions.[8] In fact, realists can readily acknowledge this phenomenon; it is the unvoiced but presupposed supervenience principle that they would deny.

Suppose we *do* accept the supervenience principle. What then are our options when confronted with epistemically equivalent but incompatible versions? There are evidently just two: since the versions cannot differ in truth value, either *both* are true or *neither* is. The "neither" option threatens to make reality indeterminate and amorphous – the world is not as either version says it is, even if the versions are contradictories. The "both" option threatens to make reality contradictory, but the contradiction is typically avoided by adopting some form of relativism – each of the theories is true, *relative* to its own conceptual scheme or what have you. Needless to say, each option has its takers on the contemporary scene. Putnam seems on the whole to prefer the relativist route, saying in more than one place that such relativity is the essence of the view he calls "internal realism."[9]

The supervenience principle is similarly at work in the philosophy of Goodman. The heart of his argument for a plurality of worlds is this: "To anyone but an arrant absolutist, alternative ostensibly conflicting versions often present good and equal claims to truth."[10] He goes on to argue that in many cases the ostensible conflict is real and irremovable. But since the versions present "good and equal claims to truth," it will (by Goodman's lights) simply not do to suppose that one is true and the other false. Hence, they are *both* true – each in its own world! Once again, the needed premise is that if two versions have equal *claims* to truth – if they are epistemically on a par – they cannot differ in truth value.[11]

2. The Principle Refuted

Some claims, like the claim that all generalizations are false, are obviously self-refuting. The principle presupposed by Putnam and Goodman, "no difference in truth value without a difference in epistemic value," is not self-refuting in the same obvious way, because it does not at first sight appear to make a claim about itself. But on further reflection we can see that it makes a claim about itself after all, as compared with its own negation: it claims that there is no difference between the two in truth value unless there is also a difference in epistemic value.

Another way to see that the "no difference" principle makes a claim about itself is to rewrite it in accordance with the logic of supervenience. "There is never a difference in A-properties without a difference in B-properties" is equivalent (given assumptions that are safe in the present context) to "Whenever anything has a given A-property, it also has a B-property that suffices for the having of that A-property." (For more on this equivalence, see Appendix 1.) The principle "no difference in truth value without a difference in epistemic value" therefore has the following corollary: if a statement is true, it has an epistemic value or status that suffices for its being true (in the sense that any statement with the same epistemic status will also be true).[12] My suggestion, of course, is going to be that the Putnam–Goodman principle has no such epistemic status itself – no epistemic status that suffices for the truth of whatever has it.

Version A

Let us begin by assuming that the supervenience of truth on epistemic status is its supervenience on *actual* evidence available *now.* (I am using 'evidence' quite broadly to cover any epistemic virtues or credentials that a statement may possess.) I ask in this case, What evidence now exists for the supervenience principle itself – evidence that suffices for its truth and gives it better epistemic standing than its own negation? There is none that I have ever seen. Antirealists tend not to argue for their principle or adduce evidence for it;[13] indeed, as we have seen, they sometimes do not even see the need to state it. But unless there is evidence for it superior to any that realists can cite on the other side, their principle is self-refuting.[14]

I suppose antirealists could reply to my challenge by saying that the supervenience principle accords well with their own philosophical sensibilities, or even that it is a self-evident principle of sound philosophizing. But the difficulty with this response is obvious: the opposing principle espoused by realists accords equally well with their sensibilities and is no less evident by their lights. So far we have seen nothing to give either side an epistemic edge over the other.[15] Realists can live with this situation, of course, since it is not part of their view that truth-value differences require epistemic differences; but antirealists ought to find it embarrassing.

To make the case as complete as I can, I will now consider two further versions of the antirealist's supervenience principle. One says the difference in epistemic value that must accompany any difference in truth value need only be a difference in *eventual* epistemic value; the other says it need only be a difference in *ideal* epistemic value.[16]

Version B

"There is never a difference in truth value without a difference in eventual epistemic value" is equivalent to this: nothing is ever true unless there one day comes to be evidence that suffices for its truth. With this formulation, the antirealist would not be refuted merely by the absence *now* of evidence for the principle. The principle would live up to its own requirements just as long as future philosophical discoveries vindicate its truth.

If we save the supervenience principle from self-refutation in this way, however, we do so at the cost of undermining its intended applications. Maybe some future philosophical genius will demonstrate to everyone's satisfaction that the supervenience principle is correct; but just so, may not some genius one day discover an argument that will settle what is at issue between Carnap and Lesniewski, or between primitive points and Whiteheadian constructions? (Metaphysicians do debate these things in the journals!) If we admit the latter possibility (say, of an eventual argument decisive in favor of Lesniewski), we cannot use the supervenience principle to argue against the realist's view of these debates. But if we reject that possibility, taking a humbler view of the power of philosophy to settle such questions, we should also be chary of the idea that sound philosophy will one day settle things in favor of the antirealist.

I would make a similar observation in response to the suggestion that antirealists could maintain that their principle applies only to contingent truths, but is itself a necessary truth. Metaphysicians who take a stand in the Carnap versus Lesniewski issue would claim for their mereological principles the status of necessary truths – and if they are not that, they are necessary falsehoods. So the suggested defense of the antirealist principle would again undermine its intended applications.

Version C

The final version of the supervenience principle I will consider is this: there is no difference in truth without a difference in *ideal* epistemic value, that is, the value that would be possessed under epistemically ideal conditions. This version fits right in with the equation often advocated by Putnam of truth with idealized rational acceptability: to say that something is true is to say that its acceptance would be warranted if conditions were epistemically ideal.[17] I will raise two difficulties for this version of the supervenience principle – or rather, one for the allied definition of truth and the other for the intended applications of the principle.

The first difficulty is that Putnam's epistemic definition of truth is demonstrably inadequate. As Ernest Sosa has pointed out, it cannot account for the truth of the proposition (call it *P*) that conditions are *not* epistemically ideal. Surely it is possible – if it is not our actual situation – that *P* is true. But under Putnam's definition, to suppose *P* true is equivalent to supposing

> If conditions were ideal it would be rational to believe that they are not ideal,

which is absurd. A proposition we ought to reckon as possibly true thus comes out under Putnam's definition as necessarily false.[18]

Some might think that Putnam has an easy escape from this difficulty. He need only insist that the conditions referred to in the consequent of the preceding conditional are not (as the pronoun 'they' suggests) the conditions obtaining in the hypothetical ideal world, but the conditions now obtaining in the actual world. The proper understanding of the entire conditional would then be the following: 'In a world where conditions were ideal, it would be rational to believe that the conditions obtaining in this, the actual world, are not ideal'. In other words, the conditional should be understood as we would understand either of the following: 'If I knew all there was to know, I would know that my current state is one of abysmal ignorance'; 'If I were six feet tall, I would be taller than I actually am'. In the first, 'current' picks out my state in the actual world, not my hypothetical state of omniscience; in the second, 'actually' directs us to my height in *this* world, not my height in the counterfactual world.[19]

I do not believe that this maneuver will save Putnam from Sosa's objection. Under the invited interpretation of Putnam's conditional, it is no longer absurd, but it also no longer captures what it is supposed to capture. What exactly is it that it would be rational to believe from the vantage point of the ideal world? I think just this: that conditions *of the sort* obtaining in our world are not ideal. In other words, Putnam's conditional is true if understood as equivalent to

> In a world where conditions were ideal, it would be rational to believe that conditions of sort S are not ideal,

where S characterizes the sort of conditions prevailing in @, the actual world. Putnam's definition of truth in terms of idealized rational acceptability thus allows for the truth of the following proposition, P^*:

> Conditions of sort S are not ideal.

But notice that P^* is a purely general or qualitative proposition, one that implies nothing as regards whether the actual conditions are ideal or not. If we want to imply that the actual conditions are not ideal, we must add that the actual conditions are of sort S. But how are we to secure the truth of this added element? That, it seems to me, is just what we cannot do under Putnam's definition. There is no way to make it part of the content of what it is rational to believe in the ideal world that conditions of sort S *actually* obtain in the sought-for sense.[20]

I come now to the other difficulty for version C. Whether Putnam's epistemic definition of truth can be saved from Sosa's objection or not, the fact will remain that version C is open to the same objection we noted against B. That is to say, by weakening the principle to save it from itself, we also spare its intended victims. Perhaps if conditions were ideal, we would see that the antirealist's supervenience principle is true; but perhaps we would also see that Lesniewski is right and Carnap wrong, or vice versa. We have no right to assume that rival ontological schemes would remain epistemically indistinguishable under ideal conditions.

3. A Difficulty

It may occur to some readers that my attempt to convict the supervenience principle of self-refutation is beset by the following problem. Suppose I am right that the principle is self-refuting. The argument establishing this would be an argument decisive against the principle. But then there would be an epistemic difference after all between the principle and its negation, constituted precisely by the existence of this argument. So the principle would live up to its own demands after all – the difference in truth value between it and its negation would be attended by a difference in epistemic value. Thus, if the principle is self-refuting, it is *not* self-refuting.

I propose the following response. When we rewrite the principle as I suggested in accord with the logic of supervenience, we see that it has two corollaries: (a) if a thesis is true, it has an epistemic value that suffices for its being true, and (b) if a thesis is false (or at any rate not true), it has an epistemic value that suffices for that. Corollaries (a) and (b) must, of course, hold for the supervenience principle itself. If I am right in contending that the principle has no epistemic status that suffices for its truth, it follows that the principle is not true. This very consideration confers upon the principle an epistemic status sufficient for its being false (or at least not true) – hence corollary (b) is satisfied, and the principle to this extent lives up to its own demands. But the fact remains that corollary (a) is not satisfied, so the principle stands refuted.

4. Conclusion

Ironically, Putnam himself has leveled the charge of self-refutation against what he calls "Quinean positivism" – the view (whether correctly attributable to Quine or not) that nothing is rightly assertible unless it is entailed by the totality of true observation conditionals. Putnam points out, quite correctly, that this view fails to be rightly assertible according to its own standard.[21] He adds that such self-refutation arguments are deep, correct, and not to be brushed aside.[22] His own position differs from Quine's in taking an enlarged and no longer narrowly empirical view of what can count as an epistemic virtue; but I suggest that it nonetheless meets the same fate of self-refutation. Whatever the virtues of the antirealist's supervenience principle, they are not such as to elevate that principle above its philosophical rivals.

Appendix 1

Jaegwon Kim distinguishes two varieties of supervenience, strong and weak, and two ways of formulating each, one in terms of possible worlds and the other in terms of modal operators.[23] Strong supervenience may be formulated as an indiscernibility or "no difference" principle that holds across possible worlds:

> (SS_w) For any worlds w_1 and w_2 and any objects x and y, if x in w_1 does not differ in its B-properties from y in w_2, then x in w_1 does not differ in its A-properties from y in w_2.

The corresponding modal operator version is as follows:

(SS$_m$) Necessarily, whenever anything has a given A-property A', it also has a B-property B' such that, necessarily, whatever has B' also has A'.

In weak supervenience, it is only *within* a given possible world that B-indiscernibility implies A-indiscernibility:

(WS$_w$) For any world w and any objects x and y in w, if x and y do not differ in their B-properties in w, then x and y do not differ in their A-properties in w.

The corresponding modal operator version is just like (SS$_m$), except that the second operator is dropped:

(WS$_m$) Necessarily, whenever anything has a given A-property A', it also has a B-property B' such that whatever has B' also has A'.

It may be shown, relative to certain closure assumptions that ought to be unproblematic in the case at hand (e.g., that the complement of an epistemic property is itself an epistemic property), that (SS$_w$) is equivalent to (SS$_m$) and that (WS$_w$) is equivalent to (WS$_m$). (See Kim 1994 for the details.) In the text I appeal to the equivalence of (WS$_w$) and (WS$_m$) – in particular, to the instance of the equivalence we get if we let the individual variables range over theories or hypotheses and take the A-properties to be truth values and the B-properties to be epistemic properties.

Appendix 2

Another leading antirealist whose views I am tempted to summarize in the slogan "truth supervenes on evidence" is Michael Dummett. Dummett (or at least the antirealist as characterized by Dummett) holds that no statement is ever true unless there is evidence for it – unless there obtains some observable (or otherwise verifiable) state of affairs knowledge of which would warrant us in asserting the statement. He also often says that the evidence in question must be "conclusive" or must be something in which the truth of the statement "consists." If "conclusive" evidence is evidence sufficient for truth (as it may not be: Dummett often sounds more like a criterialist), then Dummett holds that truth supervenes on evidence.[24]

Dummett's main argument for antirealism is the manifestation argument.[25] If this argument were sound, it might be just the thing to save the antirealist's supervenience principle from self-refutation. In fact, however, I do not believe it is sound, for reasons I set forth in "The Manifestation Argument Against Realism," forthcoming in a Festschrift for Pranab Kumar Sen.

NOTES

I am grateful to Felicia Ackerman, John Heil, Carl Posy, and Ernest Sosa for helpful discussions.

1. Hilary Putnam, *Meaning and the Moral Sciences* (London: Routledge and Kegan Paul, 1978), p. 133; and Hilary Putnam, *Reason, Truth, and History* (Cambridge University Press, 1981), p. 73.
2. Putnam, *Meaning and the Moral Sciences*, pp. 130–3; and Hilary Putnam, *Realism and Reason* (Cambridge University Press, 1983), pp. 42–4.
3. Hilary Putnam, *The Many Faces of Realism* (La Salle, Ill.: Open Court, 1987), pp. 18–19.
4. As argued by Alan McMichael in "Creative Ontology and Absolute Truth," *Midwest Studies in Philosophy*, vol. 12, edited by Peter A. French, Theodore E. Uehling, Jr., and Howard K. Wettstein (Minneapolis: University of Minnesota Press, 1988), pp. 51–74.
5. Carl Posy has suggested to me that pure mathematics may be a more fertile source of examples – e.g., the alternative set-theoretic foundations for number theory.
6. Or if the theories are logical contraries rather than logical contradictories, perhaps both are false and the truth lies elsewhere.
7. Putnam, *Realism and Reason*, p. 43.
8. He does so again quite explicitly in the following passage: "If realism is identified with the view that there is 'one true theory of everything' (and exactly one), then realism is just the *denial* that there is a plurality of 'equivalent descriptions' of the world" (Putnam, *Realism and Reason*, p. 26).
9. See Putnam, *The Many Faces of Realism*, lectures 1 and 2, especially pp. 17 and 35.
10. Nelson Goodman, *Ways of Worldmaking* (Indianapolis, Ind.: Hackett, 1978), p. 110.
11. For further illustration of this strategy, see Goodman's capsule history of pre-Socratic philosophy in ibid., pp. 97–9: "The implicit ground for rejecting Thales' theory [as well as the theories of Empedocles et al.] was that features distinguishing alternative systems cannot reflect reality as it is." Omitted from Goodman's history is the pre-Socratic philosopher he himself most emulates – that, of course, being Protagoras.
12. This is what "sufficing for" amounts to if the supervenience is *weak* in Kim's sense. If the supervenience is *strong* (see Appendix 1 again), "suffices for its being true" takes on the stronger meaning of "*entails* its being true." The difficulties I will raise in this essay for the supervenience of truth on evidence are difficulties even for weak supervenience.
13. A notable exception is Michael Dummett, whose views I discuss briefly in Appendix 2.
14. I am assuming that evidence that suffices for the truth of a hypothesis must be evidence that is superior to the evidence against the hypothesis.
15. Perhaps it will be suggested that the intuitions supporting antirealism differ in *content* from those supporting realism, even if they do not differ in quality, strength, or trustworthiness, and that such a difference in the con-

tent of the evidence is all that the supervenience principle requires by way of an epistemic difference. If we save the principle in this way, however, we deprive it of its intended applications. It will now be possible to say that "points are real" and "points are fictions," which Putnam takes to be epistemically equivalent, differ in epistemic value after all, since one is backed by the intuition that points are real and the other by the intuition that points are fictions.

16. Note that the supervenience of truth on *presently* obtaining evidence is implausible quite apart from any problem of self-refutation. Couldn't there be two predictions equally warranted by all present evidence, one of which turns out to be true and the other false?

17. See, e.g., Putnam, *Reason, Truth, and History*, pp. 55–6.

18. See Ernest Sosa, *Knowledge in Perspective* (Cambridge University Press, 1991), pp. 6–7. The point is worked out more formally in Alvin Plantinga, "How to Be an Anti-Realist," *Proceedings and Addresses of the American Philosophical Association*, 56 (1982), 47–70. Plantinga shows that Putnam's definition implies that it is a necessary truth that conditions are ideal. I observe that the same proof strategy may be used to demonstrate a more general result: that any truth definition of the form $Tp =_{df} Q > Fp$ (where the definiens is a subjunctive conditional) implies that Q (whatever is chosen as antecedent for the subjunctive conditional) is a necessary truth.

19. We are thus taking 'actual' and its cognates in what Lewis calls their primary and indexical sense. That is to say, when we say something here in our world, @, about what it would be rational to believe in some other world w about goings-on in *the actual world*, the italic phrase refers not to w, but to @. See David Lewis, *Philosophical Papers*, vol. 1 (Oxford University Press, 1983), pp. 18–22.

20. The difficulty here is that it is hard to see what appropriate sense can attach to knowing (or having rational beliefs about) what goes on in the actual world from any vantage point save that of the actual world. I thus have trouble accepting the solution offered by Dorothy Edgington in her paper "The Paradox of Knowability," *Mind*, 94 (1985), 557–68, which involves endorsing statements such as "in some world w other than @, someone knows that $\langle p \, \& \sim Kp \rangle$ is true in @." One can know in w that $\langle p \, \& \sim Kp \rangle$ is true in any world fitting a certain qualitative description, which may even be a description that the actual world uniquely fits, but that is not yet to know that $\langle p \, \& \sim Kp \rangle$ is true in the actual world.

21. Putnam, *Realism and Reason*, pp. 240–4.

22. Ibid., pp. 184–5.

23. See Jaegwon Kim, "Concepts of Supervenience," *Philosophy and Phenomenological Research*, 45 (1984), 153–76.

24. For further details, see Michael Dummett, *Truth and Other Enigmas* (Cambridge, Mass.: Harvard University Press, 1978), especially the preface and chap. 14.

25. Michael Dummett, "The Philosophical Basis of Intuitionistic Logic," in ibid., pp. 215–47.

Index